3/94

SERGEI PROKOFIEV
SOVIET DIARY 1927
AND OTHER WRITINGS

SERGEI PROKOFIEV
Soviet Diary 1927
and Other Writings

Translated and edited by
OLEG PROKOFIEV
Associate Editor
CHRISTOPHER PALMER

faber and faber
LONDON · BOSTON

First published in 1991
by Faber and Faber Limited
3 Queen Square London WC1N 3AU

Photoset by Wilmaset Birkenhead Wirral
Printed in England
by Clays Ltd, St Ives plc
All rights reserved

A CIP record for this book
is available from the British Library

ISBN 0–571–16158–8

Contents

Illustrations

Acknowledgements

The editors wish to thank David Mather for checking, revising and materially contributing to all translations and notes, George Hall and Andrew Huth for helping with the translation of *A Soviet Diary*, Alison Mansbridge for copy-editing the text, Jenny Slater and Ray Sumby for typing it, and Sarah Ereira for compiling the index.

O.P./C.P.

Introduction

I found the manuscript of this *Soviet Diary* among my mother's papers after her death in January 1989. It is a unique document which describes my father's first return visit to the Soviet Union in 1927, nearly nine years after he left in 1918. By this time he was already an international celebrity, both as a pianist in his own music (three piano concertos, five sonatas and many shorter pieces), and as the composer of the 'Classical' *Symphony*, the *Scythian Suite*, the ballet *Chout*, the opera *The Love for Three Oranges* and the First Violin Concerto. Many of his greatest successes, of course, still lay ahead – *Romeo and Juliet*, *Cinderella*, *Alexander Nevsky*, *Peter and the Wolf*, *War and Peace*, the Fifth Symphony, the Sinfonia Concertante, the last four piano sonatas.

Prokofiev kept other diaries. He had been a keen diarist ever since he was a boy and continued until he was about forty. The diaries gradually change their character. They become in the 1920s briefer and more laconic and are written in Prokofiev's characteristic shorthand, in which words are abbreviated and most vowels omitted. The comparatively detailed narrative of the *Soviet Diary* makes it exceptional for that time. The entry for 25 February begins: 'Here my shorthand diary comes to an end, and I have based my account of our ensuing stay in Moscow on Ptashka's [Prokofiev's wife's] notes and other documents.' This indicates it was Prokofiev's intention to keep an unusually detailed diary right from the beginning of his visit to the Soviet Union, as if he considered this particular journey to be special and in a totally different category from his everyday itinerant life in the West. It seems more than likely that when he returned to Paris he sat down at his desk as soon as he could and began to type it in the very form in which it has come down to us after more than sixty years (with only a few corrections made in his own handwriting).

But this diary was certainly not intended for publication, at least during his lifetime and especially at the moment when he was hoping for repeated opportunities to visit Russia to perform his music and see old friends. It is difficult to know if he was already considering returning for good. It seems unlikely, for his home was still in France. This can be deduced from the diary, which is that of a traveller, or, more exactly, the diary of a traveller's rediscovery of the country of his origins.

There is one revealing detail in the entry for the last day in Moscow. When he was taking through customs some packages of his old papers which he had retrieved from Myaskovsky, he felt relieved that the examination was formal and superficial. 'I just remembered that there are [i.e. in the old diaries] here and there some sentiments that could be considered counter-revolutionary.' (23 March)

But this remark was written when he was safely back in Paris! Also, it was in what was the first and also his only diary describing a visit to the Soviet Union (if we discount the 'papers' he refers to, which must have been the old diaries belonging to the period before he left Soviet Russia, in 1917–18). The 1927 diary was never taken back to the USSR but kept safely in the West. Prokofiev knew perfectly well that Soviet Russia was not the place for 'counter-revolutionary sentiments', even if he couldn't stop himself recording them. It seems he kept this diary separately from his others, because when after his death all his papers were sent back to the USSR this was not among them.

Perhaps one of the reasons why Prokofiev stopped keeping diaries within the next few years was that he did not want to risk putting down his feelings about the Soviet Union at a time when he was starting to make increasingly regular trips back there. After another nine years he finally became domiciled in Moscow with his family.

During these years, my father's (and my mother's) *Wanderjahre*, of which I can recall the last few before 1936, my brother and I would be left in the care of my maternal grandmother in Paris or in the South of France, in Cannes. We would occasionally receive an entertaining letter or postcard from him which brought the exciting feeling of travelling in strange countries alive for us (there would also be specially selected exotic stamps, which my brother was collecting). The text would often contain something interesting. For instance I recall the description of a visit to Hollywood, where 'the father of Mickey Mouse lives', and where 'cardboard castles and towns are made for filming'. Even the way a text was designed could sometimes be fun: one was shaped into a spiral with 'from PAPA' in the centre of the postcard.

I still have a little drawing I made in 1938 which reflects the feeling of his constant travelling as our way of life (see p. xvi). It was done after we had moved to Moscow, though, and intended for my grandmother, who had stayed behind in Paris, but the essence of my childhood is there. It pictures a train with the inscription: 'le train sur lequel Papa et Maman reviendron[t] . . .' There it is, in a nutshell, the familiar pattern of our lives as children, the abrupt comings-and-goings of itinerant parents as a recurrent feature.

Although this business of my parents' travelling regularly seemed quite natural to me, there was also something mysterious about it. Once (only once!), for some unknown reason, my father had to take me (when I was about seven) and my brother with him on a short trip abroad. I remember the strangeness of arriving in the evening in a rather large town (was it Vienna?), then being driven in a taxi through bright and unfamiliar evening streets, and finally arriving at a cosy little hotel. I was put to bed and before falling asleep got a kiss from my father who was going to his concert. But I do not recall that this made me anxious; the trip was extraordinary anyway, and being left in a strange place was accepted as something natural, as an arrangement or act of complicity between us: two boys and their companion-father together, taking part in an unusual and exciting adventure.

There was, indeed, a feeling of something special and unusual in my father's occupation. From an early age I experienced it quite clearly as being somehow out of the ordinary, almost privileged, and our family was set apart, made different by it. This feeling of being different was probably always with me, but later, in the Soviet Union, 'specialness' could sometimes be a burden.

When I read this diary for the first time I could suddenly see through my father's eyes and understand what his travels were really about. I found it particularly fascinating to be able to juxtapose the events as my father experienced them with how I imagined them as a child at the time.

But whatever my 'romanticized' reactions to it, the diary itself has a predominantly impartial and objective, descriptive character. There can be critical remarks, even a sarcastic comment, but it is rarely an over-statement or a joke at somebody's expense. Also, it is not his intention to raise problematic personal questions. Not that he is being duplicitous or trying to hide something from himself, or, for that matter, from posterity. In his diary he is absolutely honest and is ready to admit his uncertainty or failures, be it his fear before crossing the Soviet frontier or his sudden lack of confidence during his first appearances as a soloist in Moscow. But these emotions are 'objectivized': they are described as events of his life, just like the clamour of the public at the end of his first concerts, which becomes a kind of measure of the degree in which a particular recital has been successful. Here also he is not fooled or intoxicated by his successes, which must have been tremendous (he is not indifferent, either); he merely registers them, as for instance in Leningrad: 'The shouts and applause were tonight as loud as my first concert.' (22 February) We should remember also that whereas most other composer-pianists played other composers' music as well as their own, Prokofiev played *only* his own. He was thus constantly on parade, under scrutiny, in a dual role, as pianist and composer (he also conducted his own works, but not on this visit). Much therefore was expected of him, and he was under greater pressure than most visiting celebrities. He successfully coped with all these demands, and certainly from expressing these two sides of his musical genius thus powerfully there emanated an uplifting and concentrated creative energy. The contemporary poet George Obolduev expressed it vividly:

Citizen Prokofiev strangles
Our debased souls,
They have to die
To live and sing hereafter.

After expending so much energy on his work, Prokofiev in everyday life was somewhat restrained in expressing his feelings, although he never abandoned his natural directness. He had to husband his resources and showed caution and even diplomacy in certain situations; yet he was always responsive and never small-minded. When we read the diary, what we cannot fail to notice is the patience and attention that he gives to different occasional admirers, or to people who are constantly pestering him with requests, from money to fantastic artistic projects. Where is the rude and boorish Prokofiev so favoured and popularized by most biographers? He may have been irritated or annoyed by some pushy supplicant, as he is for instance by an arrogant and over-determined woman choreographer, but he patiently listens to her just the same:

'Chernetskaya's reading of the second part of her ballet proposal took place in the most adverse conditions. I could see first of all that it was worthless; meanwhile, as she went on reading, other visitors were coming in, the telephone was ringing all the time and Ptashka was busy turning away an interviewer who had arrived too late. In short the most appalling circumstances for anyone to read anything in; but Chernetskaya battled on in desperation and I for the sake of good manners was listening to her with one ear and marvelling at her heroic spirit.' (8 February)

Apart from enjoying what certainly was to be one of his happiest and most successful stays in Russia, Prokofiev had to confront some grimmer realities there too. This is exemplified in his extramusical efforts on behalf of the cousin who has been arrested. Throughout the diary the quest for help for his cousin keeps coming back like a sinister leitmotif. He does not give up and it is interesting to see here how, for the first time, he comes up against the typically Soviet reactions of evasiveness and reluctance to co-operate in such matters. Of course a few idealists – Gorki's wife, for example – hope for some positive outcome, just as he does. But they should have known better by then! After all *he* was a newcomer who could not be expected to understand how the Soviet system worked. Later he would have this understanding thrust upon him. Of course friends like Myaskovsky, Asafiev or Meyerhold *could* have explained certain things; but to understand what Soviet life really was in essence Prokofiev would have to experience it for himself. Meyerhold even promised to try to help him get his cousin out of prison, saying that he knew someone in the Secret Police in whose ear he might whisper a word. As things turned out Cousin Shurik served his term to the end, and later on Meyerhold himself, his wife and his life's work were all bloodily destroyed by Stalin.

Some details are curiously reminiscent of the Soviet Union today, albeit in a mirror image. What is coming in today as a novelty was on the wane then. Some remaining features of the NEP (New Economic Policy) of the early 1920s, very much like those being introduced now, were still in operation: for instance the co-operative restaurants which offered much better quality food and service, something which Prokofiev could not fail to notice! Experiments in art were allowed and even a certain freedom of speech was still being tolerated. Trotsky's opposition was still officially sanctioned.

On the other hand there was much more food in the shops than nowadays (at least in Moscow). And, without any doubt, a much greater number of sincere and dedicated communists of the 'old guard' – intelligent, educated people who still retained memories of their lives in the West before the Revolution – could allow themselves to have a broader view. One has only to compare the cultural level of a Lunacharsky and a Litvinov to that of a Zhdanov or a Khrushchev!

Reading this diary one must bear in mind that Stalin's rule was only beginning, the Great Famine was yet to come and so were all the hardships of industrialization, not to mention the purges of the 1930s. It is doubtful if anybody could even start to imagine what it would all turn into.

And yet the confessions of his Russian friend from the USA, who came back to work in the Soviet Union and became the director of a small factory, make things surprisingly clear: people were lazy, bureaucracy was rife, the communists wanted to control everything, spy on everybody and so on. But Prokofiev merely notes it down and is in no hurry to draw conclusions. He has not come to the Soviet Union to stay (yet) and, in fact, he records any kind of suggestion to that effect with a faintly perceptible 'Not so fast, my friends, don't be too pushy, life in Western Europe is better than you can imagine . . .' He feels he is here on a visit, to find out what the pros and cons actually are. He is a realist and prefers things to be clear; hurried decisions, therefore, are not for him. Even making up his mind to cross the border was not easy.

In fact what Prokofiev cannot stand is any kind of lethargy, sloppy thinking or dilettantism. Nor does he have any time for what he considers unnecessary complications, the fudging of clear-cut issues. His attitude to music is similar.

If 'le style c'est l'homme', this clearly manifests itself in Prokofiev's own literary style, which seems to me at times almost Chekhovian. This comes out in certain descriptions of places and events, and in situations which border on comedy. The incident in Odessa where an impostor pretends to be his secretary sounds like an episode from a Chekhov short story.

There is great economy of words and no romantic flourishes, no sentimentality, no moralistic digressions. Perhaps once or twice he treats aspects of the copyright and performance business with undue intricacy of detail, but let us not forget that he had no agent – he dealt with all these problems himself.

Perhaps the only time Prokofiev is overcome by what he sees around him and cannot find adequate words to express his feelings is when he arrives in Leningrad. Memories of the St Petersburg of his youth almost overwhelm him and the only adjective that keeps coming to his mind is 'beautiful'.

But then we come to Prokofiev's final departure from Moscow to Western Europe. After a brief, quite unsentimental description of the people who have come to see him off, some of them relatives and close friends, he concludes: 'The train moved off. It was a wonderful, clear March day and the rays of the setting sun came slanting down.' Nothing more.

It is worth mentioning that Prokofiev's skill as a writer has impressed even so stringent a critic as Robert Craft, who certainly cannot be charged with any kind of *parti pris*. In a review of *Prokofiev by Prokofiev* (the 'long' autobiography), Craft compares the latter with Vladimir Nabokov's *Speak, Memory* and describes it as the best autobiography he knows of by any composer.

Prokofiev wrote not only diaries and his own opera libretti but also fiction. Three complete (or near-complete) short stories, and fragments of two others, have so far been discovered and are published here for the first time. 'A Bad Dog' shows an accomplished story-telling technique with a strongly ironic touch. The 'Tanya' fairy-tale fragment has not gone uninfluenced by *Alice in Wonderland*, and the monstrous English governess with her lupine teeth could almost be a character in *The Love for Three Oranges*. 'The Wandering Tower' – written in a Japanese hotel, between concerts – is a symbolist-surrealist dream: is Prokofiev himself the Tower, running around the world, attracted by 'mystical sounds' to an 'Ancient Babylon'? This story in particular carries many echoes and overtones of music by Prokofiev, notably the *Scythian Suite* and the almost contemporaneous cantata *Seven, They are*

Seven – the text of which is a Balmont poem inspired by an evocation inscribed on the walls of an ancient Accadian temple. (The hero of 'The Wandering Tower', we read, digs about in the sands and ruins of Assyria, finds thousand-year-old tabulae with strange wedge-shaped inscriptions which he then deciphers, and, just before the story begins, has 'fallen entirely under the spell of the Accadians and Sumerians, with the effaced superstitions of a once so stylish culture'). The satirical treatment of the military (General Magenschmerzen's name means 'belly-ache') looks forward both to *Lieutenant Kizhe* and to *War and Peace*, and the combination of fantastic and farcical elements is strongly suggestive of *The Love for Three Oranges*. The other two stories seem to be moral fables, one on the subject of marital jealousy (cf. also 'A Bad Dog'), the other about gambling and debt. These themes recur in Prokofiev's pre-Soviet operas – jealousy in *Maddalena* and *The Fiery Angel*, gambling in *The Gambler* (and later in the film of Pushkin's *Queen of Spades*, which was never actually made but for which Prokofiev had written music in advance). Despite the variety of genres, they all have distinctive similarities – in their sharp and sometimes sardonic humour and in the simplicity of their prose style – which remind us from time to time of the *Soviet Diary*; and it is a matter for great regret that Prokofiev in later life never had the time or opportunity to develop this side of his creative talent any further.

Oleg Prokofiev, London, June 1991

A SOVIET DIARY
1927

SOVIET DIARY — EDITORIAL NOTE ON THE TRANSLATION

In translating Prokofiev's *Soviet Diary* the aim was to make it read as little like a translation as possible. Oleg Prokofiev prepared a literal version in English and we then worked together on making it idiomatic. One or two turns of phrase, though not idiomatic, were so attractive and colourful in the original that we decided not to tamper with them: for example, the notion of one of Prokofiev's works 'gobbling' up too much of a rehearsal, or of Prokofiev himself 'filling up with horror' at the prospect of having to reply to a speech.

More consistently problematic was Prokofiev's use of the 'graphic' present: that is, jumping from the past tense to the present and back again, sometimes during the course of a single paragraph. This is common in Russian (as in French), but not in English, and the effect can be disconcerting for the reader. Where we were *not* disconcerted, we left things as they were. Elsewhere we compromised: if Prokofiev changed tenses, *we* changed, but then stayed with the new tense to the end of the paragraph, even if he changed back. Ruthlessly to iron out all the inconsistencies might have been to injure the impromptu character of the work and its relaxed and informal literary style.

O.P./C.P.

A Soviet Diary: January – March 1927

Thursday 13 January

Today is the day we leave for Russia. Today also, therefore, we must empty the flat in rue Troyon and clean up, check the inventory, pack up – everything in a frantic rush. We were even worried we might not get everything done in time to catch the train. One of the suitcases we had just bought turned out not to have its keys. Gorchakov, who claims to be a scout, could not do up a single parcel properly, although he said he had learnt how to do scouts' knots. And as things turned out we did have to hurry! We had to leave various items at the Publishing House on the way to the station – suitcases, pictures etc. – and so we arrived only ten minutes before the train was due to depart. We found that quite a few people had already gathered to see us off: the Borovskys, Samoilenkos, Paichadze and others. The train was quite luxurious, blue with gold trimmings – I chose this one specially, quite adamantly, so that no one could think of us condescendingly ('Poor wretches, what must they be in for, going back to the Bolsheviks!'). Going to visit the 'proletarians' is worth the North-Express! Sweets were passed around, very good ones, and we left merrily.

Ptashka and I had separate connecting compartments. A chance for a good sleep, you might have thought, but at midnight we were awoken at the German border. Our luggage and passports were inspected, quite superficially; but when I mentioned the existence of a huge trunk the German announced that there were no such trunks in the luggage van, although I well remembered seeing it being loaded. The good German was later proved wrong but our mood and sleep were spoiled.

Friday 14 January

In the morning – Berlin. Weber and Tanya Raevsky at the station. Sashka again did not appear, giving a reasonable excuse: flu, if he were not lying. First we went to order keys for the suitcase we had bought in a hurry without any – we did not want to leave it in the left-luggage office,

3

however honest the Germans. After that we all four drank coffee at the big coffee house on the Unter den Linden. Then we shopped, mainly buying presents which we had not had time to get in Paris. For lunch I invited the same crowd plus Weber's wife to the Fürstenhof Hotel. Later we went to my publishers to discuss a number of small questions. My accounts for 1926 were not ready yet, but didn't look much like topping the previous year's. Evidently things aren't going to speed up every year the way they did in 1924–5. The sale of Stravinsky's works is down, but this is nicely compensated for by increased performance fees. From the publishers Ptashka went to the Webers' flat to rehearse and I to buy a fountain pen for Kucheryavy.

At 6.30 we left for Riga, seen off by the Webers. We ate in the restaurant car and at once went to bed, exhausted by all the bustling about in Berlin and probably in Paris as well.

Saturday 15 January

By the morning we had reached Eidkunen, the old Russian frontier which now separates Germany and Lithuania. Changed from the sleeping car to an ordinary one. Cold and chilly. Before leaving Paris I had had a new coat made, without fur – to general consternation. But I had never worn a fur coat in Russia, and decided to do the same now as before.

The Lithuanians are quiet and polite and speak Russian as if it were not Lithuania but Russia. The train drags along. In the old days trains moved much less lethargically. In the restaurant car I was approached by Piotrovsky, a tenor who was a contemporary of mine at the Conservatoire. It transpires he has taken Lithuanian nationality and, because of the poverty of musical life in Lithuania, is now the foremost musician in his adopted country. He organized the opera in Kovno and his fame spread not only all over Lithuania but to other provincial capitals like Riga and Revel. He had quite a good voice and for a tenor was actually very musical. Now he was on his way to sing in Riga. A nice man, liked talking about Russia. He had been invited to sing in Leningrad but was afraid to go there. The Lithuanian government is becoming right-wing and a while ago arrested a number of Bolsheviks;

therefore prominent Lithuanians are not advised to go to Russia in case they are taken as hostages.

The day is long and slow. The train moves sluggishly all the while. White snow everywhere. I asked Piotrovsky why the train should crawl along the way it did. He answered philosophically: 'You see, the country is small. The slower we cross it, the bigger it seems.'

Whatever the reason the train finally got us in to Riga at 11.30 p.m., a good two hours late. We were met by Maevsky and the two managers with whom I had signed contracts. It was a great pleasure to get into a sleigh – I forgot when I last did it! Maevsky's manner was that of my best friend of all time and he evidently considered himself the host, since I had been brought to Riga through his efforts. His manager–companions, who turned out to be good-natured Latvians, fed us supper with vodka which they poured out of a teapot. (Spirits are forbidden on Saturdays in Latvia to stop people being drunk on Sunday: hence this little subterfuge.)

Sunday 16 January

In the morning, interviews with three reporters, two Latvians and one Russian. Towards the end Ptashka came out looking very attractive in her blue dress, and also answered questions. Later we were photographed with the Opera House as a background, Ptashka's leopard-skin coat making a striking splash of colour. Then Shubert appeared, my former companion in Esipova's class. He turned out to be a Latvian and an important figure in musical Latvia, more important than Piotrovsky, because in comparison with Riga Lithuania is a wretched place. Shubert had already managed to get himself appointed a director of the Opera in Riga and was now Inspector of the Conservatoire. I looked at him and roared with laughter: Pavlusha, who loved playing cards, loved eating and drinking, who indulged in fact in a wide variety of the good things in life, who was never taken seriously – here now was this same Pavlusha, a respected government official, impeccably dressed in a splendid cut-away morning coat, a man of good standing, even slightly self-important. He acknowledged my outburst somewhat stiffly, but seemed a good sort just the same.

We went for a walk in the town, which is not too metropolitan in character, and not a bad sort of place. It is cold, in the air the smell of fresh snow is sometimes mixed with manure – there are no cars here and people get about on horse-drawn sleighs. This mixed smell reminds me pleasantly of old-time St Petersburg winters. I have a special memory for smells and they can sometimes reconstruct whole images.

At 2 o'clock we lunched at Maevsky's. Again Maevsky did his kind of star turn, posing as a friend of mine almost from babyhood – although we rarely met at the Conservatoire and afterwards hardly at all. Apart from Shubert there was Kreisler, not a bad fellow, with whom I always got on very well – I had addressed him as 'thou' since our times in the conducting class together. Having run away from Russia, where he lost, it seems, a considerable fortune, he could not settle anywhere for long, and even wrote to me in Ettal asking for advice and assistance. I could not do anything for him then; apart from which I remembered him as a nice chap but a poor conductor. Now he is married to a much older woman and seems to have settled down financially, but not artistically or indeed in any satisfactory domestic way. After lunch Ptashka and I rehearsed for our concert.

At Maevsky's house I saw a portrait of Myaskovsky. Myaskovsky does not like to be photographed, and until now I knew of only one portrait snapped impromptu by Derzhanovsky and later enlarged, actually quite a good one. The picture that Maevsky showed me was probably only the second ever taken of Myaskovsky. I was struck by the change: a bored expression, a heavy look, and instead of a suit he wore some kind of jacket buttoned up to the chin. I just hope he was photographed at a bad moment.

In the evening I was invited to the opera, Rimsky-Korsakov's *May Night*. There was something odd about listening to *May Night* sung in Latvian to music half of which I had forgotten. Youthful memories of the production of this opera at the Conservatoire rushed through my mind, especially during the charming first act. But then the third is tedious and absurd: the librettist did not get to grips with the plot. The production is not that bad and the singing pleasantly spirited. This can be explained by the fact that quite a number of excellent opera singers have emigrated from Russia to Riga, greatly to the benefit of local theatre. In the interval the director, Reuter, came to meet me. He had also been a student in our conducting class, but was younger than me, and I did not remember him very clearly. Now, just like Shubert, he was dressed painstakingly well, and looked very much the man to whom the fate of Latvian music had been entrusted.

Monday 17 January

In the night Ptashka felt unwell, slept badly and kept waking me up. In the morning we ordered our tickets for Moscow. In the afternoon we rehearsed and tried not to spend the time socializing that we did yesterday. Our concert was at 8 o'clock in the same opera house we had been in the day before. There were a lot of people: 1,400 the manager thought, although he immediately remarked that about 300 tickets had been distributed free.

I played rather nervously. Where was my American imperturbability, which I thought of as a permanent acquisition? The Fifth Sonata was only relatively successful, though I did not expect the Rigans to like it and included it in the programme mainly to rehearse it before Moscow. The second part of the concert was filled with my shorter pieces – the March from the *Three Oranges*, gavottes and other easily digestible things. They were received well and quite noisily, with calls and encores. Ptashka sang two sets of songs, but her voice sounded weak because she herself felt quite weak. Only mildly successful, but all things considered not too bad. After the concert, in the Green Room, quite a large number of people.

Tuesday 18 January

In the morning I received my fee and changed it into roubles. Then a Jew came to see me. He had just arrived from Moscow on his way to America, where he was going on behalf of various organizations to establish musical contacts. At least that is what he says. Others say he is lying, and on the pretext of making cultural contacts is promoting his own affairs. But he interests me: going back to my own country I'm curious to know what people coming from it are like. And this one is a special kind of person. The first thing he did was to take out his papers and set them down in front of me so that I should know who he was.

Was that because he was lying? He wanted me to give him a card for the director of the Riga Conservatoire, Vitol. In return he promised to talk to the Soviet consul about my luggage; I wanted to make sure I wouldn't encounter any problems at the frontier. He said the consul was offended that I did not go to see him.

In the evening I went with Ptashka to see A. G. Zherebtsova-Andreeva, who was extremely pleased at our visiting her and talked non-stop. She complimented Ptashka on her singing, which made her feel a good deal better.

We returned to the hotel, packed and went to the railway station – to go to Bolshevizia. Various thoughts passed through my mind: should I forget the whole thing and stay here? Can I count on coming back or will they stop me? Even if we went no further the trip wouldn't have been a waste of time since a number of concert engagements have been proposed. However I brushed these cowardly misgivings aside and we duly showed up at the station. The train was due to leave at half past midnight. There was a very heavy frost. It was nice to see Russian carriages, but they were third-class and the lighting inside was bleak. We had to go right on to somewhere near the end to find our second-class carriage. First-class does not exist in Soviet Russia; there are no 'classes' anyway, the carriages are either the hard sort or the soft. The hard ones have kept the colour of the third-class; the first-class and second-class carriages are painted yellow and are called soft.

We entered our 'soft' carriage. It was not cosy at all: cold, gloomy, no carpets, and the washbasin in our compartment was boarded up. Our three managers appeared (they run their concert-bureau together) to see us off despite the late hour. I asked all the others not to bother. The train departed and we went to bed in rather middling spirits. The Russian guard made our beds up; the sheets were rough and the beds themselves hard.

Wednesday 19 January

We had only a few hours' sleep because of crossing the frontiers early in the morning, first the Latvian, then the Russian. Since our washbasin was out of commission we had to go to the main toilets to wash, but the water there was so icy it made our fingers numb. At the Latvian border they did not look at anything and we got some coffee at the station. Again the thought occurred to us: 'This is our last chance, it's still not too late to turn back. All right, we might regret it later, but if it's virtually a matter of life or death we could do it!'

Meanwhile a tiny service steam-engine was being attached to our train. It was a glorious sunny day without a single cloud and minus 12 degrees Réaumur.

And so, turning all these thoughts over in our minds, we boarded the train and went to the intimidating, awe-inspiring USSR. Getting from the Latvian border to the Russian took about an hour. The Latvian border-post flashed by. Then a ditch covered with snow, which was the frontier; the train passed under an arch, on the top of which was written: 'Proletarians of all lands, unite!' By the rail stood a Russian soldier wearing a helmet made of textile fabric and a long ankle-length coat. The train stopped to let the soldier on and he appeared in our compartment the next minute and took away our passports.

We soon arrived at Sebezh, the Russian customs. In came a porter and took away our things. When they were piled up on the customs table I immediately asked if the customs officers had received a telegram about the Prokofievs crossing the border. They had indeed, and this gave a pleasant turn to the inspection of our luggage, which was superficial. They turned over some pages of the French books on music which I was taking for Asafiev. The large trunk and a bag for the Persimfans (with reeds) were going directly to Moscow. Nevertheless they asked me to sign a paper about the number of pieces of hand luggage we had; also they did not understand what pyjamas were, and Ptashka could not think of a translation for a nightblouse. On the whole they were polite, even to the Jewish woman next to us, a lot of whose things they confiscated. Another woman had some children's shoes taken away from her. This upset Ptashka and she thought of Svyatoslav. Once the inspection was over the porter carried our things back to the carriage. On the wall was a notice to the effect that a quarter should be paid for every item carried. Ptashka was advised to add something for a tip but I objected – so as not to do things wrong – that in a communist country, once a charge is fixed, no tips need be given, and I did not give one.

There was an hour to go before departure, so since it was noon we went to the station buffet for lunch. We observed with curiosity the various people who came in, probably officials from the station and customs who were asking for special service lunches. They all looked well, important, calm and polite. They tried to eat quietly without silly small talk. After lunch I tried to buy some chocolate, but it was five times dearer than before the war and of poor quality (though perhaps they make you pay more at a border station). We went back to the carriage and the train started.

All around there was a shroud of snow stretching as far as the eye could see. By the railway line it looked good enough to eat, like whipped cream. The train did not have a restaurant car, so at the main stations we rushed to the buffet and bought sandwiches. We got a lot of Moscow newspapers; even if the station was not particularly important, the news-stands had plenty of music and arts magazines. Looked to see if anything had been written about my arrival. Not much: the newspapers seem mainly devoted to reporting speeches of the political leaders. I spotted, though, a notice to the effect that a committee for meeting Prokofiev had been organized, with Asafiev included in it as the representative of Leningrad. I am very nervous about officialdom, but it is good to know that Asafiev will be there: he at least will tell me how to behave.

Thursday 20 January

Woke up early. It is dark outside and in the compartment too, because the gas-lamp is out of order. The guard brought a candle. Our approach to Moscow was not of a kind to draw attention to itself; I think the station was the Alexandrovsky, which has rather a provincial appearance. At 7.30 a.m. the train, slightly late, suddenly stopped at the wooden platform. While we were trying to get one of the porters (who seem to be in short supply), along came Tseitlin and Tsukker, then Derzhanovsky. Tseitlin is the chairman of the Persimfans and its guiding spirit; previously he was the leader of Koussevitsky's orchestra. Tsukker, as I learned a bit later, is an active communist. Originally he wanted to become a singer and this committed him to music. Then he took a militant part in the Soviet Revolution and is now a kind of secretary in the All-Russian Central Executive Committee. This allows him to be in touch with all the members of the government. He is the only member of the Persimfans who does not play in the orchestra: his function is to prepare programmes, give talks on the radio during the concerts and, of course, liaise with the higher authorities on all matters relating to the orchestra. He, by the way, tells me that it was Litvinov who authorized our being supplied with Soviet papers without our Nansen passports being taken away. Of course I won't be prosecuted, he says, but it would be better for me to make less use of the latter than before.

Derzhanovsky seems hardly to have changed: a bit thinner, smaller. They are all wearing felt boots and have extraordinary fur hats and sheepskin coats, just the kind of dressing up which intimidates foreigners so much.

Exclamations, greetings: 'Has Prokofiev *really* come back to Moscow?' – and, having gone through this apology for a railway station, we get a taxi. Although there are not many cars in Moscow you can find taxis. The windows are completely frozen over, so we cannot see the city we are crossing at all. Tse-Tse (Tseitlin and Tsukker) tell us about all the problems connected with our arrival, passionately interrupting each other, and of their expectations, doubts, worries and so on.

Now we have arrived at the Metropole. At the beginning of the Revolution the hotel was requisitioned for Soviet institutions and for housing those people who had responsible offices; but recently it was decided that it would be more profitable to move the whole lot somewhere else and turn the building back into an hotel. Of course it was not easy to relocate everybody and everything in Moscow, which is now badly overcrowded; only one floor has been cleared and turned into an hotel, for the time being, and this has been refurbished by the Germans.

The 'responsible people' are still living on the top floors, so there is a terrible mess everywhere – except in our corridor, which has a smart-looking carpet, a good hairdressing salon, and is very clean. Our room overlooks Theatre Square and the view is delightful. The room is impeccably clean and quite spacious, and the ceiling is unusually high. The beds are in niches and separated by a large green plush curtain which reaches almost to the ceiling. But no bathroom, only water in jugs. I order coffee for everybody, which is brought in glasses with metal glassholders. A lot of talking, but we absolutely must get down to business straight away, because tomorrow we have our first orchestral rehearsal. First I need a piano in my room: I want to be in good shape for my first appearance in Moscow. In Russia there is a chronic shortage of musical instruments; none, or at best very few, are manufactured, and no licences are given for the purchase of foreign ones. Derzhanovsky suggests we go to Kniga, a shop where they sell scores and music books; he is its director and I should be able to get a piano there.

We went there after finishing our coffee. A lot of people in the streets. On the one hand many fur collars, on the other many women in head-scarves. Much has been written about visitors from abroad being struck by the poverty of the Russians' clothing, yet I would not say *I* was struck by this; perhaps because too much fuss has been made about it, or perhaps because large numbers of head-scarves and sheepskin coats *always* walked about in Russian streets, and therefore do not surprise me now any more than before. Huge buses are driving around, the pride of Moscow. They really are large and beautiful and, though made in England, are better designed than the London ones.

The piano at Kniga was not up to much – far too 'beat-up', worn out through long use. In the shop I met Liolya, Derzhanovsky's secretary. And here, for the first time, I realized how long I have been away from Russia. I remembered Liolya as a plump thirteen-year-old girl. Now she is a large lady. Very nice meeting her again.

Went to another shop, I think it was the former Diderichs, which, since nationalization, has become a state shop. There I found a new piano with a nice, taut, clean sound, just what I wanted. I ordered it at once and they delivered it during the day. Again walked about the streets. Cold and frosty. The crowd is quiet and even-tempered. Are these the same wild beasts whose excesses have scandalized the world?

It was past 1 and we wanted to eat. Tse-Tse showed us the recently refurbished Bolshoy Moskovsky Hotel and we went there for lunch. Inside was an enormous hall with masses of tables, everything indeed completely renovated, as clean as could be and a bit on the vulgar side. In the enormous hall we were almost on our own, for here nobody eats at this hour – later is more usual, between 3 and 4 o'clock. But it fills up mainly in the evening. Russia is the kingdom of caviare, but not in this restaurant – the prices for fresh caviare were such that although we toyed with the idea we finally did not order any. On the whole prices *à la carte* are no lower than in America. Meals with the fixed-price menu are served later in the day. Waiters are polite and accept tips. The head waiter in a dinner-jacket leant on the table with fingernails so shinily varnished that they virtually lit up everything on it.

When we left the restaurant we thought we might walk about the town for a bit. Tse-Tse and Derzhanovsky had always been around us chattering mercilessly; now at last we had the chance to walk about the forbidding town on our own, and very interesting it was too. We went on to the Tverskaya, bought some cakes for our afternoon guests and returned to the Metropole: we hadn't actually walked very much, but not being in practice had got very cold. Soon Tseitlin arrived with an interviewer and a photographer. While the interviewer was asking questions guests began to arrive. They were people whom I was very interested to see, but the interviewer would not leave me alone and the situation soon got a bit ludicrous: I would be answering his question – someone knocks on the door – I rush to open it – exclamations, hugs – we come back into the room – another question from the interviewer (must take care not to say anything silly in reply) – another knock on the door – and so on.

Asafiev appeared, slightly fatter and healthier-looking; instead of a waistcoat, shirt and collar under his jacket he had a brown knitted jumper with a collar up to his chin: nice and warm and no need to worry about a clean collar! Then Myaskovsky who, despite everything, has not changed much – you wouldn't think I hadn't seen him for ten years. As for that photograph in Riga, either it lied or was taken at a bad moment. He is as refined as before, has the same charm; maybe some barely noticeable wrinkles have appeared – the kind which show up when you are tired but disappear when you are fresh, as when you come in straight from outside. Apparently Myaskovsky found many more changes in me than I in him. To begin with, at any rate, he looked intently at me for a long time, smiling all the while, probably wondering how I could have put on so much weight and become so bald.

After Myaskovsky Saradzhev came. He had a bit more grey hair and had grown to look like Nikisch. Derzhanovsky and Tsukker were also there. The interview, thank goodness, finally came to an end and we asked the photographer to take a picture of the whole group. Since group photographs are expensive in Russia and he had been ordered to photograph only the famous foreign guest, in the beginning he hesitated. Only when Tsukker insisted, explaining that all the celebrities of musical Moscow were assembled here, did he photograph us, and this group picture actually appeared in several newspapers. General conversation did not flow too easily because we were all excited and a bit flustered. Myaskovsky, Asafiev and Saradzhev pored over my new scores: the Second Symphony, the Quintet and the Overture for Seventeen Musicians.

'But it isn't complicated at all!' exclaimed Saradzhev, studying the score of the symphony: he very much wanted to perform it himself and keep the Persimfans out of it.

Most of them soon left, all rather busy people who had snatched a few minutes to come and see me. Only Asafiev and Tsukker remained. Asafiev, though, being invited somewhere else, could not stay for supper with us, and Tsukker took us to a restaurant on the Prechistenky Boulevard, which he said was less fancy and better and cheaper than in the Bolshaya Moskovskaya. All the way there he, as an active and deeply committed communist, treated me to enthusiastic descriptions of everything his Party was doing for the good of the people. It all sounded fascinating, if somewhat larger than life. It was very interesting to see the enormous building of the Comintern, a kind of huge jar full of microbes destined for world-wide distribution.

The restaurant he took us to was housed in a separate wooden building in the middle of the boulevard. Apparently in summer the tables make their way outside and then it is particularly agreeable. Tsukker lost no time in explaining that the restaurant is run by a group of 'has-beens', former rich merchants and aristocrats. Indeed we were served by pleasant and well-bred ladies. From the conversation between the cashier and the barmaid (who kept calling down to the cook in the kitchen, which was in the basement) we could tell they were not 'simple' people.

The meal was unusually delicious – hazel-grouse, whipped cream, cranberry juice (of which we drank several glasses) and many exquisite long-forgotten dishes. Tsukker would not hear of our paying. Afterwards we got into sledges and were driven home through the frost.

Going to bed we discovered the sheets were of an extraordinarily fine linen of a type we have not seen in any European or American hotel. The pillow-cases and the towels were also of first-rate quality. We feel completely stunned by Moscow, but I am at all times solidly conscious of the fact that the Bolsheviks are adept at showing off in order to impress foreigners. We compare notes in whispers. We do not believe the rumours current in *émigré* circles to the effect that the beds have microphones fixed under them; but we do notice a locked door between our room and the next through which someone could easily eavesdrop if they wanted. We fall asleep tired out.

Friday 21 January

We got up at 8.30. Tsukker came to take us by taxi to the rehearsal in the Great Hall of the Conservatoire. Few taxis are to be seen in Moscow, but there are always some on our square. They are all Renaults purchased wholesale from France.

When we were walking into the Conservatoire through the Artists' Entrance I slipped on the icy ground and nearly fell.

'You see!' said Tsukker. 'This is where Raisky was moved to tears by your arrival and his tears froze!'

Raisky is the manager of the Great Hall and the director of the Rosphil, the semi-state-owned Symphonic Society, with which the Persimfans is furiously competing.

As we were going up to the Hall Tsukker exclaimed, 'Listen! They're playing the March from the *Three Oranges*!'

I assumed we were late for the rehearsal and started to hurry, at the same time telling Tsukker the tempo was too slow and they would have to liven it up. But then it became clear that it was a fanfare: the orchestra had been alerted as to my arrival and were welcoming me with the piece of mine with which they had had their greatest success.

After finishing the March the orchestra clapped. I went up on stage. Tseitlin made a welcoming speech: what a pleasure it was to see me here in Moscow and so on. I loathe speeches because they always have to be replied to. So I decided immediately to grasp the nettle with both hands and reply: what a pleasure it is for me to be back in Moscow, particularly with the orchestra which I consider one of the best in the world . . . Applause, bows – and then straight away we begin to rehearse the Third Piano Concerto. This time it is not me who is agitated, but the orchestra, if their reluctance to keep to a steady tempo is anything to go by.

'Don't hurry so much, comrades,' shouts Tseitlin. 'Don't get excited . . .'

The rehearsal is led by Tseitlin. In front of him, on the music-stand, is not the first violin part, but the full score, into which from time to time his neighbours also peep. Sometimes the second trombone or the third horn stands up and says, 'Comrades! Here we must do this, that, or the other . . .'

Just the same, the rehearsal proceeds smoothly and agreeably. The orchestra has already played this work in public twice, once with Feinberg as soloist, and on the other occasion with the very young pianist Oborin. The problem is that both these soloists' tempi were different from mine. Oborin was not so bad – his were not too far removed from mine – but Feinberg's approach was so neurotic and mannered it almost turned the piece inside out. I wouldn't have thought there was anything 'neurotic' about my Third Concerto.

Without a conductor the orchestra took much more trouble and worked harder than it would with one; a conductor would have to battle with passages of technical difficulty and ask for important voices to be brought out. Here the players are very conscientious, play by nature musically and with great concentration; all dynamics and nuances are precisely observed. No question of learning their parts at the rehearsal; they prepare the most difficult passages at home beforehand. On the other hand, problems arise: a ritardando, for example, which with a conductor will come about quite unproblematically, may take them a good twenty minutes to straighten out, because every player slows down in his own way. This was what happened in the second movement, in the passage which leads from the last variation to the reprise of the theme, when the orchestra simply could not keep together with me. The difficulties were aggravated by the fact that Feinberg had played a ritardando which does not exist in the score; whereas I, instead, made an accelerando, which also does not exist in the score!

Feinberg had an argument about this ritardando with Myaskovsky. When I later told Myaskovsky that a ritardando would be unthinkable here he was very pleased, and exclaimed, 'I *must* remember to tell Feinberg!' But when, in order to please him more, I added that, so far from a ritardando, I even make an accelerando here, Myaskovsky (always a stickler for orthodoxy) got annoyed. 'There's really no need for it,' he said.

After the rehearsal Ptashka, Tseitlin and I went to the Persimfans's administration office, in the same building as the Conservatoire but on the floor below. The 'Persimfans Administrative Centre' sounds important, but in fact it is just a small room which also serves as the living quarters of Tseitlin and his wife, who sleep behind a curtain. After the rehearsal a whole crowd packed into the room, where there were only two chairs but also two tables, both piled high with papers. The telephone was ringing non-stop and the place was in an uproar, a complete madhouse. After having settled a few minor but pressing questions, we set off with Tseitlin for lunch in the same restaurant, on the Prechistenky Boulevard, where Tsukker had taken us the day before.

After lunch we went for a walk and Tseitlin showed us some shops in the Okhotny Row, where we bought caviare, cheese and butter. There was plenty of caviare at different prices and the shops were so full of people that we ran out of time queueing. And we thought Moscow was supposed to be starving! Admittedly there were more shoppers today than usual, because it was a holiday: not only a Sunday but also the anniversary of Lenin's death.

'You see how good it is here,' crowed Tseitlin. 'Thank God you got out of Paris. You must have read in the papers there's a shortage of coffins there . . .'

I was dumbfounded.

'A shortage of *coffins?*'

'Oh, come on, you've just come from there, you must know. What about the epidemic? The papers say so many people die there every day they can't keep up with burying them.'

Well, I could see that Moscow lied about Paris no less professionally than Paris about Moscow. As he accompanied us to the Metropole Tseitlin went on bubbling and fizzing.

'Look at the Bolshoi Theatre. It was recently refaced. They were so concerned about getting it right artistically they didn't dare reface it

17

with new stone; they wanted stone of the same vintage as the building. So the engineers went to a cemetery, found some gravestones erected in whatever year it was – and you can see how well it turned out!

'It's true, it's true!' he added, seeing that I was staring at him in utter amazement.

After saying goodbye to Tseitlin we sat for a while in our hotel room, resting and reflecting on Moscow's well-ordered and active life-style. Since we were expecting some Persimfans people in the evening we went out once more to buy a few things – ham, cakes and so on. We went to the enormous co-operative shop next to the Bolshoi Theatre. There were many shoppers, but they were all behaving in an orderly manner. Many nice things on the counter, and no shortage of very good quality paper to wrap them in.

In the evening the entire management of the Persimfans showed up – five people in all. We talked and drank tea with odds and ends to eat; they did not eat anything, probably from shyness. We discussed the tempi of *Chout* and of the *Three Oranges* Suite. Also the dates for Leningrad had to be settled. The Persimfans have booked all the best dates, the result being that Leningrad will have to wait a full two weeks before I can get there. They will not be pleased. Tse-Tse assured me that Khais (according to them a despicable character who pulls all the strings in the Leningrad Philharmonia) had already taken advantage of my reluctance to discuss money and fixed my fee lower than he should have. Even worse, Khais had already been boasting about it as an example of a very clever business arrangement. In this connection we started to talk about my contract with the Persimfans, but it was too late to get very far. Nor were we able to discuss some offers for engagements which had already come in from the provinces. To talk about the latter would anyhow have been premature at this stage.

Saturday 22 January

In the morning Tsukker came to fetch me for a rehearsal. The orchestra was learning the suite from *Chout* in its entirety except for two movements. In my opinion even that is too long – eight movements are quite enough – but Tseitlin wants to persevere and tackle all ten. The orchestral balance is good, the relationship between instruments is just right, and if it is not quite so all I need do is make the point and they *get* it right. The Persimfans's opponents say that without a conductor precision of ensemble is beyond them, and that all chords sound as if played by a drunken hussar, arpeggiato, none of the notes sounding together. Perhaps, but at least here each musician conscientiously plays all the notes in his part, thereby enabling the composer to hear what he wrote in its entirety. Whereas the attitude of players engaged on a one-off basis is often deplorable: they pretend to be playing, but in reality are leaving half the notes out and playing correctly only those passages which stand out and cannot be left unplayed. As soon as they realize they are merely accompanying they begin to slacken off and leave bits out. It goes without saying that the piece begins to sound wretched and quite different from the way the composer orchestrated it.

Feinberg was at the rehearsal. He knew I was playing my Third Concerto and came to listen jealously as to how I did it. This bothered me slightly as I rehearsed.

After the rehearsal Ptashka and I, accompanied by Tse-Tse, went to the same restaurant on the Prechistenky, but it was closed so we returned to the Metropole. There is no restaurant at the Metropole, they serve only tea and coffee, but we were able to organize a light lunch during which we discussed the dates for Leningrad and how to combine them with Moscow. During our conversation Lunacharsky, having heard I had arrived, telephoned to greet me and invited me to visit him at 7. I thanked him but explained that I was having dinner at 5 with friends and wondered if I might come at 8 instead. That suited Lunacharsky quite well; end of conversation.

Soon Asafiev arrived and we went with him to see Myaskovsky in Denezhny Lane. He lives in a big building overlooking a small garden or yard and it is very quiet there. The flat was a very nice one but, as with all flats in Moscow, several families were living there now. Myaskovsky himself had only one room; the one adjacent to his was occupied by his sister, Valentina Yakovlevna, and her daughter. Myaskovsky's room, though long and narrow, was quite large but so full of furniture – bed, washbasin, grand piano, large desk, several wardrobes and shelves with scores – that you could hardly even turn round in it. Myaskovsky complains that when he moves the piano the chair in front of it gets pushed into the desk; when he moves the desk it gets stuck against the piano. So he shunts things around according to what he needs.

We found Myaskovsky proof-reading his Seventh Symphony. I of course was very anxious to find out what had happened to the suitcase with my manuscripts, letters and diaries, which had been left during the Revolution with Koussevitsky, then given to the Musical Sector, and finally to Myaskovsky. From my correspondence with Myaskovsky I could never find out if the suitcase had been opened, and was very much afraid that it might have been ransacked. To my great joy it was in perfect order and even the sealed batches of diaries had not been opened. After all, during the Revolution, when inventories and searches were everyday events, anything could have happened.

I asked Myaskovsky what to do about Jurgenson. The problem was that all Jurgenson's publishing assets had been nationalized, but only within Russia. If therefore he were prepared to sell me the foreign rights to those early works of mine he had published, the latter could be taken over by Gutheil, who had left Russia and was carrying on his business in the West. Myaskovsky said that it was a very thorny problem. If it became known here that Jurgenson were selling off his foreign rights he could well land in prison. The only way would be for Jurgenson to express a desire to discuss the matter in strict confidence and to come to a private arrangement.

Eventually all three of us, Myaskovsky, Asafiev and I, set out for Derzhanovsky's, who lived not very far away, and by whom we had all been invited for dinner at 5 o'clock. On the way I was telling them all about Souvchinsky, how he lived, who he was married to, what he was doing, and what Eurasianism was; I stopped talking whenever other people went by because it was a proscribed topic (Asafiev remarked that letters both to and from Souvchinsky apparently get lost). However the streets we were walking through were almost deserted, so for the most part we could speak freely.

When I paused Myaskovsky looked at me critically and said, 'Well, well, things aren't as bad as I expected. At least you haven't forgotten your Russian!'

To which I reacted with acute embarrassment and even some anger. 'And why, may I ask, should you think I *would* have forgotten it?'

'When I was in Vienna and met Sashenka Tcherepnin his Russian was so fractured with Gallicisms that I could hardly understand a word he was saying.'

And to illustrate what he meant Myaskovsky gave us some examples which actually were quite amusing. And after that I must confess I began to watch what I said and to speak with some hesitation.

We found Ptashka with Derzhanovsky. He had collected her on his own and seemed to be flirting with her already. As soon as we had ended our meal Tsukker arrived and took her to the Bolshoi Theatre to see *Sadko*. I promised to come on later if the Narkompros (People's Commissariat of Enlightenment) did not keep me too long.

So Myaskovsky, Asafiev and I together again walked through the same quiet and frosty streets towards no. 7 Denezhny Lane, where Myaskovsky lived. Lunacharsky lived just a few blocks further along and Asafiev, who had been there before, volunteered to take me not only to the house but also to the very door. The house was large and obviously must once have been splendid, but now the staircase we went up to the top floor was dirty and disgusting. The lift was out of order. I rang the bell and Asafiev went downstairs. A plump maid opened the door, asked my name and went to announce me. Then she asked me to go to the sitting-room, which was furnished quite comfortably. The door to the next room was slightly ajar and somebody there was reading a poem out loud. A few minutes later the plump maid appeared again and asked me to come to the dining-room.

Lunacharsky came to meet me, very courteous as always. Looked a bit flabby compared with how he was in 1918 (when I had last seen him). About fifteen people were sitting at the large table. Some of them made as if to approach me, but the reading was not yet finished; Lunacharsky made a gesture to ask for silence and, inviting me to take a seat, begged the poet to continue.

The name of the poet was Utkin, and he read for quite some time. Naturally, having just come back to the USSR, and having tonight come to meet, of all people, the People's Commissar of Enlightenment, I expected the poetry of the rebellious proletariat to be revolutionary in character; Utkin's belonged more to what is generally classified as 'decadent'. However, once he had finished reading I was introduced to everybody. Some of the guests were half-forgotten people from the artistic world of pre-revolutionary times. The wife of Lunacharsky – or rather one of his most recent wives – was a beautiful woman from the front, much less beautiful if you looked at her predatory profile. She was an actress and her maiden name was Rozanel.

We moved into the sitting-room. One or two young men came up to me and loaded me with compliments. But Lunacharsky himself talks more than anybody: he never lets his interlocutor open his mouth. He has some interesting news for me: in spring, in Paris, an international competition between theatres from different countries will take place. Four countries, including the USSR, have already agreed to take part and as a main feature intend to present *The Love for Three Oranges*. It is not finally decided, but the wheels are greased. Several young poets and musicians surrounded me, talked to me about my compositions and asked me to play something. I sat at a rather mediocre piano and played the March from the *Three Oranges*. After that Lunacharsky asked one of the pianists present to play the Finale from my Second Sonata, which he says is his favourite work. The pianist played it quite badly. From the piano we moved to another, smaller drawing-room, quite cosily furnished. Lunacharsky showed us the first issue of the *LEF*, a new magazine published by Mayakovsky. 'LEF' means Left Front. Luna-charsky explains that Mayakovsky considers me to be a typical representative of LEF. 'So,' he adds, 'it would be good for you to listen to Mayakovsky's Address, which is published in this issue.'

Lunacharsky then reads quite well and with great enthusiasm the letter in verse from Mayakovsky to Gorky. The letter really is sharp in flavour and some of the poetic expressions are very good. The idea is: why, Alexey Maximovich, when there is so much work to do in Russia, are you living somewhere in Italy? Extremely edifying for me, and Lunacharsky, having finished the reading, laughingly recommends me to take this poem to heart. I ask him how Mayakovsky is regarded in the literary world. He answers that he is highly regarded, although some people would like to put a stick through the bars of the cage and tease the LEF.

I chat to Rozanel for a bit and at 9 o'clock excuse myself, explaining that I would like to be on time at the Bolshoi. Everybody accompanies me into the hall and a young man, a pupil of Yavorsky, comes to the theatre with me in the cab.

'We are jealous of the West having you,' he says as we drive through the streets. But the frost is terrible. I try to answer him, but am more concerned about my ears which are in danger of being frost-bitten (my Parisian coat hasn't got a fur collar).

At the Bolshoi I am shown to a box in the Dress Circle occupied by Ptashka and Tsukker. This box is next to the Tsar's in the centre, and is usually reserved for the directors. The theatre is full, but the public (judging by their clothes at least) seem rather rough-and-ready. I enjoy the scene of Sadko's departure: the music is marvellous, although many things are theatrically absurd. But then some parts of the underwater fantasy, which in the old days probably sounded quite innovatory, have lost their freshness and now strike one as boring interludes with little genuine music.

The theatre conductors, Golovanov and then later Pazovsky, visited our box during the intervals and sometimes even during the performance, and spoke about the production of the *Oranges*, which apparently will take place in the Bolshoi at the end of the season. It will be conducted by Golovanov. He asked me if I could play it to him as soon as my first concerts were over, say in a week's time, in order to show him the right tempi and generally give him directions. I also spoke to Pazovsky, and could not help remembering something written at least fifteen years ago by Kankarovich. Kankarovich had just become a music critic and, having castigated my First Piano Concerto, went on to reinforce his criticism in the following sentence: 'The conductor Pazovsky, who was sitting next to me, said it sounded to him like a lot of lunatics racing about.'

Who this conductor Pazovsky was I had not known until this evening, but now, while he was politely talking to me, the phrase about lunatics kept racing about in my mind.

Sunday 23 January

All the morning was spent rehearsing. I frequently stopped the orchestra to give instructions about tempi and balance.

Glière, my old teacher, came to the rehearsal, and we adopted the same style of addressing each other that we'd used twenty-five years ago when I was a child; that is to say, I would call him 'You' and 'Reinhold Moritsevich', and he would call me 'Thou' and 'Seryozha'. Glière is fat and middle-aged, clean-shaven and quite sleek looking, a bit like a well-fed cat. Although he is getting on for sixty, he talks a lot about his piano technique and how he has discovered a wonderful new system of exercises, according to which the back muscles influence each finger (he showed me on my back which ones influence which); and as a result of practising these he claimed to have improved a great deal of late. He has travelled across Russia with a singer, accompanying her from memory in whole evenings of his own songs, and hopes now to do the same in Germany. If he does so, pity the poor Germans and poor Glière as well! I give him news of Dukelsky (another of his pupils) and tell him how we go for walks together sometimes and amuse ourselves humming themes from his (Glière's) First and Second Symphonies, which remind us of our youth. After that I have to go on stage because most of today is to be spent rehearsing the Theme and Variations (second movement) and the Finale of the Third Concerto.

In the afternoon I rest. I begin already to feel a bit weary of all this Moscow commotion, and it's hardly begun as yet! Having had my rest I went to inspect the Bechstein piano for tomorrow's concert. Despite the poor quality of pianos in Soviet Russia this one turned out to be splendid; but to get it Tseitlin had to fight a long battle with the directors of the Conservatoire, because it belongs to them and is their prize possession. Raisky and Igumnov did not want to loan it out. Raisky I don't know about, but I thought Igumnov was supposed to be an admirer of mine. In the end Tseitlin managed to talk them round and they agreed to make the piano available, I think for 50 roubles a concert.

Later Ptashka and I set off to see Nadya Raevsky at Arbat 5. Since Shurik is in prison as a political suspect, we almost felt we were breaking the law in visiting Nadya. And what if there is a detective tailing us in another cab? Or perhaps the detective is waiting for us outside her house, knowing they are my relatives and checking on me in case I might be associating with counter-revolutionary elements. What we did in fact was to stop the cab at some distance from the house and then try to slip inconspicuously through the gates. However Ptashka's leopard-skin coat made her so obvious that no one would be likely to forget seeing us. Friends knew of only one other similar coat in the whole of Moscow, and that belonged to Nezhdanova, the wife of Golovanov.

The Raevskys occupy a flat of four small rooms on the ground floor overlooking the yard. The entrance, of course, is filthy. Inside we were met by Katyusha Uvarova, whom I remembered as a pretty fifteen-year-old girl; now she had turned into a robust but slightly coarse-featured young lady of just under thirty. She welcomed me joyfully, but when I introduced her to Ptashka she assumed that she did not speak Russian and held out her hand and said, '*Charmée.*' I nearly burst out laughing, remembering Babulenka in *The Gambler*, and explained that my wife speaks Russian like a Russian. Nadya was not at home, but in came her three daughters aged from three to twelve – puny creatures, sweet but plain and much smaller than they should be at this age. I started to explain quickly in a low voice to Katya Uvarova that we could not wait for Nadya because we were in a great hurry, but that we would like to send for Aunt Katya and Katya Ignatieva from Penza and that I can supply the money for that. If I can establish good relations with the authorities I intend to take steps to try and obtain the release of Shurik; but we cannot rush things. In short, I try to bring them up to date with everything I know to do with their family, bearing in mind that we have to be wary about coming here too often.

We said goodbye and as we were leaving ran into Nadya. She went wild with joy at seeing us, but my impression at that moment was that it was all a bit overdone. The hard years had left their imprint on her and she looked curiously like the Empress Alexandra Fyodorovna. Shurik is bravely serving his term in prison, originally ten years but now reduced by a third. In the prison common criminals are mixed with political prisoners. The latter are more or less his kind of people and they all keep together. Shurik is doing some shoemaking and also plays piano in the cinema. I hasten to explain to Nadya what I have already told Katya Uvarova, but break off because a man dressed like a *moujik* comes into the flat. He wears felt boots and a fur cap with ear-muffs, and his clothing contrasts sharply with his delicate and handsome face and slightly grizzly beard. Seeing my confusion Nadya says, 'It's all right, this is my sister's husband, Lopukhin. You can speak freely in front of him.'

We soon say goodbye and leave for the second time, because we have to hurry to the Derzhanovskys'. Madame Derzhanovsky is celebrating her fiftieth birthday today. It is very brave for a woman to celebrate her fiftieth, although venomous tongues say that she is doing that so nobody will think that she is sixty.

At the Derzhanovskys' are Myaskovsky, Asafiev, Alexandrov, Feinberg, Polovinkin, Knipper, Kryukov, Mosolov and some others, young people whose faces mean nothing to me at first. Nearly all are pupils of Myaskovsky and, of course, all have come under his aura of charm. Feinberg I recognized immediately – his face is unlike anyone else's – but not the quiet and unremarkable Alexandrov. It seems the most talented of the younger men is Mosolov, who is composing complicated works. He is good-looking, but his wife, who looks older, isn't. However, she is quite a remarkable pianist; at least, she recently gave a recital of modern sonatas – Myaskovsky, me, late Skriabin and some others of similar complexity, like six-storey buildings. What a repertoire!

Some time later Feinberg is asked to play and he performs his *Improvisations*, complicated and empty pieces. His playing is unbelievable, emotional in the most exhibitionistic way: he breathes noisily through the nose, bends right down over the keyboard and makes a long-drawn issue of every note. In short he doesn't play, he suffers. And it becomes embarrassing for the audience to watch him subjecting himself to such torture. Next they ask me to play, and I oblige with, of course, the Fifth Sonata. If I don't play it here then where should I play it? They listen silently and very attentively but express no opinion at the end. Then they ask me to play something else. This time I give them the Third Sonata, then go to the next room where Asafiev is sitting. He remarks that I play it completely differently from the way I did in 1918, before my departure for America. As a result of that – because I took a different tempo from the one he expected – he has lost a bet with somebody. He also remarks that before, when I played the introduction to the second theme, it sounded better for my putting a rest in the bass before it starts. I agree with him and promise to restore this rest.

Liolya and Madame Derzhanovsky are laying the table for supper while we are sitting in the room called Tsecooboo, which means 'Central Committee for the Improvement of Scientists' Living Conditions'. Derzhanovsky managed to keep the whole flat to himself by giving up one room to the cook. As for the Tsecooboo-room, somebody else was to have moved in, but with the help of this self-same 'Central

Committee for the Improvement of Scientists' Living Conditions' it was possible to prove that Derzhanovsky needed to concentrate on scientific-musical work, for which a separate study was required.

Supper begins. I am sitting between Myaskovsky and Asafiev. Myaskovsky has a permanent seat next to the hostess and nobody else is allowed to occupy this place. I am stunned that he addresses Liolya as 'thou' and ask her, 'How did you manage to seduce Koliechka?'

Indeed she is probably the first woman with whom he has been on familiar terms.

The young composers try to court Ptashka in every way possible, but most of all Derzhanovsky himself. Later during supper there is even champagne, a luxury in Soviet Russia; but we make a get-away before the end, because of tomorrow's dress rehearsal and my first Moscow concert.

Monday 24 January

We got home late enough yesterday, even if we did leave early. But we had to get up at 8, and at 9 the dress rehearsal began. Golovanov is sitting with the score of *Chout* and is writing in it with a pencil the notes I am giving to the Persimfans. The Persimfans people, who do not consider him a friend, make malicious fun of him, saying that he does not know how to conduct *Chout* and for that reason has to annotate every bar. While I rehearse the Third Concerto the hall is full of people, but the crowd disperses when I finish. The two suites, *Chout* and *Three Oranges*, go well, but another rehearsal wouldn't do any harm.

In the afternoon Tseitlin and I drive to the customs-house, since the trunk which was not examined at the frontier, as well as the bag with the reeds for the woodwind, are stuck in the Moscow Section. All the woodwinds of the Persimfans are waiting impatiently for these reeds because the old ones have worn out and they have to blow into God knows what. New ones cannot be found in Russia. It goes without saying that Tseitlin has provided himself with all the necessary letters of authorization and clearance, and so, in fact, hardly any examination takes place at all; they opened the trunk and undid the bag only for form's sake. Yet, having found an old silk skirt which Ptashka did not wear any more and had only packed as a present for our poor relatives, they immediately got interested and even made a fuss; but seeing how old it was they let it pass. We lunched at 3 on our own at the Bolshaya Moskovskaya. As a matter of fact, we don't really know if it is lunch or dinner – here in Moscow all the times get muddled up and they eat mainly in the middle of the afternoon (perhaps they save money by combining lunch and dinner). People at the next table turned out to be Mekler, an impresario, who already had sent me a couple of notes, and Polyakin, the violinist, once a Wunderkind in Auer's class at the same time as Cecilia Hansen, but who somehow eventually fizzled out and faded in the light of her brilliant success. After that Polyakin had managed to stay domiciled in America and even to acquire American citizenship. But American success had eluded him, and now Mekler was taking him round Russia. They came over at once and sat down at our table and Mekler lost no time going on the offensive and showering me with offers. But, seeing that I will not swallow his bait and seem indifferent to the idea of touring the provinces, he turns his attention to Ptashka. What he could do for her as a singer, he assures her – think of all the concert engagements he could secure for her! To give credence to his claims he mentions the 'artist of international stature' Marchex, whom he has already taken on tour round Russia once, and will be taking again. We laughed and explained that Marchex was no better than a third-class pianist. But Mekler would not give up and said, 'Excuse me! But he is a real gentleman . . .'

Me: 'Maybe he tries to pass himself off here as a gentleman, but in Paris he might just as well be in rags . . .'

Polyakin suddenly burst into laughter and exclaimed, 'A ragamuffin!' But then he glanced at Ptashka and looked embarrassed.

Ptashka and I finished our lunch before they did, and as we were going downstairs Mekler ran up to us and offered me 350 roubles for a concert in the provinces. By the time we were in the hallway the offer had reached 500, and going out into the street brought it up to 1,500 for Moscow and even 3,000 for two concerts. I must admit the idea of the latter sum made me feel a bit uncomfortable; yet Mekler seemed a rather pathetic character, and so, saying goodbye, I asked him to ring me in about five days, when the excitement of the first concerts was over.

Back home we rested a bit before the concert. Seryozha Serebryakov telephones, but Ptashka, not knowing who he is, tells him I do not answer the phone before a concert. Later she reports that he was obviously disappointed, so I call and ask him to meet us before the concert so we can help him get in.

Having rested we change and leave for the concert. The Great Hall of the Conservatoire is full and there are even some people standing, although this is forbidden by the fire inspector. Morolev meets us in the Green Room and I am very glad to see him, but how he has changed in these fifteen years! Yes, fifteen years is quite a long time. Now he is quite grey, and although you could not describe him as an old man, he is certainly more than middle-aged.

The concert starts with the suite from *Chout* – quite long, since they are playing ten of the twelve movements. It is perfectly audible from the Green Room, which is separated from the stage by a thin wall with gaps in it. The Persimfans's performance is excellent, clearly articulated, expressive and enthusiastic. Applause and shouts for 'the composer' follow the suite, but, as we agreed with Tse-Tse, I am not going out so as not to forestall my entrance for the performance of the concerto. Nevertheless, Tseitlin burst into the Green Room in such a state of excitement that he himself is ready to change what we agreed; he asks me if perhaps after all I should go on stage. While the applause continues we deliberate and decide that I should not.

Before going out to play my concerto I begin to get stage-fright. I work at it a bit and manage to calm down. Just the same I cannot take too light a view of the situation: I am in Moscow, where they've been looking forward so intensely to seeing me, and – worst of all – where they know my concerto so intimately I dare not play it badly.

At last Tabakov, the first trumpet (an excellent one), comes in and informs me that the orchestra is ready and I have to go on. As I appear the orchestra plays a flourish, then stands up and applauds. This turns into a large-scale and exceedingly long ovation on the part of both audience and orchestra. I stand for a long time, bow to all sides and really do not know what to do, sit down, but since the applause continues, again stand up, again bow and again do not know what to do. I have not been in Moscow for ten years, I want to concentrate in order to play properly, but a big give-and-take of emotion does not help one to become absorbed. Finally I get fed up and resolutely sit down. The applause goes on for a while, then dies away. Tseitlin, whose chair is exactly behind my back, whispers we should now sit quietly for a couple of minutes, so that I, the orchestra and the public can all get ourselves into a suitable frame of mind. I try not to look at anybody and bury myself in the piano. In about three minutes we start.

I was not at my most relaxed as I played, but did quite well. There was only one incident: at one point in the third variation I got in a bit of a muddle. I don't remember exactly what happened, but in any event it was nothing serious, and we quickly got back on an even keel again. At the end the hall shouted its head off. I don't think I ever got such a reception anywhere. I am called out over and over again. As an encore I play first the Gavotte from the 'Classical' Symphony, then the Toccata. Both these party pieces go down well. At last I retire to the Green Room while the orchestra plays the *Three Oranges* Suite. Following the tradition the March is repeated as an encore, and after that I go out several times. Once the concert is over the Green Room fills up with people. One of the first to arrive is Litvinov who at the moment, because of the prolonged absence abroad of Chicherin, is standing in as Foreign Minister. He looks a bit corpulent, is clean-shaven with thin lips and an intelligent expression, but the general impression is of a typical pharmaceutical chemist. Difficult to reconcile the portliness with his bravado in expropriating a Tiflis bank, a feat which has brought him some notoriety. But Litvinov is an important person for me, since all our passports and the various arrangements and concessions which facilitated our return to the USSR were made through him. He introduces himself and then his wife, who is English, to me. I am immediately commandeered by others: Myaskovsky, Asafiev, Morolev, Igumnov, the present Director of the Conservatoire; his predecessor Goldenweiser, with whom I have a brief conversation not about music but about chess; Glière, Feinberg, Aleksandrov and others. Having disposed of them I feel duty-bound to go over to Litvinov, who is sitting on the sofa. When I approach him he stands up; even if he does look like a pharmaceutical chemist, he is no less a diplomat, and not a bad one. I thank him for all his help, and introduce Ptashka to him and to his wife. The English lady is terribly glad to be able to speak to Ptashka in English. Then I am hauled off by another group – Golovanov, Dikij and Rabinovich. They are the conductor, the producer and the designer who will be collaborating in staging the *Oranges* in the Bolshoi Theatre. I am very pleased to meet Rabinovich, about whom I have heard many good things from Souvchinsky. (When the staging of our *Oursignol* was being planned Diaghilev couldn't decide between Yakulov and Rabinovich.) In the room Chernetskaya, who visited us on one occasion in Bellevue, mingled with the crowd. At present she has some marvellous plans for a new ballet which she can do only with me, and for which she has ideas that will turn the ballet world upside-down. She is ready to explain these ideas straight away, but by this time I am absolutely shredded and, thank God, the overturning of the ballet world is postponed. Little by little the room empties and I cool down. At last the four of us – I, Ptashka and Tse-Tse, the latter babbling enthusiastically all the way to the Metropole – are able to get away.

Tuesday 25 January

Our first day without a rehearsal; so we can rest on our laurels and take things easy. We lunched at the restaurant on the Prechistenky Boulevard with Asafiev, who gave us an enthusiastic account of his summer trip to the Far North. There, apparently, much survives from former times and the Soviet influence is mostly superficial. Ptashka liked Asafiev enormously. When she asked him about the present-day marriage-code, he explained that whatever its shortcomings it was still perhaps the best way to protect women after the dissolute years of war and Revolution when morals had grown very lax. He said that nowadays people are feeling the effects of a general policy to tighten up.

Leaving Asafiev I met Tsukker and went with him to ask for a foreign passport. Since the procedure for getting one can take a month or more, Tse-Tse had advised us to see to it without delay in order to make sure our departure was not held up. The Passport Department is supposed to be a division of the Narkomindel (the Ministry of Foreign Affairs), and the office is on their premises; but, as Tsukker explained, it is in fact under the jurisdiction of the GPU. I was quite curious to see what this special branch of the GPU was all about. We were received by Comrade Girin, a young man not without elegance, reddish in complexion, brisk in manner, well dressed, rather like a high-school student who has just joined the ranks of the civil service. Tsukker did the talking while I stood at the back. He began by speaking of Litvinov, who had organized my arrival, and made a point of emphasizing my privileged position. But Girin smiled: 'You do not need to bring Comrade Litvinov into it; just give your own account of yourself to us.'

After that he took the questionnaire (already filled out by me) and asked me to pay 6 copecks. I was surprised at the small amount, but Tsukker explained that for two passports 200 dollars will be required unless some kind of fictional business-trip classification can be arranged, in which case we would be liable to pay only a quarter of the tax. As to the 6 copecks, they are only the advance payment for the paper. The whole operation was performed swiftly and punctiliously. Seeing me to the door, Girin said that he had listened to my concert on the radio with interest. I reciprocated by praising the order in his office, which compared favourably with the confusion of the Paris Préfecture where you have to give tips all round in order to get your passport at all promptly. Girin was very pleased and asked me to come back a while later.

In the evening Mr and Mrs Mostras, both members of the board of the Persimfans, were giving a small party on behalf of the board. Also there were Tse-Tse, Yampolsky and others. The Mostras had been wealthy in the past and had a fine apartment with enormous rooms and very high ceilings. With the arrival of Bolshevism the apartment was requisitioned and they were left with only one room, albeit the biggest. Officials later decided it was too large and divided it in half, and later in half yet again. The result was something like a long and narrow corridor with an excessively high ceiling and one window.

There were extremely good hors-d'oeuvres, caviare and a marvellous white salmon, also Tokay. I received a present, a handicraft-specimen of characters from *Chout*: the buffoon himself, the merchant, the goat and others. Tsukker brought a camera with a magnesium flash and tried to take a photograph of us. The moment the lenses were open and the magnesium cord was lit, Tsukker would rush towards the group in order to get into the photograph. Then a rather comical *quiproquo* took place: Tsukker was determined, at whatever cost, to stand next to Ptashka, but his friends, who saw what he was after, contrived to thwart him every time. Tsukker would become all flustered and start another photograph.

Wednesday 26 January

We both wake up feeling sluggish. We are either worn out or have caught cold. Anyway we have to make a real effort to get ourselves back into gear.

Derzhanovsky appeared in felt boots, thin-looking with his little beard and eyes which peered out with a beadily cunning expression from beneath a shaky pince-nez. He suggested I come with him to choose a piano for tonight, but I couldn't be bothered and left it up to him.

In the afternoon Tse-Tse at last appeared to discuss terms and conditions, which we had never had time to do before. They had harsh words for the Leningrad Philharmonic and its managing director, Khais, who as I said had tried to offer me the most unfavourable terms, and had even shown off about it. As far as the Persimfans is concerned each member receives 20 roubles per concert plus expenses, and if anything is left over it is put in an all-purpose cash-box. Since they do not want to make money out of me they would like to give me all the profits after making a small deduction. However, they have to report on all their transactions with foreign musicians, and such an agreement is not possible; they have to settle on a fee and this fee has to be negotiated within certain limits. In short they suggest that the fee should be reasonably modest, but that in addition they will cover my travel, hotel and daily living expenses and anything else we can think of.

As long ago as when we were discussing the project in Paris, Yavorsky told me how important it would be to give a concert for the benefit of some good cause, and the moment Tsukker started hinting at something to this effect, I announced I would like to give one of my piano recitals for the benefit of the homeless. This instantaneously made a very good impression on Tse-Tse.

After they left I still felt rather out of sorts and fell asleep three times.

In the evening Derzhanovsky fetched us and took us to the concert at the Association for Contemporary Music, which he runs. It is to be 'a concert specifically for musicians and people in the arts', as Derzhanovsky stipulated in his correspondence with me when I was still in Paris. He had also wanted Ptashka to sing, but she did not give him a definite answer then. Since we arrived in Moscow so many demands have been made of us that she is not in very good voice; so, rather than make matters worse by straining it, we decided it would be better if she didn't sing.

Derzhanovsky was terribly worried and explained, 'The Hall seats only three hundred and fifteen hundred want to come. They all keep ringing up and those who cannot get tickets get very upset. With you I will make nothing but enemies!'

At the concert I met many acquaintances, including my niece three times removed, Shura Sezhensky, whom I remembered as a naughty little girl, and who is now a lady with greying hair; also Kostya Sezhensky, her cousin and my nephew, to whom, however, I am not blood-related, since he is an adopted son. Kostya is nearly twenty; he is ugly and acts like a buffoon. He studies at the Conservatoire and the idea of having a famous uncle seems almost more than he can cope with.

I meet Asafiev and tell him about the machinations of Khais. Asafiev gets excited: 'As a good Leningrad patriot I am appalled. I must talk to him . . .'

Derzhanovsky tells me I can go and sit down because the concert begins with the Overture on Hebrew Themes. Then a singer will be performing some of my songs, and only after that do I have to play.

The hall is not very large but is completely packed. As I walk across everyone claps, and when I sit down on the only empty seat in the front row, Saradzhev appears on the stage and makes a speech to welcome me. I am moved, but not so much that I fail to notice his making a muddle over a reference to Hans Sachs. After the end of the speech there is an ovation. Then the Overture on Hebrew Themes is performed with Igumnov at the piano. Because I am in the first row the balance is all wrong and I do not enjoy the performance. After the overture Igumnov steps down into the hall, several people change places and he sits next to me.

Igumnov is a rather curious character, lanky, clean-shaven and nervous in manner, with the remains of teeth sticking out of his mouth. I look at him with interest as I have had no news of him for a good twenty years, ever since I stayed in Sukhumi with the Smetskys. Then the singer comes on stage; she is nervous, performs the first two of my songs badly and the third one rather eccentrically.

Then it is my turn. I go up on the stage, play the Third and Fifth

Sonatas and the Toccata. The piano is tinny and pretty bad; Derzha-novsky did not excel in his choice. I am fairly calm as I play and in the Third Sonata – for no reason I can think of – begin to daydream and stop. However, I immediately collect myself and get to the end without any more mishaps. After the applause I play as an encore the Gavotte from op. 32. At the end I come off the stage and everybody pushes and crushes round me; Igumnov presents me with a book containing an article on me, and now here is old Jurgenson, once the 'Jupiter Tonans' of music publishing and now a minor clerk in the Musical Sector, which occupies his own former shop. Amid the chaos Jurgenson finds a moment to tell me that he will ring me and come for a talk. So the publishing problem, which Myaskovsky found so delicate, is probably going to be solved. Then B. B. Krasin comes to speak to me. He's already telephoned but Tseitlin, who answered the call, said I wasn't home. Krasin is connected with the Rosphil, which is at odds with the Persimfans, so Tse-Tse did everything in his power to keep him away from me. Bearing this in mind, and also remembering that a year and half ago Krasin was extremely civil to me in Paris, I am particularly attentive to him when I meet him this time. Kostya and Shura Sezhensky turn up again. Ptashka finds Kostya affected and Shura disagreeable, but when the latter mentions she has some photographs of my parents Ptashka pricks up her ears. The point is that all my family photographs disappeared when I had to abandon my Petersburg flat, and Ptashka has set herself the task of collecting from my relatives and friends whatever she can find in their albums. I question Shura as to what has happened to my other nephews and nieces in Moscow. After all, my father had a sister, she had four daughters, my cousins, and all these cousins have had numerous offspring in their turn, cousins of this Shura. But Shura says that they have all dispersed and she has lost contact with most of them; this does not upset me unduly because for the most part they were a pretty unremarkable lot. The most interesting, Nadya Faleieva, became an actress and is on tour somewhere in the provinces.

The public begins to disperse because we all have to go elsewhere for supper. We get dressed and go to a nearby club called 'For the Improvement of Scientists' Living Conditions' – i.e. the very 'Tsecooboo' which helped Derzhanovsky keep his spare room. This enormous detached house once belonged to the solitary widow of a general who died at the beginning of the Bolshevik era. Tsukker does not miss the opportunity to point out that 'in the old days a huge place like this was occupied by one solitary old woman who could not even move from one room to another. Now it is the property of writers and scientists, and they can honour Prokofiev in it.'

In an enormous hall there stands a collection of long tables on which supper is served. I am sitting between Asafiev and Mrs Derzhanovsky, Ptashka next to Myaskovsky. Also at the table are the members of the Persimfans, Yavorsky, and some young composers. Toasts are proposed and photographs taken; Derzhanovsky does his best to be photographed next to Lina Ivanovna (Ptashka). On the whole he, Mosolov and other young men try to court her in every way possible. After several toasts are drunk I get hints that it is my turn to say something. I try to get out of doing so but eventually realize I cannot without causing offence, so I stand up. Quiet quickly ensues, I hear many exclamations of satisfaction ('Ah'! etc.), and realize that much is expected of me. But to whom and to what should I drink? I guess I should drink to Musical Moscow, whose unique merits I have finally learned to recognize after my wanderings all around the world. I drink, they applaud, although they probably expected me to go into something more elaborate, with many florid expressions of appreciation. Later I go to another table where all the young composers have congregated and we are joined by Myaskovsky, Asafiev and Belyaev. We are all photographed together and I probably look like nothing on earth. So much attention is paid to me I feel completely overcome. Someone mentions that my first review appeared in the *Evening Moscow*, which shows the political importance of my arrival. By 1 a.m. I am totally exhausted, and although the feast shows no sign of coming to an end Ptashka and I decide we must leave. Everyone claps as we make our way out. Downstairs I am stopped by Kostya Sezhensky. He apparently was also present at the supper but was sitting far away, behind a palm tree, so I did not see him. He is probably quite drunk on wine and on the lionizing of his uncle and with the most absurd and rapturous expressions asks me to autograph a copy of the Third Sonata.

Thursday 27 January

Our room is quiet and peaceful, so, after yesterday's celebrations, we overslept. Tseitlin telephoned to say they had started to rehearse the second programme, including the Overture for Seventeen Musicians. I decided to sleep on during this rehearsal: let them do a bit of the sorting out without me. When I asked him what impression the overture was making, he hesitated and began to praise the other works. Probably they could make neither head nor tail of it, or are not used to the new sound it makes; or perhaps it is simply that Tseitlin, as a violinist, is not very interested in it.

Spent the rest of the morning – a good part of the day in fact – having a good go on the piano.

The weather was getting milder. It was soft and pleasant outside. Ptashka and I had our breakfast on our own. We were astonished to see the Tsar's eagles on the Iversky Gates. Apparently they were left there because it was impossible to take them down without mutilating the whole building. Besides, the official thinking, they say, is that Soviet power is so formidable that a few eagles cannot dislodge it even if they *are* crowned.

I gave an interview and in the evening went with Ptashka to Myaskovsky's. Asafiev was also invited. Since the room next to Myaskovsky's is occupied by his sister, Valentina Yakovlevna, I asked his permission to bring Ptashka with me to visit her. We also met Myaskovsky's other sister Vera and her husband, V.V. Yakovlev; but this sister is much less sensitive than Valentina and less in tune with Myaskovsky. Also present was the sixteen-year-old daughter of Valentina Yakovlevna, who with her very round, slightly puffy face and unpleasant manners seemed rather unsympathetic. Her face strangely reminded me of her father, whom I saw only once or twice many years ago at Myaskovsky's house, probably before this girl was born. It was around this time that I dropped in to see Myaskovsky and found him upset. Everybody in the house was speaking in whispers. Myaskovsky explained that Valentina's husband had shot himself. I asked why. Myaskovsky answered, 'Got in a mess over some financial transactions.'

The evening was very pleasant. The men were in Myaskovsky's

room, the women with Valentina Yakovlevna. We talked a bit about everything in general and, on the whole, about nothing in particular.

The weather being so mild we returned home on foot. I walked in front with the Yakovlevs, Ptashka behind with Asafiev. Remembering the skyscrapers in America and the way in which, in Paris, the apartment houses are built one of top of another, I admired these Moscow streets, some of which consisted of large, quiet and comfort-able-looking mansions. I mentioned this to Yakovlev and he replied, 'Yes, maybe that is how it was before. But nowadays these quiet mansions are filled to bursting with occupants; and since there are many rooms, but only one kitchen, this kitchen is often the place where the interests of all the families coincide. And you can imagine the hellish scenes there at the moment when the eighteen families living in this quiet mansion are cooking eighteen suppers on eighteen primus-stoves!'

When Ptashka and I were left on our own she gave me an interesting report of what had been going on in the ladies' room while I was with the men. Apparently Valentina Yakovlevna's daughter is a fiercely militant member of the Komsomol, has picked up a lot of Komsomol slogans and makes life a total misery for her mother. The poor woman can hardly open her mouth without getting interrupted by 'you and your bourgeois theories' or something of the kind. Her bickering spoiled the whole evening for Ptashka, although Ptashka tried to be circumspect and not get involved in this kind of conversation. At the same time this young lady lives at her mother's expense, and has money for manicures and for disappearing nobody knows where. Asafiev, walking with Ptashka in the quiet lanes of the Arbat, added that she nags not only Valentina Yakovlevna but Myaskovsky as well, and works him up to such a pitch that he shouts at her and stamps his feet. With the best will in the world I cannot imagine Myaskovsky shouting and stamping his feet. But it must all be true because it was Asafiev who told us, and he probably got it from Myaskovsky himself.

When we returned to the Metropole Ptashka and I felt very indignant and secretly hoped that the puffy-faced niece would run away with some Komsomol fellow as soon as possible and clear the air for everyone else.

Friday 28 January

In the morning the photographer came. Then, during the day, I kept myself to myself: in the evening I had my first *Klavierabend*, so I had to concentrate and get myself in good working order. I practised a fair bit. In *Izvestiya* there is an article with my portrait, which event is more significant politically than musically.

In the evening the *Klavierabend*, in agreeable Russian style, begins half an hour late. The public is probably acquainted with this custom and is in no hurry. The Great Hall of the Conservatoire filled up slowly, but every seat was taken by the time I came on.

I start with the Third Sonata. It was Souvchinsky who long ago advised me to begin all my solo concerts with the Third Sonata. After that, ten of the *Visions fugitives*. Both works are well received, if not specially warmly. The Fifth Sonata is greeted altogether with some reserve. However, a group of probably fifty people persistently claps and shouts and keeps calling me out. My real victory began with the March from the *Oranges*. The public immediately screamed its approval and I had to encore it. And so it went on, temperature at fever-pitch, for the whole of the second half of the concert, which consisted entirely of short pieces and ended with the Toccata. People shouted and roared: I never heard anything like it before. The encores were the following: the second 'Grandmother's Tale', the Gavotte from the 'Classical' Symphony and, finally, the fifth 'Bizarrerie' of Myaskovsky. So that people should know it was not one of my own works, I announced its title and the composer's name. I said it, as I thought, quite loudly, but later I was told that half of the audience did not hear. Knowing that Myaskovsky was there, and remembering of old that he was never satisfied with performances of his music, I was very worried when I played his piece; in the first half I carelessly left some notes out, but in the slow middle part collected myself and finished it quite respectably. The shouts and roars did not end after the 'Bizarrerie', which most of the audience mistook for one of my pieces; calls for encores continued, but I did not play anything else.

In the Green Room again masses of people congregated, including the wife of Litvinov, who spoke to Ptashka in English. The 'great apothecary' was absent. There was also Yurovsky, who is in charge of the State Music Publishers. He introduced himself and said that we must meet in order to legalize my relations with the State Publishing House, which prints and sells my works. Yurovsky is tall and quite elegant; his face and his head are clean-shaven. He was very gallant and said that as soon as I had some time to spare he would come to visit me, or would be glad to see me at the Publishing House.

When I returned home I got angry with myself over my nerves and stage-fright – absolutely no reason for it at all, and I made a really determined effort both before and during the concert. Last year, after those concerts in America in which I was so confident and self-possessed, I assumed I had laid that particular ghost for ever.

Saturday 29 January

We lunched with Seryozha Serebryakov at the Bolshaya Moskovskaya. I wanted to ask him about Shurik's arrest so as to work out how best to proceed in my attempts to get him out of prison. However, I did not learn anything new. Serebryakov confirmed that Shurik was not guilty of any political offence, simply got mixed up with the wrong people. Also, when questioned he did not want to give the names of people who, if implicated, could find themselves in an awkward situation.

What an extraordinary man this Seryozha Serebryakov is! Long ago he was a 'red' student and was always sounding the alarm and prophesying imminent chaos, long before the revolution of 1905. Now he is fifty, but his alarmist ways have hardly changed and, sitting in the Bolshaya Moskovskaya, he questioned me with the same conspiratorial look. Was it true that the British were quite prepared to sacrifice the entire Moscow population of two million as long as all the Kremlin got poisoned? In the end we were relieved when the lunch came to an end because, although he was talking about nothing of any significance, the expression on his face, and his conspiratorial whispering, made us seem almost like participants in this devilish 'scheme' of the British.

In the afternoon Shurik's eldest daughter, Alyona, visited us with a letter from her mother. She is a nice girl of thirteen but hardly looks more than ten. It was clear that Nadya was concerned about the steps I was proposing to take to try and get Shurik out of prison; and although I did not want to act prematurely – before I had surveyed the scene and decided whom I should approach first – I nevertheless decided to test the water with Tsukker. He was, after all, a secretary in the All-Russian Central Executive Committee and could find out something about the case easily and without attracting undue attention. It so happened he arrived that very day at 7, in order to fill out some forms for my foreign passport. In connection with a question on the form about my relatives, Shurik came into the conversation quite naturally. I asked him if he could do something to help me get my cousin released from prison. At first Tsukker was taken aback, then advised me to find out more about the court case from Nadya: when it was, what the charge was, how long the sentence, and so on.

After that Ptashka, Tsukker and I went to the MKHAT the 2nd, i.e. the Moscow Artistic Academy Theatre Number 2. They are giving *The Flea* by Leskov, adapted by Zamyatin and staged by Dikij. *The Flea* is one of the Soviet Theatre's most sensational productions; even in Riga we had heard about it. We are escorted to the director's box, which is right by the stage. There is already somebody in it but this somebody is quickly dispatched to the pit. The first act begins with a caricature of the Emperor's court and of Alexander I, but it is turned into such a pantomime that Ptashka and I can only look at each other.

'Isn't it splendid?' Tsukker gasps with excitement.

Not wishing to be impolite we concurred, though our fervour was scarcely a match for Tsukker's; nevertheless we had to admit that some of the chamberlains were actually not too bad. But the point was that we were seeing a Soviet production for the first time, and the question arose: was it typical of all such productions? However the start of the second act, with its popular humorous songs from Tula, put us in a different frame of mind straight away. The *chastushki* were utterly charming, the sound of the Cossacks approaching from a distance was rendered in a very vivid way, and in fact the production, from here to the end, was first-rate. The London scene was particularly good.

In the interval, in a little reception room adjacent to our box, tea was served with sandwiches and cakes. In came Dikij, who was not only the producer but also played the part of ataman Platov. During tea we talked about my impressions of the production of *The Flea* and also about the future production of the *Oranges* in the Bolshoi, which Dikij will be in charge of. I was also given a letter of greeting from the administration of the MKHAT. All things considered a very pleasant affair, very nice people, the more so in that this was the theatre world, nothing to do with musicians.

Sunday 30 January

In the morning I rehearsed last Friday's programme, which is to be repeated at my second *Klavierabend* at 1.30 p.m. in the Great Hall of the Conservatoire.

The hall is full. This time I feel confident, because I am beginning to get accustomed to the Russian public, and I play without incident. Audience reaction the same, the same pieces getting the most applause. Roaring and shouting at the end as never before, but I finish after playing two encores. Today in the Green Room I greet among others Meyerhold, Yavorsky, Lunacharsky and his wife, and Chernetskaya with her ballet projects that require immediate discussion. After the crowd disperses Yavorsky takes us to his home for lunch.

It is a splendidly frosty and sunny day; we go to the Zamoskvorechie in two sledge-carriages. In front of me and Protopopov are Ptashka and Yavorsky. Yavorsky lives with Protopopov and calls him 'Mussenkin'. When we cross the River Moskva I call out to Ptashka to look back at the Kremlin, which is all lit up by the sun and looks stunning. Our sledge-carriage overtakes theirs and I ask Yavorsky to show me the house of Souvchinsky; it is better here not to shout his name from the rooftops.

Yavorsky and Protopopov most graciously do not allow us to pay for the *izvozchiks* (cabs). Their flat is small and the three rooms are crammed full of furniture, including two grand pianos. Yavorsky serves an exceptionally good lunch – probably the tastiest we have had during our stay in the USSR – of *zakuski*, wonderful *blini*, incredible *pirozhki*, so good that by the middle of the meal I cannot eat another mouthful. Also present are the singer Derzhinskaya with her husband, and Protopopov's mother.

After lunch I ask Yavorsky out of politeness to show me some of Protopopov's compositions, knowing they are deadly boring. But the lunch was so good I feel I ought to make the sacrifice. Yavorsky immediately sits down at the piano and plays from manuscript a sonata by Protopopov (probably the Second). The sound of the piano is strident, the rooms are tiny, the celebrated pianist Yavorsky keeps the pedal down the whole time, the music of the sonata rolls and crashes about all over the keyboard and makes the strings and glasses resonate. Once he has finished Yavorsky apologizes for some wrong notes and also for not having clearly enough singled out the voices of a seven-part canon. In an attempt to avoid having to praise the music I show some interest in the canon, which seems in fact to be quite skilfully made. Thereupon Yavorsky and Protopopov sit at the two pianos and play 'Goudochek', an incredibly long song, approximately as long as four of my 'Ducklings' and based on a melancholy folk-tale recently collected in the north of Russia. This work is already published. Yavorsky plays the complicated accompaniment from one copy while Protopopov on the other piano takes the vocal part. Several times he goes astray, Yavorsky becomes angry and shouts at the composer. The song proceeds in an extremely slow tempo for about forty minutes. Once it is over I feel we have now paid a good price for our lunch, so now we can go into the dining-room and drink coffee. The 'Goudochek' was boring and in some places drifted into Skriabin-like harmonies; but I decided to say nothing in order not to spoil the genial atmosphere. But I muse upon the following: Yavorsky has invented some kind of brilliant theory of modality, Protopopov is a fervent exponent of this theory and after every few bars has to write down an analysis of the modes he has used. So how is it that, just the same, he cannot keep away from Skriabin's chords of the ninth?

Meanwhile the conversation turned to other topics. Derzhinskaya, a very pleasant lady, tells us how Moscow theatres are consistently packed out, despite the high prices of tickets; people would rather starve than not be able to go to the theatre. Yavorsky tells us that last May, when he returned from Paris to Moscow, it was already known in high-up circles what he and I had talked about, and in detail; for during our lunch at Du Guesclin, there sat at the next table, accidentally or on purpose, the person whose job it was to write everything down and make a report. From this, naturally, we go on to talk about the way people are 'shadowed' in Moscow, especially those from abroad. Yavorsky describes the kind of noise you hear on the telephone when a listening device is attached. In fact we have already noticed this kind of noise. Although we have not said anything anyone could take exception to, we must bear that noise in mind. We draw an unexpected conclusion from all today's conversations, namely that though Moscovites are loudly contemptuous of contemporary Moscow they are morbidly anxious for others to praise it.

We leave with the Derzhinskys, Yavorsky and Protopopov, who accompany us to the tram-stop, and the tram is jam-packed.

Monday 31 January

In the morning we have a rehearsal to brush up the programme of the last orchestral concert, which is to be repeated tonight.

In the afternoon I went to see Nadya Raevsky, and asked her to provide me with all the relevant data about Shurik in writing. Gave her 100 roubles to be sent to Aunt Katya in Penza and also 50 for herself.

An anonymous letter arrives signed 'a Russian woman'. She advises that when the dust settles and I am able to concentrate in peace and quiet, I will realize that my true metier is not composition, but the performance of Beethoven, with all his passion and titanic power; whereupon the whole world will prostrate itself in front of me. That's just what I need! Thank you, Russian woman.

In the evening we repeat the concert in the Great Hall of the Conservatoire, which is again full. From the government only Lunacharsky is present, but he does not come to see me in the Green Room. The performance of the suite from *Chout* is excellent. Before the concert Tsukker, at the request of Lunacharsky, announces from the stage that at the International Piano Competition in Warsaw the first prize was given to a Muscovite, Oborin. Oborin is apparently very young, about nineteen; he played my Third Concerto with the Persimfans before I arrived. They say he is also a composer and intends to travel to Europe to study with me.

The Third Concerto did not go as well today as the first time; but that was the orchestra's fault since I felt reasonably relaxed and played well, although a bit slower than before. Today the orchestra was a real disaster area: the first double-bass had had a heart attack, the first flute had contracted pneumonia and the first viola had broken his leg. So all those sections, deprived of their leaders, faltered. The double-basses got muddled in the difficult (for them) third variation, where I have accented syncopations and they have to play accented strong beats a quaver later. So every time my accents threw *them* they would mix me up and finally threw *me*. At last I got into step with them and everything sounded as it should. The end of the concerto brought vociferous applause and shouts for encores. In the Suite from the *Three Oranges*, at the end of the programme, the March was played as an encore, according to the now-established tradition.

Tuesday 1 February

Got up at 8 a.m. because the rehearsal of the Overture for Seventeen Musicians is to begin at 9. Many were delayed and I was the first to arrive. Their tempo was too slow and the music sounded sluggish and boring; that was why at the previous rehearsal the players hadn't warmed to it. Once I had adjusted the tempi and reinforced the accents the piece sounded much better. After that we took endless trouble with the Second Concerto. The orchestra seemed to like it and after every movement the musicians applauded loudly. However, the rehearsal turned out to be quite exhausting, since for most of it I had to sit at the piano and sort out the many problems as they arose.

After the rehearsal I feel tired and in the afternoon rest at home. As a matter of fact I have been tired ever since the first day I arrived in Moscow, and really never felt completely on top form for the whole of the two months I spent in the USSR.

Golovanov arrived at 5 o'clock and took us to his home at the Srednaya Kiselyovka to play and discuss the *Three Oranges*. Making our way there was quite a complicated business, but eventually we arrived. His flat turned out to be quite luxuriously furnished. Golovanov is probably younger than me, but he lives with Nezhdanova, who is now over fifty; it was she who set him up in the world and he occupies a position higher than his talent really justifies. And yet he is a nice chap and seemed seriously interested in staging the *Oranges*, the score of which he knew quite well. Apart from us, the producer Dikij (his name is actually not a pseudonym but his real one) and the designer Rabinovich were present. Long ago Souvchinsky had spoken in glowing terms of Rabinovich, both personally and artistically, and indeed he turned out to be a man of great charm.

We immediately got down to business: I sat at the piano and Golovanov and Dikij stood behind me with pencils. I played, explained, and enumerated the good and bad points of earlier productions. Dikij took notes and Golovanov had no trouble whatever translating my tempi into metronome marks and writing them in the score. That someone should be able to do this I found almost inconceivable: to know the exact metronomic equivalent of a tempo the moment you hear it! I could not help feeling suspicious and looking askance at his marks on the score. And yet I remember Tcherepnin telling me Rimsky-Korsakov had this ability too, and was very proud of it; he used to say he had not only absolute pitch but also absolute tempo. I have to say all three were throwing themselves into this forthcoming production with unusual enthusiasm: they wanted to do it better than Leningrad whatever it cost. Rabinovich has already been there 'to see how one should not do it', while Dikij, on the contrary, decided not to go, not to get to know anything about it so as not to be influenced by it. Golovanov was a bit dubious about an early staging; he thought the season too advanced for the opera to be put on much before May.

Between the first and second acts we had our meal. Golovanov distinguished himself by producing some remarkable hors-d'oeuvres and an old Polish vodka, which he commended to our particular attention. I took only a few sips but Dikij, not without pleasure, consumed one glass after another.

Then an Angora cat appeared on the scene; and also a camera whose extremely sensitive lenses allowed the taking of photographs even under lamp-light, and with a comparatively short (or at least not painfully long) exposure. The photograph so taken eventually got into the newspapers. Ptashka was not in it because Tsukker had come to take her to Stanislavsky's Opera Studio to see *The Tsar's Bride*. The rest of us went back to the *Three Oranges* and worked on the second act.

The idea was that after finishing the second act I would go over to see the rest of *The Tsar's Bride*. They even telephoned me from the theatre to see if I were on my way; but we didn't finish going through the second act till 10.30, by which time I felt very tired and didn't see much point in going just for the finale. However it transpired that I *should* have gone, as they were expecting me and ordered that I should be let into the theatre even during the performance itself; plus the fact that they laid on some kind of special reception. Ptashka didn't return home until 12.30, because the performance dragged on till very late and afterwards there was such a crush it was impossible to get her coat. I had words with her, telling her that because of her staying out late I hadn't been able to get to bed on time, and that tomorrow I had to be up very early in the morning to start work. So we had a row before going to bed.

Wednesday 2 February

Reconciled with Ptashka. Yesterday's production of *The Tsar's Bride* impressed her very much. Even if the singers and the orchestra were not up to par, the producer's concept and the polishing of every gesture and detail made up for it. She told Tsukker yesterday, 'I should like to work in this sort of theatre.'

Tsukker: 'Excellent. If you like, we could sign a contract tomorrow!'

In short, Ptashka is prepared to leave Paris and come and live in Moscow.

Kucheryavy telephoned. Seeing that he did not put in an appearance in person, I had written him a note. Everything is well with him. I notice that whereas his letters used to be quite strident in tone, exhorting everyone to return to the USSR and apply themselves to the recon- struction effort, he has quietened down a lot now.

I did some piano exercises and started preparing my second recital programme. Then I went to the Great Hall of the Conservatoire to rehearse with Feinberg my transcription of Schubert waltzes for two pianos. I waited for him for hours on end. At last he appeared and immediately came out with something like 'don't blame me for being late'. It seems he got held up, or his watch was slow, or something. Whatever the excuse it was by now too late to rehearse in this hall, so we went to Lamm's whose flat was nearby and had two pianos. This was the same Lamm who had accompanied the works of Myaskovsky in my first concerts in Moscow, the ones organized by Derzhanovsky.

This was supposed to be my first chance to hear my Schubert transcriptions, but in fact I did not really hear them even then. I was too preoccupied trying to keep together and play the right notes – because, of course, I had not learnt my part properly. While we were playing Myaskovsky and Lamm himself arrived and we had some tea. Myaskovsky started criticizing the Persimfans, saying that they accompanied the Third Concerto execrably.

Me: 'But it wasn't entirely their fault. Three of their most important musicians were missing.'

Myaskovsky: 'Precisely! Because the woodwinds and the strings were lacking important players, the brass kept missing the beat!'

Myaskovsky praised Oborin as a composer. Not everything of his sounds agreeable, but even what we think sounds disagreeable shows talent.

The score of Myaskovsky's Seventh Symphony has just come out in print, beautifully produced by Universal; our publishers' printing is of poorer quality.

When I returned home I found Nadya, who had brought a typed sheet of paper with all the information as to when and why Shurik was sentenced.

In the evening we did not go anywhere. We did not feel like rushing about; besides, I had to practise, since I had not done nearly enough work on the Fourth Sonata.

Thursday 3 February

In the morning I worked and put my second programme in order, mainly the Fourth Sonata. Got a letter from Gorchakov with some scribbles from Svyatoslav: 'Baby goody boy.'

In the afternoon dropped in on the Persimfans. There I read a telegram from someone called Vorobyov in Kharkov, an official in the Ukrainian Ministry of People's Education, threatening to proscribe any concert in the Ukraine in which I participate if they are not given under the auspices of the Ukrainian State Theatres. I react indignantly and say if that is the case I will dispense with the services of the State Theatres and engage a private impresario, and will announce that the concert is for the benefit of homeless children. Let them try to put obstacles in the way of *that*, if they dare. Tseitlin, though, laughs and says these threats from Kharkov are meaningless because they have no right to make them.

Rehearsed the Schubert waltzes with Feinberg on two pianos. They go well, but apparently fewer tickets for tomorrow are being sold. This may be because the poster doesn't make it clear that this is a second, new programme and the public thinks I am going to be bashing out the old one for the third time in a row.

We spent the evening in. Since I hadn't got the programme as polished as it needed to be, I had to go on practising.

Had tea with Morolev, with whom it was a pleasure to chat. He grumbles about his life, although I think he could well not grumble about it, because many are worse off. His salary is only 100 roubles a month, but he has another job as well which brings him in another 100. Besides, his eldest daughter has also just started work and gets nearly 100 as well; finally he earns from private practice yet another 100 or thereabouts. So 400 a month is not that bad.

Friday 4 February

In the morning I have a rehearsal with the orchestra, during which a cinematographic film is made of me. Altogether this gobbled up a quarter of the rehearsal, since in the beginning they filmed me with the whole Persimfans with everything going awry; then me on my own. To do this, of course, they surrounded me on every side with dazzlingly bright lamps which not only blinded me but also made me hot; then they asked me to play something featuring the hands jumping about all over the place. For that I chose the Finale of the Fourth Sonata, where scales are taken in turns by both hands; and, of course, being distracted by hissing lamps and the cameraman cranking his handle round like mad, I made a frightful hash of it. Then I thought: supposing this film is kept for posterity, and in order to find out how the composer plays his works it gets projected in slow motion? Then the full extent of my infamy will be revealed!

After the rehearsal Ptashka and I were taken to the lobby, she in her leopard-skin coat. We were seated next to each other and made to talk, and, because of the light, tears were running down my cheeks. When the film is shown the title could easily be: 'Scene with Tears in the Prokofiev Family'.

Afterward I went back with Tseitlin to the Foreign Passport Department. Comrade Girin was polite and to the point as usual. He told us they had had to speak up on my behalf in the matter of an announcement that had appeared in the *Vechernyaya krasnaya gazeta* (*Evening Red Paper*) to the effect that Prokofiev had asked for his Soviet citizenship to be returned, and that his request had been granted.

I had seen this report and was very unhappy about it. It probably originated in the fact that I had applied for a passport for going abroad. I explained to Girin that I had even been interviewed on this alleged application for Soviet citizenship, and had replied, 'Nonsense. There was nothing to apply for. I was a Soviet citizen when I left in 1918 and am still one now I have returned. Why should I put in an application for anything?'

Girin said, 'Absolutely right. We ourselves sent in a refutation to that effect to the *Vechernyaya krasnaya gazeta*.' (Incidentally I have never seen any such refutation in print there.) Some additional documents are needed for the present foreign-passport formalities, and Tseitlin will see about getting them. Girin also recommended I approach the Narkompros to see if I could get out of paying the 400 roubles for two foreign passports.

When I returned home I had to prepare for the evening concert, but still did not manage to finish learning the Fourth Sonata.

In the evening the Great Hall of the Conservatoire is again full. They say that many tickets were purchased at the last moment, although it is possible that the management of the Persimfans filled up the unsold seats by allowing people in for nothing. If this was so, Tseitlin somehow managed to keep it from me in order not to make a bad impression, or, maybe, to avoid my blaming him for piling too many concerts on top of each other.

First on the programme is the Second Sonata, which comes off quite well. After that the *Grandmother's Tales*, where, in the third one, I make a mistake, or to be precise for two bars I forget what to play with the right hand and so play with the left one only. After the concert I embrace Myaskovsky with the words 'and why on earth should I have gone wrong in the third "Tale"?'

He smiles knowingly and says, 'And it was quite obvious. But anyhow it didn't matter, didn't matter at all. You didn't play any wrong notes!'

Apart from this mishap I played the *Tales* well, 'with feeling and spirit', as the critics might say. The audience is more obviously appreciative than at the first recital, and this work goes down particularly well.

During the interval I ask that no one be allowed into the Green Room. Only Tsukker is there, very pleased with the *Tales* and their success, and is saying, 'This is the kind of music that the public should be getting!'

Whereupon I round on him, saying that the public must be educated by being made to accept more profound and complex works; but he, who I thought shared my views, now seems to be advocating that we should pander to the tastes of the crowd.

After the interval we get to the Fourth Sonata, which I do not play especially well. The first movement bores me this time and I play it without taking any pleasure in it. The second goes better, although I am fearful of making a mistake in the easiest part (in the middle). I play the Finale rather superficially, going for decorative gloss rather than for precision, as I later report to Myaskovsky. Just the same it goes down very well.

After that the second piano was opened up and Feinberg and I played the waltzes, which so far as I was concerned went well and after which the audience broke into wild applause, just as they had after all the earlier concerts. I play an encore from op.12 and then want to stop, asking for the pianos to be shut. Yavorsky bursts in and vehemently insists on our repeating the waltzes. On his instructions the pianos are opened again, he seizes the score and rushes on stage first, saying he will turn the pages. Feinberg and I force ourselves out after him and, to the great joy of the public, repeat the waltzes. This time, however, they are much less enjoyable to play, at least for me, sitting at the very edge of the stage with a huge crowd of people scrutinizing my hands and feet during the performance.

In the Green Room Yavorsky's pupils presented Ptashka with some flowers.

Saturday 5 February

An orchestral rehearsal in the morning. The overture goes better. As Tsukker advised – he even drew a plan – we made the seventeen performers sit closer together; if they remained in their usual seating they would be too far apart from each other, and the impression would be of an orchestra both depleted and downcast. So we moved them all together to form a group, and as a result the harps – in accordance with Tsukker's drawing – found themselves in the first row. Thence arose a situation both embarrassing and amusing. It became apparent that as long as they were sitting at the back they could get away with 'busking' their parts (which were difficult); but once shifted to the front there was no mistaking what they were doing, and I twice caught them playing passages full of wrong notes. They blushed and promised to take their parts home and learn them properly. On the whole we managed to get the overture better, but spent most of the rehearsal working on the Second Concerto without, however, making very much headway with it.

In the afternoon I slept and practised. Just like the other day there arrived an anonymous letter from yet another Russian woman, this time signed Pava. This communication was less high-minded, in fact a bit sexually suggestive and even diabolic in character, and gave me a number to telephone. Ptashka and I amused ourselves imagining the following method of dealing with it: Ptashka would telephone this lady, Pava, and explain that she was my private secretary who, having read the letter before referring it to me, would like to know exactly what sort of pleasure and entertainment was being offered. Then Derzhanovsky, Jurgenson and Kucheryavy began arriving and after that we forgot about it. A woman's impatient voice kept ringing up asking for me, but I did not go to the phone.

Jurgenson seems to have aged, but perhaps not so much considering that it is a full twelve years since I have seen him. He spoke rather slowly, in a convoluted and laborious manner, making so many digressions that our conversation seemed to drag on for ever. He has a minor job at the Musical Sector and, consequently, works in the very shop he owned in former times. We kept our voices down since we did not know who was in the next room, separated from us by a locked door.

The point was that after his publishing firm in Russia had been nationalized he gave his foreign rights to his friend, a German publisher, Forberg. By this arrangement Forberg reprints and sells abroad a number of works, including all those of mine formerly published by Jurgenson (with the exception of the First Piano Concerto). In return he transfers money to Jurgenson from time to time, but not very much and not on any regular basis. Of course there is no question of accounts since it is all being done semi-legally. The aim of our conversation was to try to transfer the rights from Forberg to our Publishing House, so that the royalties from the sale of my works could be divided between me and Jurgenson. That way each of us would receive 12½ per cent from the sales. The non-commercial basis of our Publishing House would guarantee Jurgenson a proper rate. Jurgenson willingly agreed to that, but the difficulty was to make Forberg cede his rights to our Publishing House. 'Although Brutus without any doubt is an honourable man', nevertheless he (Forberg) has spent money on reprinting these works and could use this as a very good excuse not to do what we want. Jurgenson was ready to contact him, although to write directly was out of the question because the letter would be intercepted by the censors. It seems the only possibility is some roundabout way, e.g. through somebody in the Germany Embassy.

Kucheryavy looked plumper than when I knew him in America, and I presented him with the fountain pen and pencil I had brought from abroad at his request. The cheerful mood of his first letters, when he first arrived in Soviet Russia and had taken up the position of director of a glue-boiling factory, has evaporated. He finds it impossible to get any work done. Everybody is lazy, bureaucratic and goes by the book; without private initiative business will come to a standstill. It goes without saying that to have to keep on good terms with the communists, who are not only in control of everything you do but are also spying on you all the time, is a real ordeal by fire.

Then, lowering his voice and changing to English, he added, 'Every sixth person here – is a spy.'

In the evening Tsukker came to collect us and we went for a visit to Kameneva, Trotsky's sister and the wife of the Soviet ambassador in Rome. She is herself the head of cultural relations with foreign countries, that is to say she has to show Soviet cultural productions to the West in their best light and, conversely, bring back anything foreign that is useful for Russia from a Soviet point of view.

Since Kameneva lives in the Kremlin we were given special passes, and this journey to the Kremlin in itself was not without interest. We went on foot and when we approached the gates handed our passes in at a little window. Some formalities ensued – I don't know what exactly, since Tsukker took care of them. I kept shuffling from foot to foot to try to keep warm (the frost was terrible). Finally we were permitted to walk through the gates, where there were soldiers standing with rifles and bayonets shining in the cold. Stepping inside the Kremlin was a strange feeling: the spirit of the old, of the past, on the one hand; on the other, the newest of the new, the Revolution. And this was the very place from which the reconstruction of the world was to be master-minded!

Tsukker meanwhile was walking next to us and pointing out things and people in a state of great excitement.

'This man who just passed us is a minister of something, and here Lenin did that, and there is where Demyan Bedny lives.'

'Imagine,' I said, 'being important enough to live in the Kremlin itself!'

'He is an old communist,' explained Tsukker, 'but it is not that convenient to live in the Kremlin, because if he wants to invite somebody to visit him, there is always this fuss about passes.'

Going down a long row of corridors in one of these enormous Kremlin buildings of somewhat ministerial type, we stopped at Kameneva's door. We were shown first into a rather incongruous lobby and after that into an enormous room, quite comfortably appointed with magnificent armchairs, sofas, many bookcases and also bookshelves. We were led in with some solemnity: we could feel that we were in an exalted place and the atmosphere was reverential.

Olga Davidovna herself seemed to be a lively, agreeable, somewhat American-style lady, although Ptashka found her neither agreeable nor American. Karakhan was also there and Litvinov with his wife came later. Both like music very much and have some understanding of it. Karakhan informed me, for instance, that in China he had a Duo-Art piano-player and a number of rolls made by me, and that in the evening, while resting from his labours, he enjoyed listening to them. Awfully touching: Karakhan, while implanting revolutionary ideals in China, finds refreshment and renewed strength in the sound of my music.

Tsukker edged cautiously towards me and gave me to understand it would be very nice if I played a bit. I obliged, and not unwillingly, since all those present were, it seemed, very fond of my music. I played them mainly small pieces and talked to Litvinov and Karakhan in between. They asked me for my impressions of the USSR and other countries.

So I criticized what was bad abroad and praised what was good in the USSR, keeping everything, needless to say, within reason. So it appeared that we agreed in principle about everything.

Afterwards the host invited us to move into the dining-room for supper. The table was laid neither richly nor poorly but with odds and ends of everything. The napkins bore the monogram A.III. A maid served us but was addressed by her first name and patronymic.

At the table, apart from Litvinov and Karakhan, there were a few other quite unremarkable people, among them the son of Kameneva. He was very young and his wife even younger: she looked about fifteen but was in fact a bit older. She is a pupil in a ballet school and is very interested in my music, but unfortunately returned tonight too late to hear me play.

After supper Kameneva asked me to play specially for this girl. But here I decide I have to take a bit of a stand. I reply that it is getting late and I am tired. The girl pulls a long face. I say somewhat reprovingly, 'You should have got back home in time.'

But it turned out that she could not get back in time because she had had to dance.

I say, 'In that case you can hear me at one of my forthcoming concerts.'

In the evening, however, she is nearly always busy. Kameneva persists and again asks me to play specially for her. I answer with some impatience, 'I am also busy tomorrow morning with a rehearsal for which I need a clear head and strong fingers' – this to the daughter – 'and if you really want to hear me as much as all that you can arrange things; but if you can't, then it can't be that important to you. And if it isn't, it certainly isn't worth my giving you a special performance now.'

After that I begin to say my goodbyes. It seems one is not supposed to talk to princesses of royal blood like that, and my obstinacy makes a bad impression on Kameneva; but I am glad I put the child in her place.

However, it is not possible to leave straight away. Apparently it is already past midnight and our passes are valid only the day they were issued, i.e. till 12 o'clock, and without a valid one we won't be let out. So we have to call the commandant's office. Litvinov is kind enough to suggest taking us in his car, since he lives outside the Kremlin.

'If you are with me nobody will ask you for your pass,' he adds.

We end up drinking some more tea while I impatiently await the arrival of Litvinov's car: I want to get to bed, and I have an early rehearsal tomorrow. At last a message comes through that the car is waiting for us, we say goodbye to Kameneva and walk through the endless corridors. Madame Litvinov is carrying her boots in her hands; it seems they are dirty and she does not want them to make a mess in the corridor. We all get into Litvinov's spacious limousine, he with his wife, I with Ptashka and also Karakhan and Tsukker.

'How I like this quiet Kremlin,' says Litvinov's wife dreamily.

Knowing the tremendous hive of activity in 'this Kremlin', I find this naïve exclamation a little bizarre.

At the Kremlin gates the guard stops our car. Litvinov, Karakhan and Tsukker get out their permanent passes. We sit quietly in hiding at the back of the car. Then the car moves on and Litvinov takes us to the Metropole.

At home we share our impressions. Ptashka enquires who that polite gentleman, who shook her hand so vigorously, was. I explain that it was the same Karakhan who has shaken up the whole of China. Ptashka is astonished and tells an amusing story about Litvinov's wife.

'You know – she was saying – it is so difficult with taxi drivers in Paris, they are all "white".'

Ptashka was about to explain that there are hardly any blacks in Paris and it is only in New York that you find black taxi drivers, but Litvinov's wife explained what she meant.

'The problem is that every third driver is a Wrangel's officer, and you're afraid that when you give the address of the Soviet Embassy he'll refuse to take you there and, even worse, is bound to be rude!'

And she invited Ptashka to call on her, probably attracted by the chance of having a chat with her in English.

Sunday 6 February

The orchestral rehearsal starts at 9 a.m. and we spend all our time on the Second Concerto. When we have finished I ask Tseitlin to advise me whether I should accept a proposition from Tutelman for six concerts in the Ukraine. Tutelman is the same man who came two years ago to Paris with Krasin and whom I did not like when I met him there.

His reputation in Moscow is not particularly good either. A year ago he was sacked from Rosphil in not altogether un-scandalous circumstances; but being an extremely cunning man he managed to get into the administration of the Ukrainian State Theatres. Tseitlin says that Tutelman is certainly a shady character, but since he proposes a contract in the name of the Ukrainian State Theatres, everything should be above board, and if he undertakes to pay in dollars and the fee he proposes is good, there is no reason why I shouldn't accept.

When I returned to the Metropole I met Mekler. He was very concerned, not wanting to lose me to Tutelman (he had got wind of the fact that Tutelman had been courting me in his usual devious manner). In his agitation Mekler proposed 1,000 roubles for each concert in the provinces – in Moscow even more – and tried to slip an advance of 1,000 roubles into my hand without any receipt simply to secure a commitment. To confirm that he really was a manager on an international scale he showed me a telegram from Marchex in which the latter agreed to twenty concerts for 110 roubles each. Poor Marchex, who boasted so much in Paris about his tremendous success in Russia: 110 roubles, and with a semi-respectable impresario at that! (Admittedly, from a French point of view, it *is* a fee of sorts.) Despite the international telegram and the 1,000-rouble fees it was supposed to guarantee, I gave Mekler back his cash-in-hand and got rid of him with some vague promises-cum-protests.

The telephone rang when I came into my room and it was Tutelman. Unable to weigh up all these propositions immediately I was just as vague and asked him to call back tomorrow. By then I will have to come to a decision, because Tutelman is going to the south and I shall be leaving for Leningrad.

I slept in the afternoon. What with getting into bed at 2 a.m. yesterday, getting out of it at 8, rehearsing all the morning, selling my services to the Ukraine afterwards: no wonder I feel weary and have a thick head.

At 5 o'clock I set out for the Bolshoi Theatre, where I was invited by a special note from the management to discuss the forthcoming production of the *Oranges*. The meeting was to take place in the director's box, or, to be precise, in the reception room adjacent to the large box on the side which is reserved for the director's use. Members of the Soviet government use this box quite often. Frequently after the end of the performance state affairs are negotiated in this reception room. In the same room theatre affairs are negotiated as well.

When I arrived for this meeting I in fact knew only Golovanov, Rabinovich and Dikij; but Rabinovich and Dikij were themselves newcomers to the Bolshoi Theatre, this being the first time they were working there. Little by little as the meeting went on I managed to work out who was who. The director, Burdyukov, was an old Party man, a communist, who knew nothing about theatre business and was some kind of foreign body, a thorn driven by the government into the live organism of the theatre. In the past he had been, I think, a military man and this, actually, served him well in that he knew how to make decisions and give orders. And yet, in trying to preserve harmony between all the artists, he behaved decently enough, even modestly, and made a rather favourable impression on me – much more so than Lossky, the chief producer, who probably resented the appearance on the stage of the Bolshoi of the new producer, Dikij, and spent all his time quietly putting spokes in his wheel.

Apart from the above-mentioned people the elderly chorus-master was present (Avranek), and a few others representing the technical and property departments, lighting effects and so on.

The aim of this meeting was to find out if it were possible to stage the *Oranges* this season. Dikij was requesting an inordinate number of stage rehearsals and Lossky immediately made it clear that in those circumstances the very thought of putting the work on would be out of the question, even in May. The others spoke too: Golovanov about the orchestral rehearsals, Rabinovich about the sets, Avranek about the chorus, the technicians about the props and costumes. *I* was in fact present only as it were in a passive capacity, and occasionally, through expressing opinions in an undertone, influenced either Golovanov or Dikij in what they said.

There was also the problem of *The Red Poppy*, a revolutionary ballet with music by Glière, whose turn it was to be staged before the *Oranges*: but Burdyukov had probably received some instruction from above to put on the latter as early as possible and, therefore, took every opportunity of insisting that the *Oranges* should be staged before the first of June. Was that why I rather liked him? Or maybe his wanting to make haste was caused by a desire to do a better production than Leningrad, which would increase the chances of Moscow's *Oranges* being taken abroad instead of Leningrad's. In short, the meeting ended happily, with everybody intent on doing whatever they could to bring the *Oranges* to fruition in May.

After the meeting I returned home to fetch Ptashka. Rabinovich joined us and we went on foot to Golovanov's for lunch. On the way Rabinovich was excitedly telling us about his project to paint all Moscow.

'Moscow looks absolutely disgraceful,' he was saying. 'Hundreds of houses are in a bad state of repair and the paint has peeled off. To reconstruct the whole town and restore its appearance will take a long time. But if meanwhile it could be painted all over according to a certain plan, it might look very striking. Imagine: one street entirely in blue, another one crosses it in two colours . . .'

I liked this idea very much, but of course it's only an idea.

Chez Golovanov the same people gathered, but there was also Nezhdanova, whom Ptashka, knowing about her famous coloratura, particularly wanted to meet. Nezhdanova is already a middle-aged lady, very tall and very lovable. People say she is already losing her voice, but Golovanov wants her to sing Ninetta. How could anyone as tall as she is, I wonder, climb into an orange?

Lunch today was as splendid as last time. When it finished Derzhanovsky arrived to collect Ptashka; they have gatherings on Sundays and he wanted to make sure she would be there. I was sorry I couldn't go, but the young composers will look after her.

After lunch I played Acts III and IV of the *Oranges*, and Golovanov, of course, had to be showing off his 'absolute tempo'; on the basis of my performance he put in metronomic marks and Dikij wrote all my comments down in his notebook. At 11 o'clock we at last finished going through the opera, and I returned home tired and with a heavy head. I went out like a light. At 1 o'clock in the morning I was deafened by the telephone ringing. I sat for some time on my bed wondering what was hitting me. But when I got round to picking up the receiver, there seemed to be nobody there.

Monday 7 February

I woke up feeling tired and lethargic but little by little came to life. Again a rehearsal, but I decided to miss the beginning. It was mainly the Second Concerto, to which we managed to bring a certain amount of coherence. These rehearsals were no less useful for me than for the orchestra, because they gave me a good opportunity thoroughly to familiarize myself with this most difficult piece and co-ordinate well with the band. At the end of the rehearsal we went through the overture once more. In the hall were Derzhanovsky, Golovanov and, later, Tutelman with a contract, which had been amended according to my wishes.

After the rehearsal I retired with Tseitlin and, after we'd both read the contract, I signed it. So, in a month's time, I have let myself in for six concerts in the Ukraine. The Ukrainian State Theatres will of course make money out of me, but what they are proposing is also quite a handsome amount and, above all, in dollars, to be paid directly by cheque and abroad.

As soon as I returned to the hotel there was a telephone call from that trickster Khais, who has contrived to pay me for my Leningrad concerts half of what Tutelman pays me for the ones in the provinces. Khais has just arrived from Leningrad and wants to pay his respects. On the pretext that I am very busy I tell him I cannot see him now. However it seems he is already in the Metropole and is calling from downstairs; besides which he has a letter for me from Asafiev. I say that unfortunately I have to go out now and that if he wants to wait a minute I will come down. In five minutes I go downstairs, exchange a few words with him on a purely official basis and go back to my room.

The second orchestral concert takes place this evening. The Great Hall of the Conservatoire is sold out. We begin with the Overture op. 42. Though all seventeen musicians try their best their playing is notably un-brilliant and the piece is poorly received. Basically this overture was conceived for the Aeolian Hall in New York which seats 250 people; of course a hall ten times larger diffuses the sound and the effect is undernourished.

After the overture much time is spent rearranging the orchestra, and then I come out to play the Second Concerto. I am nervous and ask myself why. Vanity, of course. What if they say that Prokofiev himself plays his own works badly? I try to persuade myself not to look at things in that light: supposing he does make mistakes, what does it really matter? The concerto is still the concerto. This line of reasoning is of help to me and I come out to play in a more or less calm frame of mind. But I do not manage to *stay* calm during the most difficult parts: in the cadenza (specifically where I mark it *colossale*), and at the beginning of the third movement, where the hands keep jumping over one another, I play badly. However, the rest I play well and with enthusiasm. There is no doubt that the first movement goes down well. Before the Scherzo we take a little break. After it there are shouts of 'encore' (*bis*), but of course I can't play it again. After the concerto the applause is *colossale*! No question that this concerto produces a far stronger impression than the Third. After I have come out and taken several bows, Tseitlin asks me in a whisper to consider repeating the Scherzo. I could really do with recouping a bit more strength first, but the triumphal mood of the hall and even of the orchestra spurs me on. We repeat the Scherzo, this time pushing it a bit too hard and smoothing over some of its articulated sharpness.

In the Green Room I find Yavorsky who gives me a boisterous greeting, then Myaskovsky and Madame Litvinov. Nadya Raevsky is also there, and it was very odd to see the two next to one another: one an Englishwoman who carries her overshoes in her hands, thrust by some mysterious quirk of fate into the position of a minister's wife; the other an aristocrat whose husband is in prison, not knowing which way to turn to get him out. However, it would not have done to introduce them so I had to talk to them individually in turn. Then I was called aside and introduced to Sosnovsky, an important communist, whose articles are very influential and about whom Tsukker was speaking in a reverential tone of voice. Sosnovsky asked me if I had read a revolutionary poem sent to me by the members of the Komsomol. I try to disentangle myself from this difficult situation, because, indeed, a book addressed to the Persimfans was sent to me, but I just left it in the management's office. Sosnovsky, with an incredibly boring voice, mumbles on about how meritorious this book is and that it would be a good thing for me to give it some of my attention.

My immediate reaction, however, is: how is it that both communist leaders and the books they recommend are so tedious?

At last the public begins to disperse and Sosnovsky leaves me in peace. The second part of the concert begins with the Scherzo and March from the *Three Oranges*, 'great favourites of the people', and is followed by the Suite from *Chout*. I am sitting in the Green Room and through the gaps of the thin partition I can clearly hear it. The piece sounds well and there are loud calls at the end. When I come out on to the stage it is a real celebration: the orchestra plays a flourish, the whole hall stands up and roars deafeningly. After the concert I have to go to RABIS, a club for people in the arts. Long ago I was asked to play several pieces there. Apparently I have promised to play straight after the concert, as I am now vigorously reminded. It is not far away – in a lane near Nikitskaya – and Ptashka, Tseitlin and I all walk there. We are surrounded by hordes of people leaving the concert and engaged in a lively exchange of opinions about it.

At RABIS we found an odd assortment of people, some very young, others whose appearance was not particularly intellectual. It turned out that a conference was being held, which explained the strange mixture. I ask impatiently to be allowed to play my pieces as soon as possible so I can go home. The public, who are circulating everywhere, are rounded up in the hall; I play five small pieces and immediately, despite the applause and shouts for encores, rush home as fast as I can.

Tomorrow, at last, we are to go to Leningrad. We have already received many letters and telegrams from there, including a full schedule of our stay drawn up by Asafiev. Apparently there was also to be, as it happened, a performance of Myaskovsky's Eighth Symphony. I asked Nyamochka today if he would come himself, but he is undergoing dental treatment and it looks as if he won't be able to. I am very tempted to offer to pay his fare, since money now seems to be coming my way so abundantly I can scarcely take it in. However, I don't know how to approach him without offending him.

Tuesday 8 February

Yesterday we played the second programme, today we are going to Leningrad, and yet – a rehearsal. The 14th is the fifth anniversary of the founding of the Persimfans, to mark which a gala concert has been planned in which they will be performing only two pieces: the *Scythian Suite* and Skriabin's *Poème de l'extase*. Today they asked me to come without fail to the rehearsal of the *Suite*, in order to ensure that they are playing it the way the composer wants it to be played. And, indeed, I had to correct several tempi and reinforce some of the accents in order to give more shape to the playing. The rehearsal proceeded thus: I walked about in the hall, stopping the orchestra whenever necessary.

'So, that's how it should go,' Tseitlin would cry delightedly after each comment, which he then passed on to the orchestra as 'the wish of Sergey Sergeevich'. In the sunrise Tabakov blew some marvellous B flats.

For lunch Ptashka and I went to Saradzhev's, who had been trying to invite us for ages. Although we had very little time to spare I had to find some for the man who first performed my works in Moscow, particularly in view of the fact that Saradzhev, who is by now quite grey, has never made it as an important conductor, despite his enormous musical gifts. You sense that on account of this he bears the musical world around him something of a grudge.

Saradzhev lives in the Philharmonic building and occupies an enormous room more like a large artist's studio. His daughters, who at the time of *Dreams* were tiny tots, are now very sweet and slender young girls. About Kotik, whom I remembered as a nine-year-old and who has written a whole album of quite daring pieces, I was afraid to ask. I heard rumours abroad that he was suffering from epilepsy and has turned into some kind of lunatic. Myaskovsky and Derzhanovsky had also been invited to lunch. They immediately started an endless discussion about the importance of the Persimfans. I saw at once that the house of a conductor would be the last place – *terra ingratissima*, in fact – in which to bring up the subject of an orchestra which had dispensed *in toto* with conductors. I did not make much of a contribution to this discussion; but in defence of the Persimfans I stressed the importance of playing the correct notes, which is what this ensemble makes a point of doing, and as a result the overall sound is better. After a very tasty lunch (on the whole every lunch and dinner we had in Moscow was better than the last), we moved to the piano and Saradzhev asked me to show him the tempi and how I wanted the 'Classical' Symphony and the Suite from the *Oranges* to go. The point was that, though the Persimfans had me almost completely within their grasp, the wily Derzhanovsky had managed to siphon off the Moscow première of the 'Classical' Symphony for the Association for Contemporary Music. Saradzhev would be conducting. He had sharp eyes: he pointed out a misprint in the printed score which I had already carefully proof-read.

Then Kotik appeared, a young man with a small beard, strange eyes and slightly odd in manner. I did not know how to talk to him or on what subject, and his arrival created a severe feeling of discomfort. However it was by now time to go, because a large party of visitors was expected at the Metropole and we still had to do our packing and set off for Peter.

I had arranged for the visitors all to have fixed appointments, as at the dentist, half an hour for each. But, as happens with Russian visitors, they all came late and got herded together; afterwards they all complained about getting in one another's way.

The first to arrive was Chernetskaya, the lady who was to turn the whole world of ballet upside-down. She came into the Green Room at some of my concerts and every time tried to make an appointment to go through her projects with me. None of them sound in any way convincing and what was more, I'd heard many slighting references to her. But Chernetskaya was an insistent, even somewhat demonic sort of woman; not only that, she was the former mistress of Lunacharsky and, above all, she had delayed her departure expressly to read me her manuscript. In short, I had no choice but to see her. The subject of her ballet was quite complicated and had to be expounded in great detail; reading it needed at least forty minutes. It was a nicely sugar-coated Soviet story, with noble workers and corrupt bankers, factories and luxury middle-class apartments, and so on: everything, in fact, that dyed-in-the-wool communists are by now heartily sick of. Chernetskaya's reading of the second part of her ballet-proposal took place in the most adverse conditions. I could see first of all that it was worthless; meanwhile, as she went on reading, other visitors were coming in, the telephone was ringing all the time and Ptashka was busy turning away an interviewer who had arrived too late. In short the most appalling circumstances for anyone to read anything; but Chernetskaya battled on in desperation and I for the sake of good manners was listening to her with one ear and marvelling at her heroic spirit. I must say however that some of the details were not unimaginatively conceived, but were curiously *déjà vu*. The dance of the numbers at the stock exchange, lifting the bankers on high one minute, casting them down the next, was reminiscent of the chorus and dance of the numbers in Ravel's last opera, which could well be unknown to her. The idea of the factory coming to life choreographically was also not a bad one, but Yakulov and I had used it in my last ballet for Diaghilev, something she might not have known either. When I told her she was so deflated and dismayed: 'I had no idea. You are killing me.'

But that at least put paid to the whole affair there and then.

The next visitor was Razumovsky, the secretary of the Moscow Society of Authors, a very nice man with whom I had been in correspondence abroad. I had to settle a number of questions with him: stopping my works being illegally reprinted in the Ukraine, receiving a percentage for performances of my works in concerts, also the matter of my author's fees. Since I am receiving these fees from the Mariinsky Theatre and not through the Society, the latter have no right to make any deduction from them. Razumovsky informed me that my fees for the first two symphonic concerts were 2,500 roubles each, and from the solo recitals 3,500 roubles each. Also during my visit to the USSR I will probably receive from the concerts, merely as composer, more than 1,000 roubles.

A few other people came and went in a flash, then Tsukker arrived. I asked him how the Shurik case was progressing. He answered that the paper I gave him is still on his table and that it is constantly on his mind, but the person to whom it has to be addressed is now away and will be back in four days. I begin to have doubts about Tsukker; sounds as if he's trying to wriggle out of a tricky situation.

Meanwhile Ptashka is packing all the time; we are now in a frantic hurry and fussing around like anything. The porter presents us with a bill for ironing my trousers – 2 roubles. I am indignant and say it's exorbitant.

He replies, 'That's the rate.'

Me: 'No other country charges that kind of money for pressing clothes, not even America; and if that's the rate it shouldn't be. To iron a pair of trousers you need only ten minutes; by that token a tailor can earn fully twelve roubles an hour. If that's how things are, perhaps you can tell me why the whole of Moscow isn't ironing trousers for a living?'

Here Tsukker intervenes, but the porter is rude to him. Tsukker thinks of himself as a totally committed Party-member, that is to say a Member of the Communist Elite; he states that such behaviour will be reported to the Trade Union and the porter will receive a reprimand. I do not know how it all ends, but I do not pay for the trousers and we go in a taxi to the railway station along with Tsukker.

At the Nikolaevsky station – now the October station – I see Chernetskaya, who is also going to Leningrad, apparently in connection with today's ballet; she had told me she had read the script to Lunacharsky and he had warmly recommended her to Excousovich. From the platform I look curiously at the train on which we are to travel. From the travel-book I already know its speed is the same as before the war. But the composition of the train itself has drastically changed. In the past it used to be so spick and span; not any more. It's true that the first carriage is an International Society sleeper, but the endless number which follow it are all third-class (nowadays called hard), and only somewhere far away is there a second-class carriage to be found.

We have a small International Society compartment. Tsukker, who is standing with us by the entrance, remarks, 'Excousovich is in the same carriage as you.'

I say, 'How convenient!'

We say our goodbyes and the train begins to move.

Walking along the corridor towards our compartment I greet Excousovich, but somewhat half-heartedly, not being sure that it actually is he. And in fact, seeing some surprise on his face as I do so, I decide that I have greeted the wrong man and hurry to our compartment. In about fifteen minutes I come out in the corridor again to see Excousovich next to me. It was him after all! But now he is talking to somebody else and continues to do so for some time without paying any attention to me, probably put out by my earlier stand-offishness. For heaven's sake – he puts on such a splendid production of the *Oranges*, and then all the composer can do is barely say hello and immediately rush off! He talked to the others for nearly ten minutes then turned to me and said something civil. Ptashka came out of the compartment and he bowed and scraped in front of her, the last word in gallantry; after which we had a conversation which lasted a whole hour.

Excousovich confirmed he intended to take the *Oranges* to Paris and even began to ask me some questions on various practical matters, for instance about ticket-prices at the Grand Opera and about what one might reckon a good box-office return to be. Of course I had no idea. He was also very interested in my new Soviet ballet and wanted to know if it were possible to get it away from Diaghilev for the forthcoming tenth anniversary of the October Revolution. He mentioned also a marvellous new ballerina, quite a young girl, of whom special care must be taken in case Diaghilev tried to abduct her and spirit her abroad. Basically Diaghilev is thought of here as a bird of prey, constantly on the look-out for new and good things to peck at and pin down. At 1 o'clock in the morning we at last said our goodnights and went to our compartments – but not before Excousovich had reminded me that the *Oranges* would be specially performed the day after tomorrow on the occasion of my arrival. That I knew already from Asafiev's letters. Ptashka found Excousovich very good company and by no means lacking in *chic*.

Wednesday 9 February

I jumped out of bed at 8 o'clock to shave and look through the window at the environs of Petersburg, which are so familiar to me. And yet the snow was so thick there was quite a lot I didn't recognize, including Sablino, my famous Zed.

At 10 – Leningrad! On the platform we were met by Asafiev, Ossovsky, Shcherbachev, Deshevov and some others, about six people I didn't know, representatives of various musical societies. While the porters were getting our luggage and I was embracing my friends, Excousovich said a quick goodbye and ran ahead with his little briefcase; but when we all started moving along the platform towards the exit, there he was again with a group of people whom he introduced to me saying, 'Here, Sergey Sergeevich, are the representatives of the Academy theatres who have specially come to meet you!'

I exchanged bows with everybody and we parted till tomorrow, at the *Oranges* rehearsal. Asafiev remarked, 'Yes, yes, up to every trick, isn't he, our friend Excousovich! Of course they all came to report to their director and he immediately turned it into a meeting specially organized for you!'

The familiar railway station flashes by and we are settled in a car. Leningrad is covered with snow; it's a bright day, and that gives it a clear and tidy appearance. There is the hippopotamus-like monument of Alexander III, which has been left for the edification of communist posterity to show how lacking in grace the tsars were. We drive along the Nevsky Prospect and I am full of joy and excitement. The monument to Catherine is also there, and this square with the Alexandrinsky Theatre is so beautiful. In the Gostinny dvor (the arcades) I am struck by the number of boarded-up stores. We turn up Mikhailovsky Street. When we reach the hotel the driver asks for an exorbitant price and the commissionaire at the door pays him half.

A spacious room has been reserved for us in the Hotel Evropeiskaya with a large bathroom and also beds in the same room, separated from it by a curtain. The room is much larger than the one in Moscow, but that was impeccably appointed and moreover the view from the window was stupendous. This hotel seems to have got somewhat run down since the days of its former glory, although it's still the best in town. Asafiev is thrilled to bits and goes over my Leningrad schedule with me yet again. He is particularly concerned that one day should be devoted to him and spent with him at Tsarskoe Selo.

Ossovsky and Shcherbachev arrive. I am extremely glad to see Ossovsky, who is as gentle and courteous as before; he has gone a little grey but not much. Shcherbachev's interest in me surprises me, since both at the Conservatoire and later I had hardly anything to do with him at all; but Asafiev explains that he now works closely with him in many musical affairs.

Malko is the next to turn up. He is smart as usual, only looks older. Some faces have changed little during these ten years, some, on the contrary, a good deal; and when you compare them with the way they looked before – which you clearly remember – you suddenly realize that a large quantity of water has flowed under the bridge. Malko is now the director of the Philharmonic, having replaced Klimov. Therefore, with regard to the matter of my being cheated out of my proper fee, he found himself in a pretty comfortable position.

'It was really nothing whatever to do with me, it was my predecessor, it was his estimate that was approved.'

Malko did not stay long, told us a few funny stories in his flat little voice and left; Dranishnikov took his place. Well, time hadn't touched him at all: he was just as young and merry as before – difficult times had only weathered him a bit and made him more attractive. He immediately started to talk excitedly about the *Oranges* and made no bones about telling me of all the changes and improvements he had taken it upon himself to make in staging it, all minor ones. Suddenly he got nervous and asked me not to be hypercritical during tomorrow's rehearsal.

Since it was nearly 1 o'clock I invited everyone for lunch – Asafiev, Dranishnikov, Shcherbachev and Ossovsky. The latter should long before have gone back to the Conservatoire, where he is an inspector, but rang to say he was not coming. Lunch lasted till 4.30. Ptashka was very tired and stayed in the hotel for a rest. Not me: I was burning with impatience to see Petersburg and went out with everybody else. We passed Mikhailovsky Street and on Nevsky turned to the right in the direction of the Admiralty. I could see my posters everywhere. They were of two kinds: one announcing the orchestral concerts, the other my two solo recitals.

During the many years of my travels abroad I had somehow managed to forget what Petersburg was really like; it began to seem to me that its beauty was a creation of patriotic feelings on the part of its citizens, and that, essentially, Moscow was the heart of Russia. I began to think that the European charm of Petersburg would pale in comparison with the West and that, on the contrary, the Eurasian beauty of some Moscow lanes was something unique. Now, however, strolling in this particular mood, the grandeur of Petersburg absolutely took my breath away! It looks so much more elegant and imperial than Moscow. The white snow and the clear weather contributed to this effect.

One by one Ossovsky, Dranishnikov and Asafiev went their separate ways and Shcherbachev and I went on alone. We arrived in front of the Winter Palace. Some changes here: the railings encircling the garden have been taken down and the garden is open to the public. But the disappearance of the railings does not spoil how it looks; quite the contrary, the square becomes more spacious. Shcherbachev explains that the much-enlarged Hermitage now occupies more than half the rooms of the Winter Palace.

The building of the General Staff Headquarters is painted bright yellow, with white columns. This is new – in the past it used to be dark red, the Palace as well. Is that good? I liked it dark red. But Shcherbachev explains that its original colour was different.

We got to the Neva at sunset. It is fantastic, pink all over; even the river and snow and the walls of the buildings are pink. Lit up like this the Neva and the fortress of Peter and Paul are amazingly beautiful. We walk along the embankment and turn into the Zimnaya Kanavka.

Shcherbachev, who is now teaching theory of composition at the Conservatoire, tells me with enthusiasm about his own new pedagogical system and about some even more daring innovations it authenticates. I have a very clear picture in my mind of the quiet old Conservatoire with its inevitable and unquestioned progression from harmony to counterpoint, then on to fugue and form; and it is strange and curious to me to hear about the new theories of Shcherbachev, according to which all these stages or steps or entities have been thrown overboard and completely new principles introduced. He expounds all this in a state of great excitement, for he considers me to be the leader of contemporary music.

Shcherbachev accompanied me back to the Evropeiskaya and I collapsed on the bed. I had a very demanding schedule that evening and needed a good sleep. No such luck, for on the other side of the wall a singer, a woman, was practising. Exasperated beyond description I rushed down to the lobby to speak to the hotel administration, but was told it was the tenor Smirnov. I shouted, 'It most certainly is not, I know the difference between a woman's voice and a man's!'

But they explained to me that Smirnov receives ladies in his room who are also singers. However, in a few hours he is supposed to be leaving and all will be well.

There was a telephone call from Lida Korneeva. I haven't had any news of her in a long while but it seems she is quite well, and at 10 in the evening she came to see us with her sister Zoya and also 'Grigorovich', as Zakharov used to call Lida's first husband. The girls are well-dressed and, as in the old days, I am still inclined to think of them as young ladies, although Zoya is already thirty-one and Lida thirty-three.

Lida, though, has aged a bit and yet is still beautiful, with the same charm, the same softness as before. But as for Zoya, no sign of any change in her: she blooms as dazzlingly at thirty-one as she did at twenty-one. Grigorovich has retired. I feared that for him, a naval officer, things might turn out badly, but so far so good.

Lyova was not so fortunate. The joint impact of the Revolution and an unhappy marriage affected him so badly that he nearly went out of his mind. He is much better now and has made a happy second marriage.

Lida also suffered a nervous breakdown, but she is all right now and plays in cinemas. Her younger sisters are fine and the mother is still alive.

We chatted for nearly an hour and Ptashka liked them all very much.

At 11 p.m. Asafiev, Dranishnikov and Shcherbachev came to fetch Ptashka and me to take us to the Artistic-Literary Club on Fontanka Street. About a week ago there was some correspondence about a late-evening party to be given there in my honour, and this is it. We drove past the Alexandrinsky Theatre which was all lit up, in the manner of the Grand Opera, with a bright crimson light; or rather the space behind the columns was lit up, so that the snow-covered trees and the monument to Catherine II, standing out against this illuminated backdrop, looked extremely beautiful.

At the Artistic-Literary Club there are lots of people, among whom I at once meet a number of familiar faces: Ershov, Lyonechka Nikolaev, Deshevov whom I had already seen that morning, Berlin (as beautiful as ever) with her husband, Mr and Mrs Ossovsky and many others.

The concert is extraordinarily late in starting, something like 2.30 in the morning, because the musicians have been held up somewhere. They begin with the Overture on Hebrew Themes, which they play too slowly. After that the pianist Druskin, who has graduated from the Conservatoire with a prize, plays my Fourth Sonata, not very well, all things considered, and the music sounds boring. Then four bassoons creep out and play the Scherzo – very well, boldly and dashingly; it is a big success and is performed again as an encore. After that I was given to understand it was my turn. I lost no time in playing a number of small pieces which were greeted with loud applause.

Then we were all sent out of the hall, large tables were moved in and laid for an enormous crowd of people. At our table we had the same company as in the morning for lunch, plus some others like the actor Yuriev, who still seemed able to strut around in cufflinks with crowns, Tsarist-style. The supper itself wasn't anything special, which didn't stop it costing more than the Conservatoire pupils (or rather Conservatoire *students*, as they are called now) could afford. This being the case they'd made a collection and sent two representatives, which I found quite touching. Finally Ossovsky, who was sitting next to me, got up and made a long and impassioned speech during which you could see his fingers trembling against the table-top, such was his overwrought state. This speech was addressed to me and its themes were my return to Russia, the importance of my music and even of my personality, which he characterized as unusually attractive. All the time I was filling up with horror because it all meant only one thing – that I would have to reply. A bit later I quietly asked Ossovsky, 'Alexander Vyacheslavovich, do I have to answer?'

He was embarrassed and said, 'Well, Sergey Sergeevich, it's really up to you.'

I obviously *did* have to reply, and the sooner I got it over and done with the better. So I stood up and, remembering my Moscow speech, drank this time to Leningrad and the musicians of Leningrad and talked quite a bit of noncommittal nonsense.

Ptashka was flattered when Ossovsky stood up once more and proposed a toast in her honour.

Later we were photographed but I got away as soon as I could, for I had a rehearsal in the morning. And not before time – we got back to the hotel at 3.30 in the morning. After we left the supper went on till 5.

Thursday 10 February

In the morning: first rehearsal with Dranishnikov. It isn't far to go: the Hall of the Nobility is only across the street, opposite our windows.

The Hall of Columns is so beautiful! And it has so many memories for me, going right back to childhood. What awe a large symphony orchestra spread out on stage could inspire! But nowadays the orchestra of the Philharmonic isn't first-rate. There are many young people among the musicians, including some of my former fellow pupils who once played in the Conservatoire orchestra under my baton. It's true that some of them I can hardly remember. However, the former Court orchestra in which the Philharmonic originated has also bequeathed it many old fogeys, some of whom are still not used to new music and shudder at an unresolved second as they would at the bite of a flea. The principal cello is a particular *bête noire* of Dranishnikov's. 'One day I'll kill him,' he tells me during the break.

The first half of the rehearsal is devoted to the Suite from *Chout* which Dranishnikov tackles with great enthusiasm. He has grown into an excellent conductor.

In the interval I am surrounded by the old pupils from the Conservatoire orchestra and asked if I have come to stay for good. 'Don't,' they tell me. 'If you have settled down abroad, stay there, it's no good here.'

After the break Dranishnikov works on the Third Concerto. I sit at the piano and, having played so much with the Persimfans, I feel the more how easy and simple it is to play with a conductor. But here, too, Feinberg has created difficulties. When he played it here he adopted completely different tempi; so that, after a remark by Dranishnikov, some of the old fogeys would complain, 'But last time you asked us to play it in a completely different way . . .'

Among others attending the rehearsal were Asafiev and Shcherbachev, and afterwards they, Dranishnikov, Ptashka and I set out for lunch. On the way we stopped at the hotel; and suddenly, while Ptashka was upstairs in our room and we were standing in the lobby, in came Katya Schmidthoff, of whom I had lost track in 1917. We kissed each other and sat down in a corner.

I asked her, 'So, how are you?'

But she sadly pointed to her right arm. It seems she lost it in 1922 when she fell off a tram. She jumped from the first carriage while the tram was moving and fell under the second. This accident cut short her theatrical career which up to then had been quite successful. She is married now to a retired sailor, like Lida, and has a baby slightly younger than Svyatoslav. She had been waiting for me for a long time and was happy to have caught up with me at the beginning of my stay; but since I had to go we could not talk for long and we arranged for her to come to my next rehearsal.

We all went for lunch, but in Leningrad there was nowhere as nice as in Moscow. Nobody knew where to go. We ended up in an odd place, just across the road, where we had to wait for a long time and were fed expensively and badly.

Meanwhile it was time to go to the Hermitage, where various noteworthy things were to be shown us. We all walked along the Nevsky Prospect and Asafiev pointed out various Leningrad monuments to Ptashka. Then Asafiev and Dranishnikov left and Shcherbachev took us to the Hermitage. Here he handed us over to his wife, who works there.

We were led into the Hermitage through a special entrance, having come as privileged visitors. We were met by the director, Troynitsky, a very interesting and rather elegant-looking man, who, despite being a former pupil of the Lyceum and in no way a Bolshevik, has been in charge of the Hermitage for many years and has managed to administer it with great skill and ability, avoiding all the underwater obstacles which contact with the communist government are liable to place in one's way.

Troynitsky personally showed us the most precious part of the Hermitage – the jewellery collection. This section is not easily accessible even to the director, since it is necessary as a preliminary to sign a book, pass the guards and undergo a number of formalities. In the jewel-room many curious and beautiful objects had been assembled, although I'm not normally keen on things just because their value is incalculable. Among them were tiaras all covered with diamonds, snuff-boxes and swords belonging to the tsars, everything iridescent with multi-coloured stones. Troynitsky, with a kind of nonchalance which concealed a great deal of pride, showed us all these objects with short explanations and the odd joke.

From the jewel-room, where, by the way, we were locked in while we were there, we went on to the Scythian section. Instead of Troynitsky we were shown around by a specialist working there. Here the most interesting things were articles made out of beaten gold.

After the Scythian section the Persian, and a new specialist, but our visit by now had lasted for several hours and we had grown tired. It was getting dark and we almost ran without stopping through the picture gallery. We couldn't look at everything in detail, but couldn't fail to see what a large portion of the Winter Palace had been taken over by the Hermitage.

By the time we at last got out we were completely exhausted. But we appreciated the attention given to us by the director, who had himself shown us the secret part of the Hermitage and got his two specialists to show us the rest.

After the Hermitage we decided to visit Glazunov. Right from the time when I was a student at the Conservatoire my relations with him had been somewhat strained; yet because he was still an important figure in Leningrad – despite the fact that he was no longer in the forefront of musical life – I decided as far back as Paris that when I came to Leningrad I would do the honourable thing and pay him a visit.

I did not remember the number of his house, but knew what it looked like and found it without any difficulty. The front door was boarded up. I knew that at the beginning of the Revolution all front entrances in Leningrad were shut up, but didn't realize this was still common practice. So we had to use the back door. We entered the courtyard. It was enormous, with trees; the Glazunovs, who were merchants, built spaciously and on a large scale. Having asked the *dvornik* (janitor) where to find Glazunov, we started to go up a rather disgusting and filthy staircase until we saw, on one of the doors, a copper plate with 'Glazunov' engraved (no first name or patronymic).

We rang the bell – no response; we rang again – still nothing. We decided nobody was home and started to take out our visiting cards to put through the letter-box. The frost was considerable even here, on the staircase, and as soon as you took your gloves off your fingers grew numb. We knocked once more before leaving and then heard steps behind the door. When it was unlocked we saw two ladies, one of them very young, the other older but still very young-looking. They were mother and daughter and the mother was more interesting than the daughter.

As long ago as 1918, when I arrived in New York, I heard from Vishnegradsky that Glazunov had married, but it sounded like a joke and was reported as a joke. It was said that his wife was a Conservatoire pupil and very young. Others said it was nonsense and that Glazunov had never thought of marrying. The most interesting part was that even here, in Petersburg, people didn't seem to know exactly if he were married; or, if he were, to whom – to the daughter or her mother? One thing was certain, namely that these two lively and interesting ladies had made their home here *chez* Glazunov and looked after him. The ageing composer was in need of a woman's helping hand; and no doubt life on his own in that enormous flat (of which, be it said to their credit, the Bolsheviks had left him in sole occupancy) had become irksome.

I explained I had come with my wife to pay our respects to Alexander Konstantinovich; the ladies replied that he was not at home but cordially invited us in. We were led through the kitchen towards the large drawing-room, already familiar to me from the time when I brought Glazunov my E minor Symphony (now no longer in existence except for the Andante, which I recast and used in the Fourth Piano Sonata).

We stayed for ten to fifteen minutes, during which time the ladies complained about the regime, about the difficulties of life in Soviet Leningrad, about being shadowed both visibly and invisibly; they told us of one lady who wanted to leave but at the last moment received a visit from someone, was accused of something and, so far from being allowed to go abroad, was placed under arrest; and so on.

We got up to take our leave, the ladies accompanied us to the door and we hurried home in order to rest a bit before the performance of the *Oranges*. At the hotel we found a letter inviting us both to sit in the director's box; it also offered us the use of another box for any friends we might like to invite. It was too late for that now; we could have started telephoning round, but preferred just to sit quietly and compose ourselves.

Soon Asafiev arrived and we left together for the Mariinsky Theatre. Ptashka and Asafiev took the first sledge-carriage, I followed in the second one, pressing the *izvozchik* to make haste since time was short. We quickly passed by Kazanskaya, Voznesensky, Ofitserskaya – all such familiar places. Here is the Conservatoire and here the Mariinsky Theatre painted dark red, just like the Winter Palace once was. And although I liked the Winter Palace's dark red, it's a pity the Mariinsky has lost its former yellow.

Once inside the theatre we are invited to choose between sitting either in the side box of the circle or in the stalls, so as to have the best view. I choose the stalls and the secretary shows us to the middle of the fourth row. I am happy to see my beloved Mariinsky Theatre again and look all around several times; but Dranishnikov is already at the conductor's stand, the lights go off and the performance begins. Ptashka points out the left-hand box near the stage: it seats the 'Tragicals' who are presented in this production as critics or reviewers. The 'Comicals' are at the front of the stage, but the 'Blockheads' are in the dress-circle box on the right. Hence a curious counterpoint: the right ear gets one lot of voices, the left another. When the herald appears he himself plays the trombone. Dranishnikov was very proud of this particular stunt and had told me about it in advance: 'Our singers here are incredible: they can even play trombones!'

Next to the herald is a little boy who doesn't do anything but is fun to watch. Somehow all the inventive little touches got me into the swing of the performance right from the start, and it was clear the production had been conceived with enthusiasm and talent.

Other tricks followed and each one amused me very much: Truffaldino, when summoned from the hall, actually *flew* down from the top of the stage (a doll instantly substituted by a man); there was an absolutely fantastic hell which grew to an overwhelming size with dolls floating and cavorting around on all levels of the stage; the magician Tchelio was amusingly dressed up as Father Christmas; and the table with Smeraldina hidden underneath *ran* after Leander, the better to overhear the plot he was hatching with Clarissa. The spell which ends Act I was treated very seriously in the staging: mirror lights shimmered with almost unbearable fierceness on the spell-weavers and turned them into fantastic shapes.

For the festivities in Act II the stage was hung with trapezes with actors sitting on them. I had already heard two contradictory opinions of this device: one was that it was a remarkable invention allowing the stage to fill from top to bottom with performers; others thought these performers were so paralysed by their fear of falling they looked rather pathetic. However I wasn't aware of anything of the sort and liked the effect. The monsters' fight, though, didn't work well, nor has it in any previous production. When Truffaldino pushed Fata Morgana and she had to fall down throwing her legs up in the air, you could see a second pair of artificial legs attached under her skirt and that was what she actually pulled up. This produces an incredibly funny effect. The darkness that follows somehow interrupts the action and I decide to do away with it. During the spell the little devils (as in the earlier hell scene) howl away through megaphones, just as I recommended; it is very effective and makes a frightening sound.

In Act III Tchelio, having called Farfarello, is intimidated by him; and as for Farfarello he not only sings but hops about all the time as well, something again that Dranishnikov proudly made sure I'd notice. When Tchelio halts the Prince and Truffaldino he appears on a little bridge high up at the top of the stage, talks down to them from it, and throws the red ribbon down from up there. In the castle of Creonte the Prince's conversation with Truffaldino before he steals the oranges is marvellously well done. This duel with its chipping, chirruping violin figure in the background is very difficult technically. Dranishnikov takes it at a crazy tempo, yet not only is it sung with absolute precision, it is also played on the stage with the greatest naturalness and ease. The actual stealing of the oranges also fits the music like a glove. The final words of Act III – 'His orange is rotten' – are addressed by Leander directly to the public, a bit too sarcastically, I think. In Act IV Fata Morgana has a real fight with the Father Christmas-Magician, so fierce that she tears his beard off. The Comicals lock her up, not in a dungeon but in a cage dragged out on to the stage for that purpose, and there she sits like an animal. The rat is shot at from a cannon, and the King asks for help in a frightened voice. The concluding mêlée is staged with more concentrated care than anywhere else. The acrobats make the crowd-movement livelier but diminish the sense of everyone rushing about. On the whole it's all handled quite well, yet not quite well enough. In fact it hasn't been done really well anywhere yet.

At the end of the first interval, when the public had all returned to the auditorium, Wolff-Israel came out in front of the curtain, told the audience I was present and welcomed me. The public gave me an ovation, although not as warm as when I gave my own concerts. This was quite understandable: whereas people came to my concerts specially to see me, here they came primarily for an evening out at the theatre, so to have me presented to them was not so much of a thrill. During the second act I was not in the stalls but in the box, and in response to the applause stood up and bowed from there.

As it happens this man Wolff-Israel is first cellist of the Mariinsky

Theatre Orchestra, and is the same man who made a big fuss at the time when my works were first performed in the Ziloti concerts. It was the first performance of the *Scythian Suite* which upset him more than anything. Ziloti, clever diplomat that he was, managed to shut him up by suggesting that he perform in concert in my Ballade for cello. Times have changed, and now here is this same Wolff-Israel making a speech of welcome in my honour.

During the next interval I was invited to go to the Green Room and Wolff-Israel delivered another short speech on behalf of the orchestra. I replied suitably, expressing sincere sentiments of salutation and congratulating the orchestra; then followed much kissing and conversing and everything as it should be!

During the other interval the artists dragged me to the theatre photographer on the top floor and photographed a group of those taking part in the opera with me in the middle. In a sitting-room, adjacent to the director's box, tea with cakes, *zakuski* and wine were served. Excousovich, Ershov, Malko, Ossovsky, and various conductors and producers were present – in short, a full-scale celebration. I am astonished and delighted with the ingenuity and liveliness of Radlov's production, and embrace my old chess partner. I also thank the set-designer Dmitriev, but do not pay him any meaningful compliments because the sets are unimpressive and are, on the whole, the weakest part of the production.

After the show Dranishnikov takes us for tea to his house. Asafiev with his wife comes too, and Radlov with his. Whether Dranishnikov is married or not isn't quite clear, but a rather good-looking woman lives in his flat with him. It seems she belongs to the Mariinsky Theatre Ballet and performs the hostess's duties. Suddenly a chess-set is produced but the crocodiles won't play – that is to say, Radlov and I decide we won't since our heads are full of other things; but Ptashka and Asafiev's wife try their luck, and it is hard to tell which of them plays worse.

Radlov brings up the subject of Chudovsky, who has now been in exile for several years on account of some political case in which he actually wasn't involved at all.

We returned home at 2 in the morning. Ptashka is very taken with Leningrad.

Friday 11 February

After so many hectic days in Leningrad (and prior to that in Moscow too), we have today off: at our first meeting in Moscow Asafiev set it aside for us to spend in Detskoe Selo.

We made a leisurely start to the day and at noon caught the train at the Tsarskoselsky railway station. This train, once so elegant, now consisted only of hard carriages and moved a bit more slowly. The people on the train are rather drab, but our smarter clothes and Ptashka's leopard-skin don't make any impression.

We were met by a cheerful Asafiev at the Detskoe Selo station and walked to his home over the dazzling snow. He lives in a spacious wooden house not far from the station, on the edge of Detskoe Selo, so that on one side is the town and on the other a vast expanse covered with snow. He occupies three extremely large rooms on the first floor and this is only part of the flat, which once belonged to a police officer. The atmosphere is that of a provincial Russian town and, combined with the bright sun and the snowy horizon which can be seen through the windows, transports us into a totally different world.

The first room is a dining-room which can hold up to twenty people. The second is his study, the third a bedroom; but we cannot go in, because there are two fierce dogs locked inside. Asafiev found one of them as a miserable puppy suffering from some kind of eczema and for several months he rubbed it with who knows what stinking stuff. The dog is better now but has gone wild, so it is kept away from visitors. Since we spent the whole day with Asafiev it had to be taken out twice for a walk, and bristled and growled and scratched the floor with its claws.

Asafiev told us how on one of these walks the dog attacked a goat. But the goat wasn't frightened, took up a military stance and met the dog head-on, so that a fierce fight started. But seeing the owner of the goat coming Asafiev in terror began to pull his dog back by the hind legs. One has to know Asafiev, who is such a sedentary person, in order to imagine something like this happening to him. Finally he succeeded and both dog and master vanished into the bushes before the owner arrived at the scene of the incident.

We decided to take advantage of the sunny weather and go for a walk before it got dark. Ptashka was still feeling tired from rushing around earlier and she and Asafiev's wife took a cab. I went with him on foot.

How beautiful the Elizavetinsky Palace is! We admired it for a long time. But one of the adjacent streets has been renamed Byeloborody Street in honour of the communist who authorized the shooting of the Tsar's family. This is very tactless: if for some reason it was considered necessary to shoot children as well as adults, surely you don't have to celebrate it publicly.

From the Elizavetinsky Palace Asafiev and I struggled through deep snow around the former Tsar's gardens. But it was time to go back: firstly it was very cold, secondly we were starving.

The lunch was first-rate: after the first course we didn't have enough room for a second. Then we sat down to write a letter to Excousovich.

Yesterday, after the performance, Excousovich's secretary hinted to me it would be a good idea if I wrote a few words about my impressions. This hint was not really necessary since I myself wanted to do that. I decided to enlist Asafiev's help in finalizing this letter. Afterwards Asafiev showed me the brochure he had published about me in connection with the production of the *Oranges* and asked me to correct any mistakes in it. We also wanted to look through the draft of the book about me which Asafiev was preparing for our publisher, but we chatted so much there was no time left. We set off for home at 10 p.m.

Apparently Vera Alpers, on learning we were spending the day with Asafiev, tried to intrude on the pretext of needing some information. But Asafiev, jealously protecting the day specially dedicated to him, refused to admit her. I didn't get to know about this till later, though.

When we returned to the Evropeiskaya we found two visiting cards from Glazunov. Like the gentleman he was he had called the next day. In connection with this I remembered how, nearly twenty-five years ago, my mother took me to see him for the first time; and with the same courtesy he paid a visit to my mother a few days later, although it would hardly seem necessary to pay visits to all mothers who bring young talents to a celebrity. Or was it because that was the only time when Glazunov hoped I might turn into a decent composer?

Apart from Glazunov's cards there were also two express letters from Moscow. Some five days ago in Moscow I received a letter from a certain Givnin, emotional and tearful; he is a budding talent, lives in terrible conditions and asks for help. I thought he might well be a talent deserving of support and before leaving Moscow wrote a few words asking him what amount he would like me to send him. One of the express letters was from Givnin, in which he enthusiastically, almost fulsomely, thanked me for my attention and expressed his hopes for my charity which is to start, it seems, in the region of 500 roubles, thence upwards.

The other express letter, much more educated in handwriting and style, warns me that Givnin is nothing more than a dissolute time-waster; all he wants is a few copecks to fritter away in a night-club. This denunciation is anonymous, however. So much for trying to subsidize up-and-coming talents.

Saturday 12 February

In the morning a rehearsal in the Hall of Columns. Dranishnikov, though, rehearsed yesterday as well, while we were at Detskoe, concentrating on *Chout* and the *Scythian Suite*.

Quite a number of people have gathered in the hall, but they are only allowed to sit behind the columns and are not to be a nuisance. Dranishnikov started with the *Scythian Suite* and I made some corrections concerning the tempi and orchestral balance. Then came *Chout* and the Third Concerto, which went quite well.

Malko appeared and announced that the Philharmonia is prepared to settle accounts with our publisher for all the performances of my works they had given illicitly, that is to say, the performances which used manuscript copies and not the published and printed materials.

Having placated me with this bonbon, Malko took the opportunity to ask me to be civil to Khais, 'who is upset by your indifferent attitude to him'.

Katya Schmidthoff, to whom I gave an admission card for the rehearsal, sat with Ptashka. Near Ptashka also sat Knipper, a young Moscow composer who had arrived to discuss his own ballet with Excousovich. Knipper courted Ptashka assiduously all the time.

After the end of the Third Concerto Tyulin and some others came up to me and spoke about the remarkable change in my piano-playing.

The rest of the day was spent quietly and peacefully. In view of the forthcoming concert I turned down all appointments and meetings.

When we arrived in the Green Room in the evening we met Asafiev, who said he had tactfully intimated to Malko that the fee they were paying me was inappropriate. Malko promised to think about it and, if possible, *do* something about it.

There are a lot of people in the concert hall, or rather I should say not just a lot, but a terrific lot. In Moscow fire regulations allow people only to sit, and forbid standing. But in this regard Khais turned out to be clever not only about organizing profitable fees for the Philharmonic but also in managing the public image of the concerts; he obtained permission to admit standing ticket-holders and made such capital of this concession that the hall was virtually black from all the people filling it.

First came *Chout*, at the end of which the calls for me began. But remembering the Moscow ritual, I did not go out. After the audience calmed down and the piano was wheeled out I was invited to go on stage.

When I appeared Dranishnikov started playing the *Slava* and set a colossal ovation in train, just about the same as the one at my first Moscow concert. It's not worth describing it again, except for one amusing incident: after they had played the *Slava* twice and had started it a third time, some very loud instruments came in one bar too late, and so the whole of this third rendition turned into a canon. Once started it was impossible to stop, and since they did not end together Dranishnikov had to play it a fourth time. (Three is the mandatory number of times.)

The Third Concerto goes well. I am comparatively relaxed, although nothing like the marvellous feeling of calm I had during my last American tour. No applause between movements, but at the end the same uproar as in Moscow. At first I come out to bow on my own, then several times with Dranishnikov. As an encore I play a Gavotte and two of the *Visions fugitives*. A basket of flowers is brought in, though not a large one.

In the interval Ossovsky came in, bringing greetings from Glazunov. He was at the concert but had to go to some meeting, where Ossovsky too is now going. In other words Glazunov got out of it very cleverly: on the one hand he showed up at the concert out of politeness; on the other he found a plausible excuse to avoid meeting me. After Ossovsky there appeared a group of three – Steinberg, Weisberg and Andrey Rimsky-Korsakov. Even before the Revolution these were the conservatives, the opposition, the reactionaries: they had many a stormy quarrel with Souvchinsky and Asafiev, who defended Stravinsky, Myaskovsky and Prokofiev. However this group has resigned itself to making the best of an impossible situation and welcomed me with extraordinary readiness – presumably because apart from me they have nobody to pin their hopes on.

Then appeared: the Korneevs, looking glamorous as usual; Ostroumova-Lebedeva; the Borovsky sisters, looking surprisingly well; and Vera Alpers and her brother – the former more wrinkled and shrivelled, the latter even more nervous in manner than before. From somewhere in the darkness of centuries there emerged Rudavskaya, who has changed little, though; her features may have coarsened somewhat but she still has the same lovely eyes.

The interval ends and Dranishnikov plays the *Scythian Suite*. The orchestra is nowhere near as good as the Persimfans; the players are less conscientious and the sound is different, but Dranishnikov wags the stick well and enthusiastically.

The *Scythian Suite* goes down tremendously well with the audience, better than at any of my other concerts. Everybody present, particularly the standing public, yells madly. I come out to bow on my own, then with Dranishnikov, then again on my own. This happens a countless number of times, probably at least fifteen, while the public roars continuously. Meanwhile, as I was going in and out of the Green Room, an amusing scene was taking place inside. Excousovich was in there with Asafiev and Dranishnikov on either side of him. Every time I was called out each tried to convince him how absolutely necessary it was for him to stage *The Gambler* and *Chout*. Excousovich however looked very pleased, sat down, was extremely polite to me and charm itself to Ptashka.

The Green Room is again filling with people. Eleonora Damskaya appears; she has put on weight and grown quite unattractive. I am polite to her but a bit cool and immediately turn to somebody else who wants to talk to me. But Eleonora is not to be deterred; through Asafiev's wife she is introduced to Ptashka and tells her she has kept some photographs from the time my flat in the First Rota was devastated. Ptashka thought she even mentioned some letters. A fine state of affairs, that on top of everything else correspondence of mine from my wrecked flat should now fall into *her* hands! Ptashka is not quite sure what was said about letters, but since she is very keen on photographs (she is collecting anything to do with my youth that has survived), she is very courteous to Eleonora.

After the concert, as we had earlier arranged, we go to Radlov's. He lives in a very nice flat and there is a well-served tea with *zakuski*. There I meet Professor Smirnov (the chess-player) and the poet Kuzmin. During tea the latter stammers and lisps as he reads his poems but the result is still quite expressive. I am sitting to one side and observe his skull with curiosity: it is absolutely flat up above, as if the top had been chopped off with a sabre. He is poorly dressed, with holes in his coat. When we put our coats on in the hall I somehow feel ashamed of my Paris coat with its new silk lining, which he quickly glances at. We come out of the house all together. A frosty night, 3 o'clock in the morning. As far as success with the public goes, Leningrad beats Moscow hands down.

Sunday 13 February

A much less hectic day today. I am receiving visitors. Weisberg (!) and Dobychina. I always remember Dobychina as a kind, warm and simple person. Alexander Benois had told me that she now has important connections in high communist spheres and therefore can be very useful or very unpleasant, depending on her wishes. Today she looks depressed and speaks in a quiet voice. The point is – she already hinted at this at the concert yesterday – that the Chamber Music Circle, of which she is the chairwoman, is nearly at its last gasp from lack of funds. There is no money to pay the rent, so if I don't lend a helping hand by giving a benefit concert it will fold up. Yesterday at the concert I managed to get out of the line of fire, but today she has come with Weisberg and in her quiet voice begins to apply pressure. Not only do I not want to give yet another concert (better to go to Asafiev's, to Detskoe), but I also know there are several of these circles, and that if I play for one I must play for the others. So after twenty painful minutes of having to say no I finally got rid of both ladies as another group was waiting for me.

The second group was less tiresome but more dangerous. They wanted a recital too, but this time for the benefit of the MOPR, i.e. the International Society for Rendering Assistance to Revolutionaries. In other words if I gave such a concert and the communists advertised it, not a single country would give me a visa again, this being not just a Russian society but an international organization for cultivating the microbes which start the process of fermentation. However I dispatched this business in a frank and straightforward way, saying, 'You see, I would love to help you, but I have to give many recitals abroad, and these concerts are important for Soviet Russia. For this reason it would be better for me not to get involved, so that I don't run into difficulties with my foreign commitments.'

My explanation was so clear and simple that they accepted it at once and left, giving way to Balaev, my Russian teacher at the Conservatoire.

Balaev, now an old man, is the principal of some school. My appearance on stage for the benefit of something-or-other was yet again necessary, but he added honestly that while he is fulfilling the wishes of the people who sent him he completely understands it is hopeless. So the third suitor was dealt with painlessly, and we embraced and parted.

In the afternoon we had to go to a popular Philharmonic concert: Malko had begged me to come and asked me to promise I would. We were led to the seats of honour in the Tsar's box. The concert was preceded by a talk given by Karlovich, whose Variations I conducted at the annual Conservatoire concert when he was graduating and I was a student in the conducting class. Probably according to a pre-arranged plan of Malko's he contrived to bring my name into what he said, though none of my works was being performed. It was an opportunity to point to me in the box; the public started to applaud so I stood up and bowed.

At the concert they performed several songs by Rimsky-Korsakov in his own orchestrations. The scores have only recently been dug out from the composer's archives and were being played for the first time – quite pointlessly, since the orchestration is pallid and not remotely Rimsky-Korsakovian in style.

When we got back from the concert we packed for a short trip to Moscow of just a few days, intending to return afterwards to Leningrad.

When we were on our way by sledge to the Nikolaevsky railway station our driver pulled up alongside another one and both horses suddenly reared. Either our horse suddenly became interested in the mare next to it, or simply went mad, but whatever the cause it started to leap and caper about so much that the shafts threatened to crack. Then one shaft got tangled with another and we couldn't move forwards or backwards. Ptashka, who was sitting on the side of the locked shafts, began to panic and shouted, 'Get out, get out! Come on!'

But this wasn't so easy since the cover was fastened down and all caught up in the suitcases. While I was trying to undo it the horses got separated and Ptashka discovered that in the confusion her bag had vanished. We began to search for it and then heard people shouting about fifteen feet behind us. The bag, which had fallen into the snow, had apparently been picked up by a woman who, as she started to run off, was caught by a drunk. The bag was taken from her and returned. The crowd which had gathered expressed its indignation and the drunk began to demand a rouble for saving the bag. He didn't need to be so vehement about it since I was quite willing to give him the rouble. Off he went, pursued by a chorus of voices from the crowd: 'Shame on you, citizen, forcing him to give you a reward . . .'

We again had the same compartment in the International sleeper. Excousovich, Asafiev and Rappaport, the principal artistic director of the Mariinsky Theatre (he looked just like Donner in *Rheingold*), were in the next carriage. It seems that this meeting had been planned in advance so that we could discuss future productions of my works at the Mariinsky.

Soon after the train started everyone assembled in my compartment. To begin with the conversation touched on the forthcoming production of *The Gambler*. Excousovich promised to return my original score, which was stuck fast in the library of the Mariinsky Theatre, and I promised that the première would be at the Mariinsky, something that we in fact decided two years ago in Paris. Apart from *The Gambler*, a ballet production was proposed to include *The Buffoon*, *Ala and Lolly* and, if Diaghilev gives his permission, my new Soviet ballet.

To my cautious question about having Meyerhold as the director of

The Gambler, since he was the one intended to stage it in 1917, Excousovich replied promptly in the affirmative.

All in all, Excousovich was interesting to listen to, even brilliant, and did his best to be charming. Asafiev sat in the corner and was largely silent, but what sort of man Rappaport was I couldn't really tell. I wondered about his communist inclinations, because he suddenly started saying how good it would be if I wrote something for the forthcoming tenth anniversary of the October Revolution. However, this idea found little support and was soon dropped.

They also spoke about the *Oranges*, the possibility of taking it abroad and the need to improve some aspects of the present production.

'You just wait,' said Excousovich, 'I am so fed up with being the administrative director of the theatre that one day I will become an *artistic* director. *Then* you'll see my idea of how to stage the *Oranges*.'

The meeting ended and everyone went back to their own compartments. I kept Asafiev back, and asked him if it had been awkward for Excousovich when I asked him about Meyerhold.

'On the contrary, he's delighted. Only through you can they *get* Meyerhold. To ask him directly wouldn't be on, but through you it will work out nicely.'

Monday 14 February

In the morning – Moscow; and at the railway station – Tsukker. In the Metropole – the same room, unlet during our absence and kept for us at half-price.

The telephone calls – all from people who had been put off until my return from Leningrad – began immediately. Before I left Moscow it was easy to ask everybody to telephone on the day of my return, but now I had to pay for it. Besides I had a rather heavy head, was tired and even slept in the afternoon.

In the evening, solemn celebrations of the Persimfans' fifth anniversary. I emphasized that I had come from Leningrad especially for this great event and that even my subsequent concert in aid of homeless children had been arranged to fit in with it.

The anniversary concert consisted of just two quite short pieces: the *Poème de l'extase* and the *Scythian Suite*, because the Persimfans is particularly proud of the way it performs these. In view of the solemnity of this occasion I put on evening dress for the first and last time; but perhaps this was a mistake, since I stuck out and looked foreign in the crowd. In fact nobody here wears evening dress, with the possible exception of those artists who have met with success abroad and who by wearing it probably want to draw attention to the fact. At my concerts, at any rate, I saw only two people in evening dress: Saradzhev and Yavorsky.

Our seats were in the eighth row, next to Tsukker's father and a robust-looking Red Army soldier who was clearly bored by the *Poème de l'extase* but later made a rather impressive speech as the delegate of some institution for which the Persimfans played some time ago.

After the *Poème de l'extase* the stage was cleared and a large table was placed on the right-hand side for the committee of honour. Lunacharsky was chairman and various member-delegates were to make congratulatory speeches. On the left was the Persimfans, headed by Tseitlin. Then followed a million speeches – interesting to begin with, but later one just had to sit them out since leaving was obviously out of the question.

Lunacharsky spoke well, but the Persimfans people maintain that during their whole five-year existence he has never given them any help. And yet one would think that an institution so essentially communistic in spirit would be able to rely on the support of the Minister of Enlightenment more than anyone else!

Sosnovsky also spoke – the one who bored me to distraction in the interval of one of my concerts – but this time he wasn't at all bad. The other speakers came from various theatres, the Conservatoire, workers' organizations etc. Derzhanovsky also made a speech, but his hoarse voice was almost inaudible.

Then came an interval during which the chairs and music stands were put back on the stage. In the *Scythian Suite* the Dance of the Evil Spirits won loud applause; I was repeatedly called but didn't go up since today is not my day. Even so at the end of the Suite there were renewed calls, and this time Tseitlin applauded from the stage. So I got up and walked to the stage to shake hands with him. He stretched out his hand and with a strong movement pulled me on to the stage so that we both lost our balance and nearly fell over. Before bowing to the public I

89

shook Tseitlin's hand and embraced him. I had to make some kind of public demonstration of my interest, because up to this point in the celebration I hadn't congratulated anybody on anything.

After the concert there is a supper. I have a headache and feel tired, apart from which there is tomorrow's concert; but there is no getting out of it, particularly since many important people who were expected have not turned up. At the table the places set out for Lunacharsky and Litvinov were empty. Clearly the supper is not going to be much of a success.

Many toasts, as usual. I also receive hints to propose one but explain that I did mine half an hour ago after the performance of the *Scythian Suite*. One of the critics celebrates the growing industrialization of the country and advocates that music should get more and more mechanized along with it. On hearing this I am strongly tempted to get up and propose a toast to Hanon, but am pulled back by my coat-tails and advised that such a toast would be inappropriate. By 1 a.m. the supper is getting more lively, since everybody is a bit drunk (except for me). Rather disorderly toasts follow one another; at a suitable moment I remind Tsukker of my concert tomorrow, make a sign to Ptashka and prepare to leave. However, where we are seated makes it impossible to escape inconspicuously. Tables and chairs have to be moved. Somebody else expresses a wish that Prokofiev should make a speech whereupon we disappear.

Tuesday 15 February

The headache's gone. I practise for the concert, since I didn't play at all yesterday or during the last few days in Leningrad.

We lunch at the Prechistenka with Asafiev. When we had our meeting in my compartment the day before yesterday Asafiev, Excousovich and Rappaport were all going to Moscow for an important meeting about theatre politics, a conference which would in fact decide the future of the theatre's repertoire. Well, it took place yesterday, and at lunch Asafiev told us about it enthusiastically.

The battle was between two camps: the communist one which wants to turn the theatre into a propaganda weapon ('if it uses the workers' money it must be for the benefit of the workers'), and the theatre camp, which wants the theatre to be primarily a theatre, not a political arena ('if it uses the workers' money it must offer things to interest the workers').

The root of the matter was that the 'communist' point of view was, of course, being defended by the communists and the 'theatrical' one by the non-communists, who obviously had to be very careful what they said and did.

It all began with Asafiev being prevailed upon by Excousovich to read a lecture on opera. This by his own account so bored everyone that he skipped half of it to get it over with more quickly. Then Yavorsky, who is quite a high-ranking musical official himself, was so concerned with not getting into trouble with either side that he read something incomprehensible to everyone.

As for Lunacharsky, the chairman of the conference, he preferred to keep his counsel. His official position is that of communist, but his tastes are those of an aesthete and theatre-lover; so he also had to manoeuvre to avoid taking sides. This was put to good use by the communists, who started to attack the theatre camp aggressively and rudely and showed no love for the theatrical world.

Then Meyerhold stood up. He is on the one hand a communist and an honoured Red Army soldier, and on the other a militant theatre person. He began thus:

'Comrades, first of all I will ask you not to interrupt me. I am very excited. I have just taken some tincture of valerian and I can't answer for my actions. Do you remember what happened the last time I was interrupted?'

(Asafiev doesn't know what happened because he wasn't there, but by all accounts it was something very unpleasant.)

'You, comrade communists, are probably ill-informed about what the comrade workers want.' (Meyerhold digs around in his pockets and produces a letter.) 'Here is an appeal to me from the workers of such-and-such a factory where we have performed.' (He reads out a request to perform dramas or comedies, but in no circumstances didactic or political ones.)

'Well then, comrade communists, do you want plays of the sort that will make the workers stop going to the theatre? And if the theatres are empty, the communist government will have to increase its subsidies to support them. And whose money will you spend for this purpose? The workers' money. That is to say, you will force the workers to pay for empty theatres, instead of paying for full ones, the ones that give them pleasure.'

Towards the end of his speech Meyerhold got so carried away that there was a scandal and an adjournment was called. Lunacharsky said that on balance he would like to leave the Ministry of Enlightenment, at the same time trying hard to suppress a giggle. Asafiev doesn't know how it all ended because he left too early, but in any case, he says, only Meyerhold could have made such a stunning speech. He has nothing to fear, since to imprison such an honoured Red Army soldier would cause too much political trouble; to send him into exile abroad wouldn't exactly make life difficult for him either. Meyerhold knows very well he would find a good job and only Moscow would lose out.

Asafiev went on with these stories all through lunch, and afterwards as well, when we were walking in the street.

As a result of a telegram from Diaghilev enquiring about Yakulov, I had to telephone him (Yakulov). He, however, was in Tiflis, so I spoke to his wife and then to his brother, who promised to send him a telegram. This basically means that Diaghilev has made the decision to stage my ballet and therefore to exercise his rights of exclusivity for three years. So the plan to stage it at the Mariinsky Theatre, as one of three ballets in an all-Prokofiev evening, is off.

Asafiev and I tried to come up with something to replace it, and I thought of using the Overture and a Sailors' Dance which I wrote for Romanov two years ago, adding three or four movements from the Quintet and composing one or two connecting sections using themes from both sources. If all this were orchestrated and a story invented a new ballet could be speedily created.

In the evening I sent Ptashka to the Bolshoi to see *Kitezh* while I went to the Hall of Columns to give the recital in aid of homeless children. Some sceptic said, 'It's not for homeless children but for bullets, because that's the only way to get rid of them!'

It was a pleasure to play in the elegant Hall of Columns. It is much prettier than the Great Hall of the Conservatoire, and even the piano sounds better. This evening I played the same programme as the first recital, on 4 February, only better. All the same, I came a cropper in the Finale of the Fourth Sonata, all four times when the two hands alternate the scales. Very enthusiastic response at the end. As encores I played the March from the *Oranges* and the Gavotte from the 'Classical' Symphony. The hall roared and screamed.

Nadya Raevsky was at the concert. She came to see me in the Green Room with an interesting red-haired lady from the Vakhtangov Artists' Studio, the wife of Nadya's brother-in-law Sheremetiev, whom I've already met. I don't remember her name. Then came the representatives of the Committee for Homeless Children: a man and a somewhat elderly lady. She was very affecting in what she said: 'If I die, don't forget the homeless children. You see, our plan is to do away with homelessness within three years. We are doing our best to carry it out in time but we need funds to put it into effect.' Then she thanked me once again for the concert. I replied, 'We are both interested in seeing an end to homelessness. I have worked towards it for one hour, but you dedicate all your time to it, so it's not you who should thank me, but we who should be thanking you.'

Wednesday 16 February

At 10 o'clock Asafiev and Meyerhold come bursting in. The honoured Red Army soldier is such an important person I am surprised at how little fuss he makes about coming to tell me he's agreed to direct *The Gambler*. But perhaps this is because in Paris I was the one who came to see him – to take him to Diaghilev's rehearsals. If the Mariinsky Theatre is going to the trouble of getting a big fish like Meyerhold, then the production will go with a bang. I explained to Meyerhold that before I start making revisions to *The Gambler* – and there will be many – I would like him to give me his thoughts as to what changes should be made to the old libretto. I was particularly worried about the last scene.

Meyerhold: 'As soon as you come back from your second trip to Leningrad in a fortnight, we must meet to discuss all kinds of details. Come for lunch and I will try and get hold of Andrey Bely, if you have no objection.'

Me: 'On the contrary, I would be delighted, I love Bely. But does he understand the stage?'

Meyerhold: 'Oh yes, he has a very good feeling for it. At the moment he is adapting one of his novels for me in a very interesting way.'

93

Here we parted. A bit later Myaskovsky came to collect me to take me to the Musical Sector, in what used to be the Jurgenson shop, where Yurovsky was waiting for me. He wanted us to sort out the problem of publishing those works of mine which previously belonged to Jurgenson and Gutheil but now, since the Revolution, are under the Musical Sector's control. But the Musical Sector only expropriates the publishers (the spiders, as it were) and doesn't want to offend composers. While the position of composers living abroad remains dubious, Myaskovsky (who has great influence in the Musical Sector) and all his cronies maintain that I am not an *émigré* at all, but someone with a legal Soviet passport who has been abroad a long time. My recent arrival has strongly reinforced this position, and so the Musical Sector in the person of Yurovsky has the task of legalizing their relationship with me. It wasn't an easy thing for the Musical Sector to do since it had to pay me for everything they had sold in the nine years since the Revolution, and also renew their rights for some years to come. To evaluate the payments for each work they employed a system devised by Myaskovsky. The number of notes in the work is calculated, then multiplied by the number of instruments involved (piano, ensemble, orchestra) and then multiplied again according to the 'value' of the composer. The latter would then receive between 7 and 12 per cent of the sale price of each copy.

Our discussion lasted for almost two hours. Yurovsky started by suggesting 12 per cent but seeing my expression immediately went up to 15. This 15 is more than the 25 per cent paid to me by Koussevitsky's publishers, because here it is based on the retail price of each copy; Koussevitsky's is based on the cost price to the shop, i.e. with a discount of nearly 50 per cent.

I wouldn't agree to signing a firm contract for an indefinite period, but instead suggested one limited to three years to see how things went – a compromise, but Yurovsky agreed and then asked about my writing a work for the anniversary of the Soviet Revolution, which is coming up in six months. This was the most awkward part of our conversation, because I had to refuse point-blank; at the same time my excuses had to sound polite and believable. I replied that I had no time to do a big new piece for October, being under contract to finish *The Fiery Angel* this summer. If I undertake to produce something it has to be good. Then

Yurovsky gave me to understand it was so important for them to have such a work by me they wouldn't quibble at paying a large fee. Just then I remembered my Diaghilev ballet and told him that, in fact, I had a piece on a Soviet theme already written; so the major difficulty was not just the time-factor but also the idea of composing a second work before having a chance to hear the first. All in all I got out of the situation so adroitly that when Yurovsky and I had bid a friendly farewell, his secretary caught up with me and, while I was putting on my coat in the other room, amused me by saying things like, 'Alexander Naumovich (Yurovsky) wonders if you thought he was a communist? It was merely that in his position it was his duty to talk to you about a work for the anniversary – no more to it than that.'

I met Ptashka and we went to see Rabinovich, who was very keen to show us his models for the production of the *Oranges*.

We had great difficulty finding him and were worn out by the time we arrived, but it was worth it: his models were quite brilliant. The *Oranges* has never before had such decorative sets. I particularly liked the one for the first scene which had a perspective extending to the back of the stage with mirrors. He is marvellously clever at building his models, so his ideas were beautifully presented. Rather solemnly he announced he was dedicating them to me.

After that we had to hurry home, where the secretary of the Society of Authors, Razumovsky, was expecting me. I wanted to write to the Society protesting about the deduction of 15 per cent from my forthcoming fees for the production of the *Oranges* at the Bolshoi. When it is a matter of deducting a few roubles or even copecks from my recitals, I wouldn't mind if they took 25 per cent or more. But when it comes to large sums due from the Bolshoi – and they don't even collect them, Koussevitsky's publishers do, through *Kniga* – then it's sheer robbery. The French Society of Authors takes about 2 per cent or even less.

I explained all this to Razumovsky. We wrote my submission together and he made it quite clear that the Society of Authors will probably give in, because falling out with me while I'm enjoying such success would not be in their best interests.

After Razumovsky left we had to pack, since tonight we return to Leningrad. Tsukker came to see us off. I asked him about Shurik, but he was embarrassed and kept saying that it's very difficult, it's a tricky business, one must be careful not to upset things, and that the person one has to speak to isn't yet back in Moscow. Quite obviously Tsukker wanted to keep his hands clean for fear of getting into trouble himself.

We piled our luggage into the car and drove to the station. By an odd coincidence we had the same compartment in the International carriage as on the two previous occasions, but this time there was no Excousovich. Now it was Asafiev travelling with us, though as the supplement payable to the International Society is very high, in fact several times the cost of an ordinary ticket, he was making do in a cheap carriage.

After the train had started I went to look for him. Of course it wasn't very comfy in the cheap carriages, but Asafiev had his own bench and some soft bedding. We had a little chat – I had just received a bundle of press clippings from the Moscow bureau which we looked through. I told him that today on the way to Yurovsky's I offered Nikolai Yakovlevich money for his journey to Leningrad for the performance of his Eighth Symphony, but Myaskovsky said he didn't want to go. I thought this was only because he didn't want to accept money, and he if had some he would happily go. Asafiev agreed and promised to write to him to force him to go to Leningrad for the performance.

After a discussion about the timetable of my Leningrad visit – which had actually been mapped out on my previous trip – we said goodnight and I went back to my 'aristocratic' sleeper which no Revolution had been able to take out of circulation.

Asafiev later told me that his neighbours in the carriage recognized me and after I left made a great fuss of him. They even stopped smoking because it was irritating him.

Thursday 17 February

At 10 in the morning we're in Leningrad. As we arrive I peep through the window at the snow-covered suburbs. This time despite the white covering I could make out the familiar outlines of Sablino.

From the Nikolaevsky railway station, where we and Asafiev went our separate ways, we proceeded to the Evropeiskaya Hotel. This time we were given a magnificent and spacious suite consisting of an enormous reception room, a bedroom, a bathroom, an entrance hall and even a lover's room, as I called the dark closet off the hall. The first person to call on us was Katya Schmidthoff. She told us how successful she had been in the theatre before the accident to her arm and that, while her career as an actress is clearly over, she feels she has a real vocation as a stage director and could still learn how to be one. The point being, couldn't I give a benefit concert for her, so she could train for two years as a stage director and then make a comeback in the world of the theatre which had been so tragically closed to her? All this in the same sweet unceremonious manner her brother would affect when touching me for money.

And yet, on the other hand, from her point of view it's all so simple: just another concert, does one more or less really matter? After all, I give so many of them. Then, who knows, she might begin a new career.

On thinking it over I decided that it would almost certainly turn out to be a waste of time for her: losing an arm was too severe a handicap. Besides, it wouldn't be so easy to organize a concert. So I told her that this Leningrad visit was wholly the responsibility of the Philharmonic and I was not in a position to arrange any concert except under their auspices.

I left for an orchestral rehearsal. Katya spent a long time with Ptashka telling her about her life. She is now married for the third time. She married her first husband – an actor – in 1917 or 1918, after I had left for America. It was a love match, and their trip to Siberia, where he was playing, remains one of the happiest memories of her life, despite the civil war in Russia. But her happiness lasted only a few months: her husband fell ill and died, leaving her in a desperate situation. Then, in a state of complete apathy, she married a communist whom she did not love but hoped would support her. This communist, a typical male chauvinist, was cruel and jealous and Katya was unhappy with him. He used to lock her up and all but beat her. During one of these incidents a young man tried to stand up for her but in the fight he was killed by the communist. Obviously the husband was madly jealous, although Katya assured us he had no reason to be. The communist was put in jail but reappeared a few months later, released as the result of some manifesto. Katya fled from him in horror, but he claimed her as his wife, saying, 'You won't find another husband like me in a hurry!' Nevertheless Katya never went back to him and is now married for the third time,

97

with a baby, and is quite happy, though her husband is a sailor in northern parts and is often away. She chain-smokes, deftly lighting matches with one hand.

Today's rehearsal is under the baton of Malko. The programme is new: the Suite from the *Oranges*, the 'Classical' Symphony, the new Overture and the Second Concerto. He is rehearsing *Oranges* and the Symphony: not too badly, studiously and punctiliously, but without *élan* or excitement.

I come out into the street to see an enormous line of people queuing for tickets. I am recognized and applauded. What a long-suffering lot! Even queuing for two hours doesn't stop them from clapping!

I return to the Evropeiskaya and discover to my annoyance that the piano has not yet arrived, though on my last visit I arranged with Khais for it to be sent from the Philharmonia this morning. I impatiently telephone the Philharmonia. They explain that for some reason it got delayed but it should be arriving any minute. This is a blow: tonight is my first recital and I have to practise my programme, which I haven't played for nearly three weeks.

Finally, at 4 o'clock, I am told the piano has been delivered. I open the doors, move the furniture and wait, but half an hour goes by and no piano. I go down to the lobby and see that the enormous grand piano is actually standing there, but all on its own, nobody around. Apparently while the piano was being carted into the hotel the horses which brought it bolted and the coachmen have been trying to catch them – why this has taken a good half-hour nobody knows. I ring the Philharmonia again and at last, at 5.30, the piano comes thundering into my room. It looks like a centipede and requires the combined services of nine men. I start to rehearse my programme but somehow all that farcical business with the piano has broken my concentration. Didn't have a rest, and after a bad night in the train didn't practise properly.

In the evening the Hall of Columns is packed. I play fairly well, make a few blunders at the end of the Fifth Sonata, somewhere in the *Visions fugitives*, and so on. I get the usual reception: good after the Third Sonata and the *Visions fugitives*, so-so after the Fifth, stormy outburst as soon as I start to play the March from the *Oranges* and other trifles. Three or four encores, then howling and yelling at the end until the lights are turned off, and even after.

Andrey Rimsky-Korsakov, who has already written a good review for the previous concert, starts to talk to me about writing a theatre-piece on a text by Razumnik, with sets by Petrov-Vodkin and stage direction by Meyerhold. Normally I would turn any propositions of this kind down out of hand; but since it was Andrey Rimsky-Korsakov, who until recently has been hostile on principle but is now a newly converted supporter, I fobbed him off more gently. I explained I was overloaded with work until the end of the year and therefore suggested we leave any discussion about the project until my next visit.

Then Dobychina appears and follows me about with quiet persistence, fishing for something, probably the same concert for the benefit of the chamber-music society which I thought I'd managed to get out of. As I go out for my calls she stands behind a column on the way to the Green Room and says quietly, 'Listen to them all, shouting their heads off. Perhaps you think this is success? Perhaps you think they love you? No. Love is not shouting but quiet understanding.'

I remember she has contacts with the Cheka and decide I'd better let her have her say. But there are the Korneevs, and from a distance Lidusya sees the boredom on my face. She comes up and takes me aside.

'Shall I get you out of this?'

'Oh yes, please, for God's sake, Lidusya. She will spoil my entire visit.'

She takes me by the arm and we move away from Dobychina behind the columns. Suddenly the applause, which was quietening down, breaks out again. Apparently while we were walking behind the columns we came into public view, and having seen me again, the audience starts to clap. We dodge quickly out of sight in some embarrassment.

Back in the Green Room I found a lot of people, among them Asafiev, Dranishnikov, Ossovsky, Malko, Katya Schmidthoff, Vera Alpers and her brother, Rudavskaya, and so on. Rudavskaya phoned me this morning because at our last meeting I promised her a ticket for the concert. After telling her the ticket would be left in an envelope at the hotel reception desk, I asked, 'Antonia Alexandrovna, how many times have you been married?' – a fairly normal question to any pretty woman in Soviet Russia.

But with her usual good sense she stopped me with, 'Sergey Sergeevich, we really shouldn't discuss such matters on the telephone.'

Ptashka is very fond of the Korneevs and arranged to go and see some furs tomorrow with Lidusya, who is still the same woman of fashion. Furs are what everybody from abroad buys in Russia.

Friday 18 February

The next rehearsal for the same concert. The orchestra is undisciplined, or, as Malko says apologetically, 'playful'. The musicians are inferior to the Persimfans, but the Overture op.42, which they rehearse today, goes better with a conductor than it did in Moscow without one. Apart from the overture we gave the Second Concerto a good working-over.

After the rehearsal Khais and Malko invited me to the Philharmonia office. Malko announced that the Philharmonia was going to pay my publisher for all the 'unlawful' performances of my scores, i.e. those for which they used hand-copied material. Then Khais asked where the fees should be transferred. I told him my bank in New York, and he made a note. Not a single word about any increase in my fee for the concerts, just this tense look, as if he were thinking, 'Is he going to bring it up or not?'

Meanwhile he tried to haggle with me about the amount I should receive for my trip. This infuriated me though I didn't show it. But when without any embarrassment he started talking about my concerts next year, I answered, 'I'm not sure there'll be any. Concerts with the Leningrad Philharmonic are hardly worthwhile financially. I'd do better to go to the south, to Kharkov, to the Caucasus, where I'm paid double.'

Khais collapsed in his chair. Even I could not have foreseen the effect of my words, it was so powerful. Malko is discomfited and justifies himself saying he has only recently been appointed a director and all the arrangements were made under Klimov. I reassure him by saying I am quite aware of this. Khais is stammering and Malko tries to smooth things over.

I make it plain I do not want to have any discussions about the future season with Khais but might come to some arrangement with Malko. Khais jumps up and says that in that case he will go in order not to get in the way. We say there's no need for that, but in a short time he makes some excuse and leaves.

Malko laughs. He seems to be delighted at what has happened, because in taking the stand I did I am giving him a trump card against Khais in the matter of administrating the Philharmonia. Afterwards Malko changes the subject and, after having touched on *The Fiery Angel*, tells me a story about Bryusov.

Apparently when Bryusov died his wife was asked if there were any unpublished manuscripts. There weren't any to speak of, or hardly any, but she did mention the diary which he had recently been writing in ancient Greek, showing off how learned he was. They were extremely glad to get hold of this diary and immediately started working on a translation. But then it transpired that in his diary this most revered of communists was tearing the Soviet system to shreds. What happened to the diary we don't know.

Khais came back. After exchanging a few words I said goodbye – cordially to Malko, politely to Khais.

One way and another they're a fine lot. They didn't give me a single extra copeck, and only in a roundabout way made it clear they couldn't go above the agreed amount. Any changes now would earn them a sound thrashing from the authorities.

I returned home, practised the Second Concerto and had a sleep. Ptashka had gone with Lidusya to see some sables. Katya Schmidthoff came to tell me that she had found a flat which would suit her down to the ground but that she needs 250 roubles for it, which she hasn't got. Quite clearly I'm expected to help – if not a concert for her benefit, at least something. I promised half, which I will send her from Moscow, because at the moment I haven't got much cash – all my fees are being sent directly abroad in dollars by the Leningrad Philharmonic.

I had a telephone call from Khais to say how distressed he was after our conversation today. In no way was it his fault but Klimov's, the former director who has now resigned. He's lying – of course Khais is responsible for everything. But right now, on the telephone, I behaved most correctly and said, 'You are quite right. All the letters which the Leningrad Philharmonic sent me were signed not by you, but by Klimov.'

This didn't give much satisfaction to Khais, since while I accepted his explanation from a formal standpoint I was still putting all the blame on him. So our conversation ended up achieving nothing.

A telegram from Yakulov in Tiflis. It seems that Diaghilev's staging of my ballet is coming on. In connection with this I wrote some letters and telegrams to Diaghilev in Paris and to Yakulov in Tiflis.

Ptashka returned at 7 o'clock with Lida and a sailor who is living in their flat – a very quiet and well-behaved young man. We all sat and chatted. Lidusya and I reminisced about Terioki and all the laughing and larking about we got up to in those days.

We stayed at home in the evening and went to bed early.

Saturday 19 February

Another orchestral rehearsal. They get to grips with the overture much better than the Persimfans. I play the concerto well, but the orchestra is badly behaved and does not take it seriously enough. They say that when Klemperer came he was so severe with them it was decided not to admit any of the public to the rehearsals in order not to make a spectacle of their disgrace.

Asafiev is at the rehearsal and I tell him about yesterday's clash with Khais. As a 'patriot' of his town Asafiev is very put out at the way the Leningrad Philharmonia have behaved. Khais appears, cool and curt, but only to give me the tickets for the concert. Just the same he does give me all I asked for – ten or twelve, for friends and acquaintances.

In the afternoon I practise and sleep. On the other side of the wall folk are singing and bawling gypsy songs. The Revolution may have got rid of the aristocracy with their arrogant swagger and the drunken, debauched merchants, but it has nothing to say about gypsy music, which is just as depraved.

In the evening Malko conducts the symphony concert. The programme began with the overture, played twice in succession for the public's greater understanding. However, the success it had was only slightly greater than in Moscow, which is to say small. I played the Second Concerto accurately and confidently and for the first time without anything going wrong. If I recall anything else about this evening it's all jumbled up with other concerts, and there aren't any other notes in my short-hand diary.

Sunday 20 February

Because Lunacharsky has come to Leningrad for only a few days the *Oranges*, which he hasn't seen yet, was put on for him specially this afternoon. Lunacharsky had to decide if this production was worth taking to Paris as planned.

The administration graciously made two boxes available to me and I took the opportunity to give all twelve seats to my friends, including M.G. Kilshtedt, the librettist of my childhood opera *Undine*.

When Ptashka and I arrived for the performance we met Lunacharsky, Protopopov and Excousovich in the director's room. Of course there took place a rather heated, albeit only semi-serious, discussion between Lunacharsky and the administration about sending one of the Soviet theatre companies abroad.

'But if we send *your* production of the *Oranges*, then the Bolsheviks won't let me live in peace,' he was saying. At the word 'Bolsheviks' he laughed, since he meant the Moscow Bolshoi Theatre, hurriedly mounting *their* production of the *Oranges* with Rabinovich's sets (much more lavish than the Leningrad ones).

One of the assistants came in and asked if Dranishnikov could start the performance. We were led to one of the boxes in the first circle, on the left. We sat in this order: Lunacharsky, Ptashka and myself in the first row, and in the second Excousovich and the two men accompanying Lunacharsky. Lunacharsky leaned towards me and said, 'It is a great pleasure to be listening to this opera sitting next to you,' as if he were paying a compliment to a young lady, so sweetly I couldn't think what to reply.

At a second hearing or rather viewing of the *Oranges*, when all the tricks were familiar and there were no more surprises in store, certain drawbacks started to become apparent. I pointed some of them out in a whisper to Excousovich, who was sitting behind me. The latter decided to put my critical frame of mind to practical use: in the interval he asked me to write down all my comments and recommendations so they could be taken into account and something done.

In the interval we all moved to the director's sitting room by the side-box, where tea and refreshments were served. It was there that during one of the intervals Glazunov stumbled in. It seems he wasn't at the performance but just dropped in. Lunacharsky immediately asked him how he liked the *Oranges* but he just mumbled something incomprehensible and slipped some invitations to a Beethoven concert into Lunacharsky's hands. Dranishnikov quipped instantaneously: 'He understands as much about the *Oranges* as Glazunov does,' paraphrasing the proverb 'He understands as much about oranges as a swine does.'

Excousovich took me aside and told me he had had the wonderful idea of staging *The Gambler* and *Chout* at the same time so they could be performed in one evening. I was horrified. The one would cancel out the other, and besides, it would ruin the notion of a ballet evening devoted to my works. I therefore protested energetically and immediately told Asafiev about Excousovich's project, asking him to oppose it vehemently.

At tea Lunacharsky was lavishing praise upon the *Scythian Suite*, talking about its power and force. Somebody asked, 'And what about the *Oranges*?'

'The *Oranges* is a glass of champagne, all sparkling and frothing.'

We returned to our box and the performance continued. There were calls during one of the intervals and I bowed from the box, but at the end I went out in front of the curtain with the artists. The other intervals I spent for the most part in the director's box.

In the corridor behind the box I was caught by Maria Grigorievna Kilschtedt and also by Natasha Goncharova, whom I did not at first recognize, and hardly remembered even when I did. Then Barkov brought with him Lidusya's daughter, a lovely ten-year-old girl. But all this happened in a sort of kaleidoscopic haze, and there were probably meetings with other people which I don't remember.

After the performance we went with Asafiev to Malko's for lunch. Lunacharsky said goodbye and asked if I were going to see Alexey Tolstoy tonight, the same Tolstoy I knew in Paris before he made such a song-and-dance about leaving the 'exodus' and turned into an exemplary Soviet citizen. He had indeed telephoned me yesterday inviting me to come. But my evening was already divided between Malko and Shcherbachev, and I had to refuse.

Malko lives near the Mariinsky on the Kryukov canal, in the same house where Ziloti used to live. While lunch was being prepared Malko talked to Asafiev, Ptashka to Malko's wife (a very pretty Jewish woman he met somewhere in the south) and I sat at the desk with the score of the *Oranges*, looking through it from the first page to the last and writing down, as Excousovich had asked me to, all my comments about the action on stage and the way the music should be performed.

The meal was very good, like all the others to which we have been treated in Russia. Malko is a compulsive raconteur. He has a talent for telling very amusing stories about almost nothing, and this time told so many that in the end my head began to throb. At 9 o'clock we say goodbye and drive to Shcherbachev's, where tonight all the young composers of Leningrad are gathered in my honour.

Shcherbachev lives on Nikolaevsky Street, now renamed in the usual revolutionary way. It is not far from where Lyadov used to live. We are driven on sledges right across town in a most terrible frost, Ptashka and I on one sledge, Asafiev on another. As we approach Shcherbachev's I cannot help feeling that I am in a somewhat ludicrous situation: on the one hand these young composers are coming to play me their works; on the other I have no knowledge of the ideas which are rules to them. Am I 'one of them', or am I '*not* one of them'? It's all very well being famous, but each young composer considers himself a discoverer of Americas and, apart from the fact that either he will turn into somebody or he won't, at the start he very often looks askance at an established 'maître'.

Shcherbachev has a fine apartment but like almost everywhere in Leningrad, one has to get into it through the back entrance. We arrived quite late and all the others were already there: every chair and sofa was occupied. But straight away I find the atmosphere much lighter and pleasanter than I expected, since from the start I am surrounded by old acquaintances: Deshevov, Tyulin, Shcherbachev.

Deshevov hasn't changed at all: he's just as brisk, courteous, enthusiastic and agreeable as ever. He is nearly forty, yet one is still tempted to describe him as a promising beginner. But we haven't any time to waste: there is a long list of works for me to hear, so we start immediately.

The first is Schillinger, who plays a complicated and uninteresting piece. If it's going to be like this all evening, then no thank you very much. I have no idea what to say. But Schillinger himself comes over and begins to explain the structure of the piece, which consists of various revolutionary tunes like the *Internationale*, *We Fell as Victims* and so on. This makes it in no way at all easier to understand and I try to extricate myself by asking questions, thereby covering up my real impressions.

The second person to play is Shostakovich, a very young man who is not only a composer but also a pianist. He gives me the score and plays boldly, by heart. His sonata starts with lively two-part counterpoint in Bach-like style. In the second movement, which follows without a break, the harmonic style is quite mellow and there is a melody in the middle – nice enough, but diffuse and a bit too long. This Andante changes into a fast Finale which, compared to the rest, is disproportionately short. And yet, after Schillinger, it is so much more lively and interesting that I am quite happy to start praising Shostakovich. Asafiev laughs at me, saying I like Shostakovich so much because the first movement is so clearly influenced by me.

Then follows a published collection containing works by five or six composers including Tyulin (quite pleasant but pale, a bit in the style of some of my *Visions fugitives*) and Shcherbachev, much more interesting than I expected after the experience of conducting his *Procession* at the end-of-term concert at the Conservatoire.

After tea the recital resumed. First it was the turn of Deshevov, once praised by Milhaud when he visited Leningrad. Deshevov is lively, playful, doesn't use too many dissonances, and as long as you agree that he has no claim to being a great composer it is very pleasant to listen to him. On the basis of several piquant pieces a ballet was commissioned from him; but he failed to meet the challenge of composing a large-scale piece, although some parts were successful. Deshevov did not want to leave the piano, he was keen to play this and that transcribed for two hands, for four hands. Meanwhile I was beginning to get impatient to hear the others: it was getting late and my attention was starting to wander.

When at last Deshevov was gently driven from the piano his place was taken by Popov, who had his octet or nonet to play. This was scored for a rather strange combination and written down in pencil (not very clearly). Amid some densely woven counterpoint you could distinguish a few interesting moments; I would probably have distinguished many more if it hadn't been for the throbbing in my head brought on by all the music I had already heard. At one point Popov, appreciating the indigestibility of his contrapuntal writing, introduced a rather frivolous little theme in order to entertain the public. This irritated me: the counterpoint was definitely too elaborate. Oppressed by fatigue I waited impatiently for the end of the nonet and asked Shcherbachev to play something from his sinfonietta so I could go home. But Shcherbachev said I ought to hear an organ piece by Kushnarev, very interesting and well-made; the pianist Yudina had just come specially to play it. I had to give in, and Yudina played this piece with the composer. The music was of a completely different sort, much more old-fashioned, not untouched by Rachmaninov, but not at all badly written.

By now I had become quite dizzy: every note felt as if it were being hammered into my brain like a red-hot nail. Towards the end of Kushnarev's piece I felt I couldn't stand another note, so we said goodbye and left. A pity I couldn't manage Shcherbachev's sinfonietta; it seems he is a terribly proud man, and his work above all I should have made a point of hearing.

During our musical evening the frost outside had become heavier and reached, I think, the coldest point since we came to the USSR. Whether or not this was so, the thermometer was showing below minus 20 degrees Réaumur, which in the absence of a fur hat and a fur collar starts to be a threat. While we dragged our way back to the hotel on sledges I kept my fingers and toes moving and pulled at my brow, lips and cheeks: keeping everything in motion warms the parts of the body liable to get frost-bitten. On the other hand the shock-cold of the frost helped cleanse my mind of all the sounds I'd been exposed to during the day.

Monday 21 February

This is the day we are to spend at the Conservatoire. Asafiev wrote to me about this before, when I was in Paris, and we also discussed the details in Moscow.

After yesterday's excesses we overslept and took our time getting up. We had coffee so late that when at 2 o'clock a student arrived to take us to the Conservatoire we hadn't had lunch. The student drove us there in a car and when we arrived I peered with sharp curiosity at the establishment which for ten years, between the ages of thirteen and twenty-three, was the centre of my life. It was a very strange experience seeing the same building, where every corridor and each step are so familiar, all filled with absolutely different people.

We were quickly led to the director's office, the very one where at thirteen I had my entrance examination. Several familiar professors were waiting for us and others kept arriving: Asafiev, Ossovsky, Nikolaev, Malko, Chernov, Steinberg.

Malko was already telling a story about how upset Glazunov gets when the portrait of Rubinstein hangs askew. A student once noticed that Glazunov always got up in order to straighten it; so now, whenever there is a meeting in the director's office (nowadays student representatives take part in meetings), someone slightly tilts the portrait of Rubinstein beforehand, and everybody eagerly waits for the moment when Glazunov will get up and set it straight.

Meanwhile some interesting preliminaries were taking place in the Small Hall. Ossovsky, Asafiev and Malko all kept going out and coming back in: the reason being that those students who had tickets distributed among them were playing tricks with them, since the Small Hall couldn't accommodate them all.

As long ago as last week Ossovsky asked me where I would like to play, in the Small or Large Hall, and without hesitation I chose the small one. This is a part of the students' Conservatoire and is much more a part of my life, since all my orchestral studies and exams took place there. The Large Hall has less to do with the day-to-day functioning of the Conservatoire and is normally made available for hire for concerts. And if all the students won't fit into the Small Hall it doesn't matter, they can huddle together – I remember how that happened on many occasions during my time in the Conservatoire at big events, and what fun it all was.

Finally it appeared that everything in the Small Hall was ready, and all of us – Ossovsky, Ptashka, myself, Asafiev and a few other professors making up quite a solemn procession – walked right through the Conservatoire to get there. I was, as it were, looking at this procession from the outside and remembering how in my time, when some celebrity came from abroad, there would be a similar procession, and the students who gazed at it with curiosity would then run at breakneck speed to the Small Hall in order not to be late for the beginning of the concert, and also not to miss the girl-student they were courting at the time.

When we marched into the hall, I was greeted with applause. The student orchestra was on the stage with Malko, who is the professor of orchestral classes just as Tcherepnin was in my time. The orchestra started by playing the first movement of Beethoven's Seventh Symphony, the one we studied in Tcherepnin's classes. Was that why they were playing it now? Probably not: who would have known? After the Beethoven they played the first and third movements of my 'Classical' Symphony in quite a sprightly manner. This was all very nice – it showed the Conservatoire orchestra had been preparing for my arrival.

That was the end of the first part of the Conservatoire's celebrations. We returned to the director's office, since the stage had to be cleared of the orchestra and the hall of the students; it would now be *my* turn to play. Of course this was what the students had been looking forward to most of all, and it was because of this they'd been getting up to mischief with the tickets.

This time we were met in the director's office by Glazunov, who as Master of the House was trying to be polite; but politeness did not come naturally to him, in fact it flowed very un-freely, and he muttered away unintelligibly as was his custom. Instead of his customary cigar there was a pipe in his mouth, perhaps because it is difficult to find cigars in Russia nowadays. Eventually, when the Small Hall had emptied and filled up again, we were once more led back through the Conservatoire. This time the hall was packed. The stage was densely populated as well and some people were standing by the entrance to the Green Room.

Just as I was about to leave the Green Room to go on to the stage to play I saw Glazunov. I didn't understand what he was doing there, but after all he as Master of the House can go wherever he pleases. However when I came out on to the stage and bowed after an ovation I saw that Glazunov had followed me. He addressed me in a speech which started with the words, 'Much esteemed Sergey Sergeevich . . . (look what this decadent reprobate – i.e. yours truly – has come to!)' There followed a conventional speech of welcome and, later on, a journey back into the past recalling the time 'when you, Sergey Sergeevich, brought us the . . .' Here he stumbled and started searching for a word, which might have been 'honour' or 'pleasure'. But

Glazunov couldn't bring himself to say 'honour', and as for 'pleasure', that seemed inappropriate to the solemnity of the occasion, which had far more to do with the Conservatoire than with the director personally. So Glazunov continued: '. . . gave us the joy of having him as a student in this very Conservatoire . . .' A few other remarks brought this totally unexpected speech to an end; I was left wondering if I needed to reply, and if so with what kind of nonsense. 'The joy I gave him when I was at the Conservatoire . . .' Unbelievable.

Meanwhile Glazunov shook my hand and while I was mumbling some words of gratitude left the stage. I could now happily sit down at the piano and play my short programme once the applause calmed down.

I played the Third Sonata, then the Second and a number of small pieces. These went down particularly well, and when they were over there was not applause so much as a kind of rattling. At the end Asafiev led us through staircases and corridors heavily crowded with departing students to his classroom, where my Schroeder piano, the Rubinstein prize, is standing with a silver plate attached to it. After sundry adventures this piano, salvaged by Eleonora from my looted flat, found its way to the Conservatoire. Asafiev took it into his classroom, which is on the ground floor by the entrance, near the staircase leading to the Small Hall. In this classroom the piano is well protected from rough fingers, since it's mainly Asafiev himself who plays it, and only when he is illustrating his talks on musicology. The rest of the time the classroom is locked. I tried a few chords and found the instrument in much better condition than I expected (in fact, I was sure it would be a wreck).

We sat for a while in Asafiev's classroom and then went to see Ossovsky, who now lives in the flat of the late inspector of the Conservatoire, Habel, in the same building on the fourth floor. I felt terribly hungry – we hadn't had any lunch and had expended a lot of energy – but no food was served for another hour. A lot of people were invited, including Malko, Nikolaev and Asafiev. The meal was marvellous and served in the generous and hospitable style characteristic of the Ossovskys in the old pre-revolutionary days, something I didn't fail to tell them. By the end of lunch I fell into a daze, and since the Conservatoire celebrations were far from being at an end I asked the hostess's permission to have half an hour's siesta. So we were shown into the host's bedroom, where in the darkness on a comfortable bed I went straight off to sleep and Ptashka dozed. The Ossovskys' flat is large and comfortable – when the Conservatoire was built the comfort of its staff was a priority in their eyes.

At 9 p.m. I woke up refreshed and crawled out into the dining room where some of the guests were still sitting at table. Yet to come was the concert of *my* music; this time Conservatoire students were to be the performers. I felt very proud that the students were playing a whole programme of my works, but Ossovsky explained that three times as many wanted to play as *could* play, and a selection had to be made.

Among other things the programme included the Ballade for cello and piano, the First Piano Concerto (accompanied by a second piano), the Third Sonata and some smaller pieces. We were shown to the front rows, but there weren't any special seats so I sat sometimes here and sometimes there. At one point, while they were bringing a harp on to the stage, I was talking to Professor Musina, and when the student came out and began to play I saw that my seat in the third row was occupied. I looked around and spotted an empty seat in the first row, the only one. When I sat down I found myself right at the harpist's feet, and this turned out to be fatal for the poor young girl. As soon as she noticed me she got muddled in the C major Prelude and made a hopeless mess of it (at least if she'd been playing one of the *Visions fugitives* for harp it would have been less obvious, but here, in C major!). In short the performance became an ordeal and although she improved a bit by the end and got some applause, she didn't just bow and go but simply ran away. However this was the only incident. All the others played well although some were a bit shy. As for the First Concerto, which I hadn't heard for quite a long time, it gave me real pleasure; I caught Asafiev by the elbow and asked him, as if I were talking about somebody else's composition, 'Don't you think it might sound quite good with an orchestra?'

To which Asafiev replied, 'Just what I thought when I was listening. It certainly might.'

After the concert there was supper in the conference hall, the one where thirteen years ago at my graduation I was awarded the prize amid stormy scenes. However Glazunov, whose protests had been chiefly responsible for the storminess, was absent; addressing a speech to the 'much esteemed Sergey Sergeevich' has probably been too much for him.

In the long narrow conference hall the tables are arranged in a T-shape, with a long bottom part and a short cross-bar. I was sitting between Asafiev and Nikolaev, other professors were next to us around the short cross-bar, but I couldn't see who was at the long bottom part. Ossovsky gave the first speech of welcome on behalf of the absent Glazunov. I immediately replied with a toast to 'dear, absent Alexander Konstantinovich Glazunov, the Father of the Conservatoire'. There followed many other toasts, among them one by a student-communist, the representative of the students among the professors. His speech was addressed to me and was couched in the most enthusiastic terms: I was even called upon to become the leader of the young musical communists. Well, how do you like that: come and rule! Seeing the rather strange look on my face, Asafiev whispered, 'He makes these inflammatory speeches but they don't mean very much. He's very fond of Bach and melts away at the *St Matthew Passion*. It's very easy to talk to him on Conservatoire matters, you simply have to know how to handle him.'

Ossovsky made another speech: 'I was a witness as to how difficult it was for you to carve a path for your new ideas, so unexpected were they at that time for the people who ran the fortunes of our music. But now, Sergey Sergeevich, *your* people's time has come, and our music is ruled by people who see things as *you* do.'

This might very well have been left unsaid, but, yes – during my absence my friends *have* come to prominence, they *have* taken up the cause of my music to make it accessible.

Musina-Ozorovskaya made a very convoluted speech. She is now a professor of the Conservatoire and after her divorce from Ozorovsky and his death has become simply Musina. Either she had been drinking a bit or the whole atmosphere had brought her to a state of euphoria, but her toast turned into such a succession of enthusiastic exclamations that everybody was seized with merriment and amid general laughter she could not even finish it.

There followed toasts for other people who were present and also for some of the professors. I took this opportunity to propose another toast, this time to Asafiev, 'whose opinion people in Europe take notice of'.

One o'clock in the morning came and went and still no end in sight, but I had had enough. We said goodnight, thanked everybody and went home. I had been a guest of the Conservatoire for a full twelve hours, from 2 p.m. to 2 a.m. On the one hand the place is the same, on the other it isn't at all. Many features are so typical they cannot alter: the familiar faces of professors, the same corridors, couples on the window seats, the Small Hall with the organ and the mirrors. But how many things have changed in these thirteen years! As we leave I am stopped by Chernov who presents me with several fragments from the score of my *Giant*. One of his students lived on the same staircase as my former apartment, and discovered that my manuscripts were being used as fuel during the cold weather; she managed to swap some of them for a few logs. Unfortunately she was too late to salvage anything of any value apart from a few pages of *The Giant*. The rest consisted either of fragments of orchestral scores or copies of works I already had.

Tuesday 22 February

After yesterday's excesses and because of the concert in the evening I needed a quieter day today; in spite of which I got a phone-call from Eleonora. She talked about her problems, how saving my piano cost her a lot of trouble and expense – about 12 English pounds, according to the rate of exchange at the time. Besides that she is now in a difficult situation and her mother is unwell; in short, she needs money. I told her that as soon as I returned to Moscow I would send her the 12 pounds she needed but in exchange she must return the photographs she managed to save from my ransacked flat.

In the afternoon I called the Philharmonia office who informed me that my fee had already been transferred abroad in dollars (that was why I couldn't repay Eleonora immediately). Khais, seeing that I have softened (after all, I couldn't be sarcastic all the time), asked me for a signed photograph, no doubt in order to counteract any rumours that might arise concerning alleged bad relations with Prokofiev. All he'd have to do would be to point at the photograph and say 'Look – autographed!' I answered, 'Yes, all right, next time I'm here.'

In the evening I played my second recital-programme. I sent Ptashka and Lidusya to see *Vera Sheloga* at the Mariinsky Theatre so they would be back by the end of the concert. I felt tired tonight and played sleepily. I even had to shake myself during the Fourth Sonata, but improved towards the end and got the Finale absolutely right for the first time since I arrived. I played the Schubert waltzes with Kamensky, a very gifted pianist (recommended by Asafiev), with whom they went better than with Feinberg. These had a noisily enthusiastic reception and we had to repeat them and give many other encores. The shouts and applause were tonight as loud as at my first concert.

Masses of people crowded into the Green Room and blocked the way to the stage. Madame Pototskaya told me about the tragic death of her daughter Nina, with whom I had learned to dance as a small boy. Pototskaya herself had brought her up from a safe place in the country to Petersburg where she thought there wouldn't be any danger. There however she (the daughter) fell under suspicion in connection with the Whites, was arrested, tried and shot. I heard this story in bits and pieces in between going on stage and coming off again, with the result that the public shouting itself hoarse on the one hand, and on the other images of trial and execution summoned up by a mother on the verge of tears, all became weirdly fused together.

Eleonora appeared and presented me with the photographs. They turned out to be less interesting than I thought since I had most of them already.

Ptashka and Lidusya arrived back after the concert had finished, having been delayed at the Mariinsky. Tanya and Zoya also materialized. Zoya and Lida managed to have a row just as in the good old days.

Having said goodbye to the Korneevs we went to the Artists' Club. When I was in Moscow I received a telegram expressing a wish on their part to hold a celebration in my honour. Hundreds of people were there and supper included a variety show. This consisted of music by Shaporin for the Leningrad production of *The Flea*. He used *chastushki* transcribed for a small orchestra with accordions, which made a particularly interesting sound. After that a scene staged by Radlov from a Japanese tragedy was performed.

At our table were Dranishnikov, Asafiev, Radlov and Musina. The latter's daughter Tamara Glebova, whom I remember from at least twenty years ago and with whom I used to quarrel non-stop, started to flirt with me in a very determined way. When I said something rather risky about communism during a conversation Dranishnikov leaned over and warned me in a whisper to be careful, because a communist of a particularly venomous kind was sitting at our table.

Although I had begged for an evening without any speeches they couldn't resist and started making them. One of the speakers was Brender (one of the directors of the Concerts Association), who in the past, as Asafiev and Dranishnikov told me, had put as many obstacles as he could in the way of getting the *Oranges* produced. Now he was 'expressing satisfaction at the great success enjoyed by the *Three Oranges*, on which so much effort and love has been expended . . .' During these last words Asafiev exclaimed in a low voice, 'From him, of all people!'

There was also a speech by Weisberg, who by the way has managed during these two days to change the colour of her hair from grey to black.

Yes, yes – imagine being greeted by Weisberg, my sworn enemy throughout my musical career!

Everybody very much wanted me to speak as well, but tonight I really couldn't force myself to utter a single syllable. Besides I had warned them in advance that I wouldn't. So, somewhat disappointed, they let us go home.

Wednesday 23 February

With yesterday's concert the official part of my stay in Leningrad was over. Today we had intended to go to Moscow, where rehearsals for the symphony concert should be starting, but we managed to get a day's respite and Asafiev persuaded me to come out instead once more to Detskoe Selo. I thought that a splendid idea and out we went in the morning.

It was a lovely sunny day again, and the snow was bright and white. Dranishnikov came too and we all went to the park. Ptashka and I in turn kept snapping the group with the little camera that we brought with us, but unfortunately the photographs did not come out very well.

The Radlovs and Shcherbachev arrived for lunch. Shcherbachev told us various musical anecdotes including some about Glazunov.

When he was in England and visited one of the universities – in connection with the award of an honorary doctorate, I think – the rector invited him into his study to sign the celebrities' book. When the book was opened in front of Glazunov it turned out he had to sign just underneath Richard Strauss.

'If you would prefer to sign on another page, you are welcome to do so,' said the rector.

'If you don't mind, I *would* rather sign on another page,' replied Glazunov. After that the rector (who was no great fan of Strauss either) looked out into the corridor to see that nobody was coming, shut the door, and took a bottle of Madeira and two tumblers from a cupboard, saying, 'Let's have a drink.'

And the two accomplices had a most pleasurable drink together.

The day was over before we realized, and once again Asafiev had no chance to go through the book which he is writing about me.

Dranishnikov was extremely pleasant and I was glad to hear that recently his career has been taking many turns for the better.

Again the half-wild dogs had to be taken for a walk. They growled and scraped the floor; Dranishnikov was scared of them and kept out of their way.

There were rumours that Myaskovsky might come for the rehearsals of his Eighth Symphony, and indeed in the evening we heard the voice of Asafiev's wife crying, 'Nikolay Yakovlevich has arrived! Nikolay Yakovlevich has arrived!'

Evidently he had managed to find the money to come without my help.

One by one the other visitors left and we spent the rest of the evening cosily together chatting with Myaskovsky and Asafiev. Myaskovsky told me that after my discussion with Yurovsky the Musical Sector has been trying to calculate how much they owe me for those works which they have already put on sale, and for those which I want them to put on sale now; this has been going on for several days. His sister works there and is bored to tears doing it.

At midnight it was time to return to Leningrad together with Myaskovsky. We arranged to meet tomorrow at the rehearsal of his symphony.

Thursday 24 February

When I was on my way to the rehearsal this morning I ran into Eleonora on the stairs. It seems she is very worried that she won't receive her money, that I didn't mean it when I promised to send it from Moscow, and in going there I'd get out of giving it to her. I tried to reassure her, promising I would do it as soon as I arrived in Moscow. Then we talked a bit and Demchinsky was mentioned. My point was that he had proved to be a brilliant critic, but when it came to measuring up to his own high standards one found him conspicuously wanting. Eleonora said nothing and I thought I'd have done better to say nothing as well. I was in a hurry to get to the rehearsal and didn't want to spend any more time with her, but since she had brought more photographs I sent her up to Ptashka who was staying behind in the hotel. Eleonora was there for quite a long time; she was impressed by the sheer size of our rooms and examined all the clothes from Paris with greedy eyes.

I got to the rehearsal at the beginning of Myaskovsky's Eighth Symphony which interested me greatly, more so than the earlier ones, though I have never heard the Sixth. All the same there are too many four-bar sequences and progressions from the bass up and from the treble down. There is also a tendency to draw things out, especially at the end of the Andante. The trumpet in the first movement sounds very good. In the Scherzo there are a few defects in the orchestration which can be put right in performance.

Today was the second rehearsal and although Malko was trying his best the orchestra played pretty badly. I sat next to Myaskovsky looking at his rough score. When they played wrong notes Myaskovsky groaned and buried his head in his hands. He really did get much too upset when things went wrong. One should accept the fact that at the first rehearsals new works always sound terrible. Towards the end of the symphony Asafiev arrived and he and Myaskovsky both stayed to talk to Malko. They promised to come over for lunch and I went back to the hotel.

While lunch was being served I put the brightness of the day to good advantage and took some snaps with my camera.

Myaskovsky left after lunch. Asafiev and I went to the Academy Theatre office for a meeting with Excousovich, Radlov and Dranishnikov about the possibility of producing the *Oranges* in Paris. Excousovich told us he was almost sure this would happen, and that in his briefcase (he slapped it with his hand) there was a document concerning that very matter; but from bitter experience he knows he will only believe the trip is actually on when they board the train. He then asked if I had handed over my comments on the production to Dranishnikov, and said he understood it was mainly the set-designs that needed changing. It might be that completely new sets would be required; these could be made in Paris, because materials are cheaper there.

I was asked a lot of questions, some of them so detailed I began to get confused and didn't know what to say. Then Excousovich and I exchanged letters wherein it was stated that I was giving him the rights to the first performance of *The Gambler* and he promised to give me the score of the said opera before I left for the West. I could not have it right away because some missing parts had to be copied out.

I returned to the hotel where a great number of people had congregated: Malko, Lidusya (who had been out with Ptashka choosing furs), Katya Schmidthoff, the coquettish Tamara Glebova, the taciturn Alpers. Then I suddenly remembered it was late and we had not yet packed, and exclaimed, 'Ladies and gentlemen, *please* you must leave immediately or we shall miss our train!'

'You are so firm and frank about showing us the door we cannot even take offence,' said Tamara with some disappointment in her voice.

After a frightful rush we just caught our train. Shcherbachev and Miklashevsky saw us off – the former simply out of good nature, and the latter, who complains he is given few opportunities here, obviously because he hoped through us some possibilities abroad might come his way.

Friday 25 February

Here my shorthand diary comes to an end, and I have based my account of my ensuing stay in Moscow on Ptashka's notes and other documents. Some facts may therefore have got left out, though what is recorded is undoubtedly as it happened.

When we got back to Moscow we again had the same room in the Metropole. I immediately went to my rehearsal. From now on I was no longer the responsibility of the Persimfans but of the Association for Contemporary Music, run by Derzhanovsky. The Association has fewer resources than the Persimfans so I had to be content with what they could spare. Money was also tighter, but remembering my old friendship with Derzhanovsky I was gallant in that respect and suggested they pay me whatever they can manage. Wily man that he is, Derzhanovsky had contrived to put on two concerts with almost entirely new programmes. The first was orchestral – with Saradzhev conducting, of course, since Derzhanovsky and Saradzhev are still inseparable.

In the past nine years Saradzhev hasn't got any better, if anything rather worse; he doesn't keep the orchestra together well and talks too much. This is not only my opinion but Myaskovsky's too. A pity, because he is all things considered an excellent musician and still a good conductor.

Today they are rehearsing the 'Classical' Symphony. This will be its first performance in Moscow: Derzhanovsky managed to talk the Persimfans into letting him do it. The Hall of Columns (where the rehearsal took place) was decorated with strips of red cloth hanging vertically next to the columns. This combination of red stripes and bright white columns reminded me of red-and-white blancmange. I admired the hall again, but couldn't decide which one is more beautiful, this one or Leningrad.

After the rehearsal Ptashka and I took Saradzhev and Derzhanovsky to the Prechistenka restaurant for *blini*. After lunch we left them and went to see Aunt Katya, who has at last got here from Penza and is staying with Nadya.

Our meeting was very moving. Aunt Katya has become an old lady (not surprising at sixty-nine) but despite her paralysed leg she is extremely bright in manner and is as charming as ever. Cousin Katya has grey hair; her deafness prevented us making much spontaneous contact. They liked Ptashka very much and she them.

We had a free evening and decided to go to one of Medtner's concerts. Medtner had come back to the USSR a bit later than I did and had been giving his concerts in almost the same cities, although much less fuss was being made of him. He commanded neither a large public nor a following among leading musicians – a combination I had reaped the benefits of. He was supported by a group of old theoreticians and

Conservatoire professors. They even presented him with a special address written in old Russian orthography in order to emphasize the traditional stance he represented.

Medtner's concert tonight took place in the Great Hall of the Conservatoire. His playing was good as usual, if a bit boring. But the concert was spoiled by a lame singer who, with a rasping voice and unsteady intonation, sang a song-cycle which was so monotonous it almost sent us to sleep.

In the interval we escaped to see Tseitlin, whose apartment-office is almost opposite the Green Room; we became engrossed in conversation and stayed there for the rest of the concert. Everybody is saying that my appearance at Medtner's concert was noticed favourably, especially since Medtner himself, together with the group surrounding him, was burning with unconcealed hostility towards me.

Back home I found a telegram from Diaghilev and also an anonymous letter from a woman, a mixture of salacious remarks, quotations from Wilde and a proposition. If the answer to the latter is 'yes', I should play the Scherzo from the *Oranges* as an encore, and I will be met after the concert.

Saturday 26 February

Not many details about today except that we saw Aunt Katya. In the evening we went to Meyerhold's theatre to see *The Government Inspector*. This production is the talk of Moscow and indeed of Russia: some people find it remarkable while others say it is sacrilegious and treats Gogol disrespectfully. Just the same the play is still being performed several times a week and always sells out.

We were taken straight to see Meyerhold and had a chat with him. Meanwhile the audience was waiting and the performance couldn't start. Then Meyerhold said 'begin' and as soon as the lights in the auditorium went out he took us to our seats in the front row.

I liked the production although it seemed to me overloaded and overlong. Meyerhold was so keen on inventing detail, he had forgotten about the resulting length. But my main interest in Meyerhold is in relation to the forthcoming production of *The Gambler*. Here I shan't be running this particular risk since an opera can last only as long as the music. In other words I and not Meyerhold will be in control of the timing.

This production of *The Government Inspector* doesn't have real sets. Each scene is performed on a fairly narrow platform; the scene-changes consist of blacking-out the lights and moving the platform to the back or side, while another one moves in from the opposite side with new furniture and characters on it; the inevitable dim candlelight outlines the vague silhouettes. This moving scenery was very effective and had a kind of theatrical mystery about it.

In the interval Meyerhold offered us tea and cakes; he was extremely nice but avid for compliments.

Sunday 27 February

Today Svyatoslav is three years old but it's already ten days since we had any news of him. 'Groggy' suffers from unpunctuality.

This afternoon there was an orchestral concert conducted by Saradzhev. To begin it he had dug *Dreams* out from beneath the dust of centuries. I didn't want it performed, but Derzhanovsky talked me round by saying it had been my first symphonic composition to be played in Moscow and (most important of all) by Saradzhev. If my style has changed now, so much the better: everybody will see what I represented in the past and what I have now become.

I listened to *Dreams* from the Green Room. It didn't sound too bad: sweet, gentle, rather soporific. Saradzhev conducted the 'Classical' Symphony quite well but with insufficient polish and precision. Then in the *Three Oranges* Suite he showed what he was capable of, playing the 'Infernal Scene' (which usually doesn't quite come off in a concert performance) so brilliantly the public requested an encore.

I played my Third Concerto and as before it was very successful. I gave encores, but *not* the Scherzo from the *Oranges*; although when I came on stage I did remember the anonymous letter, and thought, 'I bet that's what she's expecting. How disappointed she'll be when I play something different.' Saradzhev put his best foot forward and conducted the orchestra much better than at the rehearsal. I thanked him and promised to present him with the tie I was wearing as a memento of the first Moscow performance of the 'Classical' Symphony.

In the evening we went to see Morolev who had been insisting I visit him. He lives on Marxistskaya Street, but because this is a recent name no one knew where it was. We hired a taxi and wasted a lot of money finding it. Morolev lives with his whole family, i.e. with his wife and his more or less grown-up children. It is cosy but crowded. Among some bound scores I found some of my manuscripts, including the March op. 12 in its first version, fragments from the First Sonata (also the early version) and other odds and ends which I used to send him at the time when nobody published me.

As was our old custom we played chess and I won twice, although Morolev had a chance to draw in one game. On the whole I spent a very pleasant evening, but Ptashka was terribly bored in the company of his daughters and longed to go to the Derzhanovskys' where they were gathering tonight to discuss the afternoon concert and where, of course, her admirers, the young composers, would be. At last, late in the evening, we hurried across town to the Derzhanovskys'. But there weren't many people there and the hero of the evening was Saradzhev.

Monday 28 February

I had money transferred for Eleonora and for Katya Schmidthoff. This afternoon was the official showing of Rabinovich's models. I was invited but had problems getting into the theatre because no one was allowed in without the stage-door keeper's permission and he wasn't around at the time. Even so I arrived before the viewing had started. Needless to say it was half an hour late.

On the stairs I bumped into Excousovich who had come from Leningrad and was very keen to have a look at the various ways in which the stage had been refurbished; if I am not mistaken he trained as an architect.

Finally we all assembled and went to look at the models, which I had already seen. They were displayed in a narrow space so it was very crowded and people got in each other's way. Rabinovich had laid out his costume designs on the floor of a large room. All this viewing was pretty much a formality, since it had been decided in advance that his work would be accepted.

Excousovich suddenly took me by the arm, led me aside and said, 'I have a wonderful idea about the Leningrad production of the *Oranges*: we will commission the sets for Paris from Golovin. What do you think?'

I was stunned.

'Ivan Vassilievich, Golovin painted the sets for *The Firebird* when Diaghilev staged it nearly twenty years ago, and so far as Paris is concerned it wouldn't be anything new, just yesterday's cold leftovers. Besides, Ida Rubinstein recently staged something with sets by him and it didn't make any impression at all.'

Excousovich went off, a bit disappointed. He simply doesn't have any idea what sort of sets would attract interest in Paris.

Then old Suk came up to me and after introducing himself said that he had intended to conduct the *Oranges*, but during his absence Golovanov had appropriated the opera. 'A very crafty man, this Golovanov,' he concluded with his strong Czech accent.

We lunched with Tsukker on the Prechistenka. A lecture by Trotsky had been announced in the Hall of Columns which we very much wanted to attend as Trotsky is a first-class speaker. However Tsukker was very vague and apparently did not want to go to the trouble of obtaining tickets for us since Trotsky was at odds with the government. Finally Tsukker telephoned a friend who, he said, might be able to get tickets through someone else. But the answer was that there weren't any left, so that was that. Instead we went to a Persimfans all-Beethoven concert in which Tseitlin played the Violin Concerto. Not much fun and Tseitlin is not a first-class violinist, but because he had put himself out so much on our behalf it was impossible not to go. On the way from the restaurant to the concert I began to apply some gentle pressure to Tsukker on the subject of getting Shurik out of prison, saying it was rather a poor show if after several weeks still nothing was happening. What it boils down to is of course that Tsukker is either a coward or simply doesn't want to get involved in a 'counter-revolutionary cause'. Later this began to be obvious from his vague answers. I asked him to be frank, because if it was difficult for him I could try to find some other way while there was still time. I had heard for instance about the Political Red Cross, which helps 'politically ailing people'; or I could discuss it with Meyerhold, the 'Honorary Red Army Soldier', who probably has a few admirers in the communist élite. Tsukker reacted irritably to both suggestions, saying that the Political Red Cross was useless and Meyerhold's political reputation was not good enough to influence the release of someone politically unreliable. Basically, according to Tsukker, the entire situation was hopeless. This infuriated me and put something of a strain on our relationship.

Tseitlin was very grateful to us for coming to his concert. Afterwards when we passed the Hall of Columns there was quite a large crowd outside. One could sense that the atmosphere of Trotsky's lecture had been electric and we were glad we had not gone: we might have got into political trouble and for no good reason at all. Trying to get Shurik out of prison is quite difficult enough as it is.

Tuesday 1 March

Derzhanovsky told me that the former wife of Gorky is in charge of the Political Red Cross. He knows her and discreetly mentioned my problem to her. He says that it is possible to talk to her frankly since she genuinely devotes her life to saving people who have got into political trouble. Her organization already existed during the Tsar's time but illegally, and worked so to speak in the opposite direction, i.e. saving socialists and communists. Thanks to these services she has managed to obtain legal status from the Soviet government. The Bolsheviks put up with her reluctantly and answer her pleas as infrequently as they can. Nevertheless some results have been achieved. Derzhanovsky and I decided to go to see her because her office is on the Kuznetsky Most, not far from the Mezhdunarodnaya Kniga where Derzhanovsky works. When we were going upstairs I felt a bit uneasy, as if I were visiting some anti-government organization on a conspiratorial errand.

Peshkova received us very courteously. She vaguely remembered Raevsky's name, saying they had already appealed on his behalf. For more information she summoned her assistant – a Jew, who speaks terrible Russian – from another room. After consulting his notes he said Raevsky was one of the people they had appealed on behalf of and had obtained a reduction of his term by a third. I knew this to be true but did not know it was through the efforts of the Political Red Cross. With extraordinary candour she told me the following:

'You see, if you yourself go to the GPU to plead for Raevsky, they might agree to your request, but they would also remember they had done so and could well use it in the future against you. That is why I would not advise you to ask them personally. But it so happens I am going to the GPU on other business and will be speaking to one of Menzhinsky's closest associates (I think she named Comrade Yagoda). I will try to bring the conversation round to you, and since he might well ask the obvious question – "Well, and is Prokofiev pleased with his stay in Moscow?" – then I will say, "Very pleased, but he is upset about his cousin being in prison." So I might manage to improve Raevsky's situation without your having to intervene personally.'

I thanked her for conceiving this brilliant plan. Peshkova promised to ring Derzhanovsky tomorrow, and to avoid my becoming involved even by telephone she said that she would let him know what happened in some indirect way. Peshkova's tactfulness just goes to show how carefully one has to deal with such problems.

This afternoon Ptashka went with Tsukker to the Gostorg to look at fur coats. He pulled strings to have her shown furs which are for export only, and therefore the best, and to have them sold to her at cost price. Ptashka also visited Aunt Katya and then came home on a sledge. A runner got caught in a tram rail, the sledge overturned and she fell into the road. Fortunately the snow was quite soft and she didn't hurt herself.

That evening we were expected at the Kamerny Theatre, but I was feeling a bit low so Ptashka went on her own.

Wednesday 2 March

This afternoon I played at the Moscow Conservatoire. It is organized on different lines from Leningrad, the box-office takings being turned over for the benefit of the students. Someone rang me in the morning and asked if I were playing today. I replied I thought I was but it had been discussed a long time ago and not only had I not been told what time the performance was to take place, I didn't even know whether it would take place at all. Apparently the substance of this telephone conversation was relayed to the Conservatoire, because two hours later Director Igumnov came rushing in with a student representative. They greeted me, thanked me for agreeing to play and said a car would pick me up at 3 p.m. I felt rather embarrassed. Courtesy demanded that as a new arrival I should myself have paid a visit to the Director of the Conservatoire instead of waiting until he came to see me. When Igumnov left I decided I would have to go and see him tomorrow.

At 3 on the dot a car arrived and we were driven to the Great Hall of the Conservatoire, which was full.

When I went on stage I was welcomed with a speech and presented with a writing pad on a decorated board and a basket of flowers. Then I played much the same programme as for the students at the Leningrad Conservatoire, though I didn't have the same emotions in this 'alien' conservatoire as I had had in mine.

After the concert tea was served in the lobby with about twenty people present, including Igumnov, Yavorsky, Gnesina and Borisova. Meanwhile students were coming down the stairs towards the exit. When they saw me they gave me another ovation, which was very pleasant.

In the evening we went to see Lamm. I had got to know him a long time ago when two young composers made their Moscow débuts – Myaskovsky with *Silence* and I with *Dreams*. Lamm was of German origin, something that everyone had forgotten until war broke out in 1914 when it was discovered he had a German passport. He was interned somewhere in the Urals where he spent the whole of the war, and having nothing to do made transcriptions of symphonies for two pianos, eight hands. Eventually he had transcribed every Russian symphony in existence, and at the end of the war when he came back to Moscow, this vice had become an addiction. So he set to and transcribed every new symphony as it came out. In this way all Myaskovsky's and those of a number of young composers have been transcribed for piano. After the Revolution, with the help of Myaskovsky and others, Lamm obtained the post of director of the Musical Sector, but as a result of some unpleasant intrigue he was dismissed after various scandals, searches and arrests. Now he is simply a professor at the Conservatoire. He has two large rooms in the building and in one of them are two pianos. This inspired some of his friends to organize 'Wednesdays' there, when they meet and make music and take a collection for refreshments.

It is to one of these 'Wednesdays' that I have been invited today by Myaskovsky. Also present were Feinberg, Alexandrov, Shenshin,

Goedicke, Melkikh, Saradzhev, V. Belyaev and a few others. When I thoughtlessly said something censorious about Medtner somebody nudged me to shut up, because Goedicke is a friend of his and very sensitive to any criticism of him.

After tea and refreshments there was music: the Seventh Symphony of Myaskovsky played in the eight-hand transcription, which I was able to follow from the score. I liked this one much less than the Eighth. Then Myaskovsky asked me to listen patiently to a symphony by Shebalin which, he says, is a bit long but very interesting. Long, yes: the symphony lasted about forty-five minutes. Some parts were not without interest, but there was nothing out of the ordinary about the piece as a whole. When the composer came up to me I had no idea what to say. Knowing what to say about works when you get them played to you is surely quite an art in itself. I got out of it by asking about the state of the orchestral score and parts, in case I could generate some interest among conductors abroad. But the score wasn't finished and the parts not copied.

Tea and two symphonies took up quite a lot of time and we didn't get back home until 2 in the morning.

Thursday 3 March

At half-past 10 Protopopov came to collect Ptashka and took her to see St Basil's Cathedral. He is an expert on such things and was an interesting guide.

I went to the rehearsal of the Quintet for an evening of chamber music organized by Derzhanovsky at the Conservatoire. The players were trying their best. All were excellent musicians and the writing in the Quintet didn't worry them unduly, yet at this rehearsal it wasn't going very well. It attracted interest among the professors and some of them gathered round to listen.

Goldenweiser was sitting next to me with the score. He said nothing at all about the Quintet but asked me if there were any chance that we might, one of these days, get together for a game of chess. However I was preoccupied with other matters and as I didn't want to lose to him I put him off.

Brandukov also came. He is known for his uncompromising attitude to the Bolsheviks. 'So do you like our régime?' he began without preamble. I was only too glad when he left.

Recently five musicians were awarded the title of Honoured Artist; the list included Myaskovsky and Brandukov. But when the nominations went to the government for approval, four were accepted and Brandukov's rejected.

Igumnov buttonholed me and said he wouldn't be home at 2, the time I wanted to visit him, because of a meeting; so could I come at 4 instead? But at 4 I shall probably still be with Meyerhold, and tomorrow Igumnov himself will be busy all day. So my formal visit to the director was turning into a farce. As it turned out I never did get to see him. Meyerhold came at 3 p.m. to discuss *The Gambler*, the lithographed score of which has just arrived from the Leningrad Opera. I asked him to suggest alterations to improve the visual side of the libretto, but couldn't get anything constructive out of him. I also asked him about the end of the opera, where the love-making of Polina and Alexey seemed to me visually unpleasing. Meyerhold answered that of course it would be better to change it in some way, but he couldn't see how. It would be good to talk about it with Andrey Bely whom he will try to drag out of the Moscow suburbs (where he lives) for that purpose.

Before Meyerhold left I managed in an inconspicuous way to turn the conversation round to Shurik. Meyerhold was very sympathetic and exclaimed, 'Look, I have friends in the GPU. I will have a word with them if you give me all the details as to when and why he was sentenced.'

At this point we parted after arranging to have dinner soon. The keenness with which Meyerhold got down to business about Shurik contrasted very favourably with Tsukker's long face and negative attitude.

Ptashka wasn't home for Meyerhold's visit because she had to go to see Litvinov's wife. Litvinova was of English origin and was so delighted to find in Ptashka someone who not only speaks perfect English but who shares her Anglo-Saxon cultural upbringing that she made her promise to visit her. Litvinova herself isn't particularly interesting, but politeness from the highly-placed must be reciprocated, and today Ptashka set off to see her at the Sofiiskaya Embankment.

The Litvinovs live in a smart detached house which once belonged to the Kharitonenkos, who were rich merchants. If I am not mistaken this must be the same house in which I had lunch in May 1918, a few days before I left Russia. I was invited by Prince Gorchakov, who was related to Kharitonenko and used to live there. Ptashka found the house spacious and beautiful but so completely chaotic as to be unlivable-in. Ivy Valerovna gave us tea. Her children joined us; they looked rather grubby and were lacking in manners. Litvinova commented on their bad behaviour and said she wanted to have them educated in England. The amusing thing is that these fantasies coincided with the venomous diplomatic notes her husband was sending to England at this time.

In the evening we went to the Maly Theatre to see *Lyubov Yarovaya*, a play from the revolutionary period which is much talked about. ('Lyubov' is the first name and 'Yarovaya' the surname of the play's heroine.) The writing is very lively. It makes use of a good technical device: whenever the action is moving towards the tragic or pathetic (ruin, betrayal, violence etc.) the author interrupts it with some comic episode which instantly releases the tension and allows the action to proceed. Unfortunately the play turns into a political tract in the last act, and this spoils its general style. But perhaps the author was compelled to make this concession in order to get it staged. The heroine is a devoted revolutionary, but her appearance is distinctly off-putting. In this one can see the counter-revolutionary producers doing their best.

Friday 4 March

This morning the violinist Tsyganov came to rehearse the *Songs without Words* op.35 for the chamber concert. He plays well; I, on the other hand, have completely forgotten the piano part and keep making mistakes. Tsyganov is playing with me in one concert but in another with Medtner and has just arrived straight from seeing him. He laughs and tells me that when Medtner's wife learned he was on his way to rehearse with me she saw him to the door with a sour expression on her face.

Ptashka was with Tsukker at the Gostorg and chose an excellent blue fox fur. They promised to get some squirrel furs out of the cold store tomorrow. Squirrel used to be despised in Russia but now it is highly valued abroad and suddenly the Russians are trying to exploit the fashion and are pushing up the prices.

The Samoilenkos had made a point of asking us to find out what happened to their apartment and today we went to reconnoitre. It is of course colonized by lots of families, but the main rooms are still in the possession of their former servant. At first she didn't want to speak to us but eventually let us in; she was polite and showed us a number of photographs of Boris Nikolaevich. (He had asked us to bring some back if we could.) There was also an oil-painting in which he is depicted in full-dress guard's uniform with side-whiskers, but we could not take it for fear of problems with the customs.

We went to see Aunt Katya, taking her some fresh caviare as a Shrovetide present, while she treated us to *blini*. Then I went to see Kucheryavy while Ptashka, together with Katechka and Nadya, went to the Moscow Arts Theatre to see *Tsar Fyodor Ivanovich*. Kucheryavy lives in a rather run-down area not far from Tverskaya-Yamskaya Street in a new building mostly inhabited by workers. He has a small, tidy self-contained flat, something quite rare in Moscow now. Compared to the first letters he sent me when he returned to the USSR his mood is noticeably depressed. At that time he thought that everyone, whatever their sympathies, should return to the USSR with the aim of helping to rebuild the economy. Now he complains it is impossible to work: everyone and everything gets in the way, and the bureaucracy is unbelievable. Big projects exist only on paper. He should have stayed in America, but his wife dragged him back here only because she was nostalgic about Moscow; now she is dying to go back. Liza, whom I remember as a nine-year-old girl who used to attack me fiercely with her little fists, has grown into a fan of my music, and one of her friends is so crazy about my concerts that Liza begged me to give her an inscribed photograph. As we were leaving Kucheryavy lowered his voice and asked me if, when I go abroad, I could get in touch with the director of a large glue factory in Germany with whom he had earlier had some business connection, with a view to maintaining relations just in case he needs a contact abroad.

I walked home along Tverskaya Street buying warm *baranki*. Ptashka had enjoyed the play but was worried by the irresponsible behaviour of Katechka and Nadya, who would occasionally come out with this kind of comment in the theatre: 'Oh, how wonderful it was in those times!' (that is, of Tsar Fyodor Ivanovich) – 'Oh, I love the costumes!' – 'Yet another announcement about Red Army lotteries in the programme! I'm so fed up with it all!' Although Katya was only whispering, because she is deaf her whispering tends to be rather loud. Ptashka nudged her but she could not understand why.

Saturday 5 March

This morning I went to another Quintet rehearsal while Ptashka went to look at furs. I don't remember anything more about the first half of the day.

At 5 p.m. we dined with Meyerhold who lives on the Novinsky Boulevard in an old lop-sided house in a courtyard, quite cosy inside. Bely couldn't make it up from his suburb as he was very busy with his work and doesn't go anywhere these days. I hadn't placed much reliance on his advice about *The Gambler*, but I was sorry he wasn't there. It would have been good to meet him face to face and talk a bit. Meyerhold showed me a painting sent to him by Dmitriev, the artist who designed the sets for the *Three Oranges* in Leningrad. The style is somewhat fantastic, the subject roulette – clearly a hint that we should commission the sets for *The Gambler* from him. A gesture like this is hardly typical of a serious creative artist.

Me: 'I didn't like Dmitriev's sets for the *Oranges*.

Meyerhold: 'Neither did I. I don't understand what he's driving at.'

Me: 'But who would you like to do the sets?'

Meyerhold: 'It still has to be decided. In fact, when I staged *The Government Inspector* I managed without a set designer.'

Meyerhold's wife appeared; she was previously married to Esenin, whose two children now live in Meyerhold's house.

Our meal ended with some superb melon – very unusual in March in snow-covered Moscow. In the last act of *The Government Inspector* melon is served, and many members of the audience, their mouths watering, wonder whether it is real or just papier-mâché. Meyerhold explained that the melon was absolutely real and that he considered this kind of scenic-gustatory effect a rather good discovery. He buys the melons in the former Eliseev Stores, and when he bought the one we're eating today they asked if it should be added to the theatre's account!

Since the score of *The Gambler* was on the piano I played some excerpts to Meyerhold, mainly some of the Grandmother's music which I thought needed the fewest changes. It had been a long time since I saw the score and I played it not without pleasure.

After dinner Ptashka left for the Bolshoi to see Rimsky-Korsakov's *Snow Maiden*. She had been offered a seat in the Artistic Committee's box. She is studying the role of the Snow Maiden and couldn't miss an opportunity to see it on the Moscow stage. Meyerhold and I went to his theatre for *The Magnificent Cuckold*, a foreign play done in translation which Meyerhold wanted me to see because it was staged in a completely different way from *The Government Inspector*. While we were being driven there in a taxi his wife was saying how he loves travelling by sleeping car. Meyerhold admitted this, adding thoughtfully, 'Yes, I love it . . .'

So the Honorary Red Army Soldier has caught the bug of bourgeois tastes.

There was a lot of conventional 'theatre' (in the contemporary sense of the term) in *The Cuckold*: conventional constructivist sets and gymnastic movements which obviously fascinated Meyerhold, but once again slowed the play down terribly. This was a shame because the author of *The Cuckold*, having tied the plot up in knots rather neatly, couldn't resolve it with the same intensity so interest flags towards the end. During the intervals Meyerhold introduced me to the accordion players who were real virtuosos (they also play in his production of Ostrovsky's *Forest*). It was interesting to hear them because they have invented a lot of orchestral effects. When they asked me to suggest something of mine for them to play, I recommended Deshevov's Scherzo op.12. I think it could be great fun on accordions.

There is an attack on me in *The Life of Art*: why am I not showing my true face and speaking out openly about my real attitude to the Soviet régime? I assume the magazine didn't much want to publish this attack but couldn't refuse to. So it was published in between an article lauding me to the skies and one about Medtner which compared the two of us, coming down in my favour. I said to Meyerhold, 'I must answer this attack.'

Meyerhold made a face. 'It's not worth it. Maintain a dignified silence. I publish a small theatre magazine to join battle with those who attack me or like-minded artists. I will find a way to answer for you there.'

So I didn't answer the attack. Strangely, the *émigré* press, which didn't mention any of the laudatory articles printed about me in the USSR, reprinted only this piece. 'Look: Prokofiev goes back to Soviet Russia, and this is how they treat him.'

Sunday 6 March

This afternoon my chamber concert at the Association for Contemporary Music took place. I was pleased that it was in the Hall of Columns and not the Conservatoire. I was a bit late and didn't hear Feinberg and Shirinsky playing my Ballade. Next Tsyganov and I performed all five *Songs without Words*. Tsyganov played well (better than I did) but we got no more than a *succès d'estime*. Why was that? After the violin pieces came the Quintet, and here the Moscow musicians surpassed themselves, playing with unexpected brilliance and enthusiasm. The piece sounded excellent. Of course in time it will be played even better, but even so this performance is far superior to the one in Boston when Koussevitsky said to me, 'My dear, this thing doesn't "sound" at all.'

I was terribly pleased and enjoyed the performance; somehow or other a piece I thought dead and buried has come to life again. It had considerable success with the audience – not, of course, anything like that of my popular works, but one could nevertheless sense them listening with interest and enjoyment. The musicians congratulate me and we shake hands. Myaskovsky is in a state of unusual enthusiasm: 'Absolutely incredible! Not a single bar for one's interest to flag in!'

There is an interval after the Quintet and the Green Room is full of people, among them Rabinovich and Dikij, who sound a bit hurt when they reproach me for the letter I wrote to Excousovich praising the Leningrad production of the *Oranges*. Excousovich immediately published this letter in the papers, and Rabinovich and Dikij thought that it could be a trump card for the Mariinsky Theatre in their campaign to take *their* production abroad instead of the one being prepared in

Moscow. I tried to reassure them as far as I could. Meyerhold appeared and I introduced him to Nadya so they could talk about Shurik.

The second half begins with the Fifth Sonata, the first time I have played it decently in Moscow, but the response is lukewarm – this piece is not for the wider public. Then come pieces from op. 12 and the *Suggestion diabolique*. Knowing that this is my final performance the audience gives me an enormous ovation, as if saying goodbye. The afternoon concert ends quite early because in the evening we are off to the Ukraine. We have to hurry as there is still a lot to do.

We go to Derzhanovsky's for dinner, where the main topic of conversation is the Quintet which is praised to the skies by Myaskovsky. Then a short visit to Aunt Katya and back home to pack.

When we had left Aunt Katya's and were hailing a taxi, Mekler jumped out of nowhere and greeted us. One might be forgiven for thinking he had been spying on us. He was in a state of great perturbation over my concerts, so if I have offended him this season I must definitely do something with him in the autumn. Since we were in a rush I invited him to get into the car. On the way he talked of his plans for future concerts, proposing 1,000 roubles in the provinces and more for the ones in the capital. His proposal came to something like twenty concerts for a fee of 20,000 roubles. Later, when we had got out of the taxi and were going upstairs, he thrust a wad of notes into my hands: 'Here are a thousand roubles and tomorrow I'll bring another four thousand.'

These 5,000 roubles were supposed to be an advance for the autumn concerts. Altogether this came to a lot: for all it seemed to mean to Mekler, money could be growing on trees. And his manner was flippant, almost as if nothing need be taken too seriously. However, I didn't want to start thinking about next season or make any future commitments to Russia, where everything is so complicated and unstable. I gave Mekler back the wad of money and asked him to postpone all discussion until I returned from the Ukraine.

While we are packing we are disturbed by Razumovsky, with whom I have an involved discussion about copyright, and also by Tseitlin and Tsukker. Tsukker, in his self-awarded role of mentor, gives me to understand how advantageous it would be for me to move back permanently to the USSR if only to be able to work quietly, which he thinks is quite possible here. This man definitely annoys me.

We loaded everything into the car and set off for the Kursk railway station, which I have known well since childhood when we used to go from Moscow to Sontsovka. But there isn't much time: we quickly buy a few eatables in the buffet and go to our sleeper. The compartment is large but the carriage is old and squeaky. The train is far from smart. Ours is the only first-class carriage; all the others are third-class, and no restaurant car. At 11 p.m. the train starts moving and we begin our journey to the Ukraine for six concerts: two in Kharkov, two in Kiev and two in Odessa.

Monday 7 March

We spend the whole day travelling to Kharkov. I have known this line since childhood, and have many memories connected with the stations we pass by. We drink coffee in Kursk and buy a piece of fleshy goose. Sontsovo flashes past while I stand at the window (we do not stop). And then comes Belgorod, where we get out to stretch our legs. One can smell the south and the spring in the air, but the wind is cold. How many times did we pass through Belgorod and eat *shchi*, for which this station was famous!

We arrive at Kharkov at 5.30 p.m. On the platform we are met by Tutelman, Vorobyov and Dzbanovsky. Vorobyov is the member of the Ukrainian government who sent telegrams to the Persimfans threatening to proscribe my concerts if I performed for anyone other than the Ukrainian State Theatre. At that time Tseitlin and I, most indignant, were quite ready to take up this challenge and fight. But now, when I'm actually in Kharkov with a contract from the Ukrainian State Theatre, Vorobyov meets me at the station and turns out to be a very nice, modest man. We were driven in a rather nice open car all the way across town to the Red Hotel, which in Ukrainian is 'Chervonny'. Kharkov itself ('Kharkiv' in Ukrainian) is vast, dirty and ugly. Near the centre are buildings in the German style which aren't bad; it looks as if the Germans made a significant contribution to the architecture of Kharkov.

According to my contract the hotel is paid for by the State Theatre, but the room we have been given leaves much to be desired. It consists, in fact, of two enormous rooms with a bathroom. The bath has only hot water, so when you fill it you have to wait half an hour for it to cool down. The telephone has only an outside line, so to call room service I have to look the hotel number up in the directory and dial it through the local exchange. The piano hadn't been installed and I was taken to the hotel manager's room to practise a bit.

Then it was time for the concert. The theatre was full, the piano quite good. I played the Third and Second Sonatas, the *Visions fugitives*, some smaller pieces and the Toccata. Enormous success, cheers and encores . . .

In the interval Steiman appeared. He has become fat and seems unhappy with his lot. While he certainly hasn't fulfilled Tcherepnin's brilliant predictions he's nevertheless chief conductor of the Ukrainian Opera. After Steiman, Lapitsky. His manners are a bit rough but he's an interesting man. At one time he did a lot to enliven the theatrical side of operatic staging, something I'm very interested in.

After the concert Vera Reberg came up to me (I had received a letter from her earlier). Despite her bad health as a child she looked quite well. After promising to meet her tomorrow we went straight home as I was tired after a day and a half on the train. In fact I have been constantly tired since my arrival in the USSR.

When we returned to the hotel we wanted to have baths, but found that the enamel on the bath had broken off in places, which gave it a somewhat leprous appearance. We tried to get hold of one of the hotel staff but this wasn't so easy because some kind of elections were being held and everyone was voting. Finally we were told that the bath was pockmarked, not because it was dirty, but because it was clean: it is washed out with acid after each visitor, and this eats away the enamel. We decide to postpone the pleasures of bathing until we get to Kiev.

Tuesday 8 March

This was meant to be a free day for me to rest. Nothing of the kind: people kept coming in all the time. The most interesting was Lapitsky, who arrived with the score of the *Oranges* which he knew quite well because of the projected production in Kharkov. I had to play the opera to him and explain how this bit or that had been staged in other productions. He got carried away and said I was the only opera composer of any stature and that he would love us to work together on something entirely new. I agreed straight away without offering a firm commitment; but it did occur to me that Lapitsky, who really loves the stage, might well come up with an interesting subject and do something original with it. He hasn't too much taste but that doesn't make him less talented.

In the afternoon I went for a walk and happened to see some of my works in the window of a shop called 'Proletarian'. It wasn't the proper edition but a pirate one printed in the Ukraine, so I couldn't resist going in and asking for an explanation. After telling them who I was and what they had in their window, I asked why they were selling it.

'We are supplied by the Kiev musical organization,' was the manager's response.

'But this organization is reprinting my compositions illegally, and your shop is selling stolen goods!'

The manager looked round the shop and said, lowering his voice, 'Not so loud, please. That sort of remark could made a bad impression on our customers.'

'It's a pity that your activities are the sort one can speak of only in whispers.'

Our conversation didn't get us anywhere since it wasn't the shop's fault but the publisher's. But the manager reluctantly agreed to ask Moscow to supply him with the original edition, even though - as he pointed out - Moscow would deliver it much more slowly than Kiev.

In the evening Ptashka and I went round to the Rebergs', making our way there through the empty snow-covered streets. On the way we remembered that there were many *besprizorniye* (homeless children) in the south. They run around in large gangs; one of them jumps under your feet to knock you down while the others steal your bags and purses, often using knives or infecting you with syphilitic bites. Fortunately the streets were quiet.

Vera Reberg has followed her father into the medical profession. Her mother, Maria Iosifovna, lives with her. In old age she has become extraordinarily nice and gentle: she recalled with great animation the years of Sontsovka and Golitsinovka. Nina is married with two children and lives just a few hours from Kharkov, but Vera wasn't keen to talk about her; something is clearly wrong between them. Zina died a few years ago (she always had a weak heart). We spent a pleasant evening, and both mother and daughter were clearly moved by our visit.

Wednesday 9 March

I continued my discussions with Lapitsky and finished playing him the *Oranges*.

Rosenstein collected us to take us to the Conservatoire. I have known him for a long time, a cellist and a former student of the Petersburg Conservatoire, one of the first to perform my Ballade when we played it together at a concert as students. Now he is director of the Kharkov Conservatoire, and yesterday he burst in and begged me in the name of our old friendship (which never existed) to play for his students. I never refuse to play for students and in fact I enjoy it. So today I performed gavottes, tales, marches, in fact all kinds of this, that and the other for these nice lively young people. There was a deafening noise after I finished. One student made a speech in Ukrainian. I could hear over and over again the word '*pershy*', which means 'first'.

After the concert, the weather being sunny, we walked back to the hotel with Rosenstein and a few other professors. Some of the girl students were following us, occasionally running ahead. At first I didn't pay any attention, then it seemed amusing and later a bit trying, but finally, right in front of the hotel, they gathered in a group, pushing one another ('Well, go on!') and eventually came forward: each presented me with a little bunch of those white spring flowers they sell on street corners. It was a very nice gesture.

This evening I gave my second recital. I began with the Fifth and Fourth Sonatas, which was a mistake since nobody understands the Fifth and the Fourth is too slow to stimulate enthusiasm. Ought I to drop these? I don't have anything else ready to go in their place. When I mentioned the problem to Tutelman in Moscow he replied, 'Never mind, they'll do. Just play the Fourth and Fifth Sonatas in your second concert, so it doesn't affect the ticket sales. In any case you're leaving town afterwards.'

However, the Gavottes, some fragments from the *Oranges* and the

Suggestion diabolique got the audience going and generated the usual wild excitement. Afterwards the organizers wanted to arrange a supper for me, but I begged to be excused.

The painter Khvostov showed me his costume designs for the Kharkov production of the *Oranges* – a blend of the modern and the fantastic. It's hard to judge but I'm not very thrilled so far.

Thursday 10 March

The Leontovich Quartet visited me this morning to play some compositions by contemporary Ukrainian composers.

When I asked who Leontovich was it turned out he was the pride of the Ukraine, a composer who had died during the Revolution, apparently shot by the Bolsheviks. Now a quartet has been founded bearing his name. They played me works by Lyatoshinsky, Lisovsky, Novosatsky and Kozitsky, all of which could have been written fifty years ago and would then have sounded quite pleasant; now they all sounded provincial and rather pointless.

This afternoon I went to see Turkeltaub, the representative of the Ukrainian Society of Authors (called in fact by the pleasant acronym 'Utodik', which stands for the Ukrainian Association of Playwrights and Composers). Since this society works in tandem with the one in Moscow, I told Turkeltaub about the Kiev reprints and also enquired what fee the Kharkov State Opera would pay me if the *Oranges* is staged here. It turned out that when discussing this with Weber the State Opera proposed so little that even if the figure was doubled it was still only half what they were able to pay. Admittedly the current discussions came to nothing, but it's just as well to know this for the future.

This evening we left for Kiev, Tutelman travelling with us and Vorobyov, the important communist, seeing us off. Although we were packed and ready in time, Tutelman saw no reason to hurry and insisted on waiting for the car which was supposed to be taking us to the station. At the last moment it turned out that the car wasn't coming so we had to rush. Two smart cab drivers were found, one for Ptashka, myself and the luggage, the other for Tutelman and Vorobyov. A terrific race across town ensued. The mud was appalling, what with snow, puddles and the road full of holes. We got splashed from head to foot; even back in Paris I still found traces of Kharkov mud on my suitcase.

We made it to the station in time but then discovered that for all Vorobyov's influence a separate compartment for Ptashka and myself could not be procured. This was very disappointing because the next day I was due to arrive in Kiev immediately before my concert and I wanted a good night's sleep. Tutelman was very concerned. He ran round the station, summoned the station master, and finally we got pushed into the corridor of a carriage. It looked as if we were going to have to sleep in the corridor, but eventually everything turned out more or less all right. We didn't, in fact, have our own compartment, or sheets and pillows, but Ptashka was put in with a woman (a delegate) in one small compartment, while Tutelman and I were in a large one for four passengers. Tutelman was as solicitous as could be, letting me have the bottom couchette and offering me an inflatable cushion that he had in his suitcase. Later he entertained me with stories: about the violinist Kubelik's heavy drinking habits and how he arrived in Kharkov with a black servant. In America he probably wouldn't be allowed in any respectable hotel with a black servant, but in Kharkov it made a strong impression.

Ptashka's 'room-mate' turned out to be a very important delegate from the Ukraine connected with the Ukrainian government. She was an ordinary woman who enjoyed talking about her village and her five children.

Friday 11 March

Because there was no restaurant car in the train the first thing I did after waking up was to get out at a main station to try to find some coffee. Despite a crowd by the counter, I managed not only to drink some myself but also to take some back to Ptashka. I had to pay for the glass and the spoon. Ptashka presented them to her 'government companion' who accepted with pleasure. Not until 1 p.m. did we get to Kiev – the slow speed at which trains travel on this line has to be experienced to be believed. Outside Kiev the train slowly crossed the Dniepr which was still partly covered with ice. At this very time the ice was being blown up with dynamite in order to prevent a flood and was a very beautiful sight.

We were met at the Kiev railway station and driven in a pretty wretched car to the Continental Hotel. Unlike Kharkov which is ugly, Kiev is very beautiful. I somehow did not appreciate it in 1916 when I was last here with Glière giving concerts. The streets have lots of trees and fine buildings, but how much has been destroyed! You can certainly see the results of the city's having changed hands so many times, from the Whites to the Reds and back again. Many abandoned houses still have gaping windows with their frames knocked out.

In the afternoon I gave an interview and afterwards had a quiet respite to get ready for the evening.

The concert takes place in the Opera House. Behind the scenes are two or three dozen idle people but no manager. The hall is an elegant one and is sold out. I am playing the same programme as the first concert in Kharkov.

While I was playing, suddenly, in the prompt-box which was right beside my feet, a light came on. Then it went off, but a face appeared, listening to me intently. Then the face disappeared, but the light came on again. It irritated me terribly, so much so that I had to combat the temptation to give this importunate face a hefty kick. In the interval I ran around trying to find a manager, but nobody knew who was in charge, despite all the crowds milling about (probably theatre people), chatting, staring at me or simply paying court to each other and having a good time.

As in Kharkov this concert went down extremely well with the public. A certain Mrs Goldenberg, a teacher from the local Conservatoire, appeared in the Green Room and with uncommon persistence begged me to come tomorrow to listen to her pupils, who as it happened would also be playing some of my compositions. But tomorrow I wanted a rest from music and simply did not know how to get rid of her without appearing rude.

When we returned to the hotel Ptashka reproached me and said I *was* rude. But how else, after all, could I counter such persistence?

Saturday 12 March

Snowflakes outside the window, and we spend the whole day at home. The Malkos lunched with us. He has come here to conduct a concert whose programme includes my 'Classical' Symphony; but his concert and my recital are at the same time. How clever! At lunch he talked non-stop as usual, passing from one piece of trivia to another so skilfully that later on it's hard to remember anything very much of what he said. And yet his stories about Esenin and Isadora Duncan, whom he met in Russia many times, were very colourful. Malko described Isadora as quite an interesting woman. He quoted one of her sayings: 'Liszt reached all his life for the sky, but for Schubert the sky reached down to him' – which puts it quite brilliantly.

After the Malkos left the young composer Shipovich was brought to see me. He is twenty years old, Jewish, simple, mild and modest in manner. However his Papa was the reverse of modest, in fact he was extraordinarily pushy. Shipovich played several of his compositions which drove me insane with their two-bar phrases and crude melodic constructions; but in the march from his ballet *The Hunchbacked Horse* I thought there were some quite good moments.

Since yesterday Mrs Goldenberg again telephoned and even sent somebody to collect me. I finally decided to get dressed and go to her examination. But there was a surprise in store for me at the Conservatoire: the examination turned out to be really interesting. A very young group was performing, aged between ten and fifteen, including little fellows playing piano-duet excerpts from the score of *Chout*. Three girls delivered a lecture on the form of my Gavotte, illustrated with colour diagrams (Yavorsky's theories), but it seemed too complicated for the girls' intellects, or perhaps the author's presence intimidated them. Eventually one of the girls addressed a speech of welcome to me and I had, after all, to play three pieces myself. But it was actually a pleasure. Children surrounded the piano and screamed with excitement.

It is very good that there are establishments where young people can be trained like this. If after the Revolution, when part of the intelligentsia perished, concert audiences got depleted, such ways of educating younger people will quickly help to restore them to strength.

We parted on the friendliest terms from Mrs Goldenberg, and her examination stands out as one of the happiest memories of my Soviet trip.

Sunday 13 March

Several supplicants in the morning. Here in the south they come to the doors of newly arrived celebrities more frequently than in Moscow and Leningrad. I always felt sorry for them, and might give them 5 or 10 roubles; some would be extremely grateful, others would go away disappointed. But Ptashka was indignant, saying that an honest man wouldn't come to ask for charity at the door and only arrogant people or professional 'beggars' do it. I asked one of them to show me some identification. He readily produced a paper certifying that two years ago he had genuinely served in the GPU. I said, 'Well then, you should ask them for help. *I* help only comrades in the arts.'

Others would probably be quite easily intimidated by such unwanted soliciting (especially by the much feared and disliked class of NEP men) and would pay up promptly just to get rid of them.

In the afternoon I give my second recital in Kiev, not in the Opera this time, but in a smaller hall. At the same time the symphonic concert conducted by Malko, in which my 'Classical' Symphony is included, takes place. So stupid: either nothing, or suddenly concerts in two halls. As a result my recital is delayed by no less than an hour and a quarter. They say Malko had attracted such a small audience that his concert might have to be cancelled; therefore they hold up the beginning of mine so that the people coming to mine will have the chance to go to his too. Meanwhile: the tragedy of yesterday's pupils. I gave them cards with a request to the effect that they should be let into my concert, but they were not. One of them forced his way through and told me. I appealed to one of the managers, insisting that they should be let in. I was promised they would be, but later somebody else came and told me that they were still outside. Eventually they got in and the concert started.

Apart from the Fifth Sonata everything went down phenomenally well. The students were particularly enthusiastic: they threw themselves on to the stage (it wasn't very high) so that I had trouble elbowing my way through when I wanted to get off. One way and another the din was quite something. But after the concert we had to hurry home to pack for Odessa.

Just as we were leaving the hotel some of Mrs Goldenberg's girl

143

pupils brought me an illustrated analysis of my march from the *Oranges*, done according to Yavorsky's system of harmonic breakdown. By and large I could make neither head nor tail of it.

In the train a compartment was reserved for us in an International Society carriage, where there was hardly anybody except us.

Monday 14 March

In the morning – Odessa. We are met on the platform by a dozen people unknown to me, all representatives of the Philharmonia and the Academy Opera. It wasn't quite clear to me which of these two I was performing for, and only later did I find out that since I was invited by Tutelman that meant Acopera. But because the Philharmonia so desperately wanted to have me, Acopera resold me to it (as one of the Philharmonia's directors claimed) for double the fee I was actually paid. However the Ukrainian Acopera was paid in dollars and bought me in roubles.

Our rooms were in the Hotel Bristol, renamed the Red Hotel, but usually called by the old name. What a pity we are not on the sea-front! We have two gigantic rooms separated from the corridor only by thin doors so we can hear noise from everywhere in the hotel. What's more the telephone is opposite our door so we don't get a moment's peace.

We go for a walk in the town. Odessa means more to Ptashka than to me: this is my first visit, but she lived here in early childhood, with her grandfather, who was a Councillor of State and a President of Court. She immediately recognized the Opera building.

We made our way to the sea. The port was absolutely empty and the sea itself grey: no sign yet of spring.

In the evening, my recital in the Opera House. The hall is full and there are also about fifteen rows of seats on the stage, which always adds something rather splendid. I examine the theatre with interest: the Odessans are very proud of it. At first the public receive my programme with some reserve, but gradually warm up, although not as much as yesterday in Kiev. After the concert Pavlusha Seryakov appears in the Green Room and after the concert accompanies us back to the hotel.

Tuesday 15 March

Nothing special about today. In the evening I gave my second recital in the same hall, in the same circumstances, and got more or less the same reception.

A supper followed the recital, after which the local tenor sang the *Ugly Duckling* splendidly; only the lady accompanist spoiled it. But his performance was so good and so freely conceived that I wanted to accompany him myself, and we performed several of my songs.

Wednesday 16 March

In the morning Gorchakov's sister came to see us. Revolution and the spread of Bolshevik activity to the south have separated her from the rest of her family. Later she tried to swim across the river to Romania, but unsuccessfully. She is studying now in a medical school. She leads a half-starved existence and gave the general impression of being an unsociable and mistrustful person who needed to be spoken to very kindly indeed before she would respond in a normal human way. It became clear that what she feared most of all was being sent somewhere in the provinces after graduating. I promised to put in a word for her with the doctors who are on the Philharmonia's board of directors.

One of them, as it happened, came to visit me soon after, a Dr Goldman who wanted to take us in a car to Arcadia, a small place a few kilometres from Odessa.

Up to now we have seen very few ruined buildings in Odessa. Compared with Kiev only trees planted in the streets have suffered, most of them having been cut down for firewood. But now, on the way to Arcadia, we had to go through a street (the French Boulevard, I think), which had been the scene of a Bolshevik attack and on which both sides had engaged in heavy artillery combat. Here a great number of houses and villas, formerly quite ostentatious, had been reduced to rubble. Dr Goldman pointed out that some of the country houses had been turned into holiday homes for the workers; but compared with the general destruction it was a drop in the ocean.

There is a very pleasant beach in Arcadia protected from the winds by hills and warmed by the sun from the south. It was as if the climate had changed completely. Meanwhile Dr Goldman was telling us some fascinating stories about how he travelled last year to Transcaucasia and further to the east, beyond the Caspian Sea, to Bukhara and Khiva, where you have to go by aeroplane. This was particularly interesting in as much as living in Paris we know nothing whatsoever about these half-wild outskirts of Russia. And here you discover that Soviet citizens go there for holidays and entertainment!

After returning to Odessa and saying goodbye to Goldman we went to have lunch at the London Hotel, which has windows overlooking the sea. The former professor of eurythmics at the St Petersburg Conservatoire, Presnyakov, sat next to us. At the time we did not take to him very much but were interested in his class, since the prettiest of girls aspired to join it. When we met him he was clearly anxious to enlist advice and help, mainly on the subject of getting abroad, since he was fed up with his life in Russia.

After lunch we returned home and then Stoliarov, the present director of the Conservatoire, came for us.

I had promised to play today for the students, who gathered there in enormous numbers; they seemed particularly enormous because the Conservatoire itself is not large.

I remember Stoliarov in the violin class of the St Petersburg Conservatoire. Later he began to conduct and now he has got this directorship, but his looks are not impressive and there is nothing of the director about him – something I tried to point out in jest: 'How on earth do they ever do what you tell them? You should at least grow a beard!'

I did not play many pieces, but the response was stupendous: they shouted the place down. This of course is the southern temperament of the Odessans. When we came out into the street and took our seats in an open car to go to the hotel, the entire Conservatoire, several hundreds of people, poured out with us and shouted us along fortissimo; as the car started to move I bowed to them. In short it was a riot, but a very nice one.

Back home we packed and set off for the railway station. An amusing incident occurred just before our train left. It seemed that some strange character was already into his second day eating, drinking and ordering expensive dishes in the restaurant, saying he had come with Prokofiev and was his secretary. At the same time he was telling stories about life abroad and also about Prokofiev, while the manager and waiters were charging everything he ate and drank to my bill. When I was about to leave and it became clear that this fellow had nothing to do with me, an alarm was raised in the hotel. The maître d'hôtel was shouting, 'Just wait! I'll find him! He won't get away!'

However they put no obstacles in *our* way and we were seen off with much cordiality. At the station we found more or less the same crowd who met us, mainly doctors, because for some reason the Odessa Philharmonic Society is basically a confederation of doctors. There was also Gorchakov's sister, whom I commended to the attention of Dr Sigal, one of the influential members of the medical organizations. He of course was ready to do everything for *me* but, as I learned afterwards, did absolutely nothing for *her*. Our carriage went direct to Moscow but wasn't an International Society sleeper. However, we had a comfortable semi-compartment.

Thursday 17 March

At 11 a.m. we got to Kiev, where our carriage had to be attached to the Moscow train. This gave us an hour and three-quarters of free time, which we used to go sightseeing. We hired an *izvozchik* and went to the Vladimir Monument. Vladimir stands on his hill with a cross in his hands – revolutions and civil strife have not dared touch him. It was a warm sunny day, the snow was melting and little rivulets ran murmuring down the slope of the hill. Far away we could see a winding Dniepr, but it looked wintery and unwelcoming.

After quite a bad lunch at the railway station we returned to our carriage and discovered that our neighbour was Segovia, who had been giving recitals in Kiev and was also returning to Moscow. Segovia is a very nice Spaniard with horn-rimmed spectacles and is said to be a remarkable guitarist, but I have never heard him play. He was accompanied by a representative of the Rosphil called Kulisher, a gloomy-looking Jew. Segovia was extremely happy to meet us and chatted constantly with Ptashka in Spanish, complaining that it was impossible to get a single word out of Kulisher: he just sat there and smoked non-stop, poisoning the whole compartment with his fumes. At a main station Segovia and I rushed out to the buffet to buy a chicken. Then, leaving him with Ptashka to continue talking, I went to bed with a headache.

Friday 18 March

We arrived in Moscow at 11.30 a.m. Tsukker met us and took us back to the Metropole where we were given the same room again. He then took us straight away for a look round the Kremlin. We passed through the Armoury Museum, where we joined a group of visitors with a guide. I pointed out to Ptashka the Crown of Monomakh with its beautiful embellishments. Later we had our own guide, a certain N.N. Pomerantsev, who was in charge of restoring the paintings in the Kremlin churches. He was a very fascinating man, fanatically devoted to his craft, cultured and refined, working for an insignificant salary in extremely difficult circumstances. He was telling us with much enthusiasm how Rublyov's paintings had now been cleansed of the many layers of paint daubed over them when the churches were being restored 'in the period of uncultured Tsarism'.

I was embarrassed at entering a church in a hat and decided to take mine off. Observing this Pomerantsev said, 'We think of these churches as museums. No services take place here. And it's impossible to work here without a hat: look how cold it is.'

Indeed there was at least 15 degrees of frost. And because this was no 'church' but a 'museum' Ptashka could be led up to the altar and shown some of Rublyov's icons.

The tour was very interesting but endless. I wanted to eat, it was cold and my feet had turned into boot-trees with unbendable toes. Finally I protested and at 4 o'clock, dying from hunger, Tsukker, Ptashka and I got into the Bolshaya Moskovskaya Hotel, where we were served in a private room.

In the evening we were in the Meyerhold theatre to see *The Forest* by Ostrovsky, a very interesting and painstakingly elaborate production as is usual with Meyerhold. Shortcomings: slowness. And this slowness springs from a desire to saturate the production with detail. And Meyerhold's inventiveness may be rich but it is not unlimited, because some comes from his other productions.

Saturday 19 March

A rehearsal this morning with the Persimfans for my last concert, although there's nothing new in the programme. I lunched without Ptashka and afterwards went to see Aunt Katya.

In the evening we were at the opera workshop of the Artistic Theatre to see Tchaikovsky's *Eugene Onegin* which gave me enormous pleasure. The peasant scene in the first act was omitted: it is alleged to be insulting to the Workers' and Peasants' Government. The ball at the Larins was staged particularly well, due in part to the modest size of this theatre's stage – not a splendid ball in an enormous hall as in big theatres (with the result that you cannot find either Lensky or Onegin in the crowd), but instead a ball in an ordinary land-owner's house with a dining-room, and tea being served on a large dining-table in the foreground. The dancing was in the hall at the back of the stage, but the quarrel between Lensky and Onegin took place by the tea-table, and this focused attention on it very sharply. The small size of the stage also affected the duel scene: Lensky was left on his own while Onegin was in the wings. In this way the entire duel was shown as if from Lensky's point of view. The ball in the last act was entirely staged in a grand style so as to emphasize the stiffness of court etiquette. It was very curious to see Soviet performers in this theatre, most of them very young and completely ignorant of pre-revolutionary Russia, representing the glamorous court life of the time of Nicholas I. Some of the ladies-in-waiting were unmistakably Jewish in profile.

Lunacharsky's brother was unmistakably Jewish also. We were introduced to him in a reception room behind the stage where we had been invited in the interval for a cup of tea.

Sunday 20 March

In the morning we had a visit from Shura Sershinskaya, my niece three times removed, whom Ptashka disliked when she saw her before. But today she appeared in a much better light. Her son is a member of the Komsomol. As if in response to our surprised reaction she said, 'Well, so what? When in the past, in the grammar schools, everybody got the catechism rammed down their throats it didn't necessarily mean the children would all become religious. It's the same now: just because they get stuffed full of atheism it doesn't mean they become *anti*-religious. Political education in school now is exactly the same boring ramming and cramming of dogma it was in tsarist grammar school. At least as a member of the Komsomol my son has a better start in life.'

In the afternoon I give my last concert in Moscow – with the Persimfans in the Hall of Columns. The hall is full and the mood is that of a gala concert. In the programme is the 'Classical' Symphony which the Persimfans plays with more sparkle than Saradzhev, but in some places they are rhythmically insecure. After that comes the Second Concerto, and the *Scythian Suite* to end with. The public, knowing it is my last concert, says its farewells roaring and bellowing in triumph.

Rykov, the Head of State, was there and heard half the programme. On his way out through the Green Room Tsukker introduced me to him. Rykov was a short man with the goatee beard intellectuals often have, and rotten teeth. He asked me, 'And how did you like it here?'

'My visit here has made one of the strongest impressions on me of my whole life.' In saying which I uttered not one single word in praise of Bolshevizia yet contrived to give the impression I was overwhelmed by it. Rykov smiled and went on his way looking pleased.

In the crowd you could easily make out the red fez of Meyerhold. 'You see,' he explained, 'when spring comes I get a bit nervous and cut my hair short. But since it is still rather cold I have to wear a fez.'

There is a crowd in the Green Room: Madame Litvinov with her children, Myaskovsky, Asafiev, Belyaev, Yavorsky, Protopopov (the latter presented flowers to Ptashka, but Yavorsky, not wanting him to pay too much court to the ladies, immediately spirited him off), Saradzhev, Oborin (who looks like Dukelsky), and others. Blumenfeld came. Fifteen years ago he was already supposed to be dying from paralysis. Now he limps, doesn't move his tongue around enough in his mouth during conversation, but is just as sharp as before and his eyes light up when I introduce him to Ptashka. I speak to Saradzhev laying great stress on the fact that the first Moscow performance of the 'Classical' Symphony was the one he gave, and present him with the tie I was wearing during the performance. I introduce Nadya Raevsky to Meyerhold, asking him to assume responsibility for getting Shurik out of jail.

After the concert we looked in at the hotel and went to Prechistenka with Tse-Tse to have lunch. It was cold and I was tired after the concert. There were several taxis in the square but nobody was willing to take us according to the tariff. Tsukker, a Member of the Communist Elite, got very agitated and angry and finally took one of the cars. When we arrived at the restaurant and I wanted to pay, he shouted, 'No, no, I am paying today! Go ahead, don't wait for me.'

Quite clearly, he had had to hire a non-tariff taxi and pay triple the price, but didn't want to admit it.

We had promised to go to the theatre in the evening to see *Turandot*, but I was weary of crowds and shows and after sending Ptashka off with Nadya I went to Myaskovsky's, where we were joined by Asafiev (he has come back to Moscow for a short time). It was so pleasant to spend a quiet evening in relaxed conversation with Myaskovsky. Incidentally I brought away from him two hefty packages containing old diaries, which I decided to take abroad. To Asafiev, at his request, I handed over a bulky bound copy-book full of piano pieces dating from my young years. Later all three of us set off by a quiet route to Derzhanovsky's, where every Sunday evening there is an 'at home'.

Among others we met the Austrian pianist Wührer who in a few days' time was to give several concerts in Moscow, including a whole series of contemporary Russian sonatas. On Derzhanovsky's pretty awful piano he gave quite a good account of Myaskovsky's Fourth Sonata which, however, he played from the music.

I managed to get home reasonably early after carrying my heavy packages through deserted and ice-covered streets; as bad luck would have it there wasn't an *izvozchik* in sight.

Ptashka came back having greatly enjoyed *Turandot*. Budyonny was in the audience and everybody kept looking round at him.

Monday 21 March

Once my concert-giving was at an end pre-departure preparations took over. Our foreign passports had been collected. They had been ready and waiting for some time already – not for nothing did I hand in my application almost the day after I arrived in the USSR. Today I received the German visa and went to the Polish Consulate to get a transit visa.

This was so far away – right on the other side of town – it was like going to the ends of the earth. Tsukker maintained that in no circumstances should I go through Poland since Poland is a hostile country. I should travel through Riga, and anyhow the Poles won't give me a visa. But going through Poland would knock one day off the journey and so I ignored his protests. In fact they were very helpful in the Polish Consulate, took both passports and told me I could collect them tomorrow.

Meanwhile Ptashka was with Tsukker in Gostorg where he, through 'special dispensation', promised to get (from the state refrigerators) good squirrel furs with a reduction of 10 per cent. The best furs are set aside for export abroad, the worst for selling at home; and so his 'dispensation' consisted merely in being allowed access to the export department.

Because the Chinese revolutionaries had taken Shanghai Tsukker was beside himself with joy and even shouted out loud about it in the streets, to the great embarrassment of Ptashka.

We lunched on our own, Ptashka and I, and afterwards went to Gostorg to buy the selected squirrel.

Asafiev came in the afternoon. He was in a bad mood: on the one hand they want to send him on a mission to Vienna, on the other they give him so little money to take with him he can barely make ends meet. At first he didn't want to go, changed his mind and even agreed to put some of his own money towards the cost; then it turned out there were passport complications. In other words the whole thing is a nonsensical muddle.

At half past 6 we were collected and taken to the Artistic Theatre where I had promised to play. I was invited yesterday and even asked how much I wanted to be paid; but I answered I considered it a pleasure to play for the Artistic Theatre and would charge no fee. We were most courteously received there by Stanislavsky, Knipper-Chekhova and Luzhsky. Stanislavsky was particularly nice. Having learned that Ptashka was a singer and was excited by his opera workshop he started issuing invitations: 'How marvellous, come to Moscow and join us.'

After the performance and applause I was presented with a magnificent bouquet of white lilacs. Gathering it up we went to Aunt Katya's where we left part of it, then to the Derzhanovskys' where Asafiev, Myaskovsky and Saradzhev were assembled.

When I was leaving the Derzhanovskys' I wanted to take at least some of my flowers, but Liolya exclaimed rather angrily, 'What a greedy person! He receives a thousand roubles a concert and can't even leave us his flowers!'

Tuesday 22 March

The pre-departure rush continues. Again I sped right across town to the Polish Consulate where the visas were issued without a hitch. On the way back we bought our tickets. As soon as I returned home Tsukker telephoned. I subjected him to quite a bit of heavy teasing on the subject of the fuss he had made about my Polish visa which, in the event, was issued so easily and politely. Tsukker, a touchy man, was offended. Too bad: this kind of revolutionary watchdog irritates me and, apart from that, he has been so cagey and unwilling to commit himself in the matter of helping Shurik he is definitely in my bad books.

In the afternoon we packed. Asafiev came to say goodbye and left for the Nikolaevsky railway station to go back to Leningrad. I managed to palm a coat off on him (I had two). Then Liolya came to help Ptashka sew squirrels together, so as to make something that would look like a cloak and not just pieces of fur. She stayed late, till 9 o'clock. We smoked a lot of Russian cigarettes which I rather fancied after the foreign ones, although Russian connoisseurs have no time at all for modern tobacco. I had in my pocket a note-book from the time of my trip to Italy in 1915 which I had found in the suitcase Myaskovsky gave me. I was very amused to read the passage about my confrontation with Diaghilev at the time he was commissioning *Chout*.

The telephone rang – the Comintern. In actual fact I could not make out *who* the call was from, but the person who phoned called himself by some lengthy title in which one of the words was 'Comintern'. And one has to be cautious if the Comintern is mentioned.

It was all about my taking part, tonight, in a concert organized to celebrate the take-over of Shanghai. I was most unwilling to play, but knew I had to refuse in an indirect way. So I immediately decided to counter-attack and answered, 'But, excuse me, I would like to know who is organizing this evening's concert. Do you really think you can invite an artist to perform just a few minutes before the start of a concert? What sort of an evening would that make? I most certainly can't just drop everything, rush round and play for such an important occasion unprepared and in a state of disarray. No, please let me off and tell your organizers that next time they should prepare for such events in a more professional manner; then I would be at your service.'

(No risk at all in saying that since tomorrow we are going to Paris.)

Shortly after, Ptashka and I went for supper to the Hotel Evropeis-kaya. In the past we had only breakfasted there, but in the evening it turned out that there were also performances (uninteresting ones) on an open stage, from which we seated ourselves at a safe distance. At the end of the meal Tseitlin came to settle our accounts for all my performances with the Persimfans – a bit of a disappointment, since there was much less money to be transferred abroad than I expected. But living expenses, hotels and travel – all consume large sums of money and it melts away without your realizing it.

Wednesday 23 March

This is the day we leave and also, by a coincidence, the day of Borovsky's arrival from abroad. He is beginning a tour and is staying in the same hotel as we are, even in the same corridor. When I visited him Tsukker was going through the programme of his first recital with him, which included some of my compositions. Tsukker was very cool to me because of yesterday. How stupid.

Borovsky looked completely bemused. Arriving in Russia made a strong impression upon him and he was probably worried, not knowing if he will have any success at all, or whether the Bolsheviks might for no reason suddenly arrest him. He has already succeeded in becoming a Latvian citizen.

Tseitlin collected me and we set off for the Central Customs Administration. The point is that it is not possible to take any manuscripts out of Russia without special permission. It is, in fact, a very good rule which protects libraries from being plundered. But I had with me my old diaries and the pile of letters I'd received during my stay in the USSR, also musical manuscripts, the score of the *Gambler* with a stamp 'Property of the Imperial Theatres', and so on. I have been raising this question with Tsukker and Tseitlin for a long time, but in good Russian style they have delayed addressing themselves to it till the very last minute.

We were received politely and sent to the railway station, where my manuscripts were to be sealed on the orders of the Central Administration. Tseitlin and I could hardly carry these very heavy packages. At the station, in the customs department, an official lady poked two fingers into the cases containing letters and then ordered everything to be sealed. It might not have been so painless had she started to read my diaries. I remembered just then that there are some expressions in them which could be considered counter-revolutionary.

When it was all over Tseitlin and I, loaded with sealed bags, went back. Tseitlin was giving me an animated account of the history of the Persimfans and how some communists told him that it was, in fact, the only genuinely communistic organization in the entire USSR. Tseitlin himself is not well, his wife is also unwell, there is a re-election pending and confusion on the board of the Persimfans – but his energy is still boundless. He suffers from curvature of the spine and the doctors put a plaster corset on him; but after walking about in it for two days he threw it away and continues his activities without it.

Apparently during my absence the mother of Koshetz had come crashing in and managed to persuade Ptashka to take out a bracelet and brooch for her. Ptashka told me nothing about it and was shivering with fright all the time till we had crossed the border.

We lunched with Borovsky in the restaurant on the Prechistenky Boulevard; the Russian dishes were greatly to his liking. After that we went to say goodbye to Aunt Katya and hurried home to finish packing. Ptashka even managed to find a moment to buy herself a brocaded dressing-gown and a brooch.

At home the usual frantic pre-departure chaos. Katya and Nadya arrived, but they were more of a hindrance than a help. Katya, for instance, was determined to pack the things we were leaving behind for her. On top of everything the removal men arrived without warning to take the piano away. Somehow or other we managed – just about – to

get away at last and, accompanied by Tseitlin, drove to the railway
station. Tsukker could not see it through to the end and was absent. I
gave Tseitlin all my remaining roubles asking him, if possible, to
transfer them abroad.

The train was due to leave at 5 p.m., within minutes, in fact. At the
station, apart from Katya and Nadya loaded with presents, were
Myaskovsky, three Derzhanovskys, Tseitlin and the singer Derzhinskaya. Unlike the train in which we arrived the one we were leaving in
looked quite smart. There were several International Society carriages,
a restaurant car – in fact everything that constitutes an 'international'
train. Those seeing us off looked at us not without envy because, of
course, they knew that in two or three days we would be in Paris.
Myaskovsky brought several boxes of sweets. That morning I had
presented him with various ties, shirts and all sorts of elegant things,
knowing his penchant for them.

The train moved off. It was a wonderful, clear March day and the
rays of the setting sun came slanting down.

Thursday 24 March

In the morning first the Russian, then the Polish border: nothing worth
reporting. After my sealed packages passed through the customs I could
unseal them and put their contents into the trunk. The customs official
knew who I was and, slapping the trunk, joked, 'What is in the trunk?
Oranges?'

Then he explained that he had gone on holiday to Leningrad and
wanted to go to *The Love for Three Oranges*, but for some reason could
not get in.

On the Polish border we changed on to a through train to Paris and
got a brand-new International carriage. You might almost have thought
that people abroad were showing off on purpose in front of the shabby-
looking Russian carriages.

In the evening we get to Warsaw where we stop for quite a long time,
long enough to have supper with Madame Grossman. Warsaw has
pulled itself together these last few years and from quite a provincial
town has changed into a European capital.

Friday 25 March

In the morning – Berlin, where we had to stop whether we wanted to or
not in order to get a Belgian transit visa (there is no Belgian consulate in
Russia). Again we saw Weber, Tanya Raevskaya and Sasha, who,
however, refrained from showing off this time.

In the Hotel Fürstenhof we bumped into Sasha Tcherepnin and his
wife. The appearance of this couple, a young boy and a rich old lady,
immediately made my blood boil. Sashenka Tcherepnin had been on a
concert tour in several towns, where he happened to have played my
Ballade for cello and piano, something he was quick to tell me about. I
said, 'Well, you probably played it just as badly as you did in Paris.'

Sashenka was struck dumb. Meanwhile I started to press Ptashka to
end her conversation with 'Louisita', saying that we were in a rush for
lunch and had no time to talk. So we quickly parted company although
Ptashka remonstrated with me indignantly about my behaviour. I
answered I simply could not bear to see those two together. We had
lunch with Tanya, Sasha and Weber in some big but, as it turned out,
rather dubious café, and in the evening we set off to Paris, having
practically bankrupted ourselves on account of the Nord-Express.

Two Postscripts

The following independent accounts of events described by Prokofiev in the *Soviet Diary* were first published in Russia in 1956 in *S.Prokofiev: Autobiography, Articles, Reminiscences*, ed. S. Schlifstein (the English edition, issued by the Foreign Languages House in Moscow, appeared around the same time but is undated: the translator was Rose Prokofieva – no relation to the composer). The reader is invited to compare these accounts with Prokofiev's own, to note how they agree and disagree, and to ponder on the fallibility of memory. Whose do we rely on? Kabalevsky and Oistrakh were both writing many years after the event(s) whereas Prokofiev is supposed to have been recording his recollections at the time. In the case of Oistrakh's reminiscences it is certainly extraordinary that Prokofiev should have recalled the banquet in his honour after his recital but not Oistrakh's 'misinterpretation' of the Scherzo from the First Violin Concerto. As Oistrakh himself goes on to point out, Prokofiev remembered every detail of the Odessa tour when they became known to each other in later years, so we must assume that for some reason he failed to judge the incident worthy of mention.

I by Dmitry Kabalevsky

. . . News of Prokofiev's return to Moscow from abroad spread rapidly throughout our musical world, arousing particular excitement among the youth.

It must be said that many of us, and especially those who had taken up music only in the 1920s, had the vaguest and most inaccurate ideas about Prokofiev, both the man and the composer. The tendency in some musical circles of the time to couple Prokofiev's name with that of Stravinsky was extremely misleading, for the paths of these two composers could hardly have been more different. Stravinsky had firmly entrenched himself in bourgeois-cosmopolite positions and publicly dissociated himself from his native land, whereas Prokofiev, on the contrary, had always been deeply conscious of his ties with his native culture and had yearned with all his being to return to the Soviet Union, both as an artist and a citizen. However we did not understand all this at the time; all we knew was that Prokofiev had left Russia, that he lived abroad as a Soviet citizen and that he was about to return.

At the end of January 1927 the Association for Contemporary Music announced that Prokofiev would give his first concert in Moscow in the hall of the Academy of Arts in Ostozhenka.

I had never seen Prokofiev before, I had not even seen any photographs of him and had even a rather hazy idea of his age. Judging by the vast amount of music he had written, and also by the fact that he and Myaskovsky had attended the St Petersburg Conservatoire at the same time, I concluded that he must be at least about fifty or so. Imagine my surprise when he turned out to be no more than thirty-six, and a very youthful-looking thirty-six at that.

Prokofiev arrived long before the concert began and walked about the foyer carrying on a lively conversation with his friends. He was gay and smiling and obviously greatly moved by the warm and friendly reception accorded him. We younger musicians, who were still Conservatoire students, stood a little apart gazing with awed curiosity at the composer whose music we admired so much. My memory still retains the image of that first, purely visual impression of Prokofiev. I was rather taken aback by his appearance. His trim dashing figure, his well-cut suit, the jolly, almost boyish expression on his face – all this belied the 'Scythianism', the 'untamed character', the 'barbarism of the iconoclast of music', in a word, all that we had been accustomed to associate with the name of Prokofiev. This man, one felt, might be the composer of the spicy scherzos, or the lyrical fairy-tales, but hardly the *Scythian Suite* and the Second Concerto.

When the time came for the concert to begin, Prokofiev, still smiling, made his way through the packed hall, climbed on to the platform and, when the long ovation had subsided, sat down at the piano and played the Third Sonata.

It is hard to describe the impression Prokofiev made on us that evening. I think I shall not be mistaken if I say that that first performance of his gave many of us an entirely new understanding of his music, very different from that gained from the performance of other musicians, who tended to emphasize the elemental quality of the music, the dynamic contrasts and the mechanical elements. The music sounded far richer, far more subtle when Prokofiev played it. Everything sounded full-blooded and healthy, both spiritually and physically, everything was colourful, dynamic but without the slightest exaggeration, the slightest crudity let alone coarseness. In short, nothing 'Scythian'. And what was most important, everything was illumined by the light of sincerity, poetry and human warmth. Moreover, the whole performance was distinguished by a quiet reserve, a total absence of any external pianistic effects, conveying an impression of great spiritual calm. With his extraordinary pianistic talents Prokofiev revealed that rich lyrical feeling in his music which we had failed to notice until then. This was a joyful and unexpected discovery for us.

This impression was still further enhanced some time later when Prokofiev played his Third Concerto. I have heard him play many times since then, but I don't think he ever played with such brilliance as on that evening. And again, as after the first concert in Ostozhenka, one was struck far more by the deep feeling with which he played the lyrical episodes than by the phenomenal precision of the technically complex passages, the rich timbre and the dynamic power of his touch. The subordinate theme of the first movement, the exquisite beauty of the theme of the variations in the middle part and the variation episode in the Finale – these are what I remember most vividly from that concert. How well I understand the meaning of what Prokofiev wrote many years later in his Autobiography: 'This line [lyricism: D.K.] was not noticed until much later. For a long time I was given no credit for any lyrical gift whatever, and for want of encouragement it developed slowly. But as time went on I gave more and more attention to it.'

. . . This concert, incidentally, was notable likewise for the fact that it was the last time Prokofiev ever played music other than his own (while abroad he had played music by other composers, mainly the classics, including in his recitals a suite of Schubert's waltzes and an arrangement of an organ prelude and fugue by Buxtehude). On this occasion the work was the fifth piece from Myaskovsky's *Whimsies* cycle. When he came to the last statement of the main theme, Prokofiev lost his bearings and went back to the beginning again, then jumped to the coda

1. Prokofiev aged ten, St Petersburg.

2. Prokofiev standing, with Glazunov seated left, St Petersburg, *c*. 1909.

3. Prokofiev, *c*. 1915–16.

4. Detail from a sketch of Prokofiev
by Larionov, *c*. 1920.

5. Prokofiev in the early 1920s.

6. Prokofiev in America, early
1920s.

7. Riga – Lina and Sergei Prokofiev outside the National Opera.

Сергей Сергеевич Прокофьев
Специальный снимок для „Кр. Панорамы"

8. Postcard: Prokofiev at the piano, Moscow, 1927.

9. Theatre Square (now Sverdlov Square), Moscow, 1922: painting by
P. Kalendo, showing Metropole Hotel on left.

10. Leningrad – the Marlinsky Theatre (1920s).

11. Prokofiev with Asafiev outside Asafiev's house.

12. Moscow, 19 January 1927: seated (left to right) Tseitlin, Prokofiev, Lina, Myaskovsky; standing: Tsukker, Asafiev, Derzhanovsky, Sarajev.

13. Lina and Sergei Prokofiev, Moscow, 1927.

14. Asafiev, Myaskovsky, Lina Prokofiev (photo almost certainly by Prokofiev).

15. Golovanov, Nezhdanova, Prokofiev.

16. One of the banquets given in Prokofiev's honour in Moscow. (A) Saradfev, (B) Tzeitlin, (C) Asafiev, (D) Prokofiev, (E) Myaskovsky, (F) Lina Prokofiev (Ptashka), (G) Mosolov, (H) Derzhanovsky, (I) Feinberg.

17. Dikij, Prokofiev, Golovanov, Rabinovich.

18. Samuel Feinberg.

19. Moscow, 1927: one of
Rabinovich's costume-designs for
The Love for Three Oranges.

20. Pencil sketch by G. Vereysky, autographed by Prokofiev: Piano Concerto No. 3, first theme of first movement.

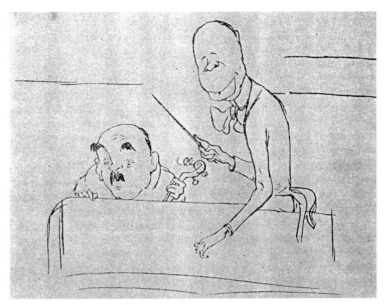

21. Tseitlin and Prokofiev, Moscow 1927, by the Kukriniksy caricaturists.

22. Page from Prokofiev's own vocal score of *The Love for Three Oranges* showing correction in his hand ('Posaune') at one bar before 15 (see p. ooo).

23. Draft of a letter written by Prokofiev (with Asafiev's help) to Excousovich.
See *Soviet Diary* for 11 February.

24. Lina and Svyatoslav, *c.* 1925.

25. Prokofiev *c*. 1936, with Svyatoslav, Oleg and Lina.

and finally wound up with some rather blurred chords. Such things never happened to him when he was playing his own music.

Many years later, walking with Prokofiev in the woods at Nikolina Gora, I reminded him of that incident. Laughing heartily as we often do when recalling some embarrassing incident long since passed, he said to me, 'You know how much I love and esteem Nikolai Yakovlevich. Frankly speaking I am even a little scared of him sometimes . . . That evening when I came to the end of the piece I suddenly remembered that he was there in the hall listening to me, and I felt so scared for some reason that the whole thing flew right out of my head. It is a good thing I managed to finish it off somehow . . .' Prokofiev played only his own compositions after that.

Prokofiev's concerts during his first visit to Moscow from abroad were a tremendous success and undoubtedly served to heighten public interest in his music . . .

I met Prokofiev during his first visit to Moscow at one of the musical evenings held regularly at the home of V. V. Derzhanovsky, one of the organizers and leaders of the Association for Contemporary Music. We younger Conservatoire composers were sometimes invited to these gatherings, at which the latest works by Soviet composers were usually performed. The most 'fashionable' composers in those years were A. Mosolov and L. Polovinkin. Their compositions were the chief attraction at these informal concerts and they themselves were treated somewhat like charming *enfants terribles*. Mossolov's *Newspaper Advertisements* set to music and Polovinkin's piano *Sensations* were considered most amusing (for one of these compositions, I remember, the lids of cigarette boxes had to be placed under the strings of the piano to obtain the desired effect).

Prokofiev arrived a little late and all the guests were already assembled. He was in his usual lively mood, very amiable and talkative. I had never met him socially before and for some reason I did not like him at all. I wanted him to be like Myaskovsky, who had taken over our composition class after the death of Katuar – serious, reserved, an extremely interesting conversationalist and a good listener. But Prokofiev was not like that at all: he told risqué anecdotes, flung his napkin playfully across the table and sedulously avoided any talk about music. What is more, he seemed to me to treat all the other composers with a certain condescension. Myaskovsky was not present on that particular evening; for him Prokofiev invariably showed the greatest respect. Prokofiev was invited to play and he declined. Whether he played later, I do not know, for feeling somehow hurt and disappointed I left the place early and went home. Many years later, when I knew Prokofiev well, I realized that I had been quite mistaken in my opinion of him at that time, that he was not a man one could judge by appearance. I saw that his simple, unaffected, almost child-like directness was indeed one of his finest qualities. I understood that a man who always worked at such high tension as he did simply had to relax occasionally. I discarded, too, my initial impression that he 'looked down' on other composers, although to tell the truth I never observed in Prokofiev that inexhaustible interest in other people's music which was so characteristic of Myaskovsky.

The association of these two distinguished composers is interesting in itself. As musicians they were totally unlike in character and disposition as well. They actually seemed to complement each other and perhaps that is the secret of their great lifelong friendship . . .

(from 'A Vivid Personality')

II by David Oistrakh

. . . Before long, in February or March 1927, the composer himself came to Odessa and gave two recitals of his works. This was a sensational event. The recitals were given in the Odessa Opera House, and the large hall was filled to overflowing long before the concert began. Practically every musician in town, all the veteran music-lovers and a host of young people came to hear the famous composer. The concert was a resounding success. For some reason I felt as excited as if I were the hero of the day. The impression made on me, not so much by the music, which by that time I had learned to understand and appreciate, as by the performance, was unlike anything I had ever experienced. What struck me about Prokofiev's playing was its remarkable simplicity. Not a single superfluous gesture, not a single exaggerated expression of emotion, no striving for effect. The composer seemed to be saying, 'I refuse to embellish my music in any way. Here it is. You may take it or leave it.' There was a sort of inner purity of purpose behind the whole performance that made an unforgettable impression.

I do not recall exactly what he played at those recitals, apart from the sonatas, the Second and Third, and, I believe, the Fifth. Of the smaller works I remember the famous Toccata, the *Grandmother's Tales*, a great many short pieces from his earlier works, and a few new things, like the Scherzo and the March from the *Three Oranges*. Coming after the dynamic Toccata, which he played with great inner force (while outwardly appearing perfectly calm and unmoved), the lyrical *Visions fugitives* made a deep impression. One of them, the piece in C major, with its beautiful lyrical episode in the middle, still rings in my ears. The tempestuous, defiant Prokofiev at such moments became as touching as a child. The fact that Prokofiev could be poetic and moving came as a surprise to many who, until they heard his music performed by himself, had refused to believe that it could have any emotional warmth.

In this connection I should like to touch briefly on some of the difficulties of Prokofiev's music, and specifically his violin music, from the standpoint of the performer. It is music in which nothing can be omitted, not a single turn of the melody, not a single modulation. It requires the strictest attention to every detail of expression, a fine, but not over-refined, execution of each individual intonation, as in the case of well-enunciated singing. The chief thing is not to permit oneself any artistic liberties. The best performance of Prokofiev's music, or of any other good music for that matter, is one in which the personality of the performer does not obtrude in any way. That is precisely what one could say of Prokofiev's playing.

After the recitals there was a banquet for Prokofiev at which local musicians gave renderings of his music. I was chosen to play the Scherzo from his Violin Concerto. I was naturally much thrilled at the prospect of meeting the great composer in person, and it was with mingled feelings of happiness and nervousness that I, then a lad of eighteen, awaited the day of the performance. At last it came. Little did I suspect how sadly it was to end for me.

The cream of Odessa public was assembled in the Scientists' Club where the banquet for Prokofiev was to be held. In the place of honour right in front of the platform sat the composer himself. As I played I observed his face grow darker and darker. When I had finished, the audience applauded, but not Prokofiev. Instead, he stepped on to the stage, paying no heed to the hubbub in the hall, sat down at the piano and, turning to me with the words: 'Young man, you don't play it right at all,' proceeded to show me how the piece ought to be played. My débâcle was complete.

Many years later when I knew Prokofiev quite well I reminded him of the incident and of his Odessa concert tour in general. To my surprise he remembered everything down to the smallest detail, including the programme and the number of encores, and Chishko, the Ukrainian composer and singer with whom he performed *The Ugly Duckling* at the banquet, and 'that unfortunate young man' whom he had given 'a fine drubbing', as he put it. His genuine embarrassment and distress when I told him that I was that young man showed me how warm and human he could be when he chose . . .

(from 'In Memoriam')

Notes

The abbreviation 'Prkfv' was devised by Prokofiev himself and frequently used by him; therefore we use it here.

3 Georgy Nikolaevich Gorchakov (born 1902), Prkfv's musical secretary, a Russian *émigré*, pianist and composer. During the Second World War went to live in Tunis. No relation so far as is known to the conductor, composer and arranger Sergey Petrovich Gorchakov who in 1954 made an alternative orchestral version of Musorgsky's *Pictures at an Exhibition*. He typed the text of the *Soviet Diary*.

3 The 'Publishing House' – in 1909 the conductor Sergey Koussevitsky (1874–1951), lifelong champion of Prkfv, founded his own publishing company, known outside Russia as the Editions Russes de Musique. He later acquired Gutheil and Belyaev (the Editions Russes was itself acquired by Boosey & Hawkes in 1947). His 'Publishing House' in Paris was at 22 rue d'Anjou. He gave the first performance of a number of Prkfv's works, among them the Second Symphony, dedicated to him, and the Fourth, commissioned by him. Ardent propagandist of Prkfv's music in both Europe and America, where he was conductor of the Boston Symphony Orchestra from 1924 to 1949.

3 Alexander Konstantinovich Borovsky (1889–1968). Russian pianist, studied together with Prkfv in Esipova's class (see note for p. 5). Performed Prkfv's music. Emigrated in 1920. He and his wife were family friends of the Prokofievs.

3 The Samoilenkos: also family friends of the Prokofievs.

3 Gavriil Grigorievich Païchadze (1879–1976), director of the Editions Russes de Musique in Paris.

3 Ptashka – an endearing name for Prkfv's wife Lina (1897–1989); in Russian it means something like 'little bird'.

3 Weber – Fyodor Vladimirovich Weber, Païchadze's opposite number in Berlin, where the Koussevitsky publishing house was known as the Russische Musikverlag. His name, like that of Païchadze, crops up frequently in Stravinsky's correspondence of the period.

3 Tanya and Sashka Raevsky – it is not known exactly who *these* Raevskys were, but see note for p. 24 on the family.

4 Kucheryavy – a Russian friend from the USA, who had recently gone back to Moscow.

4 Revel – after 1917 the Estonian capital was known as Tallin.

5 Pavlusha Shubert – unknown.

5 Anna Esipova (1851–1914), remembered more as teacher (at the St Petersburg Conservatoire) than as performer. Prkfv was one of her best-known students although he was too self-willed to derive much benefit from his lessons with her.

6 Ettal – a town in the Bavarian Alps where Prkfv lived in 1922–3 when working on his opera *The Fiery Angel*.

6 The composer Nikolay Yakovlevich Myaskovsky (1881–1950) was Prkfv's closest musical friend. They kept up a regular correspondence during Prkfv's time in the West.

6 Vladimir Vladimirovich Derzhanovsky (1881–1942), music critic, editor and long-time supporter of Prkfv.

8 Yosif Vitol [or Vitols or Wihtol or Wihtols] (1863–1948), Latvian composer. Pupil of Rimsky-Korsakov at the St Petersburg Conservatoire where he taught from 1886 to 1918. Myaskovsky and Dranishnikov (see notes for p. 6 and p. 68) were among his students, as well as Prkfv. After the Revolution he settled in Riga, where he founded the Latvian Conservatoire and developed a national school of composers.

8 Anna Grigorievna Zherebtsova-Andreeva (1868–1944), Russian singer and first performer of Prkfv's *Ugly Duckling* in Petrograd in 1915.

9 'minus 12 degrees Réaumur' – i.e. minus 15 Celsius.

9 Boris Vladimirovich Asafiev (pen-name as critic Boris Glebov) (1884–1948), eminent Russian musicologist and composer, close friend of Prkfv, class-mate at the Conservatoire. The 'Classical' Symphony was dedicated to him.

9 Svyatoslav – Prkfv's elder son, born 1924.

10 Alexandrovsky railway station – now Byelorussky railway station.

10 Lev Moiseevich Tseitlin (1881–1952), violinist, leader and organizer of the Persimfans (First Symphonic Ensemble), a symphony orchestra without a conductor which existed from 1922 to 1932.

11 Maxim Litvinov (1876–1951), first Soviet Ambassador in Britain (1917–18), later People's Commissar of Foreign Affairs.

11 Nansen passports were statutory travel documents for foreign residents in Western Europe after the First World War.

13 Konstantin Solomonovich Saradzhev (1877–1954), conductor, director of the Yerevan Conservatoire and lifelong friend of Prkfv. One of the organizers along with the critic Derzhanovsky (see note for p. 6) of the 'Evenings of Modern Music' in pre-war Moscow. He gave a number of first performances of works by Prkfv and Myaskovsky.

14 Comintern – the 'Communist International', an organization for promoting communist ideologies and activities in as many countries of the world as possible. Officially disbanded in 1943 but virtually non-functional long before (Stalin disapproved of *all* contact with foreigners, whatever its whys and wherefores).

15 N. G. Raisky (1875–1958), tenor and teacher.

16 Samuel Yevgenyevich Feinberg (1890–1962), well-known pianist, teacher and composer (principally of piano music and songs) in a post-Skriabin style. In 1925 he gave the first performance in Russia of Prkfv's Third Piano Concerto.

16 Lev Nikolaevich Oborin (1907–74), pianist and teacher, pupil of Igumnov and Myaskovsky at the Moscow Conservatoire. Among his pupils were Ashkenazy and Rozhdestvensky. Gave the first performance of the Khachaturian Piano Concerto. It was Oborin who accompanied David Oistrakh in the first performance of Prkfv's F minor Violin Sonata in Moscow in 1946 (they were long-term duo partners).

17 Okhotny Row – since 1961 Marx Prospect.

18 'Leningrad Philharmonia' – here and elsewhere Philharmoni*a* refers to the orchestra's administrative body, Philharmoni*c* to the orchestra itself.

19 Anatoly Vassilievich Lunacharsky (1875–1933), People's Commissar of Enlightenment from 1917 to 1929, early supporter of both Prkfv and Shostakovich.

20 Boris Petrovich Jurgenson (1868–1935), music publisher, son of the founder of the largest music-publishing business in Russia in the late 19th century. Most of Tchaikovsky's works were first published by Jurgenson *père*. In 1918 the firm was nationalized and became the music sector of the Soviet State Publishing House.

20 Pierre (Pyotr Petrovich) Souvchinsky (1892–1985), musicologist. A close friend of Prkfv and dedicatee of the Fifth Piano Sonata. Also noted for his passionate advocacy of the earlier Stravinsky.

20 Alexander Tcherepnin (1899–1978), Russian composer and pianist, in 1921 emigrated to France and later to the USA. His father, Nikolay Tcherepnin (1873–1945), composer, conductor of the opening season of Diaghilev's Ballets Russes and the first to complete Musorgsky's unfinished opera *Sorochintsy Fair*, was one of Prkfv's most valued teachers (primarily conducting) at the Conservatoire; Prkfv dedicated both his First Piano Concerto and Sinfonietta to him.

21 Yosif Pavlovich Utkin (1903–44), author of Soviet propaganda poems and other poetry of a more melodious and lyrical nature somewhat influenced by folksong.

22 Vladimir Vladimirovich Mayakovsky (1893–1930), famous Russian poet, began as a futurist, became a communist, committed suicide.

22 Alexey Maximovich Peshkov, known as Maxim Gorky (1868–1936). The well-known Russian writer was living at that time in voluntary exile in Italy. One of Prkfv's early admirers. He and Prkfv had participated in a concert arranged by Dobychina (see note for p. 85) in 1917 in Petrograd during which Gorky read from *Childhood* and Prkfv performed his *Ugly Duckling* and *Sarcasmes*. Prkfv visited him in Italy in 1926 and he returned permanently to Russia in 1931.

22 In Russian LEF sounds like 'lev', which means lion.

23 Nikolay Semyonovich Golovanov (1891–1953), later conductor-in-chief at the Bolshoi.

23 Ariy Moiseevich Pazovsky (1887–1953), Soviet conductor who specialized in opera.

23 Anatoly Isaakovich Kankarovich (1885–1956), composer and conductor, fellow student of Prkfv's at the St Petersburg Conservatoire.

23 Reinhold Moritsevich Glière (1874–1956), composer and conductor, Prkfv's first real teacher. (See Autobiography, p. 232.)

24 Vladimir Dukelsky [Vernon Duke] (1903–69), Russian composer, pupil of Glière, protégé of Diaghilev and Koussevitsky, settled in New York in 1922, friend of Prkfv. Composer of 'April in Paris', 'Autumn in New York' and other popular songs.

24 Konstantin Nikolaevich Igumnov (1873–1948), illustrious pianist, friend of Rachmaninov, director of the Moscow Conservatoire 1924–9. Oborin (see note for p. 16) was one of his pupils.

24 'Nadya Raevsky . . . Shurik' – 'Shurik' was Alexander Alexandrovich Raevsky (1887–1942), a cousin of Prkfv (their mothers were sisters); Nadya was his wife. The Raevskys were a distinguished aristocratic family and Sasha (Shurik) had studied at the St Petersburg Lyceum, a privileged college for the nobility. For this reason he had been arrested by the Soviets and, as we shall see, Prkfv made

many efforts during his stay in Moscow to get him released. The Raevskys feature quite prominently in Prkfv's childhood memoirs.

24 Antonina Vassilievna Nezhdanova (1873–1950), singer and leading coloratura at the Bolshoi Theatre.

25 Babulenka – in Prkfv's opera *The Gambler* (after Dostoevsky) one of the chief characters is the despotic old grandmother, the 'Babulenka'. When in Act II she is introduced to the fawning French Marquis she greets him in French with acidly exaggerated ceremony: '*Charmée!*' Seconds later everyone is conversing normally in Russian.

25 Ekaterina Grigorievna Ignatieva, née Zhitkov (1857–1929), Prkfv's aunt, his mother's sister. Ekaterina Alexandrovna Ignatieva (*c.*1885–1942) was her daughter.

25 Anatoly Nikolaevich Alexandrov (1888–1982), solo pianist, composer of late-Romantic persuasion and professor at the Moscow Conservatoire.

25 'At the Derzhanovskys' – all young Moscow composers: L.A. Polovinkin (1894–1949), L.K. Knipper (1898–1974), V.N. Kryukov (1902–60), A.V. Mossolov (1900–73). It was Polovinkin who, as director of music at the Moscow Children's Theatre, conducted the second (but first successful) performance of *Peter and the Wolf* on 5 May 1936 with Natalia Satz, who had commissioned the work, narrating.

28 Miron Borisovich Polyakin (1895–1941), violinist, later a professor at the Leningrad then the Moscow conservatoires.

28 Leopold Auer's (1845–1930) violin class in the St Petersburg Conservatoire had a world-wide reputation. Among his pupils were Heifetz and Elman (and Tseitlin).

28 Cecilia Hansen (1897–1989), Swedish violinist, was also the wife of the pianist Boris Zakharov, a friend of Prkfv at the St Petersburg Conservatoire.

28 Marchex – the reference is to the French pianist Henri Gil-Marchex who had earlier visited Russia and published a detailed account (in *The Chesterian*, no.60, Jan.–Feb.1927, pp.115–21) of his own experience of working with the Persimfans.

28 'A ragamuffin!' – the Russian derogatory expression '*goloshtannik*' almost literally means 'sans-culotte'.

28 Seryozha Serebryakov – Prkfv's second cousin who, incidentally, taught him to play chess.

29 Vassily Mitrofanovich Morolev (1880–1949), veterinary surgeon, an old friend and regular chess partner of Prkfv.

29 'Tabakov' – in his autobiography *From Russia to the West* (London, 1990) Nathan Milstein, the violinist, warmly remembers the Persimfans in general and Tabakov in particular:

'At rehearsals Tseitlin, the leader, gave instructions to the other members: he set the tempo and showed them phrasing. But in fact, there were also animated discussions and give-and-takes that would have been impossible under a conductor.

'The Persimfans members rehearsed a lot: violinists separately, cellists separately, and so on. Then they all got together and the drilling continued. During the concert the musicians formed a semicircle, the better to see one another, and the violin section sat with its back to the audience. Tseitlin gave cues with facial expressions, not with his hand, so the audience was unaware of them. Persimfans was known for its polished performances, splendid ensemble playing, and memorable orchestral solos.

'I'll never forget the golden sound of Persimfans's first trumpet, Mikhail Tabakov. He was small and plump, and when he played he puffed up and turned red. But his song was radiant, glowing and at the same time tender. The other musicians of Persimfans were comparable masters.'

30 Alexander Borisovich Goldenweiser (1875–1961), composer, writer, pianist and teacher, too strongly drawn to and influenced by Rachmaninov, Skriabin and Medtner to be very sympathetic to Prkfv. For fifty-seven years professor of piano at the Moscow Conservatoire and credited with establishing the first outstanding Soviet piano school (among his pupils were Feinberg and Lazar Berman). He was a friend of Tolstoy, of whom he published two volumes of reminiscences. Originally it was Goldenweiser who was recommended by Taneev as private tutor to the eleven-year-old Prkfv in 1902; in the event Glière went for the summer to Sontsovka, the large village in the Ukraine where the Prokofiev family had settled (Goldenweiser spent part of that summer as Tolstoy's guest at Yasnaya Polyana). At the notorious 1948 Composers' Conference chaired by Zhdanov he was far from supportive either of Prkfv or Shostakovich.

30 Alexei Denisovich Dikij (1889–1955), actor and theatre director.

30 Isaak Moiseevich Rabinovich (1894–1961), artist and theatre-designer.

31 Georgy Bogdanovich Yakulov (1884–1928), painter and theatre-designer. He created the sets for Prkfv's ballet *Le pas d'acier*, nicknamed *Oursignol*, after Stravinsky's *Rossignol* perhaps.

31 'When she asked him about the present-day marriage-code' – after the Russian Revolution divorce (and marriage) regulations were greatly simplified. For instance a single visit to the Registry office might suffice to dispatch one's business.

31 GPU – the Secret Police, then called GPU (State Political Administration), was in 1934 renamed NKVD, later the KGB.

32 Konstantin Georgyevich Mostras (1886–1965), violinist and professor at the Moscow Conservatoire.

32 Abram Ilich Yampolsky (1890–1956), violinist and well-known professor at the Moscow Conservatoire; also leader of the Persimfans.

33 Boleslav Leopoldovich Yavorsky (1877–1942), musical theorist. He created his own theory of modality. In 1964 a volume of his *Reminiscences, Essays and Letters* was published in Moscow, the editor being Shostakovich.

34 Kostya Sezhensky later became a musicologist and wrote his memoirs.

34 The Smetskys were friends of Prkfv's parents (Mme Smetskaya was at school with Prkfv's mother). They owned a large estate in Sukhumi.

35 Boris Borisovich Krasin (1884–1936), later a director of the Rosphil (Russian Philharmonic). He officially invited Prkfv in 1926 to come to the Soviet Union for a series of concerts.

36 Victor Mikhailovich Belyaev (1888–1968), musicologist.

37 'Tseitlin, as a violinist, is not very interested' – there are no violins in the scoring of this piece.

37 The Iversky Gates (completed in 1680) were demolished together with their eagles in the early 1930s.

37 Vassily Vassilievich Yakovlev (1880–1957), musicologist.

38 Komsomol – 'Communist Union of Youth'.

39 'I start with the Third Sonata': compare the account which follows with Kabalevsky's (pp. 158–60) and with Prkfv's own in the Autobiography (p. 282). Incidentally *Prichudy*, the Russian title of Myaskovsky's pieces, is difficult to translate. Oleg Prokofiev prefers the French *Bizarreries*, Rosa Prokofieva the weaker English *Whimsies*.

39 Alexander Naumovich Yurovsky (1882–1952), pianist. Director of the Publishing House between 1922 and 1944.

41 'MKHAT the 2nd': English readers will probably know it better as 'Moscow Arts Theatre', which is what Prkfv calls in on p. 130.

41 Nikolay Semyonovich Leskov (1831–95), outstanding Russian writer of short stories and novels. Shostakovich's opera *Lady Macbeth of Mtsensk* was based on one of the former.

41 Yevgeny Ivanovich Zamyatin (1884–1937), writer. Wrote an anti-utopian satire *We* (1925). In 1932 he was allowed to emigrate and died in Paris.

41 *chatushki* – urban folk-songs of a spirited and often saucy character such as form the basis of Shchedrin's well-known orchestral concerto *Naughty Ditties* (a.k.a. *Lewd Limericks*) of 1963.

42 Vsevolod Emilievich Meyerhold (1874–1940), the greatest avant-garde Russian theatre director. He probably met Prkfv for the first time at an informal run-through of *The Gambler* in Petrograd in 1916 at the apartment of the conductor Albert Coates. Meyerhold very much wanted to put the opera on at the Mariinsky Theatre but this plan – like all the others he was to make with Prkfv during the course of their twenty-two year long relationship – failed to materialize. An attempt to stage *The Gambler* at the Mariinsky again in 1929 came to nothing. Meyerhold's production of *Boris Godunov* was abandoned (for political reasons) after Prkfv had completed an original score for it; finally Meyerhold's hopes to give the première of *Semyon Kotko* in his 'Opera Studio' in Moscow were dashed when his theatre was disbanded in 1938. In June 1939 he was arrested on Stalin's orders and shot some time the following year.

42 Sergey Vladimirovich Protopopov (1893–1954), composer, pupil of Yavorsky.

42 'Mussenkin': a term of endearment ('dear little music-man' or something of the kind). Prkfv is implying that the relationship between Yavorsky and Protopopov was of an 'intimate' nature.

42 *Zkuski*, hors-d'oeuvres; *blini*, pancakes; *pirozhki*, pies, either savoury (cf. cornish pasties) or made with jam.

42 Ksenya Georgyevna Derzhinskaya (1889–1951), operatic soprano of the Bolshoi Theatre.

44 1927 was the foundation year of the quinquennial International F. Chopin Piano Competition, one of the greatest and most prestigious in the world: recent winners have included Pollini (1960), Argerich (1965), Ohlsson (1970) and Zimerman (1975). The Soviet government had set its sights on success and put a lot of effort into preparing its 'squad', which included Shostakovich, himself only twenty.

45 'his name is actually not a pseudonym' – Dikij means 'wild' in Russian.

47 Pavel Alexandrovich Lamm (1882–1951), musicologist and pianist, later became Prkfv's musical secretary or amanuensis. This involved copying out full orchestral scores from detailed sketches. In 1928 he became general editor of the Soviet

complete edition of Musorgsky, and supervised the first publication of *Boris Godunov* in its original version. He also edited Dargomyzhky, Taneev, Tchaikovsky, Rachmaninov etc.

49 'a cinematographic film is made of me' – a short fragment of a newsreel with Prkfv and members of the Persimfans performing together has survived, evidently the one referred to here.

53 Olga Davidovna Kameneva was arrested during the purges of the mid-1930s and shot.

54 Demyan Bedny (i.e. 'Demyan-the-Poor') (1883–1945), satirical and agitprop poet (propaganda jingles, Red Army songs etc). 'In' with Lenin and Trotsky, then 'out' for vilifying Russian history in a comic-opera libretto.

54 Karakhan, a prominent Soviet diplomat, was arrested and shot in 1937.

55 'A.III': since they were dining in the Kremlin the implication is that this was the linen of Alexander III.

56 'they are all "white"' – she means the white Russian *émigrés* who had fought during the civil war against the Bolsheviks, the 'reds'.

56 Wrangel was a White Russian general who took a last heroic stand against the Bolshevik forces in the South.

58 Ulric Avranek had been chorus director for Diaghilev's epoch-making season of Russian opera in Paris in 1908–9 (*Boris Godunov*, *Prince Igor* etc).

59 'How could anyone as tall' – in Act II of *The Love for Three Oranges* the three monster oranges, when sliced open, disclose three beautiful princesses.

63 'Tabakov blew some marvellous B flats' – in the Finale ('Sunrise') of the *Scythian Suite* the first trumpet has some prominent high B flats, most thrilling when finely played, as they evidently were here.

63 *Dreams*, a symphonic picture for large orchestra, composed 1910.

64 'Peter' – St Petersburg.

65 'Ravel's last opera' – *L'enfant et les sortilèges* (first produced in 1925), in which numbers from an arithmetical text-book come to life and dance and sing.

65 'my last ballet for Diaghilev' – *Le pas d'acier*, first produced in Paris later the same year (1927), is set in a contemporary Soviet factory (although the Soviets would later claim, angrily, that any resemblance between Diaghilev's conception and the genuine article was purely coincidental, so touchy and humourless were they on the subject of *émigré* Russians treating indigenous contemporary themes).

65 'the Mariinsky Theatre' – Prkfv uses the old name of St Petersburg's principal opera house. In Soviet times (1920) this was renamed the 'State Academic Theatre of Opera and Ballet'. In 1935 it added to this already cumbersome nomenclature a dedication to the recently assassinated Leningrad party boss Kirov. Its present name is the Kirov Theatre.

66 Ivan Vassilievich Excousovich (1883–1942) was at that time in charge of the Academy theatres of Moscow and Leningrad.

67 Sablino is a village a short distance from Leningrad, visible from the approaching train; but its significance for Prkfv – and the meaning of 'Zed' – is unknown.

67 Alexander Vyacheslavovich Ossovsky (1871–1957), musicologist, a pupil and friend of Rimsky-Korsakov. He helped the young Prkfv to publish his first works through writing to Jurgenson. His letter to the latter dated 5 May 1911 assures him that 'this courageous young composer' with his 'superb technique' and 'delightfully youthful determination to go his own way' has a great future before

him. Ossovsky is convinced that Jurgenson's firm would not suffer any commercial set-back through publishing Prkfv, since the latter's music 'ought to make its own way and find a market'.

67 Vladimir Vladimirovich Shcherbachev (1889–1952), composer and professor at the Leningrad Conservatoire. Like Prkfv he had studied with Tcherepnin and Lyadov; among his own pupils were the conductors Melik-Pashaev and Mravinsky.

67 Vladimir Mikhailovich Deshevov (1889–1955), composer, fellow student of Prkfv at the St Petersburg Conservatoire. Much involved in music education and with the 'Proletkult' (Proletarian Cultural–Educational Organization), a brainchild of Lunacharsky whose first aim was to train artists from members of the proletariat. As a composer he gradually dropped his modernist tendencies in favour of Soviet realism of the officially sanctioned kind.

68 The monument to Alexander III was removed in the early 1930s.

68 The Alexandrinsky Theatre had been renamed 'Pushkin Theatre' in 1919.

68 'Tsarskoe Selo' means 'Tsar's village', the country residence of the imperial family. After the Revolution renamed 'Detskoe Selo' (children's village); in 1937 renamed 'Pushkin' to mark the centenary of the death of Russia's great poet who had been taught at the famous Lyceum there. About 14 miles from Leningrad and renowned for its 18th-century palaces and parks.

68 'A spacious room' – in 1931 the German composer Berthold Goldschmidt visited Leningrad and also stayed at the Hotel Evropeiskaya: 'the well-known abode for foreign visitors like George Bernard Shaw, who had just left the place a day earlier. The scenery suddenly changed for the brilliant. The hotel was situated near the Nevsky Prospect, the famous boulevard leading down to the Baltic Sea. It offered a wide view of the domes, spires and cupolas of the cityscape, and in the glaring sunshine everything looked golden and colourful – not least the surface of the main road, which consisted neither of cobblestones nor asphalt but of wooden blocks which in the course of time had been polished by whatever traffic there may have been, and was now reflecting the light of the long summer days like a mirror. This was certainly a morale-booster, as during my walks through streets and along the canals I found no real shops apart from ironmongers, only selling tools, screws and nails.

'I was struck by the irony told by monuments when I saw the famous equestrian statue of Peter the Great pointing to the West and the nearby-anchored cruiser *Aurora*, the warship historic for its shelling of the Winter Palace at the beginning of the October Revolution in 1917. Fourteen years on, the beauty of that building appeared unimpaired, and several visits to the Hermitage with its enormous collection of first-rate paintings and *objets d'art* left me completely overwhelmed . . .' (from 'Brief Encounter, 1931', a reminiscence printed in the June 1990 issue of *Tempo* [no.173, p.4]).

68 Nikolay Andreevich Malko (1883–1961), conductor, pupil of Glazunov, Lyadov, Rimsky-Korsakov and Tcherepnin. In 1928 emigrated to the West, settling first in America then in Australia. His autobiography was published posthumously in Leningrad in 1972. Made a number of early LP recordings of Prkfv's music ('Classical' Symphony etc.).

68 Mikhail Georgiyevich Klimov (1881–1937), conductor, chorus master and teacher. Principal conductor of the Glinka Leningrad Academic Choir, 1919–35.

68 Vladimir Alexandrovich Dranishnikov (1893–1939), conductor, fellow student of Prkfv at the St Petersburg Conservatoire; he accompanied Prkfv on a second piano at the examination performance of the First Piano Concerto in 1914. From 1918 he premièred many Soviet operas in the Mariinsky Theatre in Leningrad. In 1936 he became the principal opera conductor in Kiev and died while conducting.

70 'Grigorovich' – apparently a nickname for Lida's husband, Mikhail Grigorievich Barkov, a naval officer of aristocratic origin.

70 Boris Stepanovich Zakharov (1887–1942), pianist, fellow student and friend of Prkfv.

71 Lyova: unknown.

71 'Lida . . . plays in cinemas' – almost certainly 'plays piano in cinemas'.

71 Ivan Vassilievich Ershov (1867–1943), well-known tenor.

71 Leonid Vladimirovich Nikolaev (1878–1942), pianist, composer and esteemed teacher and professor at the Leningrad Conservatoire, 1909–42.

71 'Berlin . . . with her husband' – presumably (perhaps non-musical) friends of Prkfv's from the old days.

71 The Scherzo for Four Bassoons is the same as 'Scherzo Humoristique', no.9 of the Piano Pieces op.12 (1906–13).

72 Yuri Mikhailovich Yuriev (1872–1948), well-known actor from the Alexandrinsky Theatre.

73 Katya Schmidthoff was the sister of one of Prkfv's closest friends at the Conservatoire, Maximilian Schmidthoff (1892–1913), who committed suicide. Prkfv dedicated several of his works to him, including the Second Sonata. The Second Piano Concerto and the Fourth Piano Sonata were both inscribed to his memory.

75 Ivan Alexandrovich Vishnegradsky (1893–1979), composer (born in St Petersburg), much influenced first by Skriabin then by the evolving concepts of microtonality and the quarter-tone piano. Emigrated to Paris in 1920, 'discovered' after his death by Pierre Boulez and other avant-gardists.

76 'to the daughter or her mother?' – in fact Glazunov later married the 'mother', Olga Gavrilova, and adopted her daughter Elena, a pianist (under the name of Elena Glazunov she appeared frequently as soloist in his two piano concertos, under his baton). In 1928 Glazunov left Russia and in 1932 settled in Paris with his family. He died there in 1936.

77 'the "Tragicals"' – Prkfv's adaptation of Meyerhold's adaptation (of Gozzi's play) involves, importantly, a 'Greek chorus' of spectators, representatives of various categories of theatrical entertainment – Comicals, Tragicals, Eccentrics, Lyricists (Romantics), Blockheads. All vie to impose their choice of what is to be performed and react excitedly, pro or contra, to what they see as the opera proceeds.

77 'he himself plays the trombone' – early in the Prologue Prkfv directs the curtains to open sufficiently to let a Herald *and a trumpet-player* come out. The 'trumpet'-player delivers some resounding blasts on the bass trombone, whereupon the Herald makes his proclamation. In this production the Herald and the 'trumpet'-player were clearly one and the same person. See plate no. 22 for a reproduction of this page from a vocal score belonging to Prkfv; note how in his own hand he

has corrected the 'Bass*trompete*' of the German translation to 'Bass*posaune*', i.e. trombone.

78 Yevgeny Vladimirovich Wolff-Israel (1874–1956), cellist.

79 Alexander Ilich Ziloti (1863–1945), pianist and conductor. For many years he organized series of concerts in Moscow and later in St Petersburg, where Prkfv conducted for the first time in 1915 his Sinfonietta and, in 1916, the *Scythian Suite*. As a teacher, his most distinguished pupil was his first cousin, Rachmaninov. Ziloti emigrated in 1919 and taught at the Juilliard in New York, 1924–42.

79 Sergey Ernestovich Radlov (1892–1948), theatre director, also a friend of Prkfv. Later one of the co-authors of the libretto of the ballet *Romeo and Juliet*. In 1937–8 Prkfv composed incidental music for Radlov's production of *Hamlet* at the Lensoviet Theatre in Leningrad.

79 Vladimir Vladimirovich Dmitriev (1900–48), theatre-designer.

79 'the crocodiles won't play' – reference obscure: possibly the 'real', 'professional' chess-players (as opposed to amateurs like Ptashka), those who snap at and devour each other, no quarter given?

79 'Chudovsky' – unknown; perhaps (from the context) a prominent chess-player of the time.

81 The Elizavetinsky or Great Palace was built by the architect Rastrelli in 1746–55.

81 Vera Alpers studied with Prfkv at the St Petersburg Conservatoire in 1904–9. She was much attached to him and later wrote a memoir.

82 The correspondence with Givnin (and his denouncer) is preserved in Prkfv's archive.

82 Lev Konstantinovich Knipper (1898–1974), composer, greatly influenced in the 1920s by Western avant-gardism. Later turned to folk-music research (Turkmenia, Kirgizia etc.), the fruits of which he incorporated in original works.

82 Yury Nikolaevich Tyulin (1893–1978), musicologist, occasional composer and teacher at the Leningrad Conservatoire for forty-two years, 1925–67. Contributed an interesting reminiscence of Prkfv to the symposium *Sergey Prokofiev: Materials, Articles, Interviews* (Moscow, 1978), pp. 159–64.

84 Maximilian Osseevich Steinberg (1883–1946), composer, and pupil and son-in-law of Rimsky-Korsakov. Edited the latter's works and completed his text-book on orchestration. Dranishnikov, Shostakovich and Nicolas Slonimsky were among his pupils.

84 Julia Lazarevna Weisberg (1878–1942), composer who studied with Glazunov and Rimsky-Korsakov and also with Reger and Humperdinck in Germany. She translated the musical writings of Romain Rolland into Russian (nine volumes) and in 1915–17 co-edited the journal *Muzukalnyi sovremennik* (Musical Contemporary), her co-editor being Andrey Rimsky-Korsakov (son of the composer) who was also her (second) husband. Asafiev broke with them when they refused to print his enthusiastic evaluation of the triumvirate Stravinsky–Myaskovsky–Prokofiev. No wonder Prkfv was so surprised to find the Korsakovs' opinions had changed with the times. Weisberg died in 1942 in the Siege of Leningrad.

84 Andrey Nikolaevich Rimsky-Korsakov (1878–1940), musicologist, son of the composer, husband of Julia Weisberg.

NOTES TO PP. 84–106

84 Anna Petrovna Ostroumova-Lebedeva (1871–1955), well-known engraver and watercolourist. Later painted a portrait of Prkfv.

84 Antonia Alexandrovna Rudavskaya – harpist, old acquaintance of Prkfv.

84 Eleonora Damskaya – also harpist, fellow student of Prkfv.

85 Mikhail Alexeevich Kuzmin (1875–1936), post-symbolist poet.

85 Nadezhda Yevseevna Dobychina (1885–1950). Owned an art gallery before the Revolution where she exhibited avant-garde artists and gave musico-literary soirées in which prominent writers and musicians took part. See Autobiography p. 258 for details of the recital Prkfv gave there on 12 February 1917, also note for p. 85.

85 Alexander Benois (1870–1960), Russian artist and art-historian. One of the founders of the World of Art movement. Designed sets for Diaghilev's first ballet *Le pavillon d'Armide* (music by Tcherepnin) in 1909, for *Petrushka* in 1911 and for many other productions.

86 Nothing is known of Karlovich except that he should not be confused with the important late-Romantic Polish composer Mieczyslaw Karlowicz (1876–1909).

90 Charles-Louis Hanon (1819–1900), French composer, author of a system of monotonous piano exercises often used in Russia, later parodied by Prkfv in the finale of his op.94 Flute Sonata (1943).

92 'the Overture and a Sailors' Dance' – the chamber ballet *Trapeze* (1924) for five instruments was commissioned by Boris Romanov (1891–1957), a Russian dancer and choreographer. Its music was used in the Quintet (1924) and later in the Divertissement for orchestra (1925–9).

93 'I don't remember her name' – the actress Cecilia Lvovna Mansurova.

93 Andrey Bely (1880–1934), eminent Russian poet and writer.

99 Kuzma Sergeevich Petrov-Vodkin (1878–1939), Russian painter.

99 Cheka – the Secret Police organized by the Bolsheviks in 1917 and reorganized in 1922 as the GPU.

101 Valery Yakovlevich Bryusov (1873–1924), Russian symbolist poet and writer, on whose short novel *The Fiery Angel* Prkfv based his opera.

103 Maria Grigorievna Kilshtedt (1861–?), poet and novelist.

104 Natasha Goncharova – unknown (*not* the artist Natalia, wife of Larionov, who worked with Diaghilev – *Chout, Les Noces* etc).

104 Alexey Nikolaevich Tolstoy (1882–1945), writer. Emigrated after the Revolution, but in 1923 returned to the USSR.

105 Joseph Schillinger (1895–1943), composer and theorist. In 1928 settled in the USA where he taught many 'popular' musicians including Tommy Dorsey, Vernon Duke, Gershwin, Benny Goodman, Oscar Levant and Glenn Miller (whose *Moonlight Serenade* was written as an exercise for Schillinger). In 1941 he published *The Schillinger System of Musical Composition* and in 1948 *The Mathematical Basis of the Arts*. Schillinger's *First Airphonic Suite* for theremin and orchestra (1929) was one of the first symphonic works to involve an electronic instrument.

106 Darius Milhaud describes his 1926 visit to Moscow and Leningrad in some detail in his autobiography *Notes without Music* (London, 1952). Incidentally in January 1929 Béla Bartók embarked on a three-and-a-half-week concert tour which took him to the same cities as Prkfv – Leningrad, Kharkov, Odessa, Moscow. He

175

recorded his impressions – almost completely negative – in an article printed in English in *Béla Bartók Essays* (London, 1976).

106 Gavriil Nikolaevich Popov (1904–72), composer, pupil of Shcherbachev. Among his works: a famously dissonant Septet (1927) and a Chamber Symphony (begun 1927, finished in the 1930s), considered to be two of the landmarks of 'Soviet modernism'. In 1941 he started, but never completed, an opera on the subject of Alexander Nevsky. The 'octet or nonet' to which Prkfv here refers was actually the Septet, completed that year – cf. Autobiography, p. 283, where he identifies it as such.

107 Khriztofer Stepanovich Kushnarev (1890–1960), musicologist and teacher and composer, particularly of organ music. His 1924 Passacaglia and Fugue is his best-known organ work; it may have been this or the 1925 Sonata that Prkfv heard on this occasion.

107 Maria Venyaminovna Yudina (1889–1970), pianist, noted for her eccentricities and for her championing of modern music in Soviet Russia (see Shostakovich's *Testimony* for a fascinating pen-portrait and anecdotes).

107 '20 degrees Réaumur' – 25 Celsius.

108 Mikhail Mikhailovich Chernov (1879–1938), composer, pupil of Lyadov and Rimsky-Korsakov. Translated Berlioz's *Traité d'instrumentation* into Russian.

108 'those students who had tickets' – unfortunately Prkfv does not specify the exact nature of the 'tricks', the purpose of which was presumably somehow to gain admission for more students than there were tickets.

111 'As soon as she noticed' – this 'prelude' is No.7 of the Piano Pieces op. 12. Subtitled 'Arpa', it *imitates* a harp, and can be played on the harp, but is actually a piano piece (very droll, very Prokofiev). The 'bassoon' scherzo (see pp. 71 and 173) is no. 9 in the same series.

113 'Several fragments from the score of my *Giant*' – opera by Prkfv composed at the age of eight.

113 *Vera Sheloga* – opera by Rimsky-Korsakov, composed 1877 as Prologue to *The Maid of Pskov*; partly rewritten as a separate one-act opera in 1898.

114 Alexander Danilovich Kamensky (1900–52), pupil of Nikolaev and professor at the Leningrad Conservatoire from 1934.

114 Madame Pototskaya – wife of the St Petersburg physician and surgeon Stepan Alexandrovich Pototsky. The couple had a dancing master to teach their children and Prkfv was invited to join in the lessons. There is an amusing account in the long autobiography (English edition pp. 160–61; 1982 Russian edition pp. 244–6) and even a photo (English between pp. 204–5; Russian, p. 245).

114 Yury Alexandrovich Shaporin (1887–1966), much-loved teacher and prolific composer in the epic/lyric tradition of Borodin (e.g. the opera *The Decembrists* and the oratorio *The Tale of the Battle for the Russian Land*). Closely associated with such brilliant pre-revolutionary figures as Blok and Mayakovsky. Among his pupils were Rodian Shchedrin, Karen Kachaturian and the conductor Svetlanov.

115 'including one about Glazunov' – in 1907 Glazunov came to England and received the honorary D. Mus. from the Universities of Oxford and Cambridge.

117 Boris Nikolaevich Demchinsky (1877–1942), writer, had been helping Prkfv with the libretti of the operas *The Gambler* and *The Fiery Angel*.

117 'Eleonora . . . examined all the clothes from Paris with greedy eyes' – cf.

Peter and the Wolf: 'the wolf walked round and round the tree looking at (the duck and the bird) with greedy eyes'.

118 Miklashevsky – unknown, clearly a professor at the Leningrad Conservatoire.

119 Nikolay Karlovich Medtner (1879–1951), composer, emigrated in 1921, from 1935 lived in England, lifelong friend of Rachmaninov. His outlook was so conservative he found even some of Rachmaninov's later works unacceptable; he was nevertheless within his boundaries a composer of distinguished sensibility. Cf. pp. 253 and 257 of the Autobiography, which explain his and Prkfv's dislike of one another.

120 'old Russian orthography' – i.e. pre-1918, when official changes in spelling were made (e.g. several letters were dropped from the alphabet to avoid redundancies or needless duplications).

120 *The Government Inspector* – the famous comedy by Gogol.

123 Alexander Yakovlevich Golovin (1863–1930), painter and set-designer and member of the World of Art movement.

123 Ida Rubinstein (1885–1960), dancer and actress, broke away from the Diaghilev Ballet and created a rival company.

123 Vyacheslav Ivanovich Suk (1861–1933), conductor of Czech origin who settled in Russia in 1880 and conducted opera in Kiev and Moscow.

124 'the former wife of Gorky' – Ekaterina Pavlovna Peshkova (1876–1965).

125 Vyacheslav Rudolfovich Menzhinsky (1874–1934), the head of the GPU (Secret Police) between 1926 and 1934.

125 Genrik Grigorievich Yagoda (1891–1938) succeeded Menzhinsky and was shot after a show trial as an 'enemy of the people'.

126 Yelena Fabianovna Gnesina (1874–1967), well-known pianist and music-teacher, pupil of Busoni. In 1895 she founded with her two sisters a music-school that in 1944 became the Gnesin Institute. Sister of Mikhail Fabianovich Gnesin (1883–1957), the composer hailed by Rimsky-Korsakov as the 'Jewish Glinka' (he composed some fifty works on Jewish subjects).

126 Alexander Alexandrovich Shenshin (1890–1944), composer, pupil of Glière and Gretchaninov, also theatre-conductor.

127 Alexander Fyodorovich Goedicke (1877–1957), composer and noted organist. If he was 'sensitive' to criticism of Medtner it would have been because they were not only friends but also cousins: Medtner was a nephew of Goedicke's father Fyodor (Karlovich), also a composer and organist, sometime professor at the St Petersburg Conservatoire.

127 Dmitry Mikheevich Melkikh (1885–1943), composer, pupil of Yavorsky.

127 Vissarin Yakovlevich Shebalin (1902–63), prominent composer and teacher, much admired by Shostakovich. Prolific composer in a variety of genres; also completed Musorgsky's *Sorochintsy Fair* and prepared the officially sanctioned Soviet version of Tchaikovsky's *March Slave* and *1812 Overture* in which the Tsarist anthem is replaced by a chorus from Glinka's *A Life for the Tsar* (renamed by the Soviets *Ivan Susanin*).

127 St Basil's Cathedral: celebrated 16th-century cathedral on Red Square.

127 Anatoly Andreevich Brandukov (1856–1930), cellist, pupil of Tchaikovsky (theory), with whom he played (as well as with Liszt and Rachmaninov). He was the dedicatee of Tchaikovsky's *Pezzo capriccioso* for cello and orchestra, and of Rachmaninov's Cello Sonata. Lived in Paris from 1878 to 1905.

128 'The Litvinovs live in a smart detached house' – in fact they occupied only a few rooms there. In 1930 it became the British Embassy.

129 *Lyubov Yarovaya*, a play by Konstantin Andreevich Trenyov (1876–1945), a now-forgotten playwright, much admired in his day for the exemplary nature of his 'social realism'. 'Lyubov' (noun) means love, 'Yarovaya' (adjective) spring crop: i.e. 'Spring Love'.

129 Dmitry Mikhailovich Tsyganov (born 1903), violinist, founder in 1923 of the eminent Beethoven Quartet in Moscow.

129 Gostorg: a state import/export depot.

130 *Tsar Fyodor Ivanovich*, play by A.K. Tolstoy (1817–75). It was considered one of the best productions of the Moscow Artistic Theatre (MKHAT).

130 '*baranki*' – flat bread of circular shape.

131 'Meyerhold's wife' – Zinaida Raikh (1902–39), actress. After Meyerhold's arrest she was murdered in her home in mysterious and brutal circumstances.

131 Sergey Esenin (1895–1925), celebrated Russian poet.

132 *The Magnificent Cuckold*, surreal farce by the Belgian playwright F. Crommelynck.

132 Alexander Nikolaevich Ostrovsky (1823–86), leading 19th-century playwright on whose play *The Storm* Janáček based his opera *Katya Kabanova*, and whose *Snegurochka* (The Snow Maiden) inspired both Tchaikovsky's incidental music and Rimsky-Korsakov's opera.

132 'I recommended Deshevov's "Scherzo" op. 12' – this 'Scherzo' (no.9 of the Ten Pieces for Piano op. 12) is dedicated to Deshevov. Did Prkfv remember these accordion-players when planning his monumental *Cantata for the 20th Anniversary of the Revolution* in 1936? The entry of the accordion orchestra at the climax of the 'October Revolution' movement is one of the work's great *coups de théâtre*.

133 Sergey Petrovich Shirinsky (1903–74), cellist, member of the Beethoven Quartet.

133 'this thing doesn't "sound"' – in the American sense, i.e. sound *well*.

135 'fleshy goose' – portions of cooked poultry were often on sale on Russian railway stations.

135 '*shchi*' – cabbage soup.

136 Mikhail Ossipovich Steiman (1889–1949), studied alongside Prkfv in Tcherepnin's conducting class.

136 Iosif Mikhailovich Lapitsky (1876–1944), Ukrainian opera producer.

137 Vera Reberg, daughter of A. Reberg, a doctor, who was a neighbour and a friend of Prkfv's parents in the Ukraine. Prkfv kept up a friendly relationship with her and her two sisters whenever he returned there on holiday during his years of study at the Conservatoire.

138 'nobody understands the Fifth' – towards the end of his life Prkfv made a new version of the Fifth Sonata, calling it op. 135 (1952).

139 Nikolay Dmitriena Leontovich (1877–1921), choral composer, teacher and ethnomusicologist, pupil of Yavorsky. Best known for his choral settings of folk-songs and for his 'Carol of the Bells', a popular Christmas song in the USA. Died in the Civil War.

139 Boris Nikolaevich Lyatoshinsky (1894–1968), composer and teacher, pupil of Glière at the Kiev Conservatoire where he himself later taught. Like so many of his contemporaries he began as a 'modernist' but later had to adopt a more accessible style in compliance with the demands of 'Soviet realism'. A prominent figure in Ukrainian musical life and probably the most important Ukrainian

nationalist composer. In 1986 Muzychna Ukraina began publishing his collected works in twenty-four volumes.

139 Leonid Leonidovich Lisovsky (1866–1934), minor composer and teacher.

139 Novosatsky: unknown.

139 Filipp Emelyanovich Kozitsky (1893–1960), honoured artist of the UkrSSR (1943), holder of the chair in music history at the Kiev Conservatoire.

139 'even if the figure was doubled' – unfortunately this sentence makes no better sense in Russian than in English.

140 Jan Kubelik (1880–1940), Czech violinist and composer of six violin concertos, father of Rafael Kubelik.

142 The poet Esenin was married to the dancer Isadora Duncan in 1922–3.

142 Shipovich: unknown apart from what Prkfv tells us of him.

142 'Children surrounded the piano' – a tableau strikingly prophetic of a famous photo taken nearly ten years later: Prkfv at the piano surrounded by children and by Natalia Satz. He had been writing *Peter and the Wolf* for Satz's Moscow Children's Musical Theatre .

144 Pavlusha Seryakov – a distant relative.

145 'the local tenor' – according to David Oistrakh the singer's name was Chishko (see p. 164). Alexander Semyonovich Chishko (1895–1976) was also a composer, having studied at the Leningrad Conservatoire with Kushnarev (see note for p. 106) and Tyulin (see note for p. 82) among others. His works include eight operas including the popular *Battleship Potemkin* (1937, produced 1955). He also sang the part of Pierre Bezhuhov in an early Leningrad production of *War and Peace*.

145 The sister of Prkfv's musical secretary Georgy Gorchakov.

146 Grigory Arnoldovich Stoliarov (1892–1963), conductor.

148 The Crown of Monomakh (13th–14th century), the celebrated crown of the Grand Prince of Kiev. It (or rather a reproduction of it) features prominently in the Coronation scene with which Part I of Eisenstein's film classic *Ivan the Terrible* (music by Prkfv) opens.

148 Andrey Rublyov (1360/70–1427), the greatest Russian ikon painter.

149 'unmistakably Jewish in profile' – i.e. which they could never have been in actuality since there were no Jews in the aristocracy.

150 Alexey Ivanovich Rykov (1881–1938), Soviet Premier from 1922 to 1930. He was shot after a show trial in 1938.

150 Felix Mikhailovich Blumenfeld (1863–1931), distinguished pianist, conductor and teacher (notably of Vladimir Horowitz), pupil of Rimsky-Korsakov. As a conductor he gave a number of important first performances, e.g. Rimsky-Korsakov's opera *The Legend of the Invisible City of Kitezh* and Skriabin's *Divine Poem* and *Poème de l'extase*. He composed copiously for the piano.

150 'I introduce Nadya Raevsky to Meyerhold' – it seems that Prkfv introduced Nadya to Meyerhold twice (the first time was at the concert on 6 March)! Difficult to say which date is correct.

151 *Turandot* by Carlo Gozzi (1720–1806) was staged with great success at the Vakhtangov Studio.

151 Friedrich Wührer (1900–75), Austrian pianist and teacher.

151 Budyonny was a member of the Soviet Cavalry at that time, later a marshal.

According to Solomon Volkov (*Testimony: The Memoirs of Dmitri Shostakovich*, London, 1979) he was famous for both his moustache and his outstanding stupidity.

152 'Chinese Revolutionaries': these 'Revolutionaries', of course, were not communists, but Chiang Kai-Shek's Kuomintang (Chinese National Party), which became the effective national government in October 1928. It became corrupt in its turn and was overthrown in another civil war (1945–8) and replaced by Mao Tse-Tung's communists. Both rebellions were supported by Moscow, then ever-ready to destabilize neighbouring countries.

152 'to buy the selected squirrel' – these very furs were found in Lina Prokofiev's wardrobe after her death in 1989. So antipathetic today is the idea of wearing coats made from animal pelts they proved almost impossible to dispose of.

152 Konstantin Sergeevich Stanislavsky (1863–1938), outstanding theatre director, actor and founder of the Moscow Arts Theatre.

152 Olga Lonardovna Knipper-Chekhova (1868–1959), a leading actress of the MKHAT. Wife of Anton Chekhov. In 1941 she and Prkfv (as well as Lamm and Myaskovsky) were part of a group of professors, actors and other 'artistic labourers' evacuated from Moscow (then under constant German bombardment) to Nalchik in the Caucasus.

152 Vasily Vasilievich Luzhsky (1869–1931), actor and assistant of Stanislavsky at the MKHAT.

153 'he is definitely in my bad books' – it has to be said that if Tsukker did not even try to help in this matter, even those who had promised to do something, i.e. Peshkova and Meyerhold, were unsuccessful. Shurik was freed only in 1931; his wife spent the years 1929–33 in a concentration camp set up for the construction of the Belomor Canal in Karelia. In 1928, in a letter to Prkfv in Paris, Tseitlin was informing him that 'because of his "pleasant" character, Tsukker had quarrelled with almost every member of the Persimfans, so we parted from him. We hope things will be much better without him.'

153 'I had in my pocket a note-book' – this must be one of those note-books of Prkfv's now under lock and key in TSGALI in Moscow (Central State Archives for Art and Literature).

154 Borovsky was among those who had seen Prkfv off in Paris.

155 Nina Pavlovna Koshetz (1894–1965), Russian opera singer and recitalist, emigrated in 1920, friend of the Prokofievs. She sang in many performances of Prkfv's music in the USA, including the first performance in 1921 of the *Five Songs without Words* op.35 which are dedicated to her. She sang Renata in the concert performance of Act II of *The Fiery Angel* which Koussevitsky conducted in Paris in June 1928.

156 Madame Grossman – unknown.

157 No biographies of 'Sasha' (i.e. Alexander) Tcherepnin mention this 'wife' if wife she were (as opposed let us say to a *protectrice*). What is officially recorded is that in the 1930s Tcherepnin married the Chinese pianist Lee Hsien-Ming. The two contemporary composers Ivan and Sergey Tcherepnin are their sons.

158 Postscript I by Dmitry Kabalevsky – Kabalevsky was almost certainly basing his account on Prkfv's, as recorded, not in the *Soviet Diary* (which, as we know, Kabalevsky could never have read), but in the Autobiography (see pp. 282–3), where Prkfv himself confuses or conflates the 24 January concert and the 28 January recital. However, Kabalevsky's description of the accident which befell

the Myaskovsky *Bizarrerie* bears hardly any resemblance to Prkfv's own; in other words we have a total of *three* different versions of the incident.

159 'At the end of January 1927' – see *Soviet Diary* for 26 January.

159 'Judging . . . by the fact that he and Myaskovsky' – though they were classmates, Myaskovsky was ten years older than Prkfv.

161 'Prokofiev arrived a little late' – see *Soviet Diary* for 23 January, where Kabalevsky is not mentioned. According to Prkfv, Myaskovsky *was* present and Prkfv *did* play something (the Third Sonata).

162 'Before long, in February or March 1927' – see *Soviet Diary* for 14 and 15 March. At that time Oistrakh was a violin student at the Odessa Music School.

163 'the lyrical *Visions fugitives* . . . one of them, the piece in C major' – in fact, none of the *Visions fugitives* is unequivocally in C major. Does Oistrakh have in mind the C major Prelude (Ten Pieces, op. 12 no. 7)?

164 'To my surprise he remembered everything' – compare Prkfv's account of this performance, 'spoiled by the lady-accompanist' (*Soviet Diary*, 15 March). Only afterwards did he take her place at the piano to accompany some songs. No mention of Oistrakh at all.

STORIES

A Bad Dog

It was a warm, oppressive summer evening. I was in a hurry, as I feared I would arrive at Maria's too late. The moon was shining through the trees, throwing a vivid lattice of white lights and black shadows on to the pavement. I was in a hurry, as Maria lived far away, almost on the edge of Florence. There, she said, there were fewer people, more flowers. I feared one thing: that I would again encounter that rascally lieutenant who apparently considered himself master in her little house, sitting in state like a king, talking like a Chinese emperor. No wonder. He knew he had exclusive sovereignty of her heart; and was it only her heart? I was at a loss to know how that vulgar ignoramus could have conquered her, a person of such discrimination, but whenever he came to call on her she seemed to have eyes for him alone. I felt that at those moments I turned into an item of furniture, remembered only when someone knocked against it.

Nevertheless, two days earlier, when the lieutenant had not been there, Maria had behaved quite differently towards me.

Out in the suburbs it was less oppressive: more flowers, fewer people. Maria's little house occupied a lonely site; she had only one neighbour. I pushed the gate and entered the densely flowering garden. Her house could be glimpsed only here and there, it was so intertwined with climbing plants. How often in my sketches I had traced on canvas the outline of that happy little nook.

It was as I supposed: the lieutenant was there. Of that there could be no doubt, as from the window there floated to the ear, or rather quite plainly struck it, the barbarous strains of a guitar. I knew that Maria had discriminating taste, so why did she put up with that terrible stuff? I stopped and almost felt like going away again – for indeed, who likes to play the role of a piece of furniture? But at the same time I began to feel so dismal without Maria that I was ready to consent to anything at all, just in order to be near her for a while.

When I entered the room Maria gave me a look of surprise, but said little – 'Hello, Fernando,' – and at once inclined her head over the table again, where she sat carefully cutting a pie into sections. I knew for whom that pie was intended. Oh, it was the famous apricot pie, which could be seen only at Maria's. Thin, brown on top, with juicy chunks of apricot, not overcooked, but only slightly touched by fire.

It was a wonderful pie, and the scoundrel of a lieutenant knew its value very well. Indeed, he had come here not so much for Maria's sake as for the pie and the half-bottle of Asti that always awaited him.

'Ah!' cried the lieutenant, spreading his fingers and giving the belly of his guitar a smack with his palm. 'He shall hear my new song!'

His new song was the last thing I wanted to hear. It did, however, provide some kind of escape from the situation, and so I sat down opposite him, trying to look as interested as I could. The lieutenant struck the guitar again, this time not on the belly but on the strings. A loud chord rang out. In despair I looked at Maria. Without raising her eyes she got up from the table, holding in both hands a long plate containing the pie, which she was preparing to take to the lieutenant. My heart began to beat painfully at the sight of that tender attention, but suddenly a strange sound made me start to my feet: it was as if something had jumped in through the open window. I quickly turned round and on the windowsill saw a large poodle. It had evidently not judged its leap quite correctly and was in a state of unsteady equilibrium, uncertain whether to hold out on the windowsill or to leap back down again. Maria uttered a scream, recoiled backwards and dropped the plate. That was apparently what the poodle had been waiting for. Tensing itself, it jumped down into the room. A moment later it had its mouth and paws in the pie. All this was so unexpected that I found myself rooted to the spot with surprise. Meanwhile the poodle was wagging its tail, joyfully growling as it devoured the pie, section by section.

All of a sudden the guitar went hurtling to the floor with a clatter, the lieutenant leapt up from the sofa like a wild beast, seized the poodle by its hind legs and with a herculean gesture threw it over his head and out of the window. The dog performed an improbable arc through the air and landed with a grunt in a flowerbed. There resounded a violent burst of canine squealing that passed through every harmony and modulation. From the neighbouring house came the rattle of a lock being turned, a door banged, and the owner began to call his dog. A few moments later the squealing began to grow fainter, then the door could be heard being locked again, and everything grew quiet.

The lieutenant stood over the broken plate, fastidiously holding the remains of the pie between finger and thumb.

'Thank you very much, I must say,' he said to Maria angrily. 'An excellent pie . . . you are a mistress of your art, and even better is the skill with which you threw it to the floor . . .'

'Giovanni,' she said reproachfully, 'you might at least feel sorry for me, not the pie; I got such a fright.'

'No,' Giovanni shouted, 'instead of yourself, it is me you ought to feel sorry for: do you realize that I have had nothing to eat since this morning? I am hungry and shall go to a café,' he added, putting on a hat which had feathers in it.

'Giovanni!' Maria cried beseechingly and, running up to him, seized him with both arms.

This was becoming unendurable. I leapt up from my chair and stepped forward. Of course I knew that when the lieutenant was there I turned into a piece of furniture and was ignored. But with this movement I reminded them of my existence. Maria threw me a glance, blushed and, taking a step backwards, turned away from the lieutenant.

'Goodbye,' she said to him. 'You are unfair, as ever.' And with these words, lowering her head, she went through into the other room.

The lieutenant put on his sword and, not deigning me worthy of a bow, leapt out of the window into the garden. Evidently he considered leaving by the door insufficiently dashing.

Slowly I entered the room where Maria was hiding. I was certain that I would find her stretched upon her bed, weeping inconsolably.

Instead I found her by the window. She was looking at the house of her neighbour and there was an ominous light in her eyes. (All her indignation had now been transferred to the poodle and its owner.)

'One can get no peace in one's own home for these mad dogs!' she exclaimed, in indescribable anger.

'Maria, for heaven's sake, what kind of a mad dog is that?' I said, remonstrating with her. 'Believe me: like the lieutenant, that dog was far more interested in the pie than in you! It is just a poor hungry poodle that your neighbour does not feed.'

'He's a gloomy old skinflint and a night-owl,' Maria declared. 'He doesn't feed his dog, he never receives any guests. He has been ill for a week, and now he spends all his time writing his will.'

I looked out of the window. Through the trees one could see his house and through the illuminated window there was indeed visible a figure inclined over a writing table.

'He's always writing and writing, writing and writing,' she said. 'A fat lot he must have to leave behind him after a life like that . . .'

'Well, let him write,' I said peaceably.

But the peace was soon shattered.

'He makes my life impossible!' she exclaimed. 'Yesterday he trod on my foot outside the front gate, and then today his dog attacked me . . .'

'But Maria, why did you not tell me about this earlier?' I said, beginning to feel an antipathy towards the old man.

'Because you are not the only one; there is also Giovanni. Today he threw out the dog, and tomorrow he will do the same to the old man.'

I boiled up.

'Very well. I and not he will talk to the old man and I will do it not tomorrow but right now!'

With these words I put on my hat and leapt out into the garden.

'Where are you going?' Maria called after me, and in her voice I caught a note of uneasiness. From the garden I could see her leaning over the windowsill as she said in a loud whisper, 'Fernando! Do not dare do anything silly! Where are you going?'

But I had already climbed over the wall and jumped down into her neighbour's garden. As I jumped I very nearly hurt myself, as the neighbour's garden was in a hollow and the wall was much higher on his side. I swiftly picked myself up and, hobbling slightly, approached the illuminated window in resolute fashion. The window was open, and the old man sat next to it, at his writing table, writing his will or whatever, deep in thought. The rays of an anglepoise lamp were reflected on his bald head like the sun on the ocean. The sound of footsteps seemed to alert him to my presence.

'If you do not send your villainous dog to the devil this very evening,' I shouted, 'then tomorrow I will break its legs and smash all your windows!'

At the first words I uttered the old man stood up jerkily and looked out of the window, but it was plain that in the dark he could not make me out. At the last words I uttered he extended his hand towards the window, banged it shut and lowered the blind.

Somewhat unexpectedly, I found myself in darkness. As a matter of fact this was the best response he could have devised in answer to my reprimand. I turned and walked towards the gate, but it proved locked, and was too high to be climbed. The moon had gone behind a cloud and I could make out objects only with difficulty. Nevertheless, I managed to reach the spot where I had jumped into this garden, only to find the wall was too high for anyone to scale. I tripped over a bucket that exuded a revolting smell of fresh paint and fell on to a ladder that lay beside it. Evidently the old skinflint had loosened his purse-strings and decided to have his garden wall or the walls of his house painted. The ladder served my purpose, and a moment later, having placed it against the fence, I found myself back in Maria's garden again. In excitement I hurried to see her, but the door turned out to be locked. I ran back into the garden and went round to a window. It was closed. I approached another – it was also closed. I returned to the door and cautiously knocked on it. There was no reply. The little house was fast asleep, and so was Maria . . .

Slowly I trudged off home.

II

That night I was unable to sleep. Not, of course, because of my adventure with that stupid old man. And even less because of the lieutenant. It was Maria's whisper as, flinging herself forward over the windowsill, she had said, 'Fernando . . . do not dare . . . do not dare to go!' that would not permit me to close my eyes. I had caught in it a kind of tenderness, or fear, perhaps, which I had interpreted as tenderness – but at any rate some new emotion for me, unexpectedly new, and brightening my prospects more than I had ever dared hope.

With the early morning I arose. I tried to work but it was no good; I abandoned my brushes and walked to the suburbs. When after half an hour's walking I again found myself facing Maria's little garden it was still early morning. The sun's oblique rays were bathing her little house, twined with greenery, and the garden breathed fragrance. The windows of the little house were open wide, but within reigned peace and silence. One had the feeling that the little house was nodding and basking in the rays of the morning sun. The wicket gate was open, but I could not quite bring myself to go through it. I merely stood lost in contemplation of this scene of sweet slumber, never even wondering, as I usually did, how well it would look on canvas. Thus I stood for rather a long time, and would probably have remained there had I not suddenly raised my head at the sound of human voices, which rudely dispelled the dream, returning me unceremoniously to life. The sounds were, of course, coming from next door. Giving the little house a final look I set off home. As I passed his gate I caught sight of the old man. He was standing with his back to me, and in front of him was a most charming-looking youth with blond curls and an anxious face. In a curt and methodical voice the old man was giving him a telling-off, and the youth was casting his eyes to right and to left, evidently uncertain how to escape the old man and his lecture.

'Well, that one won't get any inheritance!' I thought, and I felt sorry for the curly-headed youth.

When I got home I spent the whole day pacing from one end of the room to the other, and it was only when it had begun to grow dark that I went back to Maria's. Hardly had I grasped the handle of the gate than I had to stop, as some quite unaccustomed sounds could be heard from the window. I thought it sounded like someone inconsolably weeping, sobbing aloud. My heart tightened within me at the thought that it might be Maria. I was about to open the gate when I froze in that position. Suddenly the door screeched, opened, and out of it came the lieutenant. Some truly earth-shattering event must have taken place for him to have forgotten that it was the duty of every brave soldier to leap out through the window.

'Instead of standing there listening why don't you knock and come in?' he snapped at me immediately.

'Look here, lieutenant,' I said, 'I would ask you to . . .'

'And I would also ask you something,' the lieutenant cut in. 'I would ask you to stay at home, paint your pictures and not engage in your artistic pursuits anywhere else.'

'Now look here, sir,' I cried, jerking the gate open and directing my steps straight towards him. But he ducked out of the way and, stepping aside, flung the door wide open before me.

'Will the duke be so good,' he hissed, 'and just look how clever you have been and what the result of it is.'

With these words, rattling his sword and clicking his heels, he walked out of the garden. I rushed into the house and saw Maria stretched out upon the couch and sobbing in such despair that I came to a standstill, rooted to the spot.

'Maria, for the love of God, what has happened?' I mouthed.

'Go away . . .' I heard through sobs. I found a carafe of water, brought her a glass and helped her to sit up.

'You . . . you . . .' she said, her teeth chattering against the glass, 'have made . . . a . . . disreputable woman of me.' And instead of finishing her sentence she began a redoubled fit of sobbing.

'I? . . . of you? . . . For pity's sake, Maria,' I got out, stammering, I was so taken aback.

But Maria was not thinking, she was sobbing.

'No, I am serious, listen,' I said in a voice that was different, firm now, sitting down on the couch and taking her hands. 'Stop crying and speak properly. This is a serious matter. What was that you said about a disreputable woman?'

'I didn't say it, it was the old man . . .' Maria sobbed.

'The old man again?' I cried, starting to boil with anger. I drew her up by her arms and made her sit on the couch.

'Tell me this instant what the old man said!' I shouted, clenching my fists.

I was not shouting at Maria – heaven forbid. Was I capable of raising my voice against her even one tiny fraction? I was shouting because everything inside me was. Or, if you prefer, I was shouting at her invisible neighbour, whom I imagined before me. But whatever its motive, my shouting had an effect on Maria: she stopped crying and began to speak more coherently, though still with a break in her voice.

'Today I was standing in my garden . . .'

'Well?'

'And the old man was standing in his, near the ladder you left against the wall last night . . .'

'Yes?' I whispered, beginning to grow very excited.

'He put his hands on the ladder and said to me in a loud voice, "The difference between a respectable woman and a disreputable one is that . . ." ' At this point her voice was engulfed by a great wave of sobs.

'Yes, go on,' I said, gripping her hand.

' ". . . is that a respectable woman has respectable visitors, and a disreputable one has scoundrels." '

I leapt to my feet. Everything swam before my eyes. Maria was weeping like a child.

'He said that?' I exclaimed, still unable to believe my ears.

'Yes, he did,' Maria muttered through sobs. 'And to underline the point he struck his hand against the ladder . . .'

'Aha! Aha!' I screamed out. 'Then we shall speak to him not with words but with actions!'

Everything was dancing around me. I could not think how I could have forgotten about the ladder. I knew for certain that I was going to do something, though what exactly had not yet taken shape within my spinning head. I only felt regret that we were not living in the Middle Ages, when it was permissible to slay one's enemy at the crossroads. I looked out of the window – and again felt regret: Maria's neighbour, that brute who had dared to raise his voice against her, was slowly walking along the street and disappearing from view around the bend. The moon silhouetted his form in sharp relief. At the bend he paused, turned back, as though in reflection, then moved on further and vanished.

An unexpected realization dawned within my brain. The old man did not have his dog with him. It was plain that the dog had stayed at home. My plan was as follows: without delay, I would kill the good-for-nothing dog and leave a note on its carcass that said, 'The difference between a dog and an old donkey is that the dog is killed first, and the old donkey after.'

'Maria, I swear that the injury done to you shall receive a harsh revenge!' I cried as I ran out of the house. Maria's garden, the wall and the garden of her neighbour flashed before me. Jumping into his garden, I seized yesterday's ladder and ran over to his house with it, placed it against the balcony on the second storey and climed up on to the balcony. I found myself in the neighbour's house. He lived alone – that was well-known – and I was not afraid of meeting anyone. All I wanted was the dog, and I expected it to rush out at me, barking. I did not even have a knife on me, but I was ready to administer justice to it with my bare hands. For some reason, however, the dog was silent – asleep, perhaps. I quickly left the balcony and entered the first room I came to, the only one on the upper floor. This was the old man's bedroom. It was quiet and empty. I ran down to the ground floor, but there too silence reigned. The moon's rays, falling through the window, lit the room in long stripes. I pushed open the door of the last room and entered the study, but the dog was not in the study either. It must have run off after its owner, and I had evidently failed to notice it when I had caught sight of the old skinflint out in the street. An insane fury took possession of me: here I was, inside the dwelling, inside the very heart, one might even have said, of Maria's enemy – yet I could not put my plan into action! With all my might I struck my fist on the table, and into the blow I put all my powerless frenzy.

Suddenly my gaze fell on the papers that were lying on the table. This was the notorious will. I pounced upon the heap of closely written sheets and seized hold of them. Perhaps it was not a will at all; at any rate, there were rather too many sheets and they were rather too densely covered in tiny handwriting. It was indeed almost certain that this was not a will – I had only called it that because that was what Maria had told me it was. What difference did it make? With a sharp movement I whipped an entire bundle of papers off the table and, crumpling them up, stuffed them into my pocket, with another movement overturning an inkpot on those that remained.

In the silence I heard the sound of the gate opening. For some unknown reason the old man had already come back. I rushed headlong upstairs and found myself in the bedroom. There I stopped. It was out of the question for me to go out on to the balcony until the old man had entered the house, otherwise he might see me. I listened hard. In the silence I plainly heard first the clink of a key being inserted into the lock, and then two sonorous turns. At that same moment the poodle came rushing upstairs, barking loudly.

With one leap I was out on the balcony. Clambering down into the garden I seized the ladder and, holding it in my hands, ran over to the wall, this time, however, not the one that adjoined Maria's house, but the one that gave on to the street. The poodle was already on the balcony, and its frenzied barking filled the whole garden and the whole neighbourhood. I jumped down from the wall into the street and looked around. There was not a soul to be seen. No one had observed me on my way out of someone else's garden. I walked a few paces and slipped in through Maria's gate.

She met me in the doorway and seized my hand. Her face was pale, her eyes wide. And oh Lord, how black they were that night! An entire abyss opened before me.

'Here is the old night-owl's will,' I said, handing her the crumpled mass of papers. Amazement, suspicion and admiration – all of those things flickered at once in her eyes that were now raised to me and were as wide open as before.

'You've been inside his house?' she whispered.

'Yes, of course!' I exclaimed, kissing her hand and noticing in joyful amazement that she had not drawn it away.

'You're a madman,' Maria whispered, looking round at the window, through which her neighbour's house was visible.

'I bet he's angry now,' I smiled, 'whatever his name is . . .'

Maria's arm tenderly entwined my neck.

'Arthur Schopenhauer,' she said. 'Some foreigner.'

I really do not know how that barbarous name has remained in my memory. At that moment I felt only her arm gently, tenderly entwining my neck, all I could see were her black eyes gazing ardently at me . . .

I did not return home until late in the morning. It was the happiest night of my life.

Petrograd, 20 July – Essentuki,* 30 July 1917

(translated by David McDuff)

---

* In late July 1917 Prkfv travelled south to the Caucasus for a concert in which he played his First Piano Concerto (in Kislovodsk). Presumably this story was written on the journey. The mention of Schopenhauer reminds us that earlier that summer Prkfv had been educating himself in terms of German philosophy, particularly Kant.

Tanya and the Mushroom Kingdom

(end fragment)

. . . Tanya babbled: 'But how can you tell me I must take an oath, when I have to go home for breakfast?'

The tall mushroom angrily waved his lizard. 'Has she gone mad?' he screamed.

Mukhomor* the Seventeenth came up to Tanya. 'Tanyechka, my dear,' he said, 'we have breakfasts the like of which you haven't seen on earth. We have cakes the like of which you have never eaten. Cornflowers in fragrant snow, much better than ice cream.'

'But how can I not return home? Nyanya† will punish me . . .!' exclaimed Tanya, stretching her hand towards him, tears in her eyes.

'There won't be any Nyanya, not any more. You must give your hand not to me but to the lizard,' he said, moving away from her.

'To her? To her . . . impossible,' uttered Tanya very quietly. The tall Mukhomor blushed, his top flared with red fire.

'There is no time!' he shouted loudly. 'Farewell!' and with all his might threw the lizard on the ground.

Tanya covered her eyes with both her hands and at the same moment felt she was being lifted up. Her fingers, tightly squeezing her eyes, seemed to become bigger and bigger, her feet also were increasing in size and her head kept somehow swelling. She pressed her hands even tighter to her eyes and was on the verge of crying. But she was so frightened she couldn't even do that. Then it seemed that she was no longer being lifted up, but it still felt as though strange things were happening to her. Her head continued to swell and surely her legs were still growing.

Far away she could hear heart-rending shouts of 'Tanya, Tanya!' But

* *Mukhomor* (fly-killer), a fly-agaric, is a mushroom commonly found in Russia; it has a characteristic red top with white spots.
† *Nyanya*, or *nyanechka* as a term of endearment, is the word for an old nurse in Russian.

Tanya did not dare take her hands away from her eyes. Then she felt a breath of fresh air and a slight breeze ruffling her dark hair.

'Tanya! Tanya!' How far away it sounded. But Tanya continued to sit all hunched over, her hands covering her eyes. Something stung her on the neck: it hurt. She couldn't help touching the painful spot. An enormous ant began to wiggle and jump under her fingers. Tanya looked around. She was sitting on the grass in a real, ordinary wood. Near by a large flat meadow was shining with green grass and yellow flowers. Behind the meadow you could see Tanya's garden and, in the garden, somebody was shouting in a hoarse voice: 'Tanya! Tanya! Oh my God, Tanya!'

Tanya jumped to her feet and rubbed the bite on her neck once more, no longer tiny but her normal size. Ants were running all over her arms, and something was biting her leg sharply as well. She was standing in the middle of a large ant-hill! She jumped out and dashed through the meadow towards her home.

'Here I am, Nyanechka!' shouted Tanya as she stumbled along. About ten feet away from the garden she stopped. Papa, Mama, Boba the nurse and Dianka the dog were standing by the gate. The humans were all gesticulating angrily and shouting, and Dianka was barking.

'How dare you disappear like that, you bad girl? We've been looking for you for five hours! Grab her by the ears! Into the corner with her! Whaff, whaff, whaff!' they all screamed and barked together. Tanya took a step back, but Papa came up to her, seized her by the hand and marched her into the house in a fury. Tanya was crying, Dianka yelping, the nurse wailing, Mama drumming her fingers on the table – what an infernal pandemonium!

Then the black days began. An Englishwoman arrived, old, strict and wicked, with sallow cheeks and teeth like wolves'. Not a single word of Russian did she know. In the morning she forced Tanya to wash right down to the waist, in the afternoon tortured her with lengthy dictations, and never left her alone for a minute. The worst thing was not speaking a single word of Russian. Boba the nurse was sacked; as for Papa and Mama – silence, they refused to open their mouths. When Tanya once looked as if she was going to cry, the Englishwoman screamed some impressive-sounding gibberish at the top of her horrid nasal voice, and showed such teeth that Tanya howled and ran and hid in the wardrobe.

The Englishwoman pulled her out, undressed her and made her sit in a cold bath. Tanya did not dare cry after that and merely went around with a frightened look.

And so two weeks passed by. Two hard weeks, fourteen days, during which the horrible huge teeth never ceased gleaming. Mukhomor was a sweet dream, Tanya's only consolation; but the Englishwoman so terrified her that she was afraid even to think about him. And her night-time dreams were not about mushrooms but about the terrors of teeth.

One morning Tanya woke up earlier than her tyrant, who was sleeping in the same room. She rubbed her eyes and saw the teeth lying silently at the bottom of a glass of water on the night-table. For a long time Tanya could not believe her eyes; then she climbed out of her little bed and walked over to the night-table, taking care not to make a sound. The teeth, long and terrible, were lying at the bottom of the glass and did not move. The Englishwoman was fast asleep. Tanya stood on tiptoe and blew at the water in the glass. The teeth did not move. Then she took a button-hook off the table and carefully prodded the teeth. The teeth, long and terrible, went on lying silently at the bottom of the glass and did not move. Tanya looked at the window (which, ever since the Englishwoman had moved in, was always open during the night), caught the teeth with the hook, dragged them out of the glass, ran over to the window and threw them into the water-barrel below. The teeth gurgled and disappeared.

Tanya looked for a while at where the hateful teeth used to be, wiped the hook on her nightie, put it back on the night-table and got back into bed.

My God, what a commotion there was in the morning! The Englishwoman kicked up a terrific fuss, looked in every corner, dived under the bed. Tanya made the most of it and escaped into the garden. What a joy it was, after two weeks of prison, to be free of the Englishwoman for once! Without a moment's hesitation Tanya opened the gate and ran across the meadow into the wood, towards the very tree where she had met *him* at the entrance of the kingdom. In the distance she could see the butterfly-net she'd forgotten about. Tanya stopped by the tree, which was exactly where she expected it to be, with the butterfly-net lying next to it; but there was no Mukhomor.

'*Gribochky! Gribochky!*' (my nice little mushrooms! my mushrooms!)

cried Tanya. She did not know that a mushroom's life is short, no longer than two weeks.

'Gribochek! I am coming to your kingdom,' cried Tanya and began to dig up the ground in the place where Mukhomor had once stood. But there was no sign of the entrance to the kingdom, nor of Mukhomor – only roots of trees and plants for Tanya to stumble over.

Tanya was tired and sat down. Something licked her cheek. Next to her Dianka was looking wistfully at the hole Tanya had dug. Mukhomor's kingdom had vanished into fairy tale. Tanya clasped Dianka's shaggy neck and burst into inconsolable tears.

(1917?)

(translated by Oleg Prokofiev and Christopher Palmer)

The Wandering Tower

I

Marcel Vautour was at all events a remarkable man and his name was known in the learned circles of Paris. It was possible that armchair scholars, concealing their knowledge behind dark glasses, and refined thinkers, nursing their thoughts under the domes of their high white foreheads, found him a bit of a queer fish, but they did not deny that he had a mind that was sharp and versatile, if not always surely aimed. For this reason they would smile condescendingly and say that if his mind drew him under the earth, into the depths of the Babylonian excavations, his imagination, which was far stronger, carried him above the clouds, and very often he and his opinions floated in the air, from where, as a matter of fact, they sometimes announced the most interesting things. But the important thing was that Marcel Vautour was not a burden to anyone, did not try to thrust his opinions on anyone, but would disappear for a year or two to his beloved Assyria where, with the help of wide connections and spare cash, he was able to dig about in the sands and ruins to his heart's content, find thousand-year-old tabulae with strange wedge-shaped inscriptions, decipher them, make conjectures of genius and then, returning to Paris, burst out with a brilliant article that contained the most fantastic things. The article would cause a sensation, the issue of the fashionable journal in which it had appeared would sell out, there would be exclamations in the salons and his friends would honour him with a dinner. But he did not ascend the rostra, did not enter into disputations with the men of learning, did not try to foist his opinions on anyone – and everyone was pleased, while the scholars smiled and said that of course he was clever, but floated somewhat in the air.

II

This time he got held up in Assyria not just for a year to two, but for all of five. The publishers, who had grown peckish without a resounding article, were impatiently writing telegrams now to Damascus, now to Baghdad, but he, with his small caravan, had buried himself in the sands of Ancient Mesopotamia and, wandering between the Tigris and the Euphrates, fallen entirely under the spell of the Accadians and the Sumerians, with the effaced superstitions of a once so stylish culture. It appeared that he cared more about the fate of Nebuchadnezzar than about the fate of Paris, and that he found sandy burrows more comfortable than refined drawing-rooms. But from the depths of those burrows he talked through cunning hieroglyphs with the bygone peoples that had flourished in times so remote that Marcel's ancestors, not then having yet had time to evolve from the apes, still sat on the trees that stood in the place of Paris.

One of his assistants, who had caught yellow fever and had therefore returned to his native land, related that during the past year Marcel Vautour had settled down near the site on which Ancient Babylon had sprawled and, in the grip of a persistent idea, had been trying to unearth relics of the Tower of Babel. A whole series of newspaper columns seized on this information, there was talk in the salons, but learned Assyriologists shook their heads and, smiling, said that of course it was entertaining, the Tower of Babel, but that as usual dear Marcel, together with his many-tongued edifice, was floating somewhat in the air.

When at last the five years had passed, Marcel Vautour himself came to Paris. He arrived in a private railway carriage piled to the top with boxes large and small and with some objects that were carefully packed in thick material. From the brilliant scholar who had captivated Paris he had turned into a copper saucepan burnt by the sun, and had in addition grown a beard. But the beard could not conceal the regularity of his features, and the bronze suntan merely emphasized their sharpness. The reporters at once described all this, but that was as far as they got – in the wilds of Asia our fashionable Assyriologist had lost the habit of metropolitan politeness, received not a single one of them and gave no interviews. Only to his friends did he impart the information that the results of his investigations were significant, so significant that mankind had not even dreamt of them in such a form. Right now he was tired after the journey and subject to bouts of fever, which had not spared him either, but, none the less, starting the following day, he would begin a final setting in order of the entire vast and already well-worked-through body of material he had brought with him. At the end he would give a talk about the Tower of Babel and in that talk would impart facts that might possibly upset the whole of history, astound science and, perhaps, refute the Bible itself. He spoke seriously, in businesslike fashion, without a shadow of boasting, but so tired did he look that his friends did not force their presence on him and, taking their leave, dispersed back to their salons. There they imitated the young scholar, put on a serious air and, making gestures of helplessness, exclaimed, 'Oh, our Marcel has discovered wonderful things!'

III

Evidently, the rumours about the extraordinary materials that had been dug up in the deserts of Mesopotamia, materials that threatened to cause cracks in history and even in the legends of the Bible, promised to become a most fashionable topic in the circles of curious Paris, even before their actual publication by the newly arrived scholar. But that very same night, Paris happened to receive a fright from a certain incident, and this incident affected it more closely than distant Babylon.

At exactly 3 o'clock in the morning telephones began to ring madly, ambulances were called out, medical units went speeding. It was said that somewhere houses had been destroyed – no one knew how or why – that there were human casualties and that orders had even been given for the President to be woken. Everyone had heard something, everyone was frightened, but what had happened, no one knew precisely. In such a state of mind did Paris greet the early morning.

Marcel Vautour, his hair tousled and minus his tie, rushed out of his apartment and began to descend the stairs. In the entranceway he bumped into his mother. This elderly woman, delighted by the return of her prodigal son, had just arrived from Bordeaux and was looking forward to the pleasure of an enjoyable reunion with him. But Marcel, in response to her open embraces, shouted, 'Go away! Go away! Can you not see that I am as empty as a case from which a violin has been taken?'

Gesticulating, he ran out into the street. The confused lady sank on to a chair in bewilderment, stretching out her arms to her other son, a doctor, who had come down the stairs after Marcel.

'Auguste, for God's sake . . . has he gone mad?' asked his mother.

'I myself am hurrying after him and don't understand any of it,' Auguste replied, going over to her and kissing her hands. 'He has been complaining to me that he is subject to bouts of yellow fever, but in all my practical experience I have never heard of these bouts being expressed in such a form.'

'Perhaps something has happened to his collection?'

'His collection is intact and all of it is in our house. We stayed up until 3 o'clock in the morning putting it in order.'

Mother and son sat facing each other, raising their arms in bewilderment.

IV

Marcel Vautour set off along the street and some ten minutes later found himself beside the Seine. There an enormous crowd of astonished and excited people had gathered. The Eiffel Tower, which had hitherto stood on that spot, had vanished. The public, in confusion, were trying to spot it, but the tower had vanished as though it had dissolved into thin air.

Two gentlemen in top hats, surrounded by dense rings of curious people, were relating for the tenth time what they had seen. The gentlemen were of that type of young man who go to bed in the morning and get up in the evening, are covered in goldish pimples and are for that reason called *la jeunesse dorée*.

At 3 o'clock in the morning they had been driving from Mariette to Alexandrine and had witnessed a magical scene. The Eiffel Tower had suddenly begun to tremble, then to jump up and down, had then broken loose from its foundations and begun to stride, yes, stride on all four legs, going in a direction away from the Seine. What happened after that the gentlemen had not seen, but they were so frightened that they had leapt out of their cab and, without looking round, rushed off in flight.

No sooner had Marcel Vautour heard their story than he elbowed his way out of the dense ring and set off in the direction in which the wandering tower had gone. He soon ended up in another crowd that had gathered in front of a large building which had a gaping, ruined façade. Part of the façade had been completely broken through, revealing the interiors of rooms, studies, bedrooms. In one room a table stood set for supper. Oranges were scattered over the tablecloth and the floor. It was said that several injured people had been taken away in ambulances. Evidently the tower had stepped rather clumsily and with one leg had demolished a piece of the façade.

Marcel remained in front of this building only for a minute or so, just long enough to recover his breath. Then he at once began to hurry on his way.

V

At 11 o'clock in the morning the newspapers issued special bulletins which the public bought up in literally five minutes. According to them, the tower had left the city by the shortest route, trying to step carefully, without destroying any houses. Its iron feet had landed in the middle of streets, on empty boulevards, in courtyards, and had only in a few places trodden on buildings, usually where there was nowhere else to step.

To be sure, it had most carelessly knocked its foot into the building in front of which Marcel Vautour had stopped. This building looked on to a square and it seemed that there must have been enough room around it for the tower's feet. But one must not forget that a misunderstanding of this kind had occurred at the very beginning of the tower's running, and that, one supposed, it had grown excited after breaking loose from its foundations, or had simply, never having walked before, not yet learned to control all four of its legs, and had therefore ruined the building quite needlessly, by accident.

As for those streets on which its heavy heel had fallen, there the street lamps had been bent over, the roadways had subsided; in one street it had broken through into a station of the underground railway. Here, too, one could see a charred lozenge – the remains of a flattened car that had not been fortunate enough to get out of the way of the iron foot.

As it left the city, the tower had turned straight to the south, increased its pace and disappeared over the horizon with a speed that made it resemble a vision. Such was the story told by the inhabitants of the environs of Paris.

VI

As he approached the ticket office, Marcel Vautour wondered in alarm whether he had enough money. He could not remember whether he had put his wallet in his pocket when that morning he had so hurriedly left his apartment – indeed he could remember nothing at all – but he found a few gold coins, and they were sufficient. Vautour boarded an express train and left Paris.

Huddled in a corner, he craned his neck from time to time towards the window – from where, his gaze taking on an intelligent expression, he tried to spot the tower. Not seeing it, he again dozed off in the corner and his eyes grew vacant. They were wide open and expressed nothing. In the place of Marcel Vautour sat a case from which a violin had been taken.

At 5 o'clock in the evening the train arrived at Lyons. The newspaper boys were waving cables that had just appeared and were strenuously shouting about an extraordinary occurrence. Vautour got out of the carriage and bought a newspaper.

The tower, he read, had cut through the whole of France with extraordinary speed and had already been seen in Marseilles. It had gone in a straight line, crossing rivers and breaking through forests, but avoiding towns and villages.

A whole series of cables and telephoned reports told of the wild panic that had gripped the inhabitants of those places that had been passed by this object, which hitherto had stayed quietly in Paris.

The most interesting cable was the most recent one, from Marseilles. The tower had reached the coast, and had stepped into the waters of the Mediterranean.

VII

No one knew where the runaway tower was rushing to. No one knew either what it was or what controlled its passionate running. Perhaps only one person, Marcel Vautour, could have guessed its route, which led to Ancient Babylon, but then he was only a case from which a violin had been taken, and his actions were guided not by thoughts but by mystical sounds.

Meanwhile, the tower, which had plunged into the blue waters of the Mediterranean and gauged their depth, saw that those waters were so deep that no height would be sufficient to allow it to wade across them. The Mediterranean spread like an impassable barrier across the road to Babylon. The tower would have to pick another route, and it went by land. Here it had to go not down, but up. Crossing the Swiss Alps was not as simple as running through the level greenery of the French valleys. But neither were those Alps as impassable as the Mediterranean. And the inhabitants of Switzerland saw the iron tower climbing the mountains, sliding over the ice-covered peaks, jumping in wild leaps over gorges and torrents, sometimes carefully making its way over glaciers or wading across lakes. At times it would stop, as though puzzling out the complex labyrinths of the mountain ridges and the valleys that were squeezed between them, but at other times it would walk confidently forward, following a course to the north-east and the even, comfortable expanses of Germany.

VIII

One of Vautour's Swiss friends, coming out of his villa at a run, bumped straight into Marcel. He might have been very surprised to meet the scholar in these parts, particularly if he had taken a look at his shiny, glazed eyes, but the friend was in too disturbed a state of mind to notice his surroundings.

'Go away!' he shouted, getting into his car and loading it with wife, children and trunks. 'Go away as quickly as you can! It has appeared over there! It! The tower!'

And he vanished round the bend, not offering Marcel a lift and taking a spare suitcase instead.

'Thank you,' Vautour replied after him, turning to where the tower had appeared and from where, according to his friend, he must flee.

And indeed, a man who is afraid of a tower had better run fast, because as soon as Marcel crossed the mountain it turned out to be right there. He saw before him a long, green lawn, tightly enclosed by mountain peaks, and in the middle of the lawn the tower, moving in his direction. But what an optical illusion! The landscape was so majestic, and the mountains so enormous, that the tower seemed like a miniature compared to them . . . [*Here a part of the manuscript has been lost.*] . . . the tower was moving . . . between the mountains of northern Switzerland . . . running through valleys and making its way over ridges.

Then, as though it had decided something, the tower took a turning northwards to the right, gathered its habitual monstrous speed and leapt like a whirlwind over the German border.

IX

Hardly had the telegraph announced that the tower had appeared in the north of Switzerland than the population of the German Reich was seized by panic. In Berlin a council of war was immediately assembled, at which it was decided to meet the tower with artillery. Command was entrusted to General von Magenschmerzen, whose shining glory rested on an imposing foundation of human bones.

In spite of the swiftness of the action taken by the military authorities, they could never have managed to concentrate their forces on the possible routes followed by their agile enemy.

The tower's appearance was so lightning-swift that the advanced detachments did not have time to discharge a single shot. They succeeded merely in looking round to see that the enemy was already behind them – and the warning telegrams went flying to the north, to the general, who had dug in further away, a hundred kilometres from the border.

The tower might run fast, but electricity moved faster and Magenschmerzen managed to learn of the tower's approach a whole half-hour before it appeared.

The general looked at the map, then with an experienced gaze surveyed the surrounding district and considered that, judging by the folds in the earth's surface, the tower would not escape an ambush. At an order from him, the artillery at once prepared for battle and hurried to camouflage themselves as best they could. The tower had already appeared on the horizon and was rushing straight at them. From the elevation of the nearest hill, standing beneath the cover of a small haystack, General von Magenschmerzen personally observed the monster's approach. It was rushing so swiftly that even his well-tried and faultless eye had difficulty in calculating the ever-decreasing distance.

'Fire!' General von Magenschmerzen ordered into the telephone receiver that connected him with all the batteries.

The tower rushed straight at the positions and it seemed that any experienced artilleryman could reach it with a shell as easily as one of his own hands. A deafening volley shook the neighbourhood and a grey cloud of smoke obscured everything.

Oh, that smoke! That infinite moment that separated the volley from its consequences! There could be no doubt: the tower must be bent, mutilated, smashed to pieces. It was impossible that, having survived the tremendous volley, it could step over the heads of the artillerymen as it had done over the first ambush.

But a third thing happened. Before the smoke had yet settled, before the echo of the blast had died away, a terrible whistling sound made the general look up. The tower had flown into the air in a spiral, as though it were trying to screw itself into the sky, stretched horizontally in the air and, slipping under the clouds, disappeared in the wake of the sun that had already set.

The men of the artillery detachment stood quietly, in silence, their heads raised.

'Do you see?' General von Magenschmerzen asked his adjutant, who had of course seen everything.

'I see, your Excellency,' the meticulously disciplined adjutant replied.

'Very well then, let us go and write a dispatch,' said the general, emerging from under the haystack and setting off for headquarters.

X

Without a doubt, the tower's unexpected flight into the blue expanses of the air was an event. But even more astonishing was the fact that it had nothing whatever to do with General von Magenschmerzen's volley. The volley was one thing, and the flight another, and only chance had made them happen at the same second. In order to be more precise, it needs to be stressed that the tower left the ground a moment or two before the volley, at the very moment when the general was giving his order into the telephone receiver, and the steel disgorged from the muzzles found only an empty place under the feet of the rising tower.

But there was yet a third event, which took place at the same time as the other two, and with that third event was linked the flight that had been so unexpected: Marcel Vautour took from his pocket a book bound in snakeskin, and with the words, 'Then be you accursed!' tore it into little bits.

And at that same moment his soul left the tower into which it had earlier migrated and which it had animated by its presence. And then both the tower and Marcel rushed in a straight line to Paris, the place from which the fantastic escape had begun.

That was why the tower had soared up into the air so fast and flown westward in the wake of the setting sun. That was why General von Magenschmerzen was compelled to swallow his pride when he failed to hit it with his excellently equipped guns.

XI

Late at night, when Paris was shrouded in a thick fog that had strayed over from grey London, above it flew the Eiffel Tower. Its neck was stretched forward, its four legs were pressed behind it and its iron ribs cut the air with a whistling sound. Finding itself in its customary place of residence, it rose with its head in the air, took up a vertical position and gently sank on to its old pedestal.

A man descended the staircase concealed in one of its legs and came out on to the square. It was Marcel Vautour. He set off along the Seine Embankment and turned down a sidestreet. In Marcel's waistcoat was the key to his apartment and to the outer door. No one heard him go up to his room and, half an hour later, come back out again. On his weary, baggy face were written both mental shock and great physical tiredness, and his hands smelt of kerosene. Taking a cab, Marcel set off for an hotel, obtained a room and slept like a log.

He slept so soundly that he remained unconscious through both the hubbub that arose in Paris to greet the returning tower and the news cables that reported it in the morning.

In essence, the cables that came from Switzerland were manifestly out of date, while General von Magenschmerzen's dispatches were strange and absolutely incomprehensible. As for the news from Paris itself, it only confirmed the fact of the wandering tower's return, but the details were as obscure as the fog that had shrouded Paris at the moment of its appearance. All the reports came down to the following: when with the first morning rays the foggy curtain was torn, from behind it emerged the familiar contours of the iron skeleton, standing inanimate in its old place. And although there were a great many descriptions, a whole eight pages of them, the inhabitants of Paris did not discover where the troublesome tower had come from.

At the end of the eight pages there was also a short news item that had nothing to do with the matter in hand. The item said that in the apartment of the famous Assyriologist Vautour, at night, it was thought, in his absence, a fire had broken out, destroying all the materials he had brought from Mesopotamia. The fire was so unexpected and spread with such violence that even the Assyriologist's brother only just managed to get down the stairs and away from the blazing apartment.

12 May 1918 (Trans-Siberian Express) – Omori, 27 June 1918*

(translated by David McDuff)

---

*c.f. Autobiography p. 262, final paragraph.

Misunderstandings Sometimes Occur

I

There is a railway to be built, but all the time one's thoughts are on one's wife. It is, of course, no wonder, up here in the mountains for three months now, between an unfinished bridge and a half-finished tunnel, yet even so it would do no harm to force oneself to concentrate in order to make a clean audit of the plan of additional expenditure for a level-crossing keeper's hut, just the hut that needs to be put in this place. For really, if a thing is to be done, then it should be done well – such was the principle followed by the engineer who was building this line and who, as we have just implied, had not seen his wife for three months.

To be honest, it is not true that he had not seen her for three months. Only recently he had all of a sudden thought up some urgent business on which he had set off for the city. But that journey does not count, because, in the first place, it was of brief duration – two days – and, in the second, during the whole time the engineer was in the city he had toothache, and the journey proved not to be a journey but the devil only knows what. And, generally speaking, to build a railway competently is one thing, while to be a man who is not yet particularly old and who has moreover quite recently married is another.

The engineer had turned forty. He was a nervous, lively, sensible and stubborn man. The first of the four mentioned qualities had not prevented him, thanks to the other three, from making an excellent career or from heading, in spite of his relatively youthful age, a responsible undertaking. Of course, the word 'stubborn' should be understood not so much in a bad sense as in a good one. That is to say, if, for example, he met a mountain in the way, he would not go round it but would drill a tunnel through it, and if that tunnel were to prove to cost a million more than a roundabout route, he would dig in his heels and insist that a million be allocated to the tunnel. But such stubbornness also had its other side.

Thus, for example, if one has a toothache there is really no point in

210

making a journey to see one's wife, but he went all the same. Well, and the journey proved not to be a journey at all, but, as we have already had the honour to express it, the devil only knows what.

A hut must be planned for this place without fail. And attached to it, a small meteorological station must be set up. At first they will be unhappy about the additional expenditure, but then they will be grateful. And to force oneself to concentrate on the project is also not really so difficult. A wife, a wife – thank God, he is not a little boy and is able to pull himself together. But here there is one more attendant circumstance, namely, a light-blue envelope that, opened, lies on the table. From that same wife. And inside it says that she has resolved to surmount the difficult journey along the mountain roads (to be more precise, along the mountain lack of roads) and tomorrow expects to come and stay with him for three days, taking advantage of Monsieur Kakadu's kind company and the fact that he has offered her his assistance and services during this dreadful journey.

Now a piece of news like this gives birth within the mind and heart to a whole network of the most confused sensations. In the first place, what is Monsieur Kakadu doing here, why has he got mixed up in this affair? Until now Kakadu, as one of the less important engineers on the same construction site, has been in charge of putting the tunnel in final order, of, as it were, polishing the structures and licking them clean on the inside. A week ago he went away on leave, but now he is coming back again, together with his boss's wife. After all, one needs to know what Kakadu is. In the first place, he is a Belgian, and all Belgians and Frenchmen are excellent engineers, but even better admirers of other men's wives. In the second place, one need only take a look at him: cute, dark-complexioned, with languishing eyes, a *pince-nez* piquantly planted on his nose, his necktie piquantly stuck with a pin – a sight quite simply revolting to behold, and if the stubborn engineer tolerated such a subordinate, then it was only because the latter was a businesslike and knowledgeable fellow. But now the dear, businesslike chap was beginning to demonstrate his businesslike qualities in another field as well: just look – he is busy delivering a wife for his boss! And above all, where he is taking her – beyond the clouds, over a most mountainous pass – there are no roads of any kind. The most frightful back of beyond. The workmen and engineers live in hastily knocked-together barracks, there are no villages around, and even the mail is delivered only three times a week, with the help of a donkey and an old postman who arrives riding it. When the tunnel is opened the journey through it will be much shorter and more convenient. For the present, however, one must cross the mountain with inconveniences. And no matter how many times the engineer had hinted to his wife that, in his opinion, she might sometimes be able to come and visit her husband, that woman had always exclaimed, 'My dear, why, I should die of heart failure were I to climb such a steep slope!'

And then, all of a sudden, thanks to Monsieur Kakadu's charming good offices, there proved to be neither heart failure nor terrible steep slope, but simply and without further ado: 'Tomorrow I am coming to stay with you for three days.' Either the piquant *pince-nez* had played a role here (and, perhaps, something else that was piquant as well), or . . . she really was missing her husband very much.

The engineer caught himself up, reflecting that in all conscience he was being unfair to his wife and that, even if Kakadu did look like a scoundrel, his wife had during all three years of their married life conducted herself in exemplary fashion. She was from a patriarchal, very moral family, and so she had missed her husband and simply overcome her fear, particularly since Kakadu, for the pleasure of taking a drive with a pretty woman, had of course depicted the road as a flat tablecloth.

After all, indeed, he himself, her husband, was a man, and not a bad one either, and his wife had sufficient good taste not to pay more attention to some piquant tie-pin than to a convenient travelling companion.

The engineer went into his room in one of the barracks, and there he began to feel quite pleasantly cheerful. Although the barrack was a shambles, the engineer had spread and hung his room with rugs, and in the middle had placed an enormous leather armchair – spacious and comfortable, exactly as though it were meant for two (himself and his wife, for example). And on the whole, he reflected that if she were to come here for two or three days, that would be a very, very attractive prospect. The engineer rubbed his hands together and, having made several calculations regarding the cost of the hut and the meteorological station, went to bed.

II

Next day, at noon, Lili arrived, muffled in a large blue scarf, together with Kakadu, who was wearing high yellow boots and an especially piquantly angled tie-pin. Lili was terribly sweet, and not without tenderness did the engineer exchange kisses with her, shaking hands with Monsieur Kakadu rather sincerely, in gratitude for such an agreeable present. But one look at his bristling moustache was enough for him to realize beyond all doubt that this rascally scoundrel had made such an effort in order to ingratiate himself with his boss, and in order to hang around a pretty skirt.

Kakadu at once bowed and scraped, kissed *Madame*'s hand and set off for his tunnel in order to check that all was in order there. As for the engineer, he took his wife's hand, led her to his rug-spread room, lunched with her, *tête-à-tête*, then walked in her company over the new bridge, showed her the place where the hut and meteorological station were to be put – and, all told, permitted himself not to fatigue himself with work that afternoon, and spent the whole day so pleasantly that he did not notice night had fallen.

We shall not, of course, be indiscreet, for what can be more indiscreet than to go meddling in the married lives of others – but shall permit ourselves to suppose that after we, at nightfall, left the engineer and his Lili, they passed their time no less pleasantly than during the daytime, and perhaps even more so. The fact was that Kakadu had receded into the background and the engineer was finally convinced that all his suspicions of his sweet Lili were nothing but a vain and unworthy false accusation.

All the more unpleasant was it when at 4 o'clock in the morning the engineer received a knock at his door and was requested to come out as quickly as possible. The engineer cursed the devil, threw on his coat and stuck his nose round the door. Outside it was neither light nor dark, the dawn had barely broken, and indoors it was so nice and warm! It turned out, however, that one of the mountain rivulets, which a few days earlier had had its course blocked off by a dam in order to direct it through a stone pipe under the embankment, had burst the dam and was threatening to cause trouble.

The engineer might love his Lili any amount, but he was a man of action, and so he at once got dressed, kissed her sweet forehead and went outside. Kakadu and all the engineers were already up and about and, together with the workmen, had set off for the site of the accident.

Thus for both the end of the night, and the morning, everything was spoiled. The wretched little stream proved to be turbulent and wayward, and it took a whole eight hours to put it in order. Only towards lunchtime did the engineer and some of the workmen return, and Kakadu even stayed behind there, to make sure that a similar incident did not occur again.

Lili had woken up only a short time earlier and was hungry. The engineer at once arranged for lunch to be served, ate it with her, again *tête-à-tête*, and after lunch, making themselves comfortable on a rug, they smoked perfumed cigarettes and dreamt of how good it would be when the construction work was at an end, of how they would buy a small villa near Monte Carlo and of the charming wistarias that may be cultivated there.

Then the engineer was brought the accounts of the payment of the workmen's wages, whereupon he had to tear himself away from his pleasant talk and occupy himself with business instead. Lili, who had not yet had a walk, went outside in order to take a little fresh air, while the engineer settled down in the armchair and unfolded the papers.

He was dreadfully sleepy. Since he had been woken up in the middle of the night and had spent eight hours working on the dam, this was not at all surprising. And if one considers the fact that during the first half of the night he had, in Lili's company, slept not entirely serenely, it will at once be clear that he began the scrutiny of his business in a drowsy fashion. However, he pulled himself together, roused himself, furrowed his brow and, finally throwing off his sleepiness, plunged into the familiar region of complicated figures.

III

A certain thought suddenly cut through his head. His wife had gone for a walk, and somewhere there, at the dam, was Kakadu. Perhaps they had now met and were kissing each other.

So graphically did the engineer imagine this scene to himself that at the very same moment, without remembering how, he found himself outside, and set off between the barracks in the direction of the bridge. He did not even realize that the bridge was situated in a completely different place from the dam where Kakadu was. But instinct did not deceive, as it never ever deceives, and as he approached the river he saw, at the foot of the bank under the protectorate of a newly erected granite pier, Lili sitting on a stone and, on her knees – no, can one imagine anything more shameful? – Kakadu sitting on her knees, with both arms around her neck and kissing her on the lips in the most long-drawn-out manner! The engineer had genuine convulsions. He very nearly rushed in a straight line at the depraved couple, but suddenly he felt so ashamed of his wife, so embarrassed by her shameless pose, that somehow he involuntarily staggered back, backed away behind the barrack and from there, through the doorway, edged his way along to his room. There he awkwardly, sideways, clambered into the big armchair, thrust . . . [*The end of chapter III is missing from the manuscript.*]

IV

Next day the engineer's heart was as empty as the Gobi desert. All that had filled it in recent days had been torn out at one go, and by the roots, moreover, and in the place of flowering tenderness there spread a dry and colourless sand. Even the work itself was repulsive and had lost its savour. The construction must be finished as quickly as possible, or as a last resort the direction would have to be entrusted to someone else, since the main part of the work had already been done, and he must go elsewhere. That Kakadu with his meticulous reports, and that bridge with its granite piers – truly, to look at them was to hold the blade in the wound it had made.

In such thoughts did the day go by and the following one begin. The engineer deeply despised his wife, an unprincipled woman who had sat that vile wearer of tie-pins on her knee, and reflected that only his own infinite gentlemanly nature had saved them from the well-earned consequences.

Parallel to the thoughts about his gentlemanly nature, or, more correctly, perpendicular to them, there also appeared ideas such as: 'Just you wait, Lili. When I finish work, I'll go to the Princes Islands [Kızıl Adalar]. I'll buy a harem and then we shall see. You deal me one, I'll deal you five. Five to one, that's my style. Only the Eastern woman is truly able to love, there is the true, languorous sultriness, not among you, European cripples who have rivets where your hearts ought to be. A small harem of five. Not one of them older than fifteen. And a villa with marble steps leading straight down to the Sea of Marmara.'

The engineer went outside and saw the old postman and his donkey; both had brought the mail. From the Sea of Marmara the engineer's thoughts swiftly returned to the mainland: two days ago the postman had taken Lili to the city, and he could be asked a few questions. The engineer could find out whether his wife had reached her home again, for decency positively demanded this.

'Are there any letters, old man?' the engineer asked.

'There's not a single one for you, Mr Engineer,' the old man replied, pretending to be very saddened by this.

'What a pity!' the engineer said, affecting a jocular annoyance. 'But at any rate you delivered my wife back safely?'

'In the best condition, Mr Engineer.'

'Well, thank you.' And, trying to maintain his jocular note, he threw out a question as though it were of no significance. 'So your bag is light today? You have brought no one the happiness of a letter?'

'Almost no one, there are two letters for you all,' replied the postman, who was used to everyone being hugely pleased when he appeared and to their joking with him.

'Is one of them for Mr Kakadu?' the engineer could not refrain from asking. (This was simply stupid.)

'No, there is nothing for Mr Kakadu either.'

Through the engineer's head flashed: 'Oh, he's lying, the old fox! My wife is bound to have written to Kakadu in order to tell him about the scene she had with her husband. And of course she hasn't sent it by mail but has entrusted it personally to the postman for secret delivery. And now this old dodderer, in return for a gold coin, is acting all innocence, while I am compelled to play the cuckolded husband and fool.' Filled with indignation, the engineer abruptly turned on his heel and began to stride off in the direction of the barrack. But then he felt a desire to find fault with the postman.

'And why, good sir, why did you not deliver my newspapers last time?' he asked sternly, remembering that there had indeed for some reason been no sign of any newspapers.

'There were newspapers and I delivered them to you,' the postman replied.

The engineer was not expecting to be contradicted, and so he at once felt an attack of bile.

'I suppose you are going to tell me that you delivered them right into my hands?' he asked sharply.

The old man, surprised by such a tone, passed his hand across his beard, but then, remembering something, smiled.

'Did you not see them, Mr Engineer? I put them on your writing desk. Don't be angry, Mr Engineer, but you were asleep, and I did not want to wake you up.'

In other words, insolence upon insolence and lie upon lie. So the engineer thought.

'What, sir, did you come to me by night, then? I am a busy man and cannot sleep during the day.'

The postman was very unhappy that a conflict should have suddenly arisen. He was too used to the joyful smiles and the silver coins he was given in exchange for agreeable letters, and in the present instance it was abundantly clear that the engineer's anger was based on a misunderstanding.

The old man said, conciliatorily, 'Mr Engineer, there is no reason for you to be annoyed. I know that you have a lot of work to do, and so it's a very good thing for you to take a rest in the middle of the day. But I swear to God that when I came into your room you were fast asleep in your armchair. In order not to wake you, I put the newspapers on your writing desk. They are probably still there now.'

'Is that so?' said the engineer, his manner overbearing. 'Will you please be so good as to follow me into my barrack?'

And he went on ahead. The postman followed him.

Indeed, on one side of the writing desk there turned out to be two fresh newspapers. Because of his marital discord the engineer had been so absent-minded that he had not once touched his writing desk.

'And you assert that at the time you put them on the table I was fast asleep in the armchair?'

'In this one,' said the postman, pointing to the armchair, and remembering something even more amusing he broke into a good-natured smile. 'You were having a very bad dream,' he said, 'because you were angry in your sleep and once even said: "Scoundrel!" And your papers were scattered around your chair.'

The engineer was dumbfounded. It turned out that his wife's unfaithfulness was something he had dreamt. Tired after his work on the dam, he had fallen asleep over the checking of the accounts, and jealousy had incited him to a treacherous dream.

'And you heard me say "Scoundrel" in my sleep?' the engineer asked, his voice breaking.

'Yes, I did. And then you stretched out your leg and said, "Oh, you vile woman!"'

'And all of it in my sleep?'

'Yes, sir.'

'And you stood there admiring the performance?'

The postman was embarrassed.

'I left at once,' he said.

The engineer began to shake with indignation. He seemed to become transformed into a cloud stuffed with thunder and lightning.

'Do you know what you are? You are a simulator and a loathsome mystifier!' he cried. 'A simulator and a mystifier!'

The old man backed away, unable to believe his ears.

'I?' he whispered, not understanding the words that were being thrown at him, but sensing that in them something very offensive was concealed. 'I a simu . . . and mysti . . . mysti . . .'

'Fier! Fier! Fier!' shouted the engineer. He was beside himself. He had set too much store by his own nobleness of character and the unfaithfulness of that base woman to be able to believe that in this whole episode he alone was to blame.

The postman mournfully threw up his hands and went out of the barrack, leaving the enginer in the company of his anger and his treacherous dream.

26 May, Vladivostok – Kyoto,* 18 June 1918

(translated by David McDuff)

* Prokofiev arrived in Tokyo on 1 June 1918 and spent over two months in Japan. He probably docked in San Francisco in late August, for he had reached New York by early September.

The Two Marquises
(fragment)

I

'Very well then,' muttered the Marquis ill-humouredly, 'give it to me and I'll sign it.' He stretched out his hand for the goose-quill.

'Yes, sign, sign, your Excellency!' said the moneylender, with slightly more familiarity than was proper. 'You mustn't think I'm overcharging and be angry with me. I do charge, but not at all excessively.'

'One hundred per cent interest not excessive?'

'Oh, now, your Excellency,' smiled the moneylender, 'supposing it were not one hundred per cent but two hundred per cent? Go on, sign it, sign it!' he went on, once again a little too condescendingly. 'The *chervontsy* I'm giving you are not wood but gold; they shine like firelight and ringle-tingle like little bells.'

'They wouldn't dare not to,' said the Marquis, striking a flourish with his pen and handing over the bill.

The moneylender took hold of the document and carefully scrutinized his Excellency's autograph. 'Good, that's fine,' he said and, folding the bill in half and then in half again, he squatted down in front of a heavy iron trunk. His sparse hair, probably caught by the breeze, seemed to stick out more repulsively than ever from his skull as he bent over the trunk. He unfastened the lock with a huge key; it snapped open with a loud report. He lifted the lid slightly, dived inside and reappeared with four little packs of gold coins. The *chervontsy* were, indeed, most greatly to be desired; they shone a reddish-gold colour and rang like little bells. 'Count 'em, your Excellency; fifty in each.'

The Marquis took out a large leather purse in which a mere five *chervontsy* sat clinging forlornly to each other – the sum of his noble capital. He stowed the gold away inside, uncounted, with an indifferent gesture. 'Goodbye,' he said standing up, 'and thank you.'

'Always your Excellency's most devoted servant,' replied the moneylender; he bowed, not without humour, and added, again with a touch of condescension bordering on impertinence, 'and may Destiny send you a good hand.'

The Marquis was greatly tempted to tell him to mind his own business, but bethought himself that the man might well prove useful to him in the future, so he simply shrugged his shoulders and left. The moneylender saw him out and, though the Marquis didn't look round, for politeness' sake stood for a while by the door until he disappeared round a corner.

'Of course one hundred per cent *is* a good rate,' thought the moneylender, 'but he could easily have a hundred per cent win, too, on what I've just lent him.'

If he were willing to lend as much gold as he had today it was because up to now the Marquis had paid up on time. Presumably he would continue to do so. And scratching his head the moneylender got out a pot and started to make himself soup. 'For a good hand!' he muttered, throwing in some barley.

It has to be said that the respectable moneylender was wrong in thinking that the Marquis wanted the money for playing at cards. Of course the Marquis, just like any other ordinary person, would not have been at all averse to putting a pile of ringing gold coins on a card of seven and doubling it on the same card, but at present gambling was not a priority; he needed the money to settle some old debts. To come into a beautiful pile of cheery *chervontsy* and to dispose of it in such a stolid and unimaginative way as to pay off old creditors with it – how appalling! But the Marquis had a clear, unspotted reputation and didn't want to soil it. A great thing, a good name, especially when it came to acquiring money the way the Marquis went about it. And this way was tried and true and very simple. You borrowed money from one moneylender, and having spent it repaid it with money borrowed from another. Then from moneylender number two you went to number three, then back to one to repay three. Then to repay one you got half from number two and half from number four. Since the amounts outstanding constantly doubled and built up into awesome sums, new loans had to be raised piecemeal from different sources. You had to be discreet yet importunate and constantly widen your circle of those in a position to give credit. The annoying thing was, that these moneylenders half-killed you with their shamelessly exorbitant interest rates, so more went on paying interest than on the business of living. But somehow money came out of nowhere and it *was* possible, without undue effort, to live comfortably as a gentleman should. As to the fact that the debt was snowballing all the time, and one day would need to be taken in hand with drastic measures – the Marquis remained quite unconcerned. Why worry? You'll find a way out. There are many possibilities, surely – a rich bride, a large windfall or perhaps an inheritance from an uncle. Indeed there actually *was* such an uncle – old, childless and rich. And if all else failed, a bullet through the brain would do the trick – either yours or your uncle's. Not that difficult – hunting, at home, or admiring the family rifle in his presence.

The oil caught fire and made a stink, and the moneylender threw the window open in annoyance. However, not much fresh air got in through it so the 'respectable man' decided to have his meal in the open. He opened the door and sat down in the doorway. His home was in the suburbs, where there were more heaths and fences than houses. Not, you might think, a very good situation for a trunk full of *chervontsy*; but that would be to leave out of account the time-honoured custom whereby if a robber were caught he would lose his head, a thief merely his hand. For this reason both robbers and thieves were few in number and the iron trunk might guard its treasure undisturbed.

'Good day, your Excellency.' The moneylender got up and bowed. Another Marquis, taller than the first, was passing by.

The tall Marquis looked coldly at the moneylender and turned away. He had just encountered the first Marquis and gathered he had just been to the moneylender's. The rich jackal had skinned yet another of his victims. 'The good-for-nothing!' thought the tall Marquis and determined to pass straight on by. But at that very moment his heel caught on a stone and came off. The Marquis stumbled, stopped and picked up the heel.

'What your Excellency needs is a hammer and a nail,' exclaimed the moneylender. 'Just a moment!' – and, making a great show and fuss, disappeared into his house.

The tall Marquis, heel in hand, sat down on a stone and took off his boot. The moneylender returned. 'A hammer and a nail for your Excellency!' he repeated, pride and triumph in his voice.

'Go away!' snapped the tall Marquis, without looking up, trying to attach the heel to its former place. The nails were still in the heel so, not unsuccessfully, he began to knock them back in with the same stone that had tripped him up.

'Much better if your Excellency used the hammer and a new nail,' said the moneylender.

The tall Marquis gave him an impatient look.

'I told you to go away!' he barked angrily. 'There's your house – go back inside!'

The moneylender withdrew the arm with which he was proffering the hammer and cast down his eyes. His gestures said very plainly: I try to help you and you repay me with an insult.

The Marquis looked him up and down and said disdainfully, 'I accept help only from my friends, not from poisonous insects like you,' and turned back to trying to repair his boot.

The moneylender replied, 'Your Excellency is over-harsh in his criticism. I do my best to help people.'

So indignant was the Marquis on hearing this that the hand holding the boot dropped it.

'*You* help people! You suck their blood and their souls. You send them to prison. I can name two unfortunate men whose lives you ruined for not keeping up with your insane interest rates. Deny it if you can!'

'No, to my great regret I can't deny it,' replied the moneylender with humility, 'but they were criminals who tried to do me out of my savings.'

'And what are your savings but other people's money, money you cheated other people out of? Or perhaps it's the fruit of your honest work? A hundred per cent? You wait, my friend, they'll catch up with you. The rope has been crying out for you for years on end.'

'Everybody has to make a living as best he can,' said the moneylender, 'and to say that a rope, of all things – '

' – is singing for you loud and clear, my dear fellow,' the Marquis interrupted, 'singing its song clear as can be.' He got so excited he threw away his heel and put his boot on without it. 'What a pity our Bishop's so old. You really ought to be dealt with by him. You've got some pretty dark secrets locked up in your cupboards, even worse than your moneylending. There are all sorts of nasty rumours flying around about you. Why else do you think respectable people avoid your house and cross themselves if they pass it in the night?'

'And does arrogance and oh-such-a-ready-wit really get you that much further?' asked the moneylender.

Such a riposte took the Marquis completely by surprise, especially the sarcasm. It was as if someone had attacked the mirror of his soul with a blunt knife. He turned pale and seized the handle of his sword. 'Get out of my sight,' he shouted, 'or I'll run this right through your flabby stomach!'

Things were getting quite nasty. The moneylender stumbled up the steps, lurched through the door and locked it from the inside. Then he banged windows and shutters and turned more keys in locks. 'Can't make things too secure when you've got noblemen about, ranting and raving.'

The tall Marquis spat in his direction – much as you might after a devil who'd just vanished in a puff of smoke – and limped away on his heel-less boot. He was a man of principle and highly excitable, and took the whole business very much to heart.

II

In the evening the Marquis – not the one who spat at the moneylender's door but the other, the one who earlier that day had received the 200 gold coins – started putting his cloak on, preparatory to visiting moneylender number eight. So those ringing *chervontsy* weren't to stay in his possession very long; but if one repaid one's debts promptly more money would be forthcoming. In fact the payment didn't fall due for another two days, but the Marquis always tried to behave like a gentleman and pay in advance.

The Marquis draped himself in his black cloak and went out into the street. Number eight lived in a densely populated part of the town where one was liable to bump into acquaintances – which for various reasons the Marquis was most anxious not to do. That was why he pulled his hat well down over his eyes and followed the boulevard by various roundabout ways where it was dark and where the few oncoming pedestrians flitted by like shadows. 'This way I'm just another shadow,' thought the Marquis, quite pleased to feel the heavy weight of the purse pressing against his thigh. But alas! In a mere hour's time the sum of the last loan would have dwindled to a mere quintet of *chervontsy*, five only; and this thought filled the tender heart of the Marquis with sorrow.

Suddenly a black cat jumped out from a rubbish-bin and flashed across the Marquis's path. 'Oh no,' exclaimed the Marquis, 'I can't *stand* black cats! The idea of one of those creatures running across my path! Ugh!'

It was quiet and dark on the boulevard. Further off in a side-street the lights of the entrance to the club shone out welcomingly. 'What a pity the gold is already spoken for,' mused the Marquis. 'How handy it would come in for a nice evening at the tables over there . . . But to hell with it! I'll play when I've got the money and not before!' – and went on his way.

The cat squawked and screeched, leapt out of the bushes and went galloping off in front: probably a tom-cat was after her. The Marquis stopped and swore. 'Damn thing, rushing around all over the place! Whether you believe in portents or not, it's disgusting to see a black horror like that fouling the street.'

He looked at the brightly lit entrance to the club. 'I wonder . . . is it worth it? There are still two days to go before my time is up. If I were to lose the money there'd still be a chance to win it back or even to borrow more. With so much to place on a bet I'd stand to win a lot. I'd stand to lose a lot as well. No! *This* gold is to repay a debt, and repay it I will!'

The Marquis had an unblemished name and that meant a lot to him. One late repayment would be enough to spoil everything in his eyes, and he would never forgive himself. He wrapped his cloak tightly round him and resolutely walked on.

One step: good. Two. Three. Four, five, six, seven, eight, nine, ten, eleven, twelve, all right. Then, on the thirteenth, he stumbled across something round and small, and the cat, miaowing in bitter protest, shot out from underneath him into the bushes.

'Ugh, you spawn of Satan!' cried the startled Marquis; then, reflecting a moment, muttered 'Must be fate. There'll be a good card.' He abruptly turned on his heel and walked back in the direction of the club, ponderously and confidently: the purse of gold gave him an air of importance. In a side-room he glimpsed the profile of the tall Marquis. About ten people were standing round his table. The first Marquis's face brightened up: the other was a rich man, and since he was playing cards, what better than to play with him?

'Allow me to put this on two hundred and three,' said the first Marquis politely. He was thinking that two cards would do the trick and make a nice round sum!

But the tall Marquis knew where the money had come from and said, 'Excuse me, but I'm afraid I can't give you those cards.'

'What do you mean, you can't?' said the Marquis, a voice inside him telling him in a loud whisper that all the money lying on the table was destined for him.

'I'm sorry, but I can't give them to you,' said the tall Marquis.

The situation was becoming rather embarrassing for the other Marquis; indeed he began to feel he was being insulted. But worst of all was the idea that in being refused the cards he was simply being cheated out of money due to him.

'Perhaps you might explain to me, Monsieur le Marquis, why you're acting so ungraciously?'

'I have no wish to increase the stakes, that's all.'

'But excuse me, with so much of my money on the table you cannot refuse me. Is it something personal?' He was now getting very excited, feeling sure they were trying to prevent him getting what was his by right, so convinced he was that he would win.

The tall Marquis looked at the moneylender's money and pulled a face. 'Very well then, if you insist, yes, it *is* something personal.'

The other Marquis flushed. 'In that case perhaps you will be kind enough to give me satisfaction in another way?' he asked sharply . . .

New York, 20 October 1918*

(translated by Oleg Prokofiev and Christopher Palmer)

---

* The day before – 19 October – Prkfv had been due to make his New York début as a solo pianist. He cancelled because of illness: did he perhaps, in no mood for music, turn to writing for something to do (he could never bear to be inactive)? He recovered in time to give the postponed concert on 29 October at the Brooklyn Museum.

AUTOBIOGRAPHY

INTRODUCTORY NOTE

Prokofiev wrote two autobiographies, the 'long' and the 'short'. The 'long', enormously detailed, covers only his childhood and early student years (as far as July 1909). It was first published in a shortened version in Russia in 1973 and in America (yet further abbreviated) as *Prokofiev by Prokofiev* in 1979. The 'short' autobiography was written in 1941 and first published complete in 1956 in the Schlifstein compilation already referred to in connection with the Soviet Diary 'postscripts'. Here again the translator was Rose Prokofieva (who, incidentally, also translated the very first – 1946 – English edition of Israel Nestyev's book on the composer, the Russian original of which, so mysteriously, never appeared in Russia at all). For this edition the translation has been extensively revised and corrected with the assistance of David Mather, who has also provided many of the footnotes.

Regrettably the autobiography breaks off in 1937 in the midst of preparations for the twentieth anniversary of the Bolshevik Revolution and the Pushkin Centenary. But even had time permitted, the years between 1941 and 1953 – when he died – were both personally and professionally so embattled for Prokofiev he could probably never have written about them with the candour which is such an attractive feature of the chapters he did complete.

C.P.

Autobiography

I EARLY YEARS

I was born in the village of Sontsovka, Ekaterinoslav Guberniya, now Dnepropetrovsk Region, at 5 p.m. on Wednesday 11 April 1891, Old Style, or 23 April according to the new calendar.

My father, a Moscovite by birth and a graduate of the Petrovsko-Razumovsky Agricultural Academy, was manager of a huge estate in the steppes belonging to the Sontsov family. My mother played the piano quite well: chiefly Beethoven and Chopin, which gave me a taste for serious music from early childhood. At the age of three I struck my forehead against the edge of an iron chest and raised a bump that lasted for about twenty-five years. 'Perhaps all your talent lies in that bump,' remarked an artist who painted my portrait many years later. I used to listen with keen and even critical interest to my mother's playing. 'I like that little song,' I would announce when something took my fancy. At night I often fell asleep to the strains of a Beethoven sonata being played by my mother four rooms away from mine. When my mother played her exercises she allowed me to tap out my childish experiments in the two upper octaves. The noise was rather frightful, but my mother knew what she was doing, for before long I was sitting down at the piano by myself, trying to pick out some tune. When I was five and a half I picked out a little tune and played it several times over. My mother decided to write it down – quite a difficult task for her since she had never written music before. It was in F major without a B flat, which was no indication of my preference for the Lydian mode but rather of my reluctance to tackle the black notes. But in writing it down my mother told me it would sound better with a 'little black note', and she accordingly put it in. I called my piece the *Indian Galop*, an absurd title, evidently suggested by the famine in India which everyone was talking about at that time. The newspapers were full of it and I must have heard the grown-ups discussing it at home.

The process of writing down the music impressed me greatly, and I soon learned to 'write music' myself. At the age of six I wrote a waltz, a march and a rondo, and at seven a march for four hands. I enjoyed playing that march and hearing how all the different parts sounded when played together. After all, it was my first score.

My mother took great pains with my musical education. She believed that a child should be kept interested and not repelled by tiresome exercises, and that a minimum of time should be spent on scales so as to leave as much time as possible for reading music. At first my music lessons lasted exactly twenty minutes, and my mother took care never to exceed that time limit. She led me through the musical course of Strobel and von Ark, allowing me to play a vast number of compositions and discussing them with me, encouraging me to say why I liked or disliked one piece or another. In this way I learned to form independent judgments at an early age. The system had its disadvantages, of course – I never learned any piece properly, my playing became careless, and not enough attention was paid to the proper hand position, a fault it took me many years to overcome.

When I was eight I visited Moscow with my parents and was taken to see *Faust, Prince Igor* and *Sleeping Beauty*. I was particularly impressed by *Faust*, especially the March and Waltz, which I had learned at home, the duel scene and Mephistopheles ('a lovely Devil, but naked and without a tail'). When we returned to Sontsovka I said to my mother, 'I'm going to write my own opera.' 'How can you say that when you know you cannot do anything of the kind?' my mother chided. But I had already thought of a subject for an opera and I got to work at once. Where did the subject come from? Evidently it was invented in much the same way as the plots for the children's plays my playmates and I often used to put on at home. This is approximately what would happen: 'Stenya,' I would say, 'you're sitting and reading a book. All of a sudden a giant passes by. You look up and ask in a frightened voice, "Who goes there?" And he answers, "It's me, and I've come to get you." At that moment Yegorka and I rush in with our pistols.' 'Yes, and I fall down in a faint,' Stenya would add. And so it would go on.

In writing the music I still confused the rhythm and metre; I did not write the voice part separately but inserted it in the double-stave score after the manner of the numerous piano arrangements of operas we had in the house. In June 1900 the opera *The Giant*, in three acts and six scenes, was performed with great success for a select family audience.

This inspired me to write another opera – I called it *Desert Islands*. The subject was childish in the extreme: a ship is wrecked in a storm and the heroes are washed ashore on a desert island. The story did not hang together very well, but there was an attempt to depict the elements, the storm and rain, in the music. I worked on this opera on and off for a year and a half, but did not get beyond the overture and the first act which consisted of three scenes; true, each scene was almost as long as the whole of *The Giant*.

In the summer of 1901 I went to my uncle's estate for a visit. My cousins played the piano quite well and one of them was learning to sing, and so it was decided to put on a performance of *The Giant*. Cousin Andrey played the piano, substituting for an orchestra, I sang the leading role, my female cousin was the heroine and my aunt put on a pair of top boots and played the Giant. By evening only the first act had been learned. I was wild with excitement and impatience. 'We'd better play as much as we have learned so far, or the excitement will make him ill,' my mother said. And so we put on our make-up and costumes, the 'audience' took their seats in the hall and Andrey played the overture. Although I had directed the rehearsal and taught everyone their parts I was so nervous that when I came out on to the stage I began to sing the wrong part. 'You're singing my part,' hissed cousin Shurik and, skilfully picking up the tune, saved the situation. My uncle was very pleased with the performance. 'When your operas are performed on the imperial stage,' he said, 'remember that your first opera was staged in my house.'

In January 1902 I went to Moscow for the second time. There I met Yury, a very pleasant young man of about twenty, the nephew of the Pomerantsevs who were friends of my parents. Yury was studying composition under Taneev (he later became conductor of the Bolshoi Theatre orchestra), and he introduced me to the composer. Taneev was very kind to me, a trifle bantering in his manner, but on the whole not at all frightening. There was a bar of chocolate lying on the table, I recall, and he offered me some at once. I played him the overture to *Desert Islands*, not a very happy choice because it was rather flabby and not at all the best part of the opera. Taneev advised me to make use of my stay in Moscow to study theory with Pomerantsev. 'Above all don't let him overwork himself,' he cautioned my mother as we took our leave. Thus began my lessons in harmony with Pomerantsev. They seemed quite senseless to me. I wanted to compose operas full of marches, storms and blood-curdling scenes, and instead I got saddled with all sorts of tiresome nonsense.

In the summer of the same year, R. M. Glière came to Sontsovka on the recommendation of Taneev. A born teacher, Glière skilfully combined instruction in harmony with free composition and a study of the elements of form and orchestration. And when lessons were over he was not averse to playing a game of chess or croquet, or accepting a challenge to a duel with toy pistols. In this way he quite won my heart. He taught me song form, thus laying the foundation for a series of piano pieces which I wrote regularly over a period of about six years at the rate of about a dozen a year and under the rather inappropriate title of *Little Songs*. Playing a Beethoven sonata, Glière would give me a rough outline of sonata form, and whenever we came across a phrase characteristic of one or another instrument in a symphony orchestra, he would say, 'Now this melody could be played by a flute; the fanfare could be given to the trumpet, and in a lower register to two French horns,' etc. Of course this was only a preliminary introduction to orchestration, but many of the examples he gave me remained in my memory, so that when I went to town that autumn and heard a symphony orchestra I was already able to distinguish the different timbres. At all events that same summer I insisted on writing a symphony. After some hesitation Glière agreed, and by the time he left me in August a four-movement symphony in G major was written and half of it orchestrated. In November I showed the symphony to Taneev. We played it in a four-hand arrangement, Taneev playing the accompaniment. He praised the counterpoint (which Glière had inserted in the development), but remarked that the harmony was a little too crude. 'Mostly I, IV and V,' he said, and laughed. I was deeply offended. Not that I cried or lost any sleep over it, but somewhere the thought that my harmony was crude rankled. The seed had been planted and a long period of germination began. It was not until four years later that my harmonic experiments began to be noticed, and when some eight years later I played Taneev my *Etudes* op. 2 and he grumbled, 'Far too many wrong notes,' I reminded him of what he had said that time. Clutching his head in mock horror he exclaimed, 'So it was I who launched you on that slippery path!'

On returning to Sontsovka I composed a violin sonata, of which only the principal theme of the first movement remained and was used ten years later in the Ballade for cello op. 15. The three bars of the introduction and the first five bars of the theme are identical in both compositions, but further on the Ballade is more complex. Thus the first theme of the Ballade, composed at the age of eleven, is the earliest of my published works with an opus number.

The following summer Glière came to Sontsovka again. Under his guidance I wrote an opera on the subject of Pushkin's *Feast During the Plague*. This time it was a real opera, with vocal parts, orchestral score and an overture in sonata form. The overture was too long for a one-act opera, rather like a large head on a small body, but technically it was a step forward compared with the symphony of the previous year. For a number of years I was unable to improve on it, since it had been composed under Glière's direct supervision, whereas later on I worked quite independently.

On returning to Moscow Glière sent me the piano score of Cui's opera on the same subject (*Feast During the Plague*). I examined it eagerly with a jealous and critical eye. I found that Mary's song was written in the same key and the same time-signature as mine, and even the melodies were similar. Of course Cui's was a masterly job compared with mine, but I did not realize that at the time. 'This isn't very nice,' I said to my mother. 'Let me play you the way I have it. There, don't you like mine better?' 'Of course,' my mother replied out of politeness. 'Only do try not to play *his* opera so badly.'

Until now my parents had tutored me in general subjects themselves, devoting a good deal of time to it. But at last the time came when I had to be sent to school. The problem was which school to choose: a local Gymnasium, a provincial Gymnasium or one in Moscow or St Petersburg. Father favoured Moscow, for he had relatives there, but Mother preferred St Petersburg, where her sisters lived. In February 1904 I was taken to Glazunov who listened to my compositions and praised them, but without enthusiasm. 'He is not like dear, kind Sergey Ivanovich!' said my mother disappointedly, thinking of our visit to Taneev. A few days later, however, Glazunov visited my mother and urged her to send me to the Conservatoire. My mother voiced her doubts. What if nothing came of her son's talents and he turned out to be no more than a mediocre artist? What would become of his future? It would be wiser for him to study civil engineering or architecture or some other such profession that would enable him to continue to live in the city where he could study music if he wished, go to concerts and associate with musicians. But Glazunov pointed out that her son's talent could be fully developed only in the Conservatoire and that he had every chance of becoming a real artist. 'But if you try to prepare him for two specialities, he will end by mastering neither,' he said. My mother was not altogether persuaded. On the other hand there was the difficulty of enrolling in the Gymnasium. This was simple enough for pupils enrolling in the preparatory class, but in the higher classes, for which I had been coached, there were practically no vacancies and twenty-two of the twenty-five applicants failed the entrance exams. 'Think it over,' said Glazunov as he departed. My parents thought it over for a month or two and finally decided to take his advice, the more so since the Conservatoire course included general subjects as well.

Glazunov made me a present of the score of Glinka's *Valse fantaisie* inscribed 'To my dear confrère Seryozha Prokofiev from A. Glazunov.' Father was much amused at the idea of an Oxford and Cambridge doctor calling me his 'dear confrère'.

In St Petersburg I made the acquaintance of a 'real' poetess, M. G. Kilshtedt, whose verses were printed in the newspapers and who was about to publish a volume of poetry. She advised me to write an opera on the subject of Zhukovsky's *Undine* (after de la Motte Fouqué) and undertook to write the libretto in verse if I would sketch the plan. In May she sent me the first act, with an accompanying letter to my parents in which she expressed the hope that they would find nothing in the libretto unsuitable for a child. By August I had the score ready.

In 1904 when I was thirteen my mother took me to St Petersburg to enter the Conservatoire. Our little family was now broken up, for my father had to remain in Sontsovka. It was decided that Father would come to St Petersburg twice or three times during the winter and that my mother and I would spend the Christmas and summer holidays in Sontsovka. The entrance examination was quite sensational. The examinee before me was a man with a beard who had nothing to show the examiners but a single song without accompaniment. Then I came in, bending under the weight of two huge folders containing four operas, two sonatas, a symphony and a good many piano pieces. 'Here is a pupil after my own heart!' observed Rimsky-Korsakov who headed the examining board. They tested my ear and sight-reading in different clefs. Then I played *Undine* and while I played Rimsky-Korsakov stood beside me and made a few corrections on the score in pencil. The examination took a long time. Rimsky-Korsakov and Glazunov went out several times to talk to my mother in the next room. I have an almost stenographic report of this examination in the form of a fifteen-page letter to my father written at the time. I was enrolled in the harmony class under Lyadov. Glazunov insisted on my going through the entire course in harmony over again, since harmony is fundamental.

But there my honeymoon with the Conservatoire ended. The rest was deep disappointment. Lyadov's classes in harmony were extremely dull, he himself was disagreeable and he did not take the slightest interest in the creative aspirations of his pupils outside of the course. My old indifference to harmony returned, I began to write carelessly, and Lyadov was greatly displeased. The teaching in general subjects was poor and often the hours coincided with the harmony class. I had to continue studying general subjects at home and take examinations every autumn at the Conservatoire. 'I am thinking of engaging Chernov to come once a week to correct Seryozha's summer compositions,' Mother wrote in a letter to Father. 'They are lying about and no one is paying any attention to them.' In January the 1905 Revolution began. Rimsky-Korsakov, Glazunov and Lyadov, after a conflict with the board of directors, left the Conservatoire which closed down one day only to reopen the next. The pupils held meetings. I signed one of the protests threatening to leave the Conservatoire, much to my father's horror. That autumn I transferred to a special piano class under Winkler but continued to take private lessons from Lyadov. I was still composing piano pieces at the rate of a dozen a year and had written the second act of *Undine*. I then laid it aside for about three years, after which I rewrote the whole thing, composed three new acts and dropped it again.

In the autumn of 1906 Rimsky-Korsakov, Glazunov and Lyadov returned to the Conservatoire and I began to attend a class in counterpoint under Lyadov. Among the newcomers to the class was a composer with a little beard and a big portfolio. His name was Myaskovsky. At first he and I kept aloof from one another. In general I was not particularly popular with my classmates, especially after I took it into my head to keep a record of all the mistakes made in class, entering each one on a neat statistical chart. My classmates were furious. These boyish pranks, however, did not prevent me from taking a keen interest in new music, and the visit in December 1906 of Reger, who conducted his Serenade in G major, made a deep impression on me. Myaskovsky surprised me one day by producing from his portfolio a four-hand arrangement of the serenade. We sat down and played it then and there. Shortly after that Myaskovsky came to my house to play Beethoven's Ninth Symphony with me. He said no one had ever been able to play it with him to the end. I handed him an album with my latest pieces for piano (I called them *Little Dogs* now instead of *Little Songs*, because someone had told me that they 'snapped at you'). 'I never suspected what a little viper we had been nursing in our bosom,' Myaskovsky said when he returned them to me a few days later. But from the way he smiled into his moustache I could see that he did not think too badly of them. After that we took to showing one another our sonatas, and sometimes we played duets. On the whole there was a certain livening up in the class: Myaskovsky, two other composers and I wrote songs to one and the same text ('The Spreading Oak') and Myaskovsky's was unanimously declared the best. Then we decided to compose a violin sonata jointly. I chose the first movement and wrote it but as far as I remember the others did not write their parts. All that summer Myaskovsky and I exchanged compositions and wrote letters to each other in which we discussed music at length. This correspondence gave me much more than Lyadov's dull lessons.

Besides counterpoint we studied orchestration with Rimsky-Korsakov. He conducted two parallel groups, but instead of giving two hours to each he combined the two groups and taught for four hours. He may have believed this method to be most beneficial to the pupils, since the lessons consisted mainly in correcting the work submitted by the class. Actually, however, it was not very effective. The classroom was always full, everyone crowded round the piano at which Rimsky-Korsakov sat, so that it was hard to see or hear all that was going on. Besides, four hours of this was exceedingly tiring. Those who were conscious of the benefit to be derived from associating with Rimsky-Korsakov gained something from these lessons, in spite of the crowding. As for myself, I attached little importance to them, and thought the Schubert four-hand marches which Rimsky-Korsakov made us orchestrate extremely dull and uninteresting.

Rimsky-Korsakov did not like my orchestration. 'Instead of using your head you simply guess on your fingers – oboe or clarinet,' he once said, and closing his eyes he twirled his forefingers, brought them together and missed. I glanced triumphantly at my classmates: Aha, I had managed to annoy the old man. But their faces were grave. Rimsky-Korsakov turned over a page. 'What's this?' he said. 'Why have you only one cello playing the melody here?' 'Because I don't like it when all the cellos play together.' 'You don't? Have you ever heard them?' 'I heard them yesterday in Sibelius's symphony, and I didn't like the way they sounded.' 'Heavens! Why listen to Sibelius? What about *Ruslan*? What about the secondary theme in the overture to *Ruslan*?'

I must admit that in two years I learned nothing at those classes. I barely passed the examination in orchestration in the spring of 1908. 'Gifted but immature', is, I believe, how Rimsky-Korsakov described me at that time. However my lack of respect for Rimsky-Korsakov's teaching did not prevent me from admiring his music; I attended the dress rehearsal and three successive performances of his *Kitezh* which had its première in the spring of 1907, and applauded until my hands ached.

Besides our study of counterpoint and fugue Lyadov made us write short pieces. But he insisted on the same rigid adherence to the rules of voice-leading in the pieces as in the contrapuntal exercises. Anyone who dared to depart from the conventional path was bound to incur his wrath. Thrusting his hands into his pockets and swaying back and forth on his soft heel-less prunella boots, he would say, 'I cannot understand why you bother to study with me. Go to Richard Strauss, go to Debussy.' He might as well have said, 'Go to the devil!' Talking about me to acquaintances Lyadov would gesture hopelessly and say, 'I dare say he will get over it in time.' For all that, the fugue I wrote for the examination was quite good. As for my class pieces, some of them I later revised and used in subsequent compositions. This, for instance, is the origin of the Gavotte op. 12 and the Scherzo from the Second Sonata.

In 1908 Chernov introduced me to the sponsors of the 'Evenings of Modern Music – Karatygin, who later became one of our best music critics; Nuvel, a government official of some kind; Nurok (I don't remember what he did) and several others, all of whom had sharp tastes and even sharper tongues. They met every Thursday in the ill-lit premises of the Becker piano shop and played over all the latest compositions, choosing the most interesting to be performed at chamber concerts the next season. I have no idea how these concerts were financed; they were rather shabby affairs, held in a small hall, the tickets costing 30 copecks, I believe. Nevertheless all the leading critics and musicians attended them. Chernov took me to one of these 'evenings'. I played some of my piano pieces, most of which were subsequently incorporated, in a more polished shape, in op. 3 and op. 4. There was another little piece called *Snow-flakes* which has not survived. Myaskovsky had once suggested that we both write a piano piece on the subject of snow. His suggested what he called 'a very nasty blizzard'. I tried to convey the feeling of snow falling in large soft flakes by means of a succession of seconds descending in alternating whole-tone and diatonic scales. Word of the success of my pieces at the Modern Music Evenings reached Lyadov, and in one of his bad moments he asked me, 'Is it true that you have written a piece in which all the voices move in seconds?' and he proceeded to describe seconds in the air by closing and opening his second and third fingers.

On 31 December 1908 (18 Dec. Old Style) I made my first public appearance with seven of my piano pieces at a recital of modern music. The first public performance of Myaskovsky's compositions (four songs) was given the same evening. My mother clipped out all the reviews and pasted them into an album, the first of a whole series of such scrap-books.

One of the reviews, the first to be written about my work, read thus: 'S. Prokofiev's small pieces for the piano, played from manuscript by the composer himself, were extremely original. The young composer, who has not yet completed his musical education, belongs to the ultra-modernist trend and goes much further than the French modernists in boldness and originality. The unmistakable glow of talent shines through all the whims and caprices of this rich creative fantasy, a talent that is not yet quite balanced, and which still succumbs to every gust of feeling' etc., etc. (*Slovo* (*The Word*), 20 Dec. 1908, Old Style). This review was signed 'N. Sem.', evidently the pen-name of one of the sponsors of the concert who naturally wished to boost his own stocks. Another reviewer (*Peterburgsky Listok* (*St Petersburg Bulletin*), 24 Dec. Old Style) commented: 'If one regards these rather unintelligible compositions as a trial of the pen, so to speak, one can perhaps discern some trace of talent in them.' Curiously enough I was so absorbed in the life of the Conservatoire at this period, with its contests and diverse activities, that my performance of Rubinstein's C major *Etude* at one of our student recitals interested me much more than my first public concert.

That winter I was to hear my own music played by an orchestra for the first time. During the summer Myaskovsky and I had each written a symphony. We had corresponded regularly in the meantime, exchanging ideas and themes. Myaskovsky's symphony has survived as his First, after a few minor alterations. Of my symphony only the Andante remained, and was later used in the Fourth Sonata. In the autumn we showed our symphonies to Glazunov. By this time Glazunov had evidently heard of my activities from Lyadov and had seriously begun to suspect that he had nursed a viper in his bosom. At any rate it was only after repeated requests that he finally consented to look over my symphony and make a few trifling corrections. 'A very spirited piece of work, I should say,' Glazunov remarked to my mother, but it was obvious that the music was alien to him. Nevertheless he did arrange for the symphony to be performed at a private rehearsal of the Court orchestra conducted by Warlich. (One of Glazunov's own scores was played at the same rehearsal.) It is hard to say whether this sort of performance is of much value, since it is impossible to tell whether the music sounds badly because the orchestration is faulty or because the musicians have never seen the score before. But the fact is it nearly always sounds bad. My symphony was poorly orchestrated and the general impression was rather blurred.

That winter we studied form under Vitol who was much pleasanter in his manner than Lyadov but rather sparing with his explanations. 'Now gentlemen,' he would say, 'you all know what a rondo of the second form is. Anyone who is not quite clear about this form can examine the Andante from the Beethoven Sonata Number – . I believe that is clear? In that case I would ask you to write a rondo of this type.' Encouraged by my success with the 'modernists', I turned in pieces with confused harmonies. Vitol would listen to them, rub his forehead and say, 'I am not quite sure what you are trying to say.' 'Shall I play it again?' I would suggest. 'Oh no, thank you,' Vitol would say hastily.

My most daring compositions at this time were the Sixth Sonata and a scene from the *Feast During the Plague*. 'I don't think you ought to bother numbering your sonatas,' Myaskovsky once said to me with a smile. 'The time will come when you will cross out all the numbers and write "Sonata Number One".' That is exactly what happened, although some of the material from these early sonatas did go into later sonatas (no. 2 after some changes became no. 1, op. 1; no. 3 remained as no. 3 even after alterations; nos. 4 and 6 were lost; no. 5 was incorporated in no. 4, op. 29). The above-mentioned scene from the *Feast During the Plague* had nothing in common with the *Feast* of Glière's time. It was the final scene in which the priest wrathfully denounces the 'godless feast'. At the spring examinations in 1909 this scene and the sonata shocked the examiners profoundly. I heard Lyadov in the next room say indignantly, 'They all want to be Skriabins!' By way of punishment our whole class was given a low mark (4 out of 5), which was most unfair to Myaskovsky and myself who had written examples in all forms, whereas the others had written barely a few pages throughout the year. We felt quite badly about this until the students of the parallel class told us that they had failed their exams altogether and would have to take the course over again.

According to the new rules students who graduated from the form class did so as professional musicians and were free either to leave the Conservatoire or enrol in the free composition class. Glazunov did not conduct this class, Rimsky-Korsakov was dead (he died in 1908); there remained Lyadov, who was after all an eminent authority in his field. I spoke to him about joining his class but he would not hear of it. 'Anatoly Konstantinovich,' I pleaded with him, 'you say I have gone astray but when I ask you to lead me on to the path of righteousness you refuse.' Finally Lyadov agreed to enrol me in the free composition class beginning that autumn. For some reason, however, the class was not a success and studies were suspended after the second lesson.

In the meantime my performance of the Rubinstein *Etude* had attracted the attention of Esipova, the leading piano professor at the Conservatoire, and I moved to her class. At first we got along very well.

Esipova even boasted outside the class that she had pupils who wrote sonatas (I completed the Sonata op. 1 and played it to Esipova, who took it home and inserted pedalling). But before long trouble began. Esipova's method of teaching was to try to fit everyone into a standard pattern. True, it was a very elaborate pattern, and if the pupil's temperament coincided with her own the results were admirable. But if the pupil happened to be of an independent cast of mind Esipova would do her best to suppress his individuality instead of helping to develop it. Moreover I had great difficulty in ridding myself of the habit of careless playing, and the Mozart, Schubert and Chopin which she insisted on were somehow not in my line. At that period I was too preoccupied with the search for a new harmonic idiom to understand how anyone could care for the simple harmonies of Mozart.

Much more successful were my studies with Tcherepnin, whose class in conducting I joined at this time. Tcherepnin was a brilliant musician who could discuss old and new music with equal understanding and appreciation. His compositions may have been more eclectic than his lectures on music, his conducting less convincing than his discourses on the subject, but association with him was of inestimable value to me. Since I was far too young to direct an orchestra he made me wait a long time before he allowed me to conduct. And when at last I did mount the podium and timidly waved my baton the orchestra seemed very far away from me, and the musicians beyond the reach of my baton. Tcherepnin hastened to pronounce his verdict: 'You have no gift for conducting; but since I have faith in you as a composer and I know that you will have to conduct your own works on more than one occasion I shall teach you how to conduct.' I was thus labelled incompetent from the start, and though by the end of the course I managed to conduct a performance of *The Marriage of Figaro* I did not feel quite at home on the podium until after I left the Conservatoire and began to conduct on my own without Tcherepnin at my back.

Nevertheless Tcherepnin played a very big role in my musical development. He spoke about new trends in music with such enthusiasm that I almost felt behind the times. He gave an excellent analysis of opera which later proved very useful to me in my own work. Sitting beside me with the score at the innumerable rehearsals of our student orchestra he would say, 'Now listen to that delightful little bassoon there!' and I found myself acquiring a taste for Haydn and Mozart, which later found expression in the 'Classical' Symphony. With Tcherepnin I made up for the time wasted in Rimsky-Korsakov's orchestration class. Moreover I was writing at least one symphonic composition a year at this period, and this too helped me to master the art of orchestration. After the E minor Symphony written in 1908 I wrote a Sinfonietta in 1909, two symphonic poems, *Dreams* and *Autumnal*, in 1910 and two pieces for chorus with orchestra, the First Piano Concerto in 1911, and a second concerto in 1912/13. All these compositions had opus numbers. The Sinfonietta was an attempt to create a transparent piece for small orchestra. The attempt was not particularly successful – I had not yet learned to write light, graceful music and it was only many years later, after two revisions, that the Sinfonietta was finally whipped into shape. *Dreams*, on the other hand, was intended for full orchestra. This was a 'pensive' opus, and rather limp. 'Such unsuccessful music can only be composed in one's sleep,' quipped the critic of the *Theatre and Sport* magazine. *Dreams* was dedicated 'to the author who began with *Rêverie*', an allusion to Skriabin's first orchestral composition. I had a great admiration for Skriabin at this period, especially for his Third Symphony, the first part of which I even arranged for the piano. However, there is no Skriabin influence in the music of the *Dreams*. *Autumal* is also written in a pensive mood, more sombre than *Dreams*. This can be traced to some Rachmaninov moods, mainly to his *Isle of the Dead* and the Second Symphony, to which it is related in key as well. Like the Sinfonietta, *Autumnal* was revised twice and took final shape only twenty years later. Two female choruses with orchestra, *The Swan* and *The Wave*, were written at the time when I conducted the students' choir at the Conservatoire (I had hoped that they would be performed at a Conservatoire concert but the music proved too difficult to sing). They were settings of poems by Balmont which had a musical quality that appealed to me profoundly and had inspired me on more than one occasion.

The First Concerto was perhaps my first more or less mature composition as regards both conception and fulfilment. The conception is expressed, firstly, in some of the means used for combining piano and orchestra, and secondly in the form: a sonata Allegro with the introduction repeated after the exposition and at the end; a short Andante inserted before the development; development in the form of a Scherzo and a cadenza to introduce the recapitulation. True, this form was criticized on the grounds that the concerto consisted of a succession of unrelated episodes. But these episodes were held together quite firmly. The execution of the idea was better than in previous scores, and the concerto with a little minor retouching has remained as originally written. The charges of showy brilliance and certain 'acrobatic' tendencies in the First Concerto induced me to strive for greater depth in the Second. It seems to me that concertos (except the very best or the very worst) can be divided roughly into two categories: in the first the solo part is well co-ordinated with the orchestra but less interesting for the performer (Rimsky-Korsakov's concerto), and in the second the solo part is excellent but the orchestra serves merely as accompaniment (Chopin's concertos). My First Concerto was closer to the first type, my Second to the latter.

In the summer of 1911 I wrote a one-act opera, *Maddalena*, after the play of the same name by a Baron Lieven. I had hoped that it might be produced by the opera class of the Conservatoire; as a student of the orchestral conductors' class I was closely associated with the opera group which, besides classical works, occasionally did stage operas by Conservatoire pupils. But I was disappointed: the opera was rejected and for the same reasons as the choruses to Balmont texts. Baron Lieven turned out to be a young society lady, more charming than talented. However the action of *Maddalena*, taking place in fifteenth-century Venice, abounded in conflicts, love, treachery and murder and offered a host of interesting new problems for the composer as compared with the rather tame *Undine*. I wrote the music quickly but orchestrated only one of the four scenes. In 1913 I rewrote the music of *Maddalena* but again without orchestration.

The piano compositions of this period include the Toccata op. 11 (1912) and two one-movement sonatinas; one was subsequently lost and the other took the form of a sonata Allegro which, in turn, grew into a Sonata in four movements, op. 14 (completed in August 1912). In the same period a dozen or so pieces were combined as op. 12. They have since been smoothed out by the engraver's tool but when I prepared them for the press they presented a messy collection, being scrawled on manuscript paper of odd sizes, partly in ink, partly in pencil. Immediately after the Sonata op. 14 I wrote a Ballade for cello similar in form to a sonata in two movements. I wrote it at the request of N. P. Ruzsky, an amateur cellist and a patron of music with whom I had sometimes played chamber music. This, plus two songs (op. 9), for one of which ('There are other planets'), poor as it is, I have a paternal affection, practically completes the list of my works composed during the Conservatoire period.

Tcherepnin once gave me the task of studying a score of Berlioz in which all the brass instruments were in different keys. I wrestled with it for a long time before I could straighten it out (I would puzzle over a chord for a good three minutes only to discover that it was nothing but a C major triad). How much simpler it was with Liszt, whose clarinets and French horns are all in C! I decided that it was high time to put an end to this irrational way of scoring. If the natural key of an instrument is, say, B flat, then the part for that particular instrument should be written in B flat. But the conductor deals with the music as it sounds, i.e. in C, hence all the instruments in the score should be written in C. In that case transposition is shifted from the conductor to the copyist. I began to write all my scores this way, doing away altogether with the tenor clef (cellos and bassoons in bass and treble, trombones in alto). The English horn, which is actually an alto oboe, I wrote in alto after the manner of Bach; thus one instrument in every group was in the alto clef. When the score of the First Piano Concerto came off the press I was sure that everyone would follow my example. But I was mistaken. Though no one actually denied the convenience of my system everyone continued writing in the old way. Many years later Schoenberg published a score in which all the instruments were in C. A long explanatory note accompanied the score. I don't know whether he knew of my method or not.

I had considerable difficulty in getting my music published. In 1910 I sent two compositions to the Russian Music Publishers which had just been founded by Koussevitsky. With the best of intentions he had invited six leading musicians of the time to pass judgment on the compositions submitted – Skriabin, Rachmaninov and Medtner among them. However the individual tastes of each were so strong that what one accepted the other was bound to reject. Only Rachmaninov and

Medtner with extraordinary unanimity turned down everything that had the slightest suspicion of novelty. My two compositions were rejected. Armed with a letter from Taneev I approached Jurgenson, but he too refused them on the grounds that he had more work than he could cope with. So did Bessel. In 1911 I applied to Jurgenson again with a long and insistent letter from Ossovsky. This time Jurgenson agreed to print my first four works (a sonata and twelve pieces for the piano), offering 100 roubles for the lot – true, not without a tremor in his voice. But I agreed without hesitation, for the most important thing was to be published. For the Second Sonata Jurgenson paid 200 roubles, and for the ten pieces op. 12, 500 roubles. Nevertheless he did not accept everything I offered him; for instance I was obliged to give the cello Ballade to the St Petersburg Jurgenson, a second-rate publisher who had no direct connection with the 'big' Jurgenson.

As a rule the publication of his first opus is a landmark for the composer, a sort of dividing line between his early work and his mature compositions. With me it was different: the First Sonata, a naïve and simple little piece, marked the end of my early period; the new one began with the *Etudes* op. 2. I performed both these works during my first appearance in Moscow on 6 March 1910 (21 Feb. Old Style), at the thirteenth Musical Audition arranged by Deisha-Sionitskaya.

I continued to perform at the Evenings of Modern Music in St Petersburg. Besides my own compositions I played new music by Western composers and was the first to perform the works of Schoenberg in Russia. In 1911 I joined a similar progressive group in Moscow, headed by Derzhanovsky, publisher of *Muzyka (Music)*, an extremely lively and forward-looking magazine, and Saradzhev, who conducted symphony concerts in the Sokolniki summer park and readily performed new music. Myaskovsky made their acquaintance first and told them about me, with the result that in the summer of 1911 both the *Dreams* and *Autumnal* were performed in Sokolniki, but with little success. The First Piano Concerto, performed the following summer, had a much better reception. This was its first performance and my own first appearance with orchestra as pianist. The magazine *Muzyka* gave me a good write-up and invited me to contribute to it. 'I believe I would make quite a good music critic, and a pretty nasty one at that,' I noted at that time in my diary. However my journalistic talents, if any, remained undeveloped.

A few days after the Sokolniki appearance I played the First Concerto in Pavlovsk. The summer concerts there were conducted by Aslanov, another modern music enthusiast. The first performance of the Second Concerto took place in Pavlovsk on 5 September 1913 (23 Aug. Old Style) with Aslanov conducting. It proved quite sensational. Half the audience hissed and the other half applauded. The press was also divided. Karatygin wrote a flattering article, other reviewers were sarcastic. The *St Petersburg Gazette* came out with a feuilleton. 'On the platform appeared a youth looking like a Peterschule student. It was Sergey Prokofiev. He sat down at the piano and appeared to be either dusting the keyboard or tapping it at random, with a sharp, dry touch. The public did not know what to make of it. Some indignant murmurs were heard. One couple got up and hurried to the exit: "Such music can drive you mad!" The hall emptied. The young artist ended his concerto with a relentlessly discordant combination of brass. The audience was scandalized. The majority hissed. With a mocking bow Prokofiev sat down again and played an encore. "To hell with this futurist music!" people were heard to exclaim. "We came here for pleasure. The cats on the roof make better music!" The modernist critics were in raptures. "Brilliant!" they cried. "What freshness!" "What temperament and originality!" '

From the above it will be seen that my symphonic works (as well as Myaskovsky's) were given their first concert performance at open-air concerts in the two leading cities. These performances were not always up to scratch. One of the conductors of *Dreams* said to me, 'I hope you didn't mind the wrong notes.' 'My dear fellow,' I replied, 'there wasn't a note in the whole thing that wasn't wrong. I didn't recognize it as my own at all.' Winter concerts were closed to me altogether. The Belyaev, Count Sheremetiev and Ziloti concert managers returned all the scores I sent them. After one letter of refusal from Ziloti, in which he said he trusted that I might soon 'find myself', a vicious article signed Misanthrope appeared in *Muzyka* which sent Ziloti into a towering rage but later forced him to alter his position with regard to my music.

In the spring of 1914, at the age of twenty-three, I graduated from the Conservatoire, having completed the course in piano and conducting.

While I did not especially mind the poor rating I received for composition, this time ambition got the better of me and I resolved to win a first for the piano. There was a sporting interest involved too, for the Rubinstein Prize, a grand piano, was to be awarded for the best performance. Yet it was not so much the piano that attracted me as the tremendous excitement that the contest aroused in the Conservatoire. And so I spent the winter of 1913–14 working hard at the piano. Esipova was very ill at the time and gave only a few lessons that winter, so that to all intents and purposes the class was without a tutor. For some of the pupils this was a genuine catastrophe, but for me it was a stroke of good luck since it gave me the opportunity to prepare for the examinations without unnecessary conflicts and enabled me to carry out some plans of my own. For example, in the Bach fugue from the *Kunst der Fuge* I played all the 'subjects' *forte* and all the 'answers' *piano*. For the competition, instead of a classical concerto, I chose one of my own. While I might not be able to compete successfully in performance of a classical concerto there was a chance that my own might impress the examiners by its novelty of technique; they simply would not be able to judge whether I was playing it well or not! On the other hand, even if I did not win, the defeat would be less mortifying since no one would know whether I had lost because the concerto was bad or because my performance was faulty. Of the two concertos I chose the First. The Second would have sounded too outlandish within the Conservatoire walls. Besides the Pavlovsk experience was still too fresh in my memory. Moreover, at my request Jurgenson printed the piano score of the First Concerto in time for the examination. I bought twenty copies and distributed them to all the examiners. When I came out on the stage the first thing I saw was my concerto spread out on twenty laps – an unforgettable sight for a composer who had just begun to appear in print! My most serious competitor was Golubovskaya, a pupil of Lyapunov, a very subtle and intelligent pianist. We were extremely gallant and courteous to each other: on the eve of the examination we enquired after the condition of each other's fingers, and in the long hours of suspense while the judges were deciding our fate we played chess. After a long and stormy session the prize was awarded to me. The panel was probably divided as follows: in the first place there were a few former pupils of Esipova who would vote in principle for the

Esipova candidate; then came a group of young and progressive-minded instructors – those also voted for me; the older professors, headed by Glazunov, the director of the Conservatoire, voted against. Glazunov, who had recently expressed his opinion of my 'subjects' and 'answers', lost his temper and flatly refused to announce the results of the voting, which, he declared, encouraged a 'harmful trend'. Since, however, the 'harm' had already been done there was nothing for it but to read the announcement, which he did in a flat, toneless mumble. On 11 (24) May I played the concerto at the graduation ceremony with Tcherepnin conducting.

I should like to pause here to analyse the basic lines along which my work had developed up to this point. The first was the classical line, which could be traced back to my early childhood and the Beethoven sonatas I heard my mother play. This line takes sometimes a neo-classical form (sonatas, concertos), sometimes imitates the eighteenth century (gavottes, the 'Classical' Symphony, partly the Sinfonietta). The second line, the modern trend, begins with that meeting with Taneev when he reproached me for the 'crudeness' of my harmonies. At first this took the form of a search for my own harmonic language, developing later into a search for a language in which to express powerful emotions ('The Phantom' in the Piano Pieces op. 3, 'Despair' and 'Suggestion diabolique' in the op. 4 Piano Pieces, the *Sarcasmes*, the *Scythian Suite*, a few of the songs op. 23, *The Gambler, Seven, they are Seven*, the Quintet and the Second Symphony). Although this line covers harmonic language mainly, it also includes new departures in melody, orchestration and drama. The third line is the toccata, or 'motor' line, traceable perhaps to Schumann's Toccata which made a powerful impression on me when I first heard it (*Etudes* op. 2, Toccata op. 11, the 'Scherzo' in the Piano Pieces op. 12, the Scherzo of the Second Concerto, the Toccata in the Fifth Concerto and also the repetitive intensity of the melodic figures in the *Scythian Suite, Le pas d'acier* [*The Age of Steel*] and passages in the Third Concerto). This line is perhaps the least important. The fourth line is lyrical: it appears first as a thoughtful and meditative mood, not always associated with melody, or at any rate with long melody ('Fairy Tale' in the Four Pieces for Piano op. 3, *Dreams, Autumnal*, the songs op. 9, the 'Legend' op. 12), sometimes partly contained in long melody (the two Balmont choruses, the beginning of the First Violin Concerto, the songs to Akhmatova's poems, *Grandmother's Tales*). This line was not noticed until much later. For a long time I was given no credit for any lyrical gift whatever, and for want of encouragement it developed slowly. But as time went on I gave more and more attention to this aspect of my work.

I should like to limit myself to these four 'lines', and to regard the fifth, 'grotesque', line which some wish to ascribe to me as simply a deviation from the other lines. In any case I strenuously object to the very word 'grotesque' which has become hackneyed to the point of nausea. As a matter of fact the use of the French word 'grotesque' in this sense is a distortion of the meaning. I would prefer my music to be described as 'scherzo-ish' in quality, or else by three words describing various degrees of the scherzo – whimsicality, laughter, mockery.

II AFTER THE CONSERVATOIRE

As a reward for having done well in the final exams at the Conservatoire my mother sent me abroad. I chose London where Diaghilev's Russian opera and ballet company was having a triumphant tour that season. It was indeed a most interesting season: Chaliapin was singing, Richard Strauss was conducting and a wealth of new music was being performed. Diaghilev himself in his frock-coat and top hat, his monocle and white gloves was a sight worth seeing. Nuvel introduced us and I played him my Second Concerto. An artist who was present exclaimed in French, 'But this is a wild animal!' He apologized profusely when he learned that I understood French.

Diaghilev conceived the curious idea of trying to 'stage' my concerto, of creating a ballet pantomime to be performed on the stage while I played the concerto with the orchestra. The subordinate theme of the finale, for example, suggested to him a Pan-like creature such as Lel. But it was difficult to adapt the music to any sort of subject matter and so the idea was dropped. For some time I had been toying with the idea of writing an opera on the theme of Dostoevsky's story *The Gambler*, and I gave Diaghilev an outlined of it. He objected that opera as a form was dying out, whereas ballet on the other hand was flourishing and hence I must write a ballet. After a few talks it was decided that on my return to St Petersburg I should get in touch with some author, Gorodetsky for example, and jointly write a ballet on some Russian fairy-tale or pre-historic theme.

In between these talks with Diaghilev I heard and saw a great many new works: *Daphnis and Chloë* by Ravel, *The Firebird* and *Petrushka* by Stravinsky. The vitality, ingenuity and 'eccentricity' of these productions interested me, but I found them lacking in real thematic material. The subject matter was so 'different' that I could not accept it – my reaction, I daresay, was much the same as that of many who hear my own music for the first time.

Everything in London was so interesting that I was hardly aware of the approaching European war and it was by sheer chance that I returned to St Petersburg a few days before it broke out. As far as conscription was concerned the war did not affect me; as an only son of a widow I was exempt from service.

While Gorodetsky was searching for a Scythian theme I revised the Sinfonietta op. 5 for performance at Ziloti concerts. The article by Misanthrope in *Muzyka* magazine had its effect. 'I cannot invite Prokofiev to play the Second Concerto,' Ziloti had said, 'because I would have to conduct the orchestra and that is beyond my power. Debussy's music has a pleasant aroma, this music stinks. But since everyone insists I can invite the composer to conduct his Sinfonietta himself.' I decided to make the most of this opportunity and polish up the Sinfonietta thoroughly.

Notwithstanding Diaghilev's condemnation of opera it continued to interest me. But since I could not afford to start on anything big at the time I composed some long vocal pieces, *The Ugly Duckling* and *Under the Roof*. Gorodetsky had dug up a few good Scythian characters but could not think of a plot, and it was only after many joint sessions that we finally pieced together some sort of story. We called it *Ala and Lolli*. I wrote the music as soon as I received the text. I wanted to try my hand at something big. I had already heard Stravinsky's *Sacre du printemps* but I had not understood it. It is quite possible that I was now searching for the same images in my own way. Nurok and Nuvel came and listened to the music but made no comment, and Nuvel later wrote to Diaghilev that Prokofiev was turning out some weird stuff on a weird subject. Diaghilev wrote urging me to come to Italy where he was touring at the time. He promised to arrange a concert for me in Rome and to pay my fare. I went, travelling through Romania, Bulgaria and Greece which had not yet entered the war. Diaghilev heard the unfinished sketches for the ballet and did not approve of either the music or the plot which he declared 'trite'. 'You must write a new one,' he said.

On 7 March 1915 I performed my Second Concerto in Rome, in the Augusteum under the direction of Molinari. This was my first foreign appearance. The audience, which was not very large, split into 'for' and 'against', but there were no demonstrations of the kind that had occurred at the first performance of the concerto in Pavlovsk.

War or no war, Diaghilev was preparing for another season. He was negotiating with the Italian futurists and had induced Stravinsky to come to Italy from Switzerland. I had already met Stravinsky two years before in St Petersburg. He had played the introduction to *The Firebird* on the piano and it did not sound well without the orchestra. I told him there was no music in the introduction, and if there was any it was from *Sadko*. Stravinsky had taken offence at the time, and Diaghilev was afraid that there might be a clash between us. But Stravinsky seemed to bear me no grudge; he praised the Second Concerto and we played a four-hand arrangement of *Petrushka* for the futurists. Of all the futurists the one who impressed me most was Marinetti, who spoke a rapid, voluble French that was almost impossible to follow. But it was all very new to me and I was greatly thrilled to be associating with such an extraordinarily 'progressive' person, though his theories passed way over my head. I wrote an article for *Muzyka* about the musical instruments, mainly percussion, which the futurists demonstrated for us.

After Stravinsky's departure Diaghilev and I sat down to examine a collection of Russian folk-tales by Afanasiev which Stravinsky had brought and came across a series of tales about a buffoon. It did not take us long to map out a ballet plot in six scenes out of two of these tales, and this time Diaghilev signed a proper contract with me for 3,000 roubles. 'Only please write music that will be truly Russian,' he said. 'They've forgotten how to write Russian music in that rotten Petersburg of yours.'

Besides being an impresario Diaghilev was a very fine artist. He had a thorough knowledge of music and painting and choreography. His opinions were as sharp-edged as they were paradoxical. He reproached me with a fondness for too many different kinds of music. 'In art you must know how to hate,' he said, 'otherwise your music will lose all individuality.' 'But surely that will lead to narrowness,' I objected. 'The cannon shoots far because it doesn't scatter its fire,' he retorted.

On my return to Petrograd I noticed that my stocks there had risen. Even Jurgenson had changed 'from Jupiter to Venus', which, however, did not prevent him offering me very unfavourable terms for my new ballet. I refused. Little by little I settled down to composing the thematic material for *Chout*, trying to make it as truly Russian as possible. In my childhood in Sontsovka I had often heard the village girls singing in chorus on Saturday evenings or on Sundays. I do not know whether Sontsovka was especially poor in folk-songs, or whether it was the crude, raucous manner of the local singers that irritated me – they always yelled at the top of their voices – but their performance had not impressed me with the beauty of Russian folk-music and I did not remember a single tune. It is possible, of course, that subconsciously I was affected by the village songs, for now the Russian national idiom came quite easily to me. It was as if I had stumbled upon an unsuspected store of wealth, or planted seeds in virgin soil that were now bearing rich fruit. By the end of the summer all six scenes were finished.

I had agreed with Diaghilev that I would go to Italy again to complete the ballet together with the choreographer. In the meantime, however, the Balkan route had been closed and the North Sea was dangerous on account of mines. In any case musical life in Petrograd attracted me far more than the glittering prospects Diaghilev held out to me abroad – and so I sent the manuscript with the choreographer Grigoriev who was going to Rome.

While working on *Chout* I returned to my sketches for *Ala and Lolli* and found that if a few uninteresting passages were deleted the rest of the music was well worth saving. A slight revision here and there resulted in a four-movement *Scythian Suite* with the material laid out in approximately the same order as in the ballet. By this time I knew enough about orchestration to be able to write for full orchestra and I had a few ideas of my own which I wished to try out. The first two movements came quite easily; the last two gave me much more trouble but were far more interesting in texture. I spent nearly as much time on the sunrise Finale as on half of the suite. Ziloti invited me to conduct the suite that same season.

It was Ziloti, too, who introduced me to Albert Coates, who was gradually taking the place of the ageing Napravnik as conductor of the Mariinsky Theatre orchestra. Coates was not afraid of new music. 'Write your *Gambler*,' he said, 'and we'll stage it.' A more favourable opportunity could hardly be imagined. I re-read the story, wrote the libretto and in the autumn of 1915 set about composing the music (I began from the middle of Act I, from the words 'good *Vater*').

That same year I met Rachmaninov. He was very pleasant to me, offered me his huge paw and chatted graciously with me. That autumn he gave a concert in memory of Skriabin at which, among other things, he played the Fifth Sonata. When Skriabin had played this sonata everything seemed to be flying upward; with Rachmaninov all the notes stood firmly planted on earth. There was some confusion among the Skriabinists in the hall. Alchevsky, the tenor, whom someone tried to hold back by the lapels, shouted, 'Wait, let me have a word with him!' I tried to be objective and argued that although we were accustomed to the author's interpretation there could obviously be other interpretations. I was thinking of this when I remarked to Rachmaninov after the concert, 'After all, Sergey Vasilievich, I think you played it very well.' 'Did you think I would play it badly?' replied Rachmaninov with a wry smile, and turned away from me. This ended our good relations. A contributing factor no doubt was Rachmaninov's dislike for my music, which irritated him. Some time later I had a little tiff with Medtner too. I had hoped that he would play his A minor Sonata, which I liked. But he had limited himself to one of the more straightforward sonatas which one could have easily played oneself at home. I told him as much. 'And what do you think of the one I played?' 'That is more suited for domestic use,' I replied. Rachmaninov, to whom Medtner passed on the incident, later related indignantly that Prokofiev divided sonatas into ordinary sonatas and sonatas for domestic use.

In the autumn of 1915 I conducted the revised version of the Sinfonietta at Ziloti's concerts, and on 16 (29) January 1916 the *Scythian Suite*. The suite caused almost as much of a scandal as the first performance of the Second Concerto in Pavlovsk, but this time the whole musical élite of Petrograd was present. Glazunov, whom I had personally invited, lost his temper again and walked out, unable to endure the sunrise Finale, eight bars before the end. 'The director of the Conservatoire did not mince words in appraising the new composition,' commented the newspapers. The kettle-drummer banged right through his drum, and Ziloti promised to send me the torn skin as a keepsake. There were a few feeble attempts at obstruction on the part of the orchestra. 'If I didn't have a sick wife and three children I should never stand for this!' groaned the cellist, nearly deafened by the trombones behind him. Ziloti paraded the hall in fine good humour, saying, 'A slap in the face! A slap in the face!' meaning that he and Prokofiev had given the public a slap in the face. 'A scandal in high society,' *Muzyka* somewhat gleefully remarked.

Between concerts I worked hard at *The Gambler* and by March three acts were ready. I hit a snag, however, in the roulette scene in the fourth act – the general plan did not work out. B. N. Demchinsky came to the rescue by adding something I had not been able to find in the Dostoevsky story. Encouraged by the interest shown in the *Scythian Suite* I chose an ultra-left idiom for *The Gambler*. 'There are no limits to his creative imagination and it is impossible to foretell whither it will lead him,' wrote *Muzyka* in support of me. 'A catharsis of panicky laughter at the transient canons of artistic idiom,' raved Karatygin. 'Stupendous!' wrote Igor Glebov, but owing to a typographical error the word 'stupendous' appeared as 'stupid'. One day my mother, coming into the room where I was composing *The Gambler*, exclaimed in despair, 'Do you really understand what you are pounding out of that piano of yours?' We didn't speak to each other for two days after that. True my search for a powerful idiom found expression mainly in the form of strong emotion or mockery. At the same time I did succeed in finding musical expression for the Russian image of the 'Granny' (*babulenka* – the action takes place abroad and describes the sudden arrival of an old Russian granny from Moscow). I must confess, however, to a great deal of modernistic padding which was merely fatiguing without adding anything, and only complicated the vocal score.

I composed the entire music for *The Gambler* in five and a half months. In the spring Telyakovsky, director of imperial theatres, held an audition of new operas for the coming season. Knowing that the panel would include such stumbling blocks as Cui, Glazunov and several others Coates deliberately said nothing about *The Gambler*. But when the panel had finished its work and departed he told Telyakovsky about my opera. An additional session was arranged with the young conductors of the Mariinsky Theatre also present, with Ziloti as the presiding bigwig. Telyakovsky's reaction to *The Gambler* was negative, but since the others praised it he decided to take the risk of signing a contract. This brought with it a substantial advance and the printing of the piano score in a hundred copies. I spent the entire summer of 1916 on the orchestration, doing about ten pages of score a day, and in the less complicated sections up to eighteen pages. My mother once asked Tcherepnin how much he managed to orchestrate in a day. 'No more than a single chord sometimes,' replied Tcherepnin who prided himself on his thoroughness. 'My Sergey does eighteen pages a day!' said my mother proudly.

In between the larger forms I continued to write piano pieces and songs, primarily the *Sarcastic Pieces* (1912–14), subsequently renamed *Sarcasmes* on the advice of Nurok and Nuvel. The pieces were a big success with the 'modernists', perhaps because the search for a new musical language was more strongly evident in them than in other works of the same period. Tcherepnin said, 'All his life Nurok longed for new music and in his old age God sent him Prokofiev.' I still have the programme of one of the *Sarcasmes* (no. 5): 'We often indulge in malicious laughter at someone or something, but when we pause to look we see how pitiful and sad is the object of our ridicule: and then we grow ashamed, the mocking laughter rings in our ears, but it is we who are its object now.' The other *Sarcasmes* had no programme. There is a certain affinity between the *Sarcasmes* and the Songs, op. 23: the very long one 'Under the Roof', 'The Grey Dress', 'The Wizard'. But there were some with lyrical themes as well: 'In My Garden' and 'Trust in Me'. Incidentally Karatygin discovered some lyrical touches in the *Sarcasmes* too (in no. 3). Curiously enough, 'Under the Roof' was the only piece that Karatygin did not understand. And although I had taken the greatest care to reflect in the music every nuance of thought and feeling contained in the text Karatygin said, 'To my mind, while the voice sings words of definite meaning, the piano plays a scherzo having nothing whatever to do with it.'

A certain 'softening of temper' may be noted in *Visions fugitives*, op. 22, a series of twenty miniatures composed over a period of two years (1915–17). No. 5 was composed first, no. 19 last; the order in which they appear in the collection was dictated by artistic and not chronological considerations. The title was suggested by Balmont's poem:

> In every fugitive vision I see worlds,
> Full of the changing play of rainbow hues.

The 'softening' was even more noticeable in the Songs op. 27, written in November 1916, i.e. after *The Gambler* was completed. Many people at last began to believe that I really could write lyrical music. Unlike the songs of op. 23 they were composed very quickly: the entire cycle was written within five or six days. They were entered in the catalogue as op. 27, which suggests that I had already begun work on the Violin Concerto op. 19, the Third Piano Concerto op. 26 and the 'Classical' Symphony op. 25; but being occupied with large theatrical forms I was unable to complete them.

In the latter part of 1916 I changed publishers, going over from Jurgenson to Koussevitzky. The judges of the Editions Russes de Musique, with their conflicting opinions, did not satisfy Koussevitzky and he decided to do without them. He had taken over the publishing business from Gutheil, who being an Austrian citizen had been forced to wind up his affairs when the war broke out. I was not getting along very well with Jurgenson and a conflict was brewing over the printing of scores which Jurgenson fought shy of. Koussevitzky set a definite fee for each category of composition and agreed to print everything. That is how I shifted to Gutheil (the name of the firm remained). The first things I published there were the Songs op. 9, op. 23 and op. 27, and the *Visions fugitives*.

On 12 (25) December 1916 Koussevitzky was to have given a performance of the *Scythian Suite* in Moscow, but shortly before the concert a large number of the musicians in his orchestra were drafted into the army. And since the *Scythian Suite* required a large orchestra Koussevitzky decided to postpone the performance until the next season and substitute something simpler. The next day, however, an article by Sabaneev appeared in the Moscow paper *Novosti sezona (News of the Season)* in which he condemned the suite in the most violent terms, the word 'barbarous' being the most moderate of the epithets used. He had written the review in advance, had not taken the trouble to go to the concert and knew nothing about the change. Sabaneev was a cultivated musician and a mediocre composer. He could not stand my music and had repeatedly attacked it in the press, declaring that, like Petrushka, I had shavings inside me in place of a soul. Derzhanovsky had once offered me a chance to take my revenge by writing a review of Sabaneev's music for *Muzyka*. I did so, taking great pleasure in pointing out all the defects ('it sounds more like spiders crawling about than music') but Derzhanovsky did not have the courage to print it, and hence I was robbed of my revenge. And now the enemy had dug his own grave! The most curious thing is that although Sabaneev had never heard the suite or even seen the score he had been accurately informed about it and I doubt whether he would have changed a word in his article had he actually heard the music. This blunder of his forced him to resign from several newspapers and his reputation as a music critic was badly damaged for a long time.

In place of the Petrograd Evenings of Modern Music, which were petering out, a new association was formed under the auspices of the magazine *Muzykalny sovremennik* (*Musical Contemporary*) which also arranged concerts of modern music. It was headed by two progressive-minded musicologists – Souvchinsky and Igor Glebov – and the conservative A. Rimsky-Korsakov (son of the famous composer), Julia Weisberg and others. Perpetual differences of opinion regarding the music of Stravinsky, Myaskovsky and myself led to a split within the magazine. But Souvchinsky and Igor Glebov took a different view of my music from the 'modernists': whereas Nurok and Nuvel were interested chiefly in the impetuous spirit and novel harmonies, the others concentrated their attention on the Songs op. 27.

On 5 (18) February 1917 the Association for Contemporary Music held the first chamber evening of my music in Moscow. Among those present were Rachmaninov and Medtner. Medtner fumed throughout the performance and said, 'If this is music then I am no musician.' Rachmaninov, on the other hand, sat as motionless as a carven image, and the Moscow public, which had been more or less favourably disposed toward my music, kept casting anxious glances at their idol.

About this time my first piano recital took place in Saratov, followed by a small literary and musical evening in Petrograd on the occasion of an exhibition of paintings arranged by Dobychina. The programme also included readings by Maxim Gorky and a farewell performance by Jascha Heifetz on the eve of his departure for America. Gorky showed much interest in the *Sarcasmes* and *The Ugly Duckling*. At the same time or thereabouts there appeared an interesting article by Amfiteatrov in which, while reproaching me for larking about and poking my tongue out at the public, he wrote, 'But in the meantime talent effervesces like young beer in a barrel, and when poured into a goblet spatters the foam and blows its white head so high that sometimes underneath that tall white cap of foam one finds barely a drop of beer or none at all . . . But alas! – youth is a vice we lose with each passing moment and as a virtue never regain . . .'

The February Revolution found me in Petrograd. I and those I associated with welcomed it with open arms. I was in the streets of Petrograd while the fighting was going on, hiding behind house corners when the shooting came too close. No. 19 of the *Visions fugitives* written at this time partly reflected my impressions – the feeling of the crowd rather than the inner essence of the Revolution.

Telyakovsky left the Mariinsky Theatre. Ziloti took his place but was unable to overcome the reluctance of the singers and the orchestra to penetrate the maze of *The Gambler*. And so the production had to be postponed.

I spent the summer of 1917 in the country near Petrograd all alone, reading Kant and working a great deal. I deliberately did not take my piano with me, for I wished to try composing without it. Until this time I had always composed at the piano, but I noticed that thematic material composed without the piano was often better. At first it seems strange when transferred to the piano, but after one has played it a few times everything falls into place. I had been toying with the idea of writing a whole symphony without the piano. I believed that the orchestra would sound more natural. That is how the project for a symphony in the Haydn style came into being: I had learned a great deal about Haydn's technique from Tcherepnin, and hence felt myself on sufficiently familiar ground to venture forth on this difficult journey without the piano. It seemed to me that had Haydn lived to our day he would have retained his own style while accepting something of the new at the same time. That was the kind of symphony I wanted to write: a symphony in the classical style. And when I saw that my idea was beginning to work I called it the 'Classical' Symphony: in the first place because that was simpler, and secondly for the fun of it, to 'tease the geese', and in the secret hope that it would prove me right if the symphony really did turn out to be a piece of classical music.

I composed the symphony in my head during my walks in the country. The Violin Concerto op. 19 was orchestrated at the same time. Its first theme had been composed for a concertino in the beginning of 1915 and I had often regretted that other work had prevented me from returning to its 'meditative opening'. Gradually, by the summer of 1917, the concertino had grown into a concerto, and during the summer of 1917 I completed the score. The third part of the 'Classical' Symphony, the Gavotte, had likewise been written earlier, and later on, in 1916, I sketched the first and second movements. But a good deal of work still remained to be done when I returned to it in the summer of 1917. I crossed out the first version of the finale and wrote a completely new one, endeavouring, among other things, to avoid all minor chords.

When the music of the 'Classical' Symphony was written and part of the orchestration done, I conceived the idea of writing a similar miniature 'Russian' Symphony and dedicating it to Diaghilev in recognition of his concern for my 'Russian style'. But the desire to create something huge, something cosmic eclipsed the idea. Moreover I too had been subconsciously affected by the revolutionary events that had shaken Russia to its foundations, and now all this clamoured for expression. I did not know how to do it and my mind, paradoxically enough, turned to ancient themes. The fact that the thoughts and emotions of those remote times had survived through the ages captured my imagination. A Chaldean invocation engraved in cuneiform charac- ters on the walls of an ancient Akkadian temple which had been deciphered by Winkler and which Balmont had expressed in the poem 'They are Seven' inspired me to write a cantata for choir and full orchestra. I planned to do the work in three stages: firstly, make a rough skeleton of the whole text (working without the piano), plan the climaxes and anti-climaxes, sketch the general outline of the different parts, jot down fragments of melodies, phrases, accompaniments and ideas for orchestration. Without a text this would have been rather difficult, but having the text it was possible to lay out the whole content of the piece bar by bar, and so exactly that it required no alteration. The second stage: detailed work on the music, at the piano, following the skeleton outline – putting flesh on to the bones, so to speak. The third stage, again without the piano, was the orchestration. I completed the first stage in one week in September, working at fever pitch and visualizing some passages with such startling clarity that I would find myself breathless with excitement and would have to leave my desk and go for a walk in the woods to calm down. The general outline was now ready, and although there was still very little music in it I felt that the main work was done.

Then came a break. Our western front had collapsed; it was rumoured that Petrograd was in danger of being taken by the Germans. My mother, who was taking a cure in the Caucasus, decided to remain there for the autumn and I went down to join her, first sending a suitcase with my manuscripts to Moscow, where it was deposited in the vaults of the Gutheil publishing house. In Essentuki, and later in Kislovodsk, I worked on the second stage of *Seven, they are Seven*, but this turned out to be more difficult. I had trouble with the harmony and at times I began to think that I was producing ideas but not music. At the same time I revised a Conservatoire sonata which now became Sonata no. 4, op. 29. I had revised no. 3 that spring, making the technique more suitable for the piano, more elaborate, modifying the development and recapitulation somewhat but leaving the general design unchanged. I made more changes in the Fourth Sonata (conceived at the same time as the Third), especially in the Andante, taken from the 1908 symphony, and in the Finale, which had remained incomplete since the Conservatoire period.

From Petrograd came confusing reports about the October Revolution and the formation of the 'Lenin Government', as the Soviet Government was called in the local papers. The news was exciting, but so contradictory that it was impossible to make out what was happening. Kislovodsk was full of Whites who interpreted the events in their own way. I decided to go to Petrograd, although it seemed unlikely that the proposed performance of my Violin Concerto with Ziloti and my piano recitals with the Third and Fourth Sonatas and the *Visions fugitives* would take place. I was told that it was madness to think of travelling. A train with smashed windows arrived and a panic-stricken bourgeois crowd poured out. 'There's shooting in the streets of Moscow and Petrograd. You'll never get there,' people said. It indeed looked as though this was hardly the time for concerts even if one could reach the capital cities. Before long the Kaledin front was formed near Rostov and all news from Petrograd ceased. I stayed on in Kislovodsk and wrote the score of *Seven, they are Seven*. Kislovodsk was now a cul-de-sac from which there was no way out.

After the score of *Seven, they are Seven* was finished I was left with nothing to do and time hung heavily on my hands. I had not the slightest idea of the scope and significance of the October Revolution. It never occurred to me that like any other citizen I might be of use to it. And hence the idea of going to America took root in my mind. I believed that Russia had no use for music at the moment, whereas in America I might learn a great deal and interest people in my music at the same time. The previous summer I had met an American named McCormick who had come to Petrograd with a delegation led by Senator Reid to welcome the advent of our Republic. McCormick was a big manufacturer of agricultural machinery – I remembered the name from the trade-mark on farm machines I had seen in Sontsovka in my childhood. He was interested in music and had asked me to give him a list of the best of our new music and to have a copy of the score of the *Scythian Suite* made at his expense. I complied with his request and on leaving he had said, 'If ever you wish to come to America, wire me. I have connections in the musical world.'

In March 1918 the Kaledin front was broken and I started out. I had to go to Moscow and Petrograd first, to arrange for a passport and attend to money matters. The journey to Moscow took eight days. Once or twice the train was fired at, but otherwise the journey passed without mishap. I had in my pocket a safe-conduct pass from the Kislovodsk Soviet of Workers' Deputies. In Moscow I did not have much difficulty in persuading Koussevitzky to advance me 6,000 roubles on account for the *Scythian Suite*, *Chout* and *The Gambler*. This was at once a generous gesture and good business, for the rouble was falling rapidly and nobody had any faith in the Kerensky currency, whereas there was a fair chance of my music retaining its value. While my financial affairs were being settled I had some interesting meetings with Mayakovsky and his friends Burlyuk, Vasily Kamensky and the others. I had met Maya-kovsky the previous year during his appearances in Petrograd which had impressed me greatly. Now our acquaintance deepened; I played for him and he read me his verses, and on parting he presented me with a copy of his *War and the Universe* inscribed: 'To the World President for Music from the World President for Poetry. To Prokofiev from Mayakovsky.'

I gave two piano recitals in Petrograd on 15 and 17 April 1918, playing the Third and Fourth Sonatas and the *Visions fugitives* for the first time. Although the Soviet Government had been in power for half a year, private enterprise still existed in the concert world. On 21 April I gave a première performance of the 'Classical' Symphony with the former Court orchestra (the one which had played my youthful symphony ten years before at a rehearsal). Lunacharsky was present. He had his office in the Winter Palace at that time. Alexander Benois was then repairing the damage done to the palace by shellfire from the *Aurora*; Gorky, too, often came there on business. They both introduced me to Lunacharsky. 'I have been working rather hard,' I told him, 'and I would like to get a breath of fresh air.' 'Don't you think we have enough fresh air here now?' 'Yes, but I would like the physical air of seas and oceans.' Lunacharsky thought it over for a few minutes and then said gaily, 'You are a revolutionary in music, we are revolutionaries in life. We ought to work together. But if you want to go to America I shall not stand in your way.' Thus I missed my chance of becoming part of the life of the new Russia at its very birth. I received a passport for foreign travel and an accompanying document to the effect that I was going abroad on an art mission and to improve my health. There was no indication as to the length of my stay. In vain did one wise friend warn me, 'You are running away from history, and history will never forgive you: when you return you will not be understood.' I paid no heed to these words and on 7 May 1918 I set out on my journey, intending to return within a few months. I took with me the *Scythian Suite*, the 'Classical' Symphony, the First Concerto and my piano pieces.

The journey to Vladivostok was painfully slow (eighteen days), but otherwise uneventful. I sat in my compartment reading about Babylo-nian culture and it was only much later that I realized how risky it had been to journey by train across Siberia, then seething with unrest. At one point we were held up for a long time by trainloads of Czechoslovak troops. When at last we were allowed to pass the Czechoslovak front closed immediately behind us. Beginning from here the postcards I sent my mother at Kislovodsk did not reach her until a year later. At Chita we were held up again – Soviet detachments were engaging Ataman Semyonov's forces further up the line. At last Semyonov retreated to Harbin and we went on to Khabarovsk.

On 1 June I arrived in Tokyo. I had intended to go to South America where the winter season had already opened, and had been learning Spanish on the way in preparation. But I discovered that the boat to Valparaiso had just left and the next would not be leaving for a month. Moreover since the voyage would take six or seven weeks I would arrive at the end of the season. On the other hand it was too early for North America. And so I stayed on in Japan until August, giving two concerts in Tokyo and one in Yokohama. Since several books on modern music had already appeared in Japan and one of them, by M. Otaguro, included a whole chapter devoted to myself, I was given the Imperial Theatre in Tokyo for my concerts. The Japanese did not understand much about European music but they listened quietly and attentively and applauded the virtuoso passages. The audiences, however, were small and I earned very few yen.

From Yokohama I sailed to San Francisco with a delightful stop-over at Honolulu. In San Francisco I was not allowed to go ashore at first, having come from Russia where the 'Maximalists' (as the Bolsheviks were called in America at that time) were in power – a strange and evidently dangerous lot. After being held for three days on an island and subjected to close questioning ('Have you ever been in jail?' 'Yes.' 'That's bad. Where?' 'Here on your island.' 'Oh, you are joking!') I was admitted to the United States. By this time I was penniless, but some people I had met on the boat loaned me 300 dollars, and early in September 1918 I arrived in New York.

III–IV THE YEARS ABROAD AND AFTER MY RETURN HOME

I had expected my musical career to be as smooth-sailing in America as it had been in recent years in Russia. But I was mistaken. I found myself in a musical world where everything was excellently organized but utterly different from what I had been accustomed to.

In my own country for a whole century composers had been continually creating something new, offering the public new problems to solve, giving rise to heated controversies. The outcome of these controversies was not always the same: sometimes the composers talked nonsense and were soon forgotten, sometimes it was the public that talked nonsense and the composers who were remembered. But discussion of new music, new trends and composers had become an integral part of our musical life. America, on the contrary, had no original composers, apart from those who came from Europe with ready-made reputations, and the whole accent of musical life was concentrated on execution. In this field the standard was rather high: a carelessness of performance which Moscow would have overlooked was not forgiven here.

I evoked some interest at first. My initial piano recital in New York on 20 November 1918 was on the face of it a success. There were many musicians present and the New York press, whose opinion was decisive in procuring provincial engagements, was on the whole satisfactory. Even its unfavourable comment was served up in a somewhat sensational manner. In appraising my music the critics wrote a good deal of nonsense; for example, the best of them maintained that the finale of the Second Sonata made him think of a herd of mammoths charging across an Asiatic plateau. Of my playing they said that it had too little gradation, but that I had 'steel fingers, steel wrists, steel biceps and triceps'. No wonder the black lift attendant in the hotel touched my sleeve and remarked with some awe, 'Steel muscles . . .' He evidently thought I was a boxer. At the insistence of my manager I included some Skriabin and Rachmaninov since a whole programme of new music would be tiring for the public. Actually this was too little. Rachmaninov, who arrived in New York about this time, acted more wisely: he added only two or three of his own preludes to an otherwise all-classical programme.

The piano recital did not cover expenses but it bore fruit in other respects. I procured a rather profitable contract for pianola recordings. Two publishing firms ordered several piano pieces, and I wrote my *Grandmother's Tales* and the Dances op. 32 for them. But the terms finally offered me were so unfavourable that I withdrew. In general the system of contracts, terms and agreements I encountered in America was quite new to me. A manager would offer me a two- or three-year contract for concerts. 'I know I shall lose on you the first year,' he would say, 'but I hope to make up for it the next.' But I was so sure that I would be returning home shortly that I did not want to bind myself for any length of time. I was introduced to Damrosch, one of the leading American orchestral conductors. 'Don't play him the *Scythian Suite*, he won't understand it,' I was advised. But even in the First Concerto he did not turn the pages over in time, and his comment on the 'Classical' Symphony was: 'Delightful, just like Kalinnikov.' I went off in a huff, but it turned out that he had intended this as a compliment; he had toured the whole of America with Kalinnikov's symphony.

I gave two concerts in December with the Russian Symphony Orchestra conducted by Altschuler. Altschuler was a good musician but a poor conductor. He took pride in the fact that ten years before he had played with Rachmaninov and Skriabin. Since then, however, his orchestra had deteriorated. New Yorkers did not see why anyone needed a Russian orchestra in which most of the musicians were Americans, and with a mediocre conductor besides. After these concerts the press was unanimous in its abuse of both the orchestra and its conductor, with myself thrown in for good measure.

I had better luck in Chicago. McCormick, who lived there, kept his promise and put me in touch with Stock, conductor of the Chicago Orchestra, and with Campanini, conductor of the Chicago Opera. My two appearances with the Chicago Orchestra were far more successful than those in New York. The newspapers described the *Scythian Suite* as 'Bolshevist music'.

Campanini was interested in *The Gambler*. I had the piano score with me but how was I to get the orchestral score from the Mariinsky Theatre? An idea occurred to me: on leaving Moscow I had taken with me a theatrical magazine called *Love for Three Oranges*, after the play by Carlo Gozzi printed in its first issue. The play, with its mixture of fairy-tale, humour and satire, had a strong appeal for me, and during the long journey I had even sketched a plan of sorts in my mind. I put the idea to Campanini. 'Gozzi!' he cried. 'Our dear Gozzi! But that is wonderful!' We signed a contract in January 1919. The opera was to be ready by the autumn. After my unsuccessful New York appearance I had few concert engagements at this time, and having little inclination to learn other people's music for mixed programmes I snatched at this opportunity to work on an opera, the more so since the contract gave me sufficient means to work without interruption. Taking the tastes of the American audience into account I chose a simpler musical idiom than in *The Gambler*, and the work proceeded without difficulty. The theatrical aspect interested me tremendously. The three different planes in which the action developed were a novelty in themselves: (1) the fairy-tale characters, the Prince, Truffaldino etc.; (2) the forces of the nether world (Tchelio the sorcerer, Fata Morgana); and (3) the comic characters, like the representatives of the management who comment on everything that takes place.

In March I fell ill with scarlet fever and diphtheria combined, plus an abscess in my throat that very nearly choked me. 'I thought you were dying so I sent you some roses,' one American lady later confessed to me, obviously a little sorry that she had taken all that trouble for nothing. When I recovered I could barely wait for the doctor's permission to get back to work. I had slowed down a little before my illness, but the fever seemed to have cleansed me and I returned to work with renewed vigour. By June the music was all composed. The summer was spent on orchestration. By 1 October the score was ready, exactly as the contract stipulated. The theatre had spared no expense; the sets had been ordered from Anisfeld. Everything was going splendidly when Campanini died suddenly in December, and the theatre, being afraid to continue with the production without him, postponed it until the following season. I was left high and dry without the opera and with no concerts to speak of.

In the autumn of 1919 the Jewish 'Zimro' ensemble came to America. It consisted of a string quartet, a clarinet and piano, all of them fellow students of mine at the Petersburg Conservatoire. The official purpose of their concert tour was to raise funds for a Conservatoire in Jerusalem. But this was merely to impress the Jewish population of America. Actually they barely made enough to keep themselves alive. They had a repertoire of rather interesting Jewish music for diverse combinations of instruments: for two violins, trio etc. They asked me to write them an overture for six players and gave me a notebook of Jewish themes. I refused at first on the grounds that I used only my own musical material. The notebook, however, remained with me, and glancing through it one evening I chose a few pleasant themes and began to improvise at the piano. I soon noticed that several well-knit passages were emerging. I spent the next day working on the themes and by evening I had the overture ready. It took ten more days to whip it into final shape. I did not attach much importance to the Overture on Hebrew Themes but it was quite a success.

In December a new subject engaged my attention – Valery Bryusov's *Fiery Angel*. After the gay and frivolous *Oranges* it was interesting to turn to the wild and passionate Renata. The medieval setting, with wandering Fausts and the fulminating archbishops, also appealed to me. Unfortunately my interest was not altogether timely. I had had a contract in my pocket when I started working on the *Love for Three Oranges* and yet nothing came of it. To start on a major work now without any prospects was unwise to say the least. But apparently the stubborn streak in my nature was asserting itself – one opera had failed: I would write another. I worked altogether seven years on *The Fiery Angel* with long intervals in between. I wrote a great deal of music for it, far more than for the *Oranges*, but I never had any luck with it. The plot is partly to blame, for it does not fit easily into a libretto, as is the case with all stories told in the first person: because that person is constantly in the foreground, the story tells us little about the other characters and one has to invent situations for them.

Nevertheless the opera did fill the gap left by the *Oranges*. At times, as I roamed New York's Central Park and looked up at the skyscrapers facing it, I would think with cold fury of all the wonderful orchestras in America that cared nothing for my music; of the critics who never tired of uttering platitudes such as 'Beethoven is a great composer' and who balked violently at anything new; of the managers who arranged long tours for artists playing the same old hackneyed programme fifty times over. I had come here too soon; the child (America) was not old enough to appreciate new music. Should I go home? But how was I to get there? Russia was blocked on all sides by White Guard fronts, and besides who wants to return home a failure!

At the beginning of 1920 I had a rather pleasant trip to Canada giving concerts in Montreal and Quebec. A very amusing thing happened in one small town. Before I left for this town my New York manager had warned me to be sure to collect my fee in advance, otherwise I might not be paid. When I arrived and made this stipulation to the local concert manager he shrugged his shoulders but promised to attend to the matter. The concert hall was huge and tickets were sold at 25 cents, chiefly to students. Before the concert began the manager came into the dressing room carrying a small valise. 'Students pay for their tickets in silver,' he said. 'I shall have to pay you the same way.' He handed me 25 huge silver dollars, 100 50-cent pieces and 100 quarters. I stuffed them into my pockets until I felt as if I had a hundred poods of silver on me. A terrible thought occurred to me: What if my pocket seams gave way in the middle of the recital and a heap of coins spilled on to the floor. I would be the laughing-stock of America! 'I shall try to change the rest of the silver for you by the intermission,' the manager said. But I never saw him again and returned to New York with only one-third of the receipts due to me.

In April I went to Paris and London where I met Stravinsky and Diaghilev. The latter had revived his ballet season after the interval caused by the war and was preparing to stage *Chout*. The piano score I had sent him five years before was intact and had been neatly bound but there was still a great deal of work to be done. In the first place Diaghilev pointed out a number of places which had to be rewritten. He was a subtle and discerning critic and argued his point with great conviction. I, too, had learned enough in the past five years to be able to distinguish good from bad in *Chout*. So we had no difficulty in agreeing on the changes. Secondly, there were five entr'actes to be written, since Diaghilev wanted all six scenes to be presented without intermission. Thirdly, the whole thing had to be orchestrated. I settled for the summer in Mantes, near Paris, and set to work. In rewriting the ballet I endeavoured to replace the unsuccessful parts with development of the music of the other parts. Here and there some new music had to be composed, and the final dance entirely rewritten. The very beginning – the whistling and clattering which sounded like dust being wiped off the orchestra before the performance – remained unchanged.

Since the American public demanded classical music as well as my own compositions I tried to introduce a novelty by arranging a Buxtehude organ fugue for the piano (I had played a fugue by

Buxtehude at the Conservatoire in Taneev's class). Stravinsky gave me the idea of hunting up some of Schubert's waltzes and Ländler. I selected the most interesting of these and combined them in a suite, leaving the fabric of the original almost unchanged.

In the autumn of 1920 I returned to America where I had a battle royal with the director of the Chicago Opera. He was prepared to stage the *Three Oranges* that season but refused to pay me compensation for the year's delay. I would not agree. 'You ruined a whole season for me,' I said. 'In that case we shall be obliged to produce the opera without your consent,' he replied. 'In that case I shall be forced to take legal action to stop the production.' As a matter of fact the contract was not quite clear on that point – they could have produced it without my consent – but I could make plenty of trouble for them. Both sides refused to yield in the negotiations. I was ready to sacrifice the production rather than allow them to wipe their boots on me. The director was ready to sacrifice the 80,000 dollars he had invested in the sets rather than allow money to be pumped from him. And so again the opera was not staged, but this time, I must confess, the fault was mine.

In December and January I had some concert engagements in California. The concerts were not so interesting in themselves but the six months I spent in that delightful state were a pleasant vacation after my Chicago disappointments. In California, and partly in Chicago, I wrote *Five Songs without Words* (op. 35). However, the form proved to be impractical, and later I rewrote them for violin and piano, with the help of the violinist Kochanski. On my return to New York I learned that Mary Garden, the famous American singer who could sing the part of the tender Mélisande in Debussy's opera and that of the temperamental Salome in Richard Strauss's with equal mastery, had been appointed director of the Chicago Opera. She was not afraid of modern music and at once signed a new contract with me for the production of the *Three Oranges* the following season. My American stocks rose again.

I went to France. Diaghilev had begun rehearsing *Chout* in Monte Carlo. He had gone to great pains to turn out a brilliant performance. At his request Matisse, who lived nearby in Nice, made a pencil portrait of me. Diaghilev was much perturbed by the news that Koussevitzky, recently arrived in Paris, had decided to give the *Scythian Suite* a fortnight before the scheduled première of *Chout*. These two popularizers of Russian art exchanged several acrimonious telegrams on the subject of which of them should introduce me to Paris. But Koussevitzky would not yield and on 29 April 1921 the *Scythian Suite* was performed. On 17 May Diaghilev opened his season with *Chout*. I conducted. The entire musical world of Paris was present. The production was very well received by both public and press. The Paris public is extremely sensitive and progressive in its musical tastes: it knows 'when to turn the page' not only in the score but in music in general. Diaghilev, who toured in many countries, always tried to give his premières in Paris, for he believed that Paris set the tone. I must say, however, that I found it less pleasant to work with French orchestras than with American, since the French have the most distressing practice of allowing every musician to absent himself from rehearsals or performances whenever he pleases, provided he finds a substitute. I saw at least three different leaders during the rehearsals and four performances of *Chout*.

On 9 June the ballet had its première in London. At the dress rehearsal, held the day before the opening, I stopped the orchestra at one point noticing that something was wrong. The next moment Diaghilev came up to me, his face contorted with rage, and hissed, 'I have gathered the cream of London society for you and now you have ruined the whole impression. Now, please continue and do not stop on any account.' The public received the ballet very well but press comment was most unfavourable, quite abusive in fact. The English are supposed to be very polite but that certainly does not apply to their music critics. English critics are the most impolite in the world, with the possible exception of the Americans. Even as experienced a person as Diaghilev once lost his patience and committed an unheard-of breach of etiquette: he did not send an invitation to the leading music critic of *The Times*. The point was that if a critic is invited he is expected to express his opinion and is at liberty to praise or not as he sees fit, but if he buys a ticket and abuses the performance he may be sued for damages. The London musical world is more conservative than the Parisian, the British are slow to accept anything new, but once they have accepted it they are less apt to change their minds so quickly.

After the excitement of the theatre I moved to the coast of Brittany for the summer and set to work on the Third Piano Concerto. Much of it had already been composed at various times over a long period. As far back as 1911, while working on the First Piano Concerto, which like the First Violin Concerto was conceived originally as a concertino, I had planned a large virtuoso concerto. I made very little progress with this work, however, and only one passage of parallel ascending triads had survived. This I now inserted at the end of the first movement of the Third Concerto. In 1913 I had composed a theme for variations which I kept for a long time for subsequent use. In 1916–17 I had tried several times to return to the Third Concerto. I wrote a beginning for it (two themes) and two variations on the theme of the second movement. At about the same time I contemplated writing a 'white quartet', i.e. an absolutely diatonic string quartet that could be played only on the white keys of the piano. The quartet was to have consisted of two movements, a slow first movement in sonata form and a 3/4 finale. Some of the 'white' themes were composed in St Petersburg, some on the Pacific Ocean and others in America. However I found the task too difficult, I was afraid it would prove too monotonous, and now in 1921 I decided to split up the material: the subordinate theme became the theme of Renata in *The Fiery Angel*; the principal theme I used for the monastery; the first and second themes of the finale went into the finale of the Third Concerto. Thus when I began working on the latter I already had the entire thematic material apart from the subordinate theme of the first movement and the third theme of the finale.

That summer I wrote Five Songs (op. 36) to verses by Balmont who happened to be staying further up the Atlantic coast. Some of the verses were old, others (e.g., 'The Butterfly') were written on the spot. While I played him fragments from the Third Concerto he dashed off a sonnet dedicated to it. But soon afterwards Balmont turned his pen against his 'suffering homeland' (as he called it) and we parted ways.

In October 1921 I went to America, this time with greater pleasure than the previous year: the production of the *Three Oranges* was already in full swing, I had a number of concert engagements and I was taking my new concerto with me. The rehearsals of the opera soon began, with myself conducting. Mary Garden turned out to be a director who liked to make generous gestures but who was chiefly concerned with her own roles and was never available when wanted. The singers were good, the settings superb, but the director, Coini, was a colourless personality: he was one of those professionals who know a hundred operas by heart but have nothing new of their own to offer. At first I merely grumbled at his lack of originality, but after a while I went backstage and explained the parts to the singers myself, and instructed the chorus right on the stage. Once when I got excited and made a mistake in English one of the members of the chorus said, 'You needn't bother trying to talk English to us, half of us here are Russian Jews!' Finally Coini lost his temper. 'Who is in charge here, you or I?' he demanded. 'You are,' I replied, 'but you are here to carry out my wishes.'

Fortunately the dress rehearsal was held without the public, for I was obliged to start the prologue four times before I was satisfied with the chorus. The première on 30 December 1921 brought a full house and on the face of it was a big success. The Chicagoans were both proud and embarrassed to be presenting a 'modernist première' which, according to the newspapers, had already cost some 250,000 dollars.

On 13 January I took part in a grand concert arranged by the Chicago branch of the Friends of Soviet Russia. Besides my own compositions I played Musorgsky's *Pictures at an Exhibition*. The printed programmes bore the emblem of the society – two hands clasped in friendship. After that I went to New York to be followed shortly by the Chicago Opera Company, which, after several postponements, gave a single perfor-mance of the *Oranges* on 14 February 1922. Owing to these changes in the date of the performance I happened to have a piano recital as well on the day of the opening. Since I was to conduct the opera that evening I followed Capablanca's advice and spent the time between the recital and the opera taking a hot bath and resting. The opera was again warmly received by the public, but, heavens, what a press it had the next day! It was as if a pack of dogs had been suddenly unleashed at me and were tearing my trousers to bits. If the opera had not been too well understood in Chicago at least the production, being their own, had been spared. But New York did not need to spare anything; on the contrary the rivalry of the two cities made itself felt. 'You wanted to show us something we hadn't thought of producing ourselves – well, here's what we think of it!'

A similar fate awaited the Third Concerto, which I played in Chicago on 16 and 17 December with Stock and in New York on 26 and 27 January with Coates. In Chicago there was less understanding than support ('the composer whose opera we produced'); in New York there was neither understanding nor support. I had to face the truth: the American season, which had begun so promisingly, fizzled out completely for me. My last hope was that Mary Garden would put on *The Fiery Angel* the following season and sing the main role, but unfortunately for me she resigned the directorship. I was left with a thousand dollars in my pocket and an aching head, to say nothing of a fervent desire to get away to some quiet place where I could work in peace.

In March 1922 I settled in southern Germany on the slopes of the Bavarian Alps, not far from Ettal Monastery and three kilometres from Oberammergau, famed for its *Festspielen* – medieval Passion Plays held once every ten years. It was a picturesque and peaceful spot, ideal for work. I set to work on *The Fiery Angel* – incidentally, the Witches' Sabbaths described in it must have taken place somewhere in these parts. Ettal became my headquarters for the next year and a half; from here I made trips to other towns for concerts. In April I played the Third Concerto in Paris and London. In both cities it was well received and even the English press was 'less worse' than after *Chout*. The critic to whom Diaghilev had omitted to send a ticket discovered that Prokofiev was endowed with a little talent after all and that one could endure listening to his music for about fifteen minutes. In June Diaghilev revived *Chout* in Paris and asked me for the *Three Oranges*, but when I played him the music Stravinsky, who happened to be present, sharply criticized it and refused to listen to more than one act. In some respects he was right: the first act is the least successful. But on that occasion I hotly defended my opera and the result was a quarrel. For my part I did not approve of Stravinsky's predilection for Bachian techniques – his 'pseudo-Bachism' – or rather I did not approve of adopting someone else's idiom and calling it one's own. True I had written a 'Classical' Symphony myself, but that was only a passing phase. With Stravinsky this 'Bachism' was becoming the basic line of his music. After this encounter our relations became strained and for several years Stravinsky's attitude toward me was critical, though not altogether unfavourable. I met Diaghilev once more in Berlin when Mayakovsky was there, and we spent some interesting evenings together. On one of these occasions Mayakovsky and Diaghilev got into

a furious argument on the subject of modern art; on another Mayakovsky read his verses to which we listened with intense interest.

In Ettal, besides working on *The Fiery Angel*, I polished up the piano
score of *Chout* and the *Three Oranges* and arranged a symphonic suite
from *Chout*. I included everything in the latter that could be used as
symphonic music. There were twelve movements – too many and too
varied to be performed in succession, but I did not intend all of them to
go into one programme; five or eight numbers of the conductor's
choosing is quite enough. These three pieces plus the score of the
Scythian Suite and a number of smaller pieces were published at this
time by Gutheil, who had resumed their activities and had been
showering me with proofs. This time they had moved to Paris and
become a shareholding company with French participation since the
French do not allow purely foreign companies in their country.
However the shareholders had been carefully chosen to enable the
publishing house to adhere to its principal purpose: to work for
composers and not for profit.

While living in Ettal I corresponded with my Moscow and Petrograd
friends and began to write for several Soviet magazines. In May 1923
my report of my work abroad appeared in the journal *K Novym beregam
(To New Shores)*. My latest compositions began to be performed in
Moscow, and the Petrograd Philharmonic invited me to come and give a
few concerts. Why did I not return to my native land? I believe the chief
and basic reason was that I had not yet fully grasped the significance of
what was happending in the USSR. I did not realize that the events
there demanded the co-operation of all citizens, not only men of
politics, as I had thought, but men of art as well. Moreover it was hard to
break away from the routine of the life I was leading: publishing
compositions, correcting proofs, giving concerts, endeavouring to hold
my own against other composers and other musical trends. Family
affairs, too, played no small part: the long illness of my mother, her
subsequent death, my marriage and the birth of my son.

My concert engagements at this period took me all over France,
England, Belgium, Italy and Spain. Strange to say, though I lived for a
year and a half in Germany within two hours' ride of a city like Munich,
I did not establish any contacts whatever with the German musical
world. The March and Scherzo from the *Three Oranges* and the

Overture on Hebrew Themes had been performed in Berlin, and one or two piano pieces were played by professional pianists, but they did not make much impression and Paris remained my musical centre. The first performance of the *Scythian Suite* in Brussels on 15 January 1923 under the baton of Ruhlmann was rather stormy, the audience very nearly coming to blows. In 1923 I revised the Second Concerto, the score of which had been lost, and wrote the Fifth Sonata.

In October 1923 I moved to Paris where the first performance of my Violin Concerto took place on 18 October (soloist Darrieux, conductor Koussevitzky). Hubermann and some other violinists flatly refused to learn 'that music' and the solo part had to be given to the leader, who did quite well with it. The critics were divided; some of them commented not without malice on its 'Mendelssohnisms'. The Fifth Sonata, written in an entirely different and more intricate style, was also coolly received.

Living in Paris does not make one a Parisian, and France having been victorious on the battlefield wanted to be the victor in the field of music as well. Hence the exceptional attentions showered upon the 'Six' (Honegger, Milhaud, Poulenc etc.), which the 'Six' did not altogether deserve. On 8 May 1924 my Second Piano Concerto had its première in Paris, and on 29 May the cantata *Seven, they are Seven*, played from the printed score received from Moscow. This was my first composition to be published under Soviet auspices. Both were extremely successful and the public was even slightly offended when Koussevitzky played the cantata twice on the same programme – to drive it home better, as he thought. It was at this time, however, that I first heard a reproach that was to be cast at me more than once subsequently: namely, that I was living off my old compositions. This decided me to write a large symphony 'to be made of iron and steel'. I had already composed the main theme. It was somewhat similar in outline to that of Beethoven's Sonata op. 111.

In order to earn some money while working on the symphony I accepted a commission to write a short ballet for a travelling ballet troupe which wished to present a performance of several short ballets accompanied by an ensemble of five instruments. I suggested a quintet consisting of oboe, clarinet, violin, viola and double-bass. The simple plot from circus life, entitled *Trapeze*, served as a pretext for composing a chamber piece that could be performed as pure music. This explains the impractical rhythms, like the numbers written in 10/8 (3-4-3) which gave the choreographers a great deal of trouble. Nevertheless the *Trapeze* ballet ran in several cities in Germany and Italy with some success. For the same troupe I arranged Schubert's waltzes for two pianos, which were to stand on the stage and form part of the set. In the earlier version, arranged for one piano, I had preserved Schubert's texture, but since a large number of waltzes played in succession sounded rather monotonous, in adapting them for two pianos I endeavoured to liven up the music with harmonic and contrapuntal additions.

While the Quintet op. 39 gave me comparatively little trouble, the Second Symphony (the 'Classical' Symphony though not strictly symphonic in form was a symphony nevertheless, and hence I had decided to consider it the First) turned out to be a long and complicated piece and occupied me throughout the autumn and winter. After an energetic first movement I wanted to relieve the tension at least in the beginning of the second movement which I had conceived as a theme with variations, and for this I chose a quiet theme I had composed in Japan. But on the whole the Fifth Sonata, the Quintet and the Second Symphony, continuing from the *Sarcasmes* through the *Scythian Suite* and *Seven, they are Seven*, were the most chromatic of all my compositions. This was the effect of the Parisian atmosphere where complex patterns and dissonances were the accepted thing, and which fostered my predilection for complex thinking.

Of my concert appearances that season mention might be made of a piano recital, or rather a sonata evening, in Paris on 5 December 1924, in which I played the Second, Third, Fourth and Fifth Sonatas, and my first piano recital in Berlin on 24 January 1925. I particularly remember the latter occasion because, having been warned that I would probably not be paid, I asked for the money in advance, only to find that the impresario had vanished. In the meantime the audience was getting impatient and I finally went on and played. The next day the newspapers reproached me for having turned up late for the concert, and I never did get any money for that performance.

In the summer of 1924 Szigeti played my Violin Concerto at a festival of modern music in Prague and afterwards toured all the main cities of

Europe with it. When he came to Paris and I expressed the desire to attend the rehearsal his face fell. 'You see,' he said, 'I love that concerto and I know the score so well that I sometimes give pointers to the conductor as if it were my own composition. But you must admit that under the circumstances the presence of the composer would be embarrassing for me.' I agreed and went to the concert instead. Szigeti played superbly.

On 14 March 1925 the European première of the *Three Oranges* took place in Cologne with Szenkar conducting. This was an excellent production, far superior to the American (if less lavish). Both public and press showed greater understanding than in New York or Chicago.

The Second Symphony was performed on 6 June 1925, in Paris. It was too densely woven in texture, too heavily laden with contrapuntal lines changing to figuration to be successful, and although one critic did comment admiringly on the septuple counterpoint my friends preserved an embarrassed silence. This was perhaps the first time it occurred to me that I might perhaps be destined to be a second-rate composer. Paris as the undisputed dictator of fashion has a tendency to pose as the arbiter in other fields as well. In music the refinement of French tastes has its reverse side – the public are apt to be too easily bored. Having taken up with one composer they quickly tire of him and in a year or two are searching for a new sensation. I was evidently no longer a sensation. Diaghilev too had deserted me after my quarrel with Stravinsky.

However Diaghilev returned to me periodically and in the summer of 1925, soon after the performance of the Second Symphony, he broached the subject of a new ballet. 'But I cannot write in the style you approve of,' I said, hinting at the rather banal stuff Auric and Milhaud were composing for him. 'You must write in your own style,' Diaghilev replied and suggested that I write a ballet on a Soviet theme. I could not believe my ears. It was as if a fresh breeze had blown through my window, that fresh breeze of which Lunacharsky had spoken. It was decided to invite Yakulov as the artist; he had recently exhibited in Paris with great success.

Sitting in a tiny café on the banks of a river half an hour outside Paris, Yakulov and I roughly sketched several draft librettos. We assumed that the important thing at this stage was not to provide mere entertainment but to show the new life that had come to the Soviet Union, and primarily the construction effort. It was to be a ballet of construction, with hammers big and small being wielded, transmission belts and flywheels revolving, light signals flashing, all leading to a general creative upsurge with the dance groups operating the machines and at the same time depicting the work of the machines choreographically. The idea was Yakulov's, who had spent some years in the Soviet Union and described it all most vividly. It was easy to see that the libretto had been written not by a playwright but a painter guided by his visual impressions. 'The ballet consists of two acts,' he wrote in the magazine *Zhizn iskusstva (Art Life)*, 'the first showing the breakdown of the old order, its deterioration, and the enthusiasm of the revolutionaries against the background of this decaying old order, and, in contrast, the uplifting influence of organized labour.' My job consisted in organizing the rather haphazard material Yakulov had given me and arranging it in the form of musical numbers in a harmonious succession leading to a culmination.

As soon as the libretto had been worked out and more or less approved by Diaghilev I turned my attention to the music, and here I must record some serious changes in my approach as compared with the Quintet and the Second Symphony. The first was a turn towards Russian musical idiom, this time not the idiom of Afanasiev's fairy-tales, but one that could convey the spirit of modern times. The second radical change was from the chromatic to the diatonic: this ballet – which Diaghilev for some reason proposed calling *Le pas d'acier (The Age of Steel)* – was in a large measure diatonic and many of the themes were composed on the white keys only. I worked at a good speed and by the autumn I was already able to play the entire piano score to Diaghilev. The latter as usual made a number of very useful suggestions and after a few alterations I started on the orchestral score.

The ballet was not my only contact with the USSR at this time. Negotiations were in progress for the production of the *Three Oranges* in Leningrad. On 19 November 1925 a suite from this opera was performed in Paris for the first time. This suite was more difficult to do than the one from *Chout* since here some of the movements, the 'Odd Fellows' and 'The Prince and Princess', for instance, had to be pieced together from fragments taken from various parts of the opera, and this meant much new composition.

In the latter part of December 1925, after a four-year interval, I went to the United States on a concert tour. I gave fourteen concerts, seven of them (in five cities) with the Boston Symphony Orchestra which Koussevitzky had been conductor of for two years. I played the Third Piano Concerto. Six concerts were sponsored by the Pro Musica, a society for modern music which was founded by a Frenchman named Schmitz, with branches in several cities. My wife Lina Llubera took part in these concerts. She sang songs by Myaskovsky and Taneev as well as my own. I also played Myaskovsky's *Bizarreries*. In one provincial town all the members of the society (there were 300 of them) expressed the desire to shake hands with us. The ceremony proceeded thus: a member of the society would approach the secretary and say, 'I am Mr Smith.' The chairman would say to me, 'Let me introduce you to Mr Smith.' I would shake hands and say, 'Happy to meet you, Mr Smith!' Whereupon Mr Smith would say, 'Happy to meet you, Mr Prokofiev!' and pass on to my wife. In the meantime Mr Jones would be approaching in the same manner and so on, 300 times!

I continued to work on the orchestration of the ballet during the tour. Since the branches of the Pro Musica society were scattered all over the United States, from New York to San Francisco, and a good deal of my time was spent in railway carriages, I endeavoured to utilize the time by scoring my ballet. The shaking of the car made it difficult to write the score so I decided to do all the preliminary work *en route*, not only choosing the instruments but scoring each bar complete in every detail, including the instrumentation of chords, bowing, accents and nuances. In this way all that remained was the mechanical job of copying on to the orchestral score what had been sketched out in pencil on the piano score. At first it seemed impossible to map out all the instruments on the piano score but after a little practice I learned to do this without much difficulty. Moreover between the braced staves I always had an extra stave on which to insert additional voices or accents, and if there was not enough room I would make a note and carry over the extra passages or complex string chords on to a separate stave. This method proved extremely useful in later years.

My American tour was followed in 1926 by a tour of Italy. After a matinée recital in Naples Maxim Gorky came to see me and took me off to his place for dinner. He lived in a typical but rather uncomfortable Italian house. He was in good form and I spent a most pleasant evening in his company.

On 18 February 1926 the *Three Oranges* opened in Leningrad, and on 9 October in Berlin. In Leningrad the opera was a success and the press gave it a good deal of space. The comments of some reviewers were very sensible; others wanted to know whom I was laughing at: the audience, Gozzi, the operatic form or those who had no sense of humour. They found in the *Oranges* mockery, defiance, the grotesque and what not; all I had been trying to do was to write an amusing opera. At about the same time the conductorless orchestra, the Persimfans, gave several concerts of my music in Moscow and I was very pleased to learn that Moscow showed serious interest in my work.

In October I went to Berlin for the opening of the *Three Oranges*. I did not like the sets. As I was walking across the stage about fifteen minutes before the curtain rose I overheard an old stage-hand remark, 'All that good German money wasted on these sets when the whole thing will be scrapped after one or two performances.' We'll see about that! I said to myself. But the stage-hand's prediction was not far wrong. The opera was not a success and after eight performances was taken off. The direction was so obviously poor that when the head of the company proceeded to praise the elderly producer in my presence I could not force myself to make a single flattering comment. Blech, who conducted the orchestra, was perfect, so perfect indeed that he took all the life out of the score. 'Take this passage a little faster,' I suggested at the final rehearsal. 'Can't be done,' he replied, 'the orchestra is bound to make a mess of it.' 'Let them make a mess of it,' I said, and I felt that from that moment Blech ceased to respect me. In the Cologne production the general conception was more harmoniously integrated and the opera was consequently much more successful.

I spent the summer of 1926 near Paris again, orchestrating *The Fiery Angel* in which Bruno Walter, who was the head of another Berlin opera house, was now interested. Taking into account a few scenic defects I revised the libretto and rewrote some of the music. In orchestrating it I used the method I had worked out on American trains, but this time I had my piano-score sketch copied by someone else. This cut the work to nearly half and relieved me of a great deal of purely mechanical labour.

In between periods of work on *The Fiery Angel* I wrote the Overture op. 42. The story of this overture is as follows: my contract with the American pianola company was still valid, but by now player pianos had gone out of style and the company had begun to diversify; among other things it was building a concert hall in New York. Instead of playing a new batch of pieces for recordings (which could have been done in London) the company asked me to write an overture for the opening of the new hall. I eagerly seized on the idea, for I much preferred composing to making recordings.

Since the hall was to be of medium size I chose an ensemble of seventeen musicians. I planned the music as follows: the main instruments would be two pianos, two harps and a celesta; the latter, used mainly in the lower registers, would serve as a sort of resonator for the pianos; there would be five woodwinds to carry the horizontal music; two trumpets and a trombone used with caution to add power and emphasize the rhythmic passages; and finally for the bass, three double-basses, now soft, now blatant (the highest was subsequently replaced by a cello). The seventeenth performer would play several percussion instruments (hence an overture for seventeen *musicians* and not seventeen *instruments*, as it has sometimes mistakenly been called). The music would be definitely tonal; all three themes without accidentals, the second in the Dorian mode, very little development and no coda. Later this form of ensemble turned out to be impractical (too small for a symphony concert, too large for a chamber concert), so I made a different version for full symphony orchestra.

During the autumn of 1926 I corresponded with the Persimfans and the Leningrad Philharmonic and in January 1927, accompanied by my wife, I went to the USSR, giving one concert in Riga *en route*. Before leaving America I was interviewed by a New York magazine. Among other things I was asked to give a definition of the classics. Wishing to poke a little fun at the Americans I gave this reply: 'A classical composer is a madman who composes music that is incomprehensible to his own generation. He has succeeded in discovering a certain logic that is still unknown to others and hence these others cannot follow his reasoning. Only after some time the paths he has charted, provided they are genuine, will become clear to everyone else. To write only according to the rules laid down by classical composers of the past means to be only a pupil and not a master. Such a composer is easily understood by his contemporaries but he has no chance of outliving his generation.'

On 18 January I stepped on Soviet soil at Bigosovo, and on the 19th I arrived in Moscow. How can I describe my feelings on returning to my native land! I was met by the Persimfans people and driven in a car with frost-coated windows straight to the Metropole Hotel where I found many old friends awaiting me – Myaskovsky, Derzhanovsky, Saradzhev, Asafiev. With L. M. Tseitlin, the moving spirit of the Persimfans, I went to a rehearsal of the orchestra. As we approached the hall I heard the March from the *Three Oranges* being played. 'They are taking it a little too slow,' I said, thinking they were rehearsing it, but it turned out that the orchestra was playing the March in my honour. The conductorless orchestra coped splendidly with difficult programmes and accompanied soloists as competently as any conducted orchestra. Their main difficulty lay in changing tempo, for here the whole ensemble had to feel the music in exactly the same way. On the other hand, difficult passages were easily overcome, for each individual musician felt himself a soloist and played with perfect precision. The programme of the first concert held on 24 January 1927 consisted of the *Chout* Suite (ten numbers), the Third Concerto and the Suite from the *Three Oranges*. The reception I was given in Moscow was tremendous. For an encore after the Third Concerto I played Myaskovsky's *Bizarreries*, but knowing that the composer was present I lost my nerve and muffed it so badly that he hardly recognized his own work. Altogether two symphony programmes (in the second I played the Second Piano Concerto) and two piano recitals had been prepared for Moscow. Each programme was given twice, making a total of eight concerts.

At the rehearsal of each new piece the musicians expressed their enthusiasm, but after the 'American' Overture op. 42 they preserved an awkward silence: they did not understand it. Neither did the public. What was the trouble? The themes were almost entirely diatonic and there was no complex development. I purposely dwell on this point because it was to affect a whole period of my work, beginning roughly with that overture. I believe the trouble was this: having turned from the chaos of chromaticism toward diatonism I had begun to search for new melodic designs. But novelty of design is something that does not strike the attention. The listener, unable to grasp it at once, will pass it by without noticing it. It is the same with a melody: if it follows a familiar pattern it will be easily understood, but will soon just as easily find its way into the waste-paper basket. A melody of an unaccustomed design is not accepted as a melody at all at first because it consists of phrases hitherto not considered melodious. But if the composer is right he will have extended the range of melodic possibilities and the listener is bound to follow him, if only at a respectful distance. It sometimes happened that coming across one of my own compositions of this period after a lapse of several years I would be unable to make head or tail of it at first. But after playing it once, twice, three times, the thing would suddenly emerge, everything would fall into place and I would see that all was exactly as it should be. Now if I myself cannot always immediately comprehend something that was perfectly clear to me before, how can I expect the listener to grasp it at once, especially if he is not particularly discerning? I might perhaps wish that he would have a little more faith in the 'trade mark' instead of protesting that the firm used to turn out decent goods and has now gone berserk. If he would bear in mind that music which the ear takes in at once is not necessarily good music (history teaches us that) and would give a little more serious attention to my 'incomprehensible' composition I am sure we could speedily understand one another.

From Moscow I went to Leningrad where the same four programmes were given. The reception in Leningrad was even more enthusiastic than in Moscow. In the intervals between concerts I roamed the streets and the embankments with tender memories of this city where I had spent so many years of my life. The young Leningrad composers showed me their compositions. Of these the most notable were a sonata by Shostakovich and a septet by Gavriil Popov. At the performance of *The Love for Three Oranges* I sat next to Lunacharsky who said that the *Scythian Suite* was elemental and the *Three Oranges* was like a 'glass of champagne'. The production, staged by two friends of my youth – Dranishnikov, a fellow student, and Radlov, a chess partner of mine – was brilliant from the point of view both of smooth performance and of respect for the composer's wishes. It was undoubtedly the best of all the productions of the opera I had seen. Here is a bit of verse that was current at the time:

> Three oranges upon the stage,
> One orange in my hand,
> Me up in the gallery
> Clapping to beat the band.

After Leningrad I toured Kharkov, Kiev and Odessa, giving two piano recitals in each city. I gave three more concerts in Moscow: two for the Association for Contemporary Music (*Dreams* and the 'Classical' Symphony for the first time in Moscow on 27 February and the Quintet, also for the first time, on 6 March) and a final concert with the Persimfans on 20 March. After that I went to France where Diaghilev had started rehearsals of *Le pas d'acier*.

The ballet had its première in Paris on 7 June 1927. Like all Diaghilev productions it was magnificently staged and was a great success. 'A queer production,' the French press commented, 'beginning with the title and ending with the music and the choreography. Can it possibly be intended to replace *A Life for the Tsar*?' The White Guard press scoffed at this 'prickly flower of proletarian culture'. Stravinsky was disgusted by the hammering on the stage. But the young people were ecstatic. On 4 July the ballet opened in London. The theatre was full of lords and ladies and a dazzling display of diamonds. 'The packed hall rocked with applause,' wrote the newspapers. 'Sergey Prokofiev deserves to be famous. As an apostle of Bolshevism he has no peer.' 'Prokofiev travels through our countries but refuses to think as we do.'

Other premières in this period besides *Le pas d'acier* were *Ala and Lolli* on 7 May 1927, in Berlin under the title of *Die Erlösten* (being in Magdeburg on a concert tour I attended the première incognito, but it was so bad that I hurried away without making myself known); *Love for Three Oranges* (of which more below) on 19 May in the Bolshoi Theatre in Moscow; *Ala and Lolli* on 11 October in Buenos Aires, well received; *Chout*, in January 1928 in Kiev, which used the suite and not the complete ballet.

In the summer of 1927 I completed the orchestration of *The Fiery Angel*. The piano score with the text in German was printed for the production in Berlin but the orchestral parts arrived too late and it was cancelled. After the success of the *Three Oranges* Leningrad wanted to produce *The Gambler* and with this in view I decided to revise it. Ten years had passed since it was written and now I saw quite clearly what was genuine in it and what was sheer padding disguised by thunderous chords. I discarded these parts and replaced them by new ones built mainly on the material which I considered worth preserving. I also polished up the vocal parts and simplified the orchestration. I had been given the score in Leningrad, and now that *The Fiery Angel* was finished I at once began work.

In December I was to have undertaken another concert tour in the USSR but it fell through for practical reasons. On 16 February 1928 my Second Symphony was played for the second time in Paris under the baton of Straram, after eight rehearsals. It sounded better this time. But I intend to return to it one day and try to express the same ideas more lucidly. On 28 November it was performed in Leningrad.

The following spring selections from *The Fiery Angel* were given in concert performance in Paris. They were well received and I was sorry the opera had not been staged and that the score lay gathering dust on the shelf. I was about to make a suite out of it when I remembered that for one of the entr'actes I had developed themes from the preceding scene, and it occurred to me that this might serve as the kernel for a symphony. I examined the themes and found that they would make a good exposition for a sonata allegro. I found the same themes in other parts of the opera differently expressed and quite suitable for the recapitulation. In this way the plan for the first movement of the symphony worked out quite simply. The material for the Scherzo and for the Andante was also found without difficulty. The Finale took a little longer. I spent far more time whipping the thing into final shape, tying up all the loose ends and doing the orchestration. But the result – the Third Symphony – I consider to be one of my best compositions. I do not like it to be called the 'Fiery Angel' Symphony. The main thematic material was composed quite independently of the opera. Used in the opera it naturally acquired its colouring from the plot, but being transferred from the opera to the symphony it lost that colouring, I believe, and I should therefore prefer the Third Symphony to be regarded as pure 'symphony'.

Besides the symphony I worked on two rather long pieces for the piano in which I wished to indulge in a little musical introspection without trying to find some easily accessible shape for my ideas. (I do not wish to defend this method of composition but I do think that having written quite an amount of simple comprehensible music I might occasionally be permitted the luxury of composing something for myself.) I called the pieces *Things in Themselves*, op. 45. The first and longer piece contained a substantial amount of thematic material, rather diatonic in parts and not too complicated, or so it seemed to me at the time. The second had two elements, chromatic and lyrical, the latter recurring three times in slightly altered form. Unfortunately the title created the mistaken impression that these were abstractions, mere juggling with sounds. After reading the title and noticing some complexities in the texture, people did not take the trouble to try to understand the music itself. After all, the thinking of one and the same composer can be both complex and simple. Take the second volume of Beethoven's sonatas. No one would go so far as to claim that the simple sonatas in that volume are better or more necessary than the complex ones. Hence the barbs so frequently levelled at *Things in Themselves* usually fall wide of the mark since the criticism is based on a false premise, on a misunderstanding.

Early in the autumn of 1928 Diaghilev commissioned me to write a new ballet on a biblical subject: the parable of the prodigal son. The moral of the elder brother was discarded and the story went thus: the prodigal son leaves home, goes on a spree and yields to the charms of a beautiful maiden. At last, robbed and destitute, he crawls home to his father who welcomes and forgives him. It was a brief plot in three scenes but it contained all the necessary elements. This made the job both easy and interesting. When Diaghilev called me up in November to ask how the work was progressing I was able to tell him that the rough draft of the piano score was ready. He was amazed. 'What, already!' he gasped. 'Then it cannot be good.' But when he heard the music he was satisfied. To my mind the final scene, the return, was the best. Choreographically, too, this scene was excellently done: the prodigal son crawled across the whole stage on his knees, staff in hand, the upper part of his body moving with remarkable plasticity. I spent the whole winter on the orchestration, using the now routine 'speed' method. It should not be thought that this method led to carelessness or inaccuracies. On the contrary it made for a smoother flow of ideas, unencumbered by purely mechanical work.

The spring of 1929 brought three premières. Since Leningrad's interest in *The Gambler* had gradually waned it was first produced on 29 April 1929, in Brussels, whose opera theatre, though modest in resources, was considered progressive. It did a thorough job with the production and the opera had a successful run for two years. For me the main source of satisfaction was that the dramatic tension was built up gradually and was sustained until the very end. The reviews were on the whole favourable; some critics, in fact, were even too lavish in their praise. 'Listening to *The Gambler*,' one of them wrote, 'one experiences a delight comparable, though in modern forms, to that evoked by the music of Mozart.' Although *The Gambler* is the least Dostoevskyan of all Dostoevsky's stories, many of the spiritual perturbations described by the author would have evoked an entirely different reaction in Russia than was the case in Brussels, which was too ready to regard them as interesting but incomprehensible manifestations of the Slav soul.

On 17 May the Third Symphony was performed for the first time in Paris under the baton of Monteux. I worked a great deal on the Scherzo between rehearsals, increasing or decreasing the number of bars and trying to find the correct proportion. Opinion about the symphony was divided but on the whole it was treated with respect. The composer was given credit for 'original thinking amidst the thousands of modern Parisian influences', which was said to be 'a rare virtue in our days'. 'The Scythian,' another critic wrote, 'has come down to the southern shores and become more human.'

On 21 May *The Prodigal Son* opened in Paris. The sets by Roualt, one of France's leading artists, were excellent. I conducted the orchestra, following Stravinsky who conducted his ballet *Renard*. Rachmaninov sat in the front row and condescendingly applauded a few numbers. The public and press were most enthusiastic. I was not altogether satisfied with the choreography; it did not always follow the music. Having been occupied with *The Gambler* I was too late in contacting the producers to be able to change anything. I had a clash with Diaghilev on this account. Stravinsky too had been having some trouble with him. After Paris *The Prodigal Son* was performed in Berlin and London.

In August of that year Diaghilev died in Venice. Here in Russia his work has not been properly appreciated and many are inclined to regard him merely as an impresario who exploited the talents of his artists. Yet his influence on art and his services in popularizing Russian art cannot be over-estimated. He left no money after his death, only a very interesting collection of books and sketches made by the artists he worked with. He had been in constant touch with our representatives in London and Paris and, had he lived, would no doubt be working with us now.

In the summer of 1929 I decided to tackle the backlog of old musical material that had been piling up for some time, chiefly the Divertissement and Sinfonietta. The Divertissement had grown out of four numbers written at various times. The first and third had been composed as far back as 1925 when the troupe that had produced the *Trapeze* had asked for two additional numbers. That explains why both numbers had originally been conceived for a quintet. The first was very successful and Diaghilev had included it as an intermezzo dance between two scenes of *Le pas d'acier*. The Larghetto was sketched in rough in 1928 and the fourth number emerged from music intended for *The Prodigal Son*. The following summer I put all this material in order and orchestrated it. The title Divertissement is not altogether happy: it applies to the first number but not to the piece as a whole. The tone-colour of the orchestration was subdued, though in this it bore some traces of the influence of Stravinsky with whom I was now on good terms. At this period Stravinsky insisted on austere instrumentation. 'Surely I cannot be expected to go in for the pageantry of Rimsky-Korsakov?' he would say.

I was not satisfied with the 1914 version of the Sinfonietta and so I took it apart and put it together again, rewriting some sections but adding no new material. I gave it a double opus number – 5/48 – which evoked some ironical smiles, being taken as a sign that I was trying to pile up my opus numbers. Incidentally the Sinfonietta has been comparatively rarely performed, whereas the 'Classical' Symphony, written in the same manner, has been played everywhere. I cannot quite understand why the fate of these two pieces should be so different.

The Boston Symphony Orchestra, one of the best orchestras in the world, commissioned Stravinsky and myself to write symphonies on the occasion of its fiftieth anniversary. I thought of making a symphony out of *The Prodigal Son*, but people began to tell me I was turning theatre music into symphonies rather too often. I was prompted to this by a dual motive: the possibility of building a sonata Allegro and the desire to subject the material to symphonic treatment. The idea turned out to be impractical and I abandoned it. Now, however, music that had been written for but not included in *The Prodigal Son* proved perfectly suitable for the first movement of the Fourth Symphony (I composed a new introduction). The music of the Son's homecoming was used for the second movement, that of the Beautiful Woman for the third. The Finale was the most difficult part. Much of the ballet music was unsuitable for a symphony and I used it for a separate symphonic suite. I worked on this symphony in the autumn of 1929 and the spring of 1930. First performed in Boston on 14 November 1930, it was not a success, but I have always liked it for its restrained tone and the wealth of material it contains.

In October 1929 the motor-car in which I was travelling with my family overturned. Fortunately no one was badly hurt, but I struck my hands heavily against the hard pavement and was unable to play the piano for two months. In November I went to Moscow, this time without any concert engagements. I was very glad, for on my previous visit I had had no chance to see anything. Incidentally, one concert did take place: Saradzhev conducted and the Sinfonietta was played twice. This was the first time it had been performed since I had revised it. On 13 November the Bolshoi Theatre revived the *Three Oranges*. The highlight of the production was the extremely interesting décor by Rabinovich; however it was so complicated that the intervals lasted longer than the acts. 'Love for three intervals,' joked the weary spectators as they wandered about the foyers between the acts.

Though more lavish than the Leningrad production Moscow's was not quite as smooth. Some of it was a little overdone, for instance when the Prince, on seeing Fata Morgana tumble over, not only laughed but imitated the actor playing the part of the laughing Prince.

The Bolshoi decided to stage *Le pas d'acier* which had been performed three times in Moscow on the concert stage. However after some rather sharp criticism by members of the Association of Proletarian Musicians the Bolshoi Theatre changed its mind and I had to content myself with foreign productions for the time being. An excellent production was given in 1931 in the New York Metropolitan Opera with Stokowski conducting. It was thrilling to see a tremendous red flag flying on the stage of this most bourgeois of bourgeois theatres!

At the beginning of 1930 I went to America on an extended concert tour consisting of twelve symphony concerts and eleven chamber recitals in which my wife also took part. The reception by both the public and the press was quite serious this time. I was well known by now: moreover in the twelve years since my first visit musical America had made considerable progress and had begun to cultivate its own modern composers. My European reputation, too, had something to do with it. Although Americans like to form their own judgments ('We are the richest country in the world, we invite whom we please and we have the right to our own opinion'), nevertheless to be on the safe side they keep an eye on Europe. At any rate it was a pleasant tour almost without reservation and with none of the petty irritations of the previous tours. It took me not only across the whole country from east to west but to Canada and Cuba as well.

There was some talk of the Metropolitan staging *The Fiery Angel* but nothing came of it. The patroness who provided most of the funds to keep the theatre going said to me, 'Our theatre is so big that we sit in boxes near one street and the singers sing at the end of the next street. How do you expect us to catch all the fine points of your music?' The trouble was that *The Fiery Angel* was not dynamic enough for the stage – parts of it were too static. One of the artists of the theatre suggested that if the action could not be livened up the dull spots might be improved visually. In other words with a few slight alterations in the text and the music a slow-moving act could be broken up into three scenes, each with different décor, and these novel impressions would have the effect of speeding up the tempo. It was a good idea and I worked out a new plan requiring a moderate amount of revision. But since the New York production did not materialize the plan was never carried out; however I intend to return to it.

On my return from America I worked on the String Quartet op. 50, commissioned by the Library of Congress in Washington. This huge library has a much poorer collection of original manuscripts than most European libraries. To remedy this a special fund has been set up for purchasing original manuscripts of modern composers. Of course in time hardly more than one out of ten compositions will be of any value, but by then it will be worth ten times what was originally paid for it. The new compositions are performed with a great deal of ceremony at music festivals in Washington to which musicians from New York and other cities are invited. Before starting work on the quartet I studied Beethoven's quartets, chiefly in railway carriages on my way from one concert to another. In this way I came to understand and greatly admire his quartet technique. Perhaps this explains the somewhat 'classical' idiom of the first movement of my quartet. It has, however, two distinctive features: firstly, the Finale is the slow movement and, secondly, the key of B minor is one rarely chosen for quartets. I ended the quartet with a slow movement because the material happened to be the most significant in the whole piece. As for the key, the tonic of B minor is just half a tone below the limits of the cello and viola range. This involves a number of difficulties in writing the music. I tried out the Andante from the quartet with a full string group, rewriting some of the cello part and adding double-basses. One would think that this Andante, being for the most part melodious, ought to sound richer in the orchestra, but it is in fact better as a quartet. The first performance of the quartet took place in Washington on 23 April 1931. Besides this the Roth Quartet was sent to Europe with a programme of music written for the Library of Congress and, on 9 October 1931, played my quartet for the first time in Moscow.

While working on the quartet I was planning a symphonic suite based on the music of *The Gambler*. But I could not make much headway with it. The close interweaving of the music and the text resulted in an intricate pattern from which it was hard to pick any thread for a single symphonic line. In the end I discarded the idea of a suite in favour of portraits of the individual characters. This however was not so simple either, in as much as the music of the different characters was scattered throughout the opera. I devised the following method: I took the score apart, picked out everything relating to a given character and spread the sheets out on the floor. Seated on a chair I studied the pages for a long time until gradually the interrelated episodes began, as it were, to coalesce. This gave me sufficient concentrated material to work with. Even so a great deal of time passed before more or less rounded portraits of Alexey, Granny, the General and Paulina began to emerge. I added a fifth movement, 'Denouement', consisting of the music of two entr'actes. I had to reorchestrate the whole thing and the work was not finished until 1931. The first performance took place on 12 March 1932, in Paris.

In the summer of 1930, at the suggestion of the Paris Grand Opéra, I started a two-act ballet *On the Dnieper* (*Sur le Borysthène* in the French translation: Borysthène is the ancient name for the Dnieper). Here in Russia we like long ballets lasting the entire evening; abroad they prefer short ones and it is customary to give either three one-act ballets in an evening or a one-act ballet and a short opera. The reason for this I believe is that while we lay more emphasis on plot and its development, in the West plot plays a secondary role, and it is felt that three one-act ballets by different artists, choreographers and composers offer a greater variety of impressions than one long one. The lyrical subject for this ballet was chosen chiefly with a view to striking the right balance between the music and the choreography. The music came easily to me and I enjoyed writing it. In style it is similar to *The Prodigal Son* but the fate of the two ballets has been altogether different: whereas *The Prodigal Son* was an immediate success in the three big capitals of Europe, *On the Dnieper*, in spite of the admirable production by the Grand Opéra (on 16 December 1932, with sets by Larionov and costumes by Goncharova), was dull, and although warmly defended by the Paris composers was taken off after a few performances. However considering that ten years elapsed before my early lyrical music was noticed I presume this ballet's turn will come some day, too.

I attribute the cool reception given to *Sur le Borysthène* to the fact that I was too preoccupied with the subject matter to pay sufficient attention to form. Originality of form is hardly less important for a composer than inner content. The great classics were also great innovators. True, the composer for whom originality of form takes precedence over content is working primarily against himself, for others will take his new ideas and clothe them with meaning and they, not he, will be writing for posterity. But equally unfortunate is the composer who is afraid or incapable of originality, for whereas the creator of new harmonies is bound to be eventually acknowledged, the composer who has nothing new to offer will sooner or later be forgotten. In 1933 I made a symphonic suite out of *Le Borysthène* which is a selection of the more symphonic parts of the ballet.

In 1931 I wrote a piano concerto (no. 4) for the left hand at the request of the Austrian pianist Wittgenstein, who had lost his right hand in the war. He was concentrating all his energy on developing his left hand and building up a concert repertoire. In the latter respect he was not very successful. Richard Strauss had written some symphonic études for an orchestra with quadruple woodwinds. 'How can I with my one poor hand hope to compete with a quadruple orchestra!' Wittgenstein said in despair. 'But it is not for me to tell Strauss how to orchestrate . . .' Ravel composed a concerto beginning with a tremendous cadenza for the left hand. Wittgenstein was furious. 'If I wanted to play without the orchestra I would not have commissioned a concerto!' he said. He demanded that Ravel rewrite the piece. But conductors supported the composer and insisted that the concerto be played exactly as he had intended. I sent Wittgenstein my concerto and received this answer: 'Thank you for the concerto, but I do not understand a single note and I shall not play it.' And so this concerto has never been performed. I have not formed any definite opinion about it myself: sometimes I like it, sometimes I do not. I intend to write a two-hand version of it some time. The general plan is as follows: four movements: the first a swift running movement built mainly on finger technique; the second an Andante developing with calm solemnity; the third a sort of sonata Allegro (although deviating from this form); and the fourth a reversion to the swift first, but in abbreviated form and *piano* throughout.

Other piano pieces of this period include Six Pieces op. 52 and Two Sonatinas op. 54. Actually the six pieces are transcriptions of some orchestral or chamber compositions, but I took care to make them sound quite independent and gave each a title of its own without any reference to the work from which they were taken. All are difficult to play and are intended for concert performance, with the exception of the Andante, which is an almost literal transcription of the Andante from the quartet. I have always had a weakness for sonatina form – I like the idea of writing an utterly simple piece in the elevated sonata form. I have the same fondness for the concertino, although my concertinos have usually grown into concertos and in the sonatinas the melodies lacked the simplicity I strove for. In both sonatinas the best movements are the slow middle ones.

Periods of composition alternated with concert tours. I visited all the principal cities of Europe giving concerts in all except Athens, Oslo and Helsinki. On 5 March 1929 I gave a recital at a big diplomatic reception in the Soviet Embassy in Paris. This was the first of many subsequent appearances in our embassies – six in Paris, two each in Rome and Washington, as well as in London, Berlin and other cities. In May 1931 a ballet was made of the 'Classical' Symphony. It was not at all bad but the production soon folded up for reasons having nothing to do with the music.

In 1932 I wrote the Fifth Piano Concerto. If we discount the Fourth Concerto for left hand, more than ten years had passed since I had written a piano concerto. Since then my conception of the treatment of this form had changed somewhat, some new ideas had occurred to me (a passage running across the entire keyboard, with the left hand overtaking the right; chords in the piano and orchestra interrupting one another etc.) and finally I had accumulated a good number of vigorous major themes in my notebook. I had not intended the concerto to be difficult and at first had even contemplated calling it 'Music for Piano and Orchestra', partly to avoid confusing the concerto numbers. But in the end it turned out to be complicated, as indeed was the case with a good many other compositions of this period. What was the explanation? In my desire for simplicity I was hampered by the fear of repeating old formulas, of reverting to the 'old simplicity', which is something all modern composers seek to avoid. I searched for a 'new simplicity' only to discover that this new simplicity, with its novel forms and, chiefly, new tonal structure, was not understood. The fact that here and there my efforts to write simply were not successful is beside the point. I did not give up, hoping that the bulk of my music would in time prove to be quite simple when the ear grew accustomed to the new melodies, that is, when these melodies became the accepted idiom.

I played the Fifth Concerto for the first time on 31 October 1932, with the Berlin Philharmonic Orchestra conducted by Furtwängler. I was late coming from another concert and reached Berlin in time for only the final rehearsal. 'I left one rehearsal for you, but that is of course not enough for such a difficult score,' Furtwängler said. 'But we shall all try to do our best.' They had indeed worked very hard and the concert went very well. In November I played the concerto in Moscow, in December in Leningrad. The programmes of both concerts included the 'Portraits' from *The Gambler* and the Suite from *Le pas d'acier*. Formerly *Le pas d'acier* had been given in concert performance from the abbreviated ballet score but this had been unsatisfactory. It was not until the spring of 1931 that I saw clearly how to make a four-movement suite. The first and third parts of the suite remained as in the ballet, the second and fourth were rearranged. This time *Le pas d'acier* was well received.

I was very anxious to start working on Soviet themes. In an article published in *Vechernyaya Moskva* (a Moscow evening newspaper) on 6 December 1932 I wrote: 'What kind of subject am I looking for? Not caricatures of shortcomings, ridiculing the negative features of our life. I am interested in a subject that would assert the positive elements. The heroic aspects of socialist construction. The new man. The struggle to overcome obstacles. These are the sentiments and emotions which I should like to embody in large musical canvases.' So far this was only a general principle, the ideas out of which the *Cantata for the Twentieth Anniversary of the October Revolution* was gradually to take shape. But the musical idiom in which one could speak of Soviet life was not yet clear to me. It was clear to no one at this period, and I did not want to make a mistake. Hence I was much pleased when the Belgoskino Studios asked me to write the music for the film *Lieutenant Kijé*. This gave me a welcome opportunity to try my hand if not at Soviet subject matter then at music for Soviet audiences, and for the mass audience at that.

A society called 'Triton' had been formed in Paris for the performance of new chamber music. Honegger, Milhaud, Poulenc, myself and others joined it. Listening to bad music sometimes inspires good ideas: that's not the way to do it, one tells oneself, it should be done this way. That is how I happened to write my Sonata for two violins. After once hearing an unsuccessful piece for two violins without piano accompaniment, it struck me that in spite of the apparent limitations of such a duet one could make it interesting enough to listen to for ten and fifteen minutes without tiring. The sonata was performed at the official opening of the 'Triton' on 16 December 1932, which chanced to coincide with the première of my *Dnieper* ballet. Fortunately the ballet came on half an hour later, and so immediately after the sonata we dashed over to the Grand Opéra – musicians, critics, composer all together.

The following morning I left for America to give a series of concerts with leading American orchestras. I played my Third and Fifth Piano Concertos. In Chicago I made a mistake in the middle of the fourth movement, stopped and began again, but Stock caught on at once and carried on as if nothing had happened. In New York Bruno Walter played the 'Portraits' from *The Gambler* which he had conducted with some success in Leipzig and Berlin. The performance was excellent but the reception was poor. As I was coming out of my box after the performance a splendid specimen of the prosperous American came out of the next box and remarked in a loud voice to someone inside, 'I'd like to meet that guy. I'd tell him a thing or two about his music!' I hastily withdrew.

On returning to Moscow I eagerly set to work on the music for *Lieutenant Kijé*. I somehow had no doubts whatever about the musical language for this film. I went to Leningrad for the recording of the score. Dunayevsky conducted the orchestra rather well. Unfortunately the ending was altered so many times that the film became confused and heavy as a result. The following year I made a symphonic suite out of the music. This gave me much more trouble than the music for the film itself, since I had to find the proper form, re-orchestrate the whole thing, polish it up and even combine several of the themes.

After *Lieutenant Kijé* I wrote music for *Egyptian Nights* produced by the Moscow Kamerny Theatre. This was an interesting attempt to combine Bernard Shaw's *Caesar and Cleopatra*, describing Cleopatra's youth, Shakespeare's *Antony and Cleopatra*, which deals with the end of her life, and a monologue from the poem *Egyptian Nights* by Pushkin. However, notwithstanding the delightful humour of Bernard Shaw, old Shakespeare turned out to be so much of a titan by comparison that he willy-nilly crowded out poor Shaw, who as a result got whittled down to one brief, unimportant episode tacked on at the beginning. Tairov, who staged the production, paid a great deal of attention to the music, and the conductor A. Medtner, brother of the composer (and the first performer of my *Autumnal* many years earlier), did his best to do justice to the score within the limits of a small theatre orchestra.

In 1934 I made a suite out of *Egyptian Nights* as I had done with *Lieutenant Kijé*, again spending considerable time on it. The first part, 'Night in Egypt', was suggested by a poem of M. Kuzmin's about Egypt, in which a flute sounds at dead of night. The number for percussion alone sustained the feeling of alarm on the stage rather well. I hesitated before including this in the suite and added a note saying that the conductor might omit it if he wished. But it was invariably well received in all countries. The best part of the suite is 'The Decline of Cleopatra', which involves her entire musical material. Besides the suite the music for the Pushkin monologue *The Shining Palace* is also performed in concert. However there is little novelty in this music compared with the suite.

Some thoughts about the future of Soviet music were contained in an article of mine published in the 16 November 1934 issue of *Izvestiya* where among other things I wrote: 'The question of what kind of music should be written at the present time is one that interests many Soviet composers today. I have thought a good deal about this during the past two years and I believe that the following is the correct solution. What we need is great music, i.e. music that will be in keeping both in conception and technical execution with the grandeur of the epoch. Such music would be a stimulus to our own musical development; and abroad too it would reveal our true selves. The danger of becoming provincial is unfortunately a very real one for modern Soviet composers. It is not so easy to find the right idiom for this music. To begin with it must be melodious; moreover the melody must be simple and comprehensible, without being repetitive or trivial. Many composers have difficulty in composing any sort of melody; all the harder is it to compose a melody that has a definite function. The same applies to the technique and the idiom: it must be clear and simple, but not banal. We must seek a new simplicity.' I have taken the liberty of quoting this excerpt published seven years ago because it seems to me that these ideas are still timely, and because they anticipate certain views that came many years later to be recognized as valid.

In 1934 Grabar and Konchalovsky painted my portraits. Konchalovsky's portrait (in an armchair, full length) was done in the garden during a succession of cool April days while I was working on the orchestration of the Overture on Hebrew Themes op. 34. 'Well, how are the Jews getting along?' Konchalovsky would ask me every now and then. 'Thanks, they're coming along gradually. How about yourself?' 'Stop, don't move! Magnificent!' Konchalovsky would shout suddenly and begin to work furiously with his brush. I would freeze in one position, trying my best to look intelligent. For a while Konchalovsky would go on working with great concentration, then at last he would lean back exhausted. 'What's magnificent?' I would finally venture to inquire. 'The boot,' he would reply.

In 1933 I wrote a rather large orchestral piece which I called *Symphonic Song* op. 57. This was a serious piece of work and I took great care in choosing the thematic material. In form it consists of three closely integrated parts. Although there is no programme the mood of the three parts might be defined thus: darkness – struggle – achievement. The music is similar in character to that of op. 62, three pieces for piano under the general title of *Thoughts*. The second of the three I consider one of the best things I have ever written. More simple are the Three Piano Pieces op. 59: 'Promenade', 'Landscape' and 'Pastoral Sonatina'. This one-part sonatina is purer and more typical of the sonatina form than the previous two, op. 54.

In 1935 a group of admirers of the French violinist Soetens asked me to write a violin concerto for him, giving him exclusive rights to perform it for one year. I readily agreed since I had been intending to write something for the violin at that time and had accumulated some material. As in the case of the preceding concertos I began by searching for an original title for the piece, such as 'concert sonata for violin and orchestra', but finally returned to the simplest solution: Concerto no. 2. Nevertheless I wanted it to be altogether different from no. 1 in both music and style.

The variety of places in which that concerto was written is a reflection of the nomadic concert-tour existence I led at that time: the principal theme of the first movement was written in Paris, the first theme of the second movement in Voronezh, the orchestration I completed in Baku, while the first performance was given in Madrid, in December 1935. This was part of an extremely interesting concert tour which I made together with Soetens through Spain, Portugal, Morocco, Algeria and Tunisia. Besides my own compositions we played Debussy and Beethoven sonatas.

In the latter part of 1934 there was talk of the Kirov Theatre of Leningrad staging a ballet of mine. I was interested in a lyrical subject. Shakespeare's *Romeo and Juliet* was suggested. But the Kirov backed out and I signed a contract with the Moscow Bolshoi Theatre instead. In the spring of 1935 Radlov and I worked out a scenario, consulting with the choreographer on questions of ballet technique. The music was written in the course of the summer but the Bolshoi declared it impossible to dance to and the contract was cancelled.

There was quite a fuss at the time about our attempts to give *Romeo and Juliet* a happy ending – in the last act Romeo arrives a minute earlier, finds Juliet alive and everything ends well. The reasons for this bit of barbarism were purely choreographic: living people can dance, the dying cannot. The justification was that Shakespeare himself was said to have been uncertain about the endings of his plays (*King Lear*) and parallel with *Romeo and Juliet* had written *Two Gentlemen of Verona* in which all ends well. Curiously enough, whereas the report that Prokofiev was writing a ballet on the theme of *Romeo and Juliet* with a happy ending was received quite calmly in London, our own Shakespeare scholars proved more papal than the pope and rushed to the defence of Shakespeare. But what really caused me to change my mind was a remark someone made to me about the ballet: 'Strictly speaking your music does not express any real joy at the end.' That was quite true. After several conferences with the choreographers it was found that the tragic ending could be expressed in dance and in due course the music for that ending was written.

I made two symphonic suites from this ballet, each consisting of seven movements. They do not follow each other consecutively; both suites develop parallel to each other. Some numbers were taken directly from the ballet without alteration, others were compiled from different sources within it. These two suites do not cover the entire music and I shall perhaps be able to make a third. Besides the suites I compiled a collection of ten pieces for piano, selecting the parts best suited for transcription. The suites were performed before the ballet was produced. The ballet itself was rather unlucky. In 1937 the Leningrad Ballet School signed an agreement undertaking to produce it on the occasion of its 200th anniversary, and in 1938 the Brno Opera (Czechoslovakia) agreed to stage it too. The Ballet School violated the agreement and so the première took place in Brno in December 1938. The Kirov Theatre produced the ballet in January 1940 with all the mastery for which its dancers are famed – although with some slight divergences from the original. One might have appreciated their skill more had the choreography adhered more closely to the music. Owing to the peculiar acoustics of the Kirov Theatre and the need to make the rhythms as clear-cut as possible for the dancers I was obliged to alter a good deal of the orchestration. This explains why the same parts in the suites are more translucent than in the ballet score.

In the summer of 1935, besides *Romeo and Juliet*, I also wrote a number of small pieces for children. My old love for the sonatina form helped me to convey the true flavour of childhood. By autumn I had a whole dozen of them, subsequently published in a volume entitled *Music for Children*, op. 65. 'The last of the pieces, 'The Moon Goes Over the Meadows', was written on an original and not a folk theme. I was staying in Polenovo at the time in a little cottage with a balcony overlooking the Oka, and in the evenings I often watched the moon floating over the fields and meadows. There was a big demand for children's music and in the spring of 1936 I started a symphonic tale for children entitled *Peter and the Wolf* op. 67, to a text of my own. Every character in the story had its own motif played each time by the same instrument: the duck was played by the oboe, the grandfather by the bassoon etc. Before each performance the instruments were shown to the children and the themes played for them; during the performance the children heard the themes repeated several times and learned to recognize the timbres of the different instruments. The text was read during the pauses in the music which was disproportionately longer than the text – for me the story was important only as a means of inducing the children to listen to the music.

I composed the music quickly, approximately in one week, and another week was spent on the orchestration. It was first performed at a Moscow Philharmonic matinée concert on 2 May 1936, but the performance was rather poor and did not attract much attention. Another piece written at this period was 'The Chatterbox' op. 68, a song for children about children, with piano accompaniment or small orchestra. To this I added at a later date 'Sweet Song' and 'The Piglets'.

Besides music for children I wrote in 1935 and 1936 several marches for military band and several mass songs op. 66, of which 'Anyutka' was awarded a second prize at a *Pravda* contest (no first prize was awarded).

In 1936 preparations began for two major jubilees – the twentieth anniversary of the coming to power of the Soviets and the centenary of Pushkin's death. For the latter occasion I undertook to write the incidental music for productions of *Eugene Onegin* and *Boris Godunov* on the dramatic stage and for a film of *The Queen of Spades*. Of these three *Eugene Onegin* interested me the most. As I wrote in an article published at the time in *Vechernyaya Moskva*, 'the play *Eugene Onegin*, adapted for the stage by S. D. Kryzhanovsky, highlights those parts of Pushkin's poem which are not included in Tchaikovsky's opera. I believe it will be interesting to see Lensky arguing with Onegin over a bottle of Ay; Tatyana visiting his empty house, or Onegin "on the banks of the Neva". It is a well-known fact that opinions about Tchaikovsky's opera were divided. Some considered the composer's interpretation to be perfect; others, on the other hand, believed that it robbed the novel of the intrinsic humour peculiar to the poet and gave it the pessimistic touch characteristic of Tchaikovsky. I personally shall endeavour to capture the true spirit of Pushkin. To write the music for *Eugene Onegin* is a tempting proposition, but at the same time perhaps a thankless task. However successful I might be our theatre-goers love Tchaikovsky too well to be willing to part with the familiar musical images.'

I enjoyed writing the music very much and believed I had found some true images, although not without considerable trouble. In some cases I had to rewrite the themes and make several sketches before I found what I wanted. But none of my Pushkin pieces was ever produced. The music lay for a long time on the shelf and was gradually incorporated in other compositions. Only three songs of mine (op. 73) were performed during the Pushkin centenary, my one tangible contribution to the occasion.

Notes

231 Shurik is the same cousin whose release from prison Prkfv tries hard to engineer in the *Soviet Diary*.

231 Sergey Ivanovich Taneev (1856–1915) – composer, Director of the Moscow Conservatory 1885–9, a teacher of great influence (pupils included Skriabin and Rachmaninov).

231 Yury Nikolaevich Pomerantsev (1878–1933), pupil of Taneev and Skriabin for composition and of Nikisch (in Leipzig) for conducting. Conducted at the Bolshoi (1910–18) then settled abroad. Frequently performed with Medtner.

232 Reinhold Moritsevich Glière – see *Soviet Diary*, note for p. 23.

233 César Cui (1835–1918) – composer and critic, of French descent, member of the Russian 'Mighty Handful' group of nationalist composers.

234 In fact Glazunov received his honorary Oxbridge doctorates only in 1907. See *Soviet Diary*, p. 75.

235 Mikhail Mikhailovich Chernov – see *Soviet Diary*, note for p. 108.

235 Alexander Adolfovich Winkler (1865–1935), pianist, composer and professor at the St Petersburg Conservatoire (1896–1924). Settled in France in 1924. Myaskovsky was another of his students.

236 Nikolay Yakovlevich Myaskovsky – see *Soviet Diary*, note for p. 6.

237 Vyacheslav Gavrilovich Karatygin (1875–1925), music critic, edited the music section of the newspaper *Rech*. From 1916 taught history of music at the St Petersburg Conservatoire.

238 Walter Fyodorovich Nuvel (1871–1949) was an amateur composer and prior to 1917 held a position in the Office of the Ministry of the Court. Friend of Diaghilev, later one of his circle in the West.

238 Alfred Pavlovich Nurok (1860–1919) was a bibliophile and music-lover who, so far as we can ascertain, never precisely 'did' anything.

239 'Of my symphony only the Andante' – in 1934 Prkfv re-transcribed this Andante for orchestra, calling it op. 29 bis.

239 Yosif Vitol (or Vitols or Wihtol or Wihtols) – see *Soviet Diary*, note for p. 8.

241 Anna Esipova – see *Soviet Diary*, note for p. 5.

241 Alexander Tcherepnin – see *Soviet Diary*, note for p. 20.

241 The student performance of *The Marriage of Figaro* which Prkfv conducted took place on 24 March (Old Style) 1914. This was not Prkfv's first appearance as an opera conductor. He had conducted the first scene of the second act and the fourth act of a Conservatoire performance of *Aida* given in memory of Verdi (on 8 December 1913). While at the Conservatoire Prkfv conducted the following symphonic works: the first movement of Schubert's 'Unfinished' Symphony (at a student concert on 6 November 1909), *Lyrical Poem* op. 12 by Glazunov (25 April 1910), *Ivan the Terrible*, tone poem by Anton Rubinstein (16 December 1912, at a concert held on the occasion of the fiftieth anniversary of the St Petersburg

Conservatoire), Haydn's Symphony in G major (19 February 1913), *Fantasia on Finnish Themes* and *Ukrainian Kazachok* by Dargomyzhsky (1913, at a concert dedicated to the centenary of the composer's birth), Beethoven's Seventh Symphony (14 November 1913); new music – his own symphonic poem *Dreams* (22 November 1910), Variations for Orchestra by Karlovich and *Introduction* and *Dances of the Maidens* from the ballet *The Royal Feast* by Shaposhnikov. The last two compositions were performed at the graduation ceremony at the St Petersburg Conservatoire on 12 May 1913. The mysterious Karlovich turns up again in Leningrad in 1927, but as we explain (note for p. 86) nothing more is known of him.

Shaposhnikov (Adrian Grigorievich: 1887–1967) settled in Turkmenia in 1937, where he organized professional music and composed the first Turkmenian opera.

Prkfv gained considerable experience as a conductor in the sphere of orchestral accompaniment as well. During his Conservatoire years he conducted piano concertos by Weber, Liszt, Saint-Saëns and Tchaikovsky, and violin concertos by Beethoven and Brahms.

242 *The White Swan* and *The Wave* – these two choruses remained unpublished and unperformed until 1989.

243 'acrobatic' – in Russian literally 'footballistic'.

243 *Maddalena* was first performed in England in 1979 by Edward Downes, who orchestrated the scenes which survived only in piano score. It is now published by Boosey & Hawkes.

243 'Baron' Lieven – pen-name of Magda Gustavovna Lieven-Orlov, of whom nothing more is known.

243 Sonata op. 14 – i.e. the Second Piano Sonata, which Prkfv played several times during his 1927 (*Soviet Diary*) tour.

244 'I don't know whether he knew of my method' – only today, in the 1980s–90s, is Prkfv's method starting to be widely adopted.

244 Sergey Koussevitsky – see *Soviet Diary*, note for p. 3.

244 Nikolay Karlovich Medtner – see *Soviet Diary*, note for p. 119.

245 Boris Petrovich Jurgenson – see *Soviet Diary*, note for p. 20.

245 Alexander Vyacheslavovich Ossovsky – see *Soviet Diary*, note for p. 68.

245 Maria Adrianovna Deisha-Sionitskaya (1861–1932), singer (dramatic soprano) and teacher, member of the company of the Mariinsky Theatre in St Petersburg, and later (1891–1908) of the Bolshoi Theatre, Moscow. In 1907–13 arranged free performances of the vocal and instrumental works of Russian composers. Taneev, Ippolitov-Ivanov, Vasilenko, Glière, Spendyarov and many other composers first performed their compositions at these 'auditions' which played an important role in popularizing Russian chamber music. The young Prkfv too made his first appearances in Moscow here.

245 Derzhanovsky – see *Soviet Diary*, note for p. 6.

245 Konstantin Solomonovich Saradzhev – see *Soviet Diary*, note for p. 13.

246 Pavlovsk – a country spot near St Petersburg noted for its 18th- early 19th-century palace and park.

246 Mitrofan Petrovich Belyaev (1836–1900), well-known music publisher.

246 Alexander Dmitrievich Sheremetiev (1859–1931) was the nephew of Count N. P.

Sheremetiev, a man of immense wealth who owned several famous serf theatres and orchestras. Alexander Sheremetiev was an 'amateur' in the best sense: a dedicated composer, conductor, entrepreneur and ardent supporter of Russian music and of the idea, the ideal, of 'educating' the people. In 1882 he founded a symphony orchestra which from 1889 combined with the forces of the Imperial Chapel to give public concerts. In 1900 the 'Symphony Concerts Accessible to All' were founded, which from 1910 to 1917 were completely free. Sheremetiev emigrated in 1918.

246 Alexander Ilich Ziloti – see *Soviet Diary*, note for p. 79.

247 'Subject' and 'answer' – the Russian terms are much less dusty: 'leader' (*vozhd*) and 'companion' (*sputnik*).

247 Sergey Mikhailovich Lyapunov (1859–1924) – composer, pianist and conductor. He studied at the Moscow Conservatory and taught and conducted in St Petersburg.

247 First Piano Concerto – Prkfv does not explain that at this competition performance the orchestral part was played on a second piano.

249 Prkfv's visit to London. The first sentences of this chapter could easily mislead people into thinking this was Prkfv's first major trip abroad. In fact the previous year he had visited Paris, London and Geneva.

249 'wild animal' – if the word the Frenchman actually used was *fauve* the remark acquires a somewhat different significance (artistic rather than abusive).

250 Sergey Mitrofarovich Gorodetsky (1884–?). 'Acmeist' poet and well-known (Soviet) opera librettist and translator.

251 Bernadino Molinari (1880–1952), Italian conductor, artistic director of the Augusteo Orchestra in Rome, distinguished exponent of modern music. Transcribed Debussy's *L'isle joyeuse* for orchestra with the composer's approval.

251 Filippo Tommaso Marinetti (1876–1944), Italian writer, leader of the futurists.

251 Alexander Nikolaevich Afanasiev (1826–71), collector and student of Russian oral folk-lore, mainly fairy-tales and legends. Stravinsky drew on his collection for the scenarios of *Les noces* and *The Soldier's Tale*.

253 Albert Coates (1882–1953), English conductor and composer working in St Petersburg from 1911 to 1919 (principal conductor at the Mariinsky Theatre). Introduced Prkfv's Third Piano Concerto to Britain with the composer as soloist.

253 Eduard Napravnik (1839–1916) – Czech conductor and composer, studied in Prague. In 1869 he became principal conductor of the Mariinsky Theatre.

254 Boris Nikolaevich Demchinsky – see *Soviet Diary*, note for p. 117.

254 Igor Glebov – i.e. Asafiev. See *Soviet Diary* note for p. 9.

256 Konstantin Dmitrievich Balmont (1867–1942), Russian virtuoso symbolist poet (also prolific Anglophile translator and novelist) whose works attracted Stravinsky (the cantata *King of the Stars*) and Rachmaninov (*The Bells*, after Poe through Balmont) as well as Prkfv. Settled permanently in Paris in 1920. Believed in 'revelation', 'ecstasy' and 'inspiration', was an 'artist-sorcerer' like Skriabin.

256 Leonid Leonidovich Sabaneev (1881–1968), musicologist, critic and composer, early champion of contemporary music in Russia – 'contemporary' in terms of Skriabin rather than Prkfv, at least at first. Later he became a supporter of Prkfv and Shostakovich. Left Russia in 1926.

257 Pierre (Pyotr Petrovich) Souvchinsky – see *Soviet Diary*, note for p. 20.

257 Andrey Nikolaevich Rimsky-Korsakov – see *Soviet Diary*, note for p. 84.

257 Julia Lazarevna Weisberg – see *Soviet Diary*, note for p. 84.
258 Nadezhda Yevseevna Dobychina – see *Soviet Diary*, note for p. 85.
258 Alexander Valentinovich Amfiteatrov (1862–1923), popular bourgeois journalist and novelist, one of the owners of the reactionary newspaper *Russkaya volya*. His son was the composer and conductor Daniele Amfiteatrov (1901–83) who studied with Respighi and later became a composer of film-scores in Hollywood.
259 Hugo Winkler (1863–1913), German orientalist, archaeologist, author of many books on the history and archaeology of the Orient.
261 Vladimir Vladimirovich Mayakovsky – see *Soviet Diary*, note for p. 22.
262 Anatoly Vassilievich Lunacharsky – see *Soviet Diary*, note for p. 19.
262 Alexander Benois – see *Soviet Diary*, note for p. 85.
264 'Dances' op. 32 – the title of this opus is actually *Four Pieces* although all four are dances ('Dance', 'Minuet', 'Gavotte', 'Waltz').
265 Walter Damrosch (1862–1950), composer and conductor, associated primarily with the Metropolitan Opera, the New York Symphony Society and with founding the American Music School at Fontainebleau in France.
265 Modest Altschuler (1873–1963), cellist and conductor, educated at the Conservatoire of Cologne. In 1895 went to America. In 1903 founded the Russian Symphony Orchestra with which he toured many countries. Gave the first performance of the *Poème de l'extase* (1908) and the American premières of other works by Skriabin. In 1925 settled in Los Angeles, where he taught.
265 Frederick August Stock (1872–1942), conductor and composer, educated at the Conservatoire of Cologne. In 1895 went to the United States where he joined the Chicago Symphony Orchestra as violinist. In 1905 became chief conductor of the orchestra. Stock was the first to perform the works of many American composers and was also an ardent popularizer of Soviet music, especially of Myaskovsky's.
265 Cleofonte Campanini (1860–1919), Italian opera conductor. Made his début in Parma in 1883. The same year was appointed assistant conductor at the Metropolitan Opera in New York. In 1906–9 he was conductor of the Manhattan Opera; in 1910 he joined the Chicago Opera Association where he remained until his death.
268 'poods': a Russian weight, *c.* 36 lb avoirdupois.
269 'Buxtehude's organ fugue' – Prkfv has actually confused several things here, which are unravelled by the long autobiography. In March/April 1908 he had to take two exams to admit him to the advanced piano class. He was told by Winkler that at the second public exam it was customary to play Bach. By chance Prkfv met Taneev, who was visiting St Petersburg and who advised him to play not Bach but Buxtehude, which would be a novelty for the examiners. When Prkfv asked if there was any keyboard music, Taneev replied there was plenty of organ music which he could easily transcribe for piano. Prkfv accordingly transcribed an A minor fugue which he played for the exam. Later, trying to think of some 'old' pieces to play in his recitals in North America and Canada, he remembered Buxtehude, but arranged a different fugue, one in D minor, which was subsequently published. Taneev never held a class at the St Petersburg Conservatoire.
269 Pawel Kochanski (1887–1934), Polish violinist. Between 1913 and 1919 lived in Russia and taught at the St Petersburg and Kiev Conservatoires. His association

with Szymanowski brought forth the latter's *Mythes* (violin and piano) and First Violin Concerto.

272 José Raúl Capablanca (1888–1942), the great Cuban chess-player, at that time world champion. Prkfv competed against him in simultaneous displays given in St Petersburg on 11, 13 and 15 May 1914: he managed to win the last of these, a fact of which he was inordinately proud.

275 Bronislaw Hubermann (1882–1947), Polish violinist, whose concert appearances in the USSR in 1926 and 1929 were a great success.

277 Joseph Szigeti (1892–1973), violinist, born in Budapest, pupil of Jeno Hubay. Inspired interpreter of classical music, especially the sonatas of Bach. Also known as an advocate of new music. Gave the first American performances of Prkfv's two violin sonatas (op. 80 and op. 94) in the 1940s.

278 Georgy Bogdanovich Yakulov – see *Soviet Diary*, note for p. 31.

280 Persimfans – see *Soviet Diary*, note for p. 10.

280 Leo Blech (1871–1958) – German conductor and composer.

282 'As we approached the hall' – compare this account with the *Soviet Diary* pp. 15–16) and with Kabalevsky's (pp. 158–60); see also note for p. 39.

283 Vladimir Alexandrovich Dranishnikov – see *Soviet Diary*, note for p. 68.

283 Sergey Ernestovich Radlov – see *Soviet Diary*, note for p. 79.

284 *Ala and Lolli*: the point here – easy to miss – is that this was the first time a ballet was danced to the *Scythian Suite* which, as Prkfv has explained, was originally *conceived* as a ballet (for Diaghilev).

285 Walther Straram (1876–1933), French conductor born in London. His 'Concerts Straram' series in Paris was highly regarded. In 1928 he conducted the première of Ravel's *Boléro* for the Ida Rubinstein company.

285 'But I intend to return to it' – towards the end of his life Prkfv came close to starting work on this revision, since he assigned it an opus number (136 – in three movements, not two) in his list of works. However this was as far as it went.

289 Isaak Moiseevich Rabinovich – see *Soviet Diary*, note for p. 30.

290 'however I intend to return to it' – he never did.

292 Mikhail Larionov (1881–1964) and Natalia Sergeevna Goncharova (1881–1962), his wife, were the founders of neo-primitivism in Russia. Goncharova's interests also included rayonism and futurism. In their work for Diaghilev (*Coq d'or, Aurora's Wedding, Les noces, Chout, On the Dnieper*, etc.) she and her husband made many innovations in the field of theatrical design.

293 Paul Wittgenstein (1887–1961) – Austrian pianist. He lost his right arm in the First World War, but soon acquired great virtuosity with his left hand and commissioned works from Franz Schmidt, Strauss, Ravel and Britten, as well as Prkfv.

293 Strauss and his quadruple woodwinds – the work referred to is the *Panathenäenzug* ('symphonic études in the form of a passacaglia') op. 74. However, the woodwind (at least in the published score) is 'triple' (i.e. three members of each family), not quadruple.

293 'I intend to write a two-hand version' – this plan was never carried out. The Concerto itself was not performed until 1956, three years after Prkfv's death.

294 Isaac Osipovich Dunayevsky (1900–55), the most popular composer of 'popular music' during the Stalin era. Deliberately cultivated a style of strong mass appeal in his songs and twelve operettas. The main theme of the Finale of Prkfv's

oratorio *On Guard for Peace* is probably modelled on the style of Dunayevsky's
mass songs.

296 Alexander Yakovlevich Tairov (1885–1950), celebrated Soviet theatre producer.
Founder and director of the Moscow Kamerny Theatre (1914–50).

296 Alexander Karlovich Medtner (1877–1961), viola-player, teacher and conductor.

297 Mikhail Alekseevich Kuzmin (1875–1936), lyric poet, prose-writer, playwright
and critic associated first with the symbolists then with the acmeists. Also a minor
composer who had studied with Rimsky-Korsakov. His role in *Egyptian Nights* is
unclear: the first movement of Prkfv's suite is essentially the same as the first
section of the complete incidental music, which relates to Shaw, not Kuzmin.
Perhaps Prkfv means that Kuzmin's poem was his personal inspiration for the
music.

297 *The Shining Palace* is now published as part of the complete *Egyptian Nights*
music.

297 Igor Emmanuelovich Grabar (1871–1960), Russian painter who started his career
as an impressionist – many fine snow-scenes – but later became equally
celebrated as an art-historian. He was an active member of the society for
preserving and restoring historical monuments, and a member of the USSR
Academy of Sciences.

297 Peter Petrovich Konchalovsky (1876–1956), outstanding Russian post-
impressionist painter and art-historian who unlike many contemporaries found
favour with the Soviets.

297 Overture on Hebrew Themes: Prkfv was making a version for larger orchestra of
the 1919 sextet.

299 Kirov Theatre – i.e. the Mariinsky so beloved of Prkfv (see *Soviet Diary*, note for
p. 65 Mariinsky Theatre).

299 A third *Romeo and Juliet* Suite was compiled in 1946.

301 'The music lay for a long time on the shelf' – e.g. Prokofiev drew on *Eugene
Onegin* for *War and Peace* and *Cinderella* and on *Boris Godunov* for *Ivan the Terrible*
and the opera *Semyon Kotko*. In 1962 Gennadi Rozhdestvensky published a suite
of selections from *The Queen of Spades*, *Eugene Onegin* and *Boris Godunov* under
the title of *Pushkiniana*.

Index

Biographical material can be found in the notes, which are in two sections: after the *Soviet Diary* (p. 165), and after the *Autobiography* (p. 302). Prokofiev's musical works are grouped under 'Prokofiev'.

Winkler, Alexander Adolfovich, 235
Wittgenstein, Paul, 293
Wührer, Friedrich, 151

Yakulov, Georgy Bogdanovich, 31, 65,
    92, 102, 278
Yavorsky, Boleslav Leopoldovich:
    Prkfv's visit to, 42–3
    theatre conference, 91
    theories, 142, 144

passing references, 33, 36, 51, 61, 89,
    126, 150
Yudina, Maria Venyaminovna, 107
Yurovsky, Alexander Naumovich, 39,
    94–6, 116

Ziloti, Alexander Ilyich, 79, 104, 246,
    250, 253–4, 255, 258, 260
'Zimro' ensemble, 266